STUDIES IN CHRISTIAN HISTORY AND THOUGHT

D1375874

The Puritan Millennium

Literature and Theology, 1550-1682

STUDIES IN CHRISTIAN HISTORY AND THOUGHT

STUDIES IN CHRISTIAN HISTORY AND THOUGHT

The Puritan Millennium

Literature and Theology, 1550-1682

Crawford Gribben

MILTON KEYNES · COLORADO SPRINGS · HYDERABAD

Paternoster is an imprint of Authentic Media
9 Holdons Avenue, Bletchley, Milton Keynes, MK1 1QR, UK
1820 Jet Stream Drive, Colorado Springs, CO 80921, USA
OM Authentic Media, Medchal Road, Jeedimetla Village,
Secunderabad 500 055, A.P., India

www.authenticmedia.co.uk
Authentic Media is a Division of IBS-STL UK, a company limited by guarentee
(registered charity no. 270162)

14 13 12 11 10 09 08 7 6 5 4 3 2 1

British Library Cataloguing in Publication Data
A catalogue record for this book is available from the British Library

ISBN 978-1-84227-372-2

Typeset by the Author
Printed and bound in Great Britain
for Paternoster
by Nottingham Alphagraphics

Series Preface

This series complements the specialist series of *Studies in Evangelical History and Thought* and *Studies in Baptist History and Thought* for which Paternoster is becoming increasingly well known by offering works that cover the wider field of Christian history and thought. It encompasses accounts of Christian witness at various periods, studies of individual Christians and movements, and works which concern the relations of church and society through history, and the history of Christian thought.

The series includes monographs, revised dissertations and theses, and collections of papers by individuals and groups. As well as 'free standing' volumes, works on particular running themes are being commissioned; authors will be engaged for these from around the world and from a variety of Christian traditions.

A high academic standard combined with lively writing will commend the volumes in this series both to scholars and to a wider readership.

Series Editors

Alan P.F. Sell, Visiting Professor at Acadia University Divinity College, Nova Scotia, Canada

David Bebbington, Professor of History, University of Stirling, Stirling, Scotland, UK

Clyde Binfield, Professor Associate in History, University of Sheffield, UK

Gerald Bray, Anglican Professor of Divinity, Beeson Divinity School, Samford University, Birmingham, Alabama, USA

Grayson Carter, Associate Professor of Church History, Fuller Theological Seminary SW, Phoenix, Arizona, USA

for Pauline and Daniel

Contents

Abbreviations

AV	Authorised (King James) Version of the Bible
Brooks	*The Works of Thomas Brooks*
Bunyan	*The Works of John Bunyan*
DNB	*Dictionary of National Biography*
GA	John Bunyan, *Grace Abounding*
Geneva Bible (1560)	*The Geneva Bible: A facsimile of the 1560 edition*, intro. Lloyd E. Berry (Madison: University of Madison Press, 1969)
Geneva Bible (1602)	*The Geneva Bible: The Annotated New Testament, 1602 edition*, intro. Gerald Sheppard (New York: Pilgrim Press, 1989)
Gillespie	*The Works of George Gillespie*
Goodwin	*The Works of Thomas Goodwin*
Hist. Cat.	*Historical Catalogue of Printed Editions of the English Bible*
Manton	*The Complete Works of Thomas Manton*
Milton	*The Works of John Milton*
PL	*Paradise Lost*, in Milton ii
Owen	*The Works of John Owen*
Rutherford	*Letters of Samuel Rutherford*
Sibbes	*The Complete Works of Richard Sibbes*
STC	*Short-Title Catalogue*
TCD	Trinity College, Dublin
Ussher	*The Whole Works of James Ussher*
WCF	*Westminster Confession of Faith*, in Hall (ed.) (1842): 574-604

Unless otherwise specified, all Old Testament quotations are taken from *Geneva Bible* (1560), and New Testament quotations are taken from *Geneva Bible* (1602). Quotations from other translations are noted appropriately.

Preface to the Revised Edition

The first edition of this book was published by Four Courts in 2000, and this revised edition appears with their permission to reflect developments in my thinking about puritan millennialism in the last six years. The most significant change has been my increasing reservation about the usefulness of the terms 'amillennial', 'premillennial' and 'postmillennial', which are often unsuitable to describe the much wider range of eschatological options in the early modern period. The new appendix to this volume comments on the use of these terms.

This edition retains the interdisciplinary approaches of the first. There are a number of reasons for its so doing. Firstly, its interest in the form of puritan apocalyptic texts could not be easily eliminated. Secondly, these discussions of literary form relate closely to the historical argument of the book, which examines the relationship between form and content in puritan apocalyptic writing. This edition also presents an updated bibliography. A number of important studies of puritan millennialism have appeared since the publication of the first edition. While they have not changed the basic argument of this book, they have prompted some re-thinking.

As I reflect on the experience of the last six years, I would like to thank those who have provided the greatest encouragement in and best examples of scholarly work on this tradition, particularly John Coffey and Michael Haykin, and the students who have helped to shape my thinking on puritan and apocalyptic textual cultures, particularly Joel Swann, currently a doctoral student at Keele University, whose work on the Geneva Bible has influenced my own thinking on the subject. I would also like to thank Mark Sweetnam and Anthony R. Cross for their help in the preparation of this edition. As always, my final thanks are to those without whom I could not accomplish anything, Pauline and Daniel. *Soli Deo Gloria.*

CHAPTER 1

Introduction

'An early tea could be advisable today', suggested the front page of the *Irish Times* on 22 October 1996; 'the world may end at 6pm'. The supposed claims of Archbishop James Ussher - the basis of the report - were 'only the latest in a long line of end-of-the-world-prophecies' and, readers were reminded, 'none of the prophets have hit the jackpot yet.' One year later, on the 24 October 1997, Glasgow's *Herald* observed that 'The world did not come to an end at noon yesterday. Archbishop Ussher was wrong.' Each article was apparently based on the same calculations, combining Ussher's dating of Creation at 4004 BC with a supposed six thousand-year-span of human history. Each arrived at different conclusions. But it is not only in its mathematics that puritan apocalyptic thought has become confused.

The foundations of the contemporary interpretation of puritanism were laid in the nineteenth century by S. R. Gardiner, whose carefully crafted Whig historiography cast an incalculable influence over succeeding explorations of the seventeenth century. But Gardiner, while founder of the most enduring meta-historical paradigm, was not a neutral in the debates he reconstructed; he was a member of the Catholic Apostolic Church, a radically apocalyptic group established when Rev. Edward Irving was expelled from the Church of Scotland in 1830.[1] No analysis exists of the influence of Irving's apocalyptic eschatology upon Gardiner's framework of Whig progress, although his historiography has proved paradigmatic for succeeding generations of scholars. Certainly the two most influential misinterpretations of puritan thinking were constructed upon the paradigm of Gardiner's Whig historiography. R.H. Tawney's *Religion and the Rise of Capitalism* (1926) and Max Weber's *The Protestant Ethic and the Sprit of Capitalism* (1930) both posited a controversial link between puritan Calvinism and the development of free enterprise. Perhaps the greatest usefulness of these texts was their illumination of the possibilities of a 'social' history, a history 'from below'. With Tawney and Weber began the struggle to wrestle the English revolution away from its traditional political meta-

---

[1] John Kenyon, *The History Men: The Historical Profession in England since the Renaissance* (London: Weidenfeld and Nicolson, 1983; 2nd ed. 1993), p. 224.

narrative.

Two of the most seminal texts in puritan studies were published in 1938. A. S. P. Woodhouse's *Puritanism and Liberty* was an annotated transcription of the army debates of 1647-49, bound together with other documents explaining the period. Woodhouse's introduction was a long essay on civil war puritanism, erudite and engaging. Millenarian concerns were highlighted in his citations from *A Glimpse of Sions Glory*, and their centrality in puritan thought was not obscured by extensive quotations from other documents explicating the panoply of puritan worldviews. In the same year William Haller published *The Rise of Puritanism* which was, once again, rooted in Gardiner's system. Haller's book - ostensibly all background to a study of Milton's poetry - revitalised puritan studies but underplayed the centrality of apocalyptic thought in seventeenth-century England. Haller followed this with *Liberty and Reformation in the Puritan Revolution* (1955), a collection of important primary sources from the civil wars republished in facsimile. The other most important studies dating from that period - *The New England Mind* (1939) and *Errand into the Wilderness* (1956), authored by another American professor of English literature, Perry Miller - were vitally concerned with the establishment of godly societies in the New World and consequently paid little attention to the apocalypticism of the old.

In the context of the 'three kingdoms', however, the most significant development of the 1950s was Christopher Hill's slow turning towards the experience of the ordinary people behind what he called the English Revolution. Hill's brand of Marxist social history illuminated and challenged many of the assumptions which Gardiner's Whig thesis had long taken for granted. Hill was early interested in the ideology pervading the first bourgeois revolution - and millenarianism emerged as a key factor in his analysis.

Perhaps the publication of Norman Cohn's *The Pursuit of the Millennium* (1957) stimulated his thinking. Cohn was concerned to explore the roots of the twentieth century's two largest millenarian societies - Nazi Germany and Soviet Russia. Cohn documented the rise and progress of various medieval and Reformation radical movements, concluding his study with the observation that 'again and again one finds that a particular outbreak of revolutionary chiliasm took place against a background of disaster.'[2] The implications for seventeenth-century England Cohn left unspoken. Only an appendix documenting 'The 'Free Spirit' in Cromwell's England: the Ranters and their literature' hinted at a three-kingdom context.

---

[2] Norman Cohn, *The Pursuit of the Millennium* (1957; rpr. London: Mercury Books, 1962), p. 315.

Studies of the native apocalyptic tradition in this period were often fragmentary and untried. S.A. Burrell's essay on 'The Apocalyptic Vision of the Early Covenanters' (1964), for example, disappointed the hopes its title raised. Burrell offered a rather sketchy overview but usefully pointed out that millenarianism was not limited to the lunacy of extremists. Burrell's documentation of eschatological hopes traced their implications throughout the Scottish Covenanting movement and demonstrated that the Scottish revolution was grounded in the hope of a better - and solely Presbyterian - world. Nevertheless, historians in general were slow to recognise the wider significance of apocalyptic thought. In 1971 Bernard Capp was correct to note that 'The rôle of millenarianism has, to date, received more attention from the anthropologist than from the historian.'[3]

The review article in which Capp made his dramatic claim, *'Godly Rule* and English Millenarianism' (1971), was taking account of a very sudden and unparalleled burst of enthusiasm for the topic among his contemporaries. It was at the height of the influence of Hill's socio-historical narrative, in the early 1970s, that scholarly interest in millenarianism experienced its first peak. A flurry of titles had emerged which would endure as standard works on the subject. John Wilson's *Pulpit in Parliament: Puritanism during the English Civil Wars, 1640-1648* (1969) was a study of the sermons preached to the Long Parliament. William Lamont's *Godly Rule: Politics and Religion, 1603-60* (1969) traced the impact of eschatology upon puritan theories of government. Paul Seaver's *The Puritan Lectureships: The Politics of Religious Dissent, 1560-1662* (1970) analysed the ideologies of these alternative and uncontrolled pulpits. The lectureships were preaching stations established by the voluntary subscriptions of local puritans, who thus maintained the independence of the preacher from the Church of England's demands for conformity. That they continued to be voluntarily maintained suggests that these preachers successfully mirrored the concerns and hopes of their subscribers. Seaver, significantly, discovered a substantial millennial component in their thought.

Puritans, the Millennium and the Future of Israel: Puritan Eschatology 1600 to 1660 (1970) was a highly useful selection of essays edited by Peter Toon. This volume was the first to chart the theological developments within the puritan apocalyptic tradition, from the re-birth of millenarianism to the beginnings of its various Quaker expressions. This project constructed a meta-narrative of theological evolution which would be echoed in future studies of the subject. Nevertheless, as we

---

[3] B. S. Capp, *'Godly Rule* and English Millenarianism', *Past and Present* 52 (1971), p. 106.

shall see, it was an attempt at scholarly comprehension which seemed to raise as many questions as it answered.

Toon's text was immediately complemented by James de Jong's *As the Waters Cover the Sea: Millennial Expectations in the Rise of Anglo-American Missions, 1640-1810* (1970). This text provided an excellent overview of the seventeenth-century development of puritan eschatology, highlighting general expectations of Jewish conversions. This theme was picked up in Iain Murray's *The Puritan Hope: Revival and the Interpretation of Prophecy* (1971), which included a useful survey of puritan expectations as part of a larger polemical interest in re-establishing eschatological optimism among evangelical Christians. Christopher Hill's *Antichrist in Seventeenth Century England* (1971) was a delightfully inter-textual compilation which excelled in quotations but was meagre in analysis. Much of the value of Hill's text was in this lack of overt systemisation; his study was less the history of an idea than a wonderful collage of citations and quotations.

Capp's review article was followed by the publication of his own researches into *The Fifth Monarchy Men* (1972), one of the best titles among the secondary studies of puritan millenarianism. Capp traced the beginnings of the Fifth Monarchist movement, detailed their ideology and social composition, and reflected on their place within the puritan apocalyptic tradition. It was, in many ways, a model of socio-historical analysis.

Hill followed his *Antichrist* with *The World Turned Upside Down: Radical Ideas during the English Revolution* (1972), which included a short section distilling millenarian thought from various prominent figures in the period. Tai Liu's *Discord in Zion: The Puritan Divines and the Puritan Revolution* (1973) was a far more substantial exploration of the crucial rôle played by puritan apocalyptic thought – nevertheless, as we shall see, minor problems of terminology beset a thoroughly convincing argument. Liu's analysis of the complex matrix of events between 1640 and 1660 is memorable and penetrating. Marjorie Reeves' essay on 'History and Eschatology: Medieval and Early Protestant Thought in Some English and Scottish Writings' (1973) was useful only insofar as it reminded scholars of the importance of the Scottish dimension - by then largely forgotten – in the apocalyptic conflagration of the three kingdoms.

This breathtaking charting of the puritanism's apocalyptic basis was cut short with the sudden rise of the revisionists. Conrad Russell and John Morrill led the way in a series of texts which challenged Gardiner's foundational assumptions about the inevitability of civil war by repudiating the search for long-term factors of dissent. The revolution which the revisionists discovered was the immediate result of problems which only surfaced in the early 1640s and which could have been entirely avoided. By contrast, writers on puritan apocalypticism had traced a grand meta-narrative of gradual change and incessant evolution, in which long-term elaborations of religious doctrine enabled the discourses of civil war. It was several years before attempts were made to regain the momentum captured by the previous millenarian studies. The late 1970s produced a clutch of important new works in Bryan W. Ball's *A Great Expectation: Eschatological Thought in English Protestantism to 1660* (1975), Paul Christianson's *Reformers and Babylon: English Apocalyptic Visions from the Reformation to the Eve of the Civil War* (1978), Richard Bauckham's *Tudor Apocalypse* (1978) and Katherine Firth's *The Apocalyptic Tradition in Reformation Britain, 1530-1645* (1979).

Firth and Christianson returned to the narrative established in Toon's collection. Covering much of the same material, both texts had the advantage of emanating from a single author, and consequently their material is more closely organised and systematically interrogated. Bauckham's *Tudor Apocalypse*, on the other hand, consists of several chapters examining discrete elements of the sixteenth-century tradition - the notion of an imminent end, for example - which are followed by relevant selections from both major and minor texts. Since its publication, investigations of puritan eschatology have tended to work across disciplinary boundaries.

The literary focus had already been well established among the historians of puritan eschatology. A.C. Dobbins, in 1975, produced *Milton and the Book of Revelation*, whose success might be gauged by Hill's complaint in *Milton and the English Revolution* (1977) that 'there is no work on Milton and contemporary millenarianism'.[4] These texts were followed in 1979 by William Lamont's analysis of *Richard Baxter and the Millennium*. Margarita Stocker's exposition of *Apocalyptic Marvell* (1986) demonstrated the extensive influence of eschatological ideas in this most influential of civil war poets. Each of these texts pushed into the foreground their subjects' interest in eschatological themes and demonstrated that they pervaded every aspect of seventeenth-century life. More ambitiously, both *The Apocalypse in English Renaissance Thought and Literature: Patterns, Antecedents and Repercussions* (1984), edited by C.A. Patrides and Joseph Wittreich, and *Millenarianism and Messianism in English Literature and Thought, 1650-1800* (1988), edited by Richard Popkin, attempted to engage with the implications of eschatology in the periods both before and towards the end of the chronological scope of this thesis. Apart from Hill's essay on Marvell in Popkin's collection, neither text offered much investigation of the puritan apocalyptic tradition. Theodore Dwight Bozeman's *To Live*

---

[4] Christopher Hill, *Milton and the English Revolution* (London: Faber and Faber, 1977), p. 6.

Ancient Lives: The Primitivist Dimension in Puritanism (1988) was, by contrast, a thorough historical-theological investigation, offering a challenge to previous models of the relationship between millennial eschatology and the 'errand into the wilderness'.

More recently several studies have emerged which more helpfully blur the distinctions between literary criticism and historical analysis. Michael Wilding's *Dragon's Teeth: Literature in the English Revolution* (1987) complemented Neil Keeble's *The Literary Culture of Nonconformity in Later Seventeenth-Century England* (1987) in explicating the various factors operating on puritan literature from the 1640s to the turn of the century. Keeble's text is wider in scope and usefully includes puritan theologians and their writings among the corpus of texts which literary critics can approach with profit. Nigel Smith's *Perfection Proclaimed: Language and Literature in English Radical Religion, 1640-1660* (1989) and his later *Literature and Revolution in England, 1640-1660* (1994) offer some fascinating and important insights into the hermeneutics of the radical groups of the civil war, pointing out that their methods of reading and writing were politicised tools employed to renew a fragmented and disparate world. Similarly, a number of the essays in *Milton and the Ends of Time* (2003), an interdisciplinary collection edited by Juliet Cummins, point to the lack of serious attention given to Milton's eschatology, echoing the argument of Hill's *Milton and the English Revolution* (1977).[5]

Most recent scholarship has emerged from within the community of historians. Irena Backus's influential work on *Reformation Readings of the Apocalypse: Geneva, Zurich and Wittenberg* (2000) has provided important new insights into the reformation origins of the puritan apocalyptic tradition, emphases developed in Howard Hotson's intellectual biography of *Johann Heinrich Alsted, 1588-1638* (2000) and its companion volume, *Paradise Postponed: Johann Heinrich Alsted and the Birth of Calvinist Millenarianism* (2000). A major article by Richard Cogley has outlined the central elements of puritan ideas of Israel's restoration and the fall of the Ottoman empire (2003), and Jeffrey K. Jue has offered a revision of a number of scholarly assumptions in *Heaven upon Earth: Joseph Mede (1586-1638) and the Legacy of Millenarianism* (2006).[6] Warren Johnston's doctoral thesis and its published outputs, including 'The

---

[5] See, for example, Juliet Cummins, 'Introduction: "Those thoughts that wander through eternity', in Juliet Cummins (ed.), *Milton and the ends of time* (Cambridge: Cambridge University Press, 2003), p. 1.

[6] Jue's fine work of historical-theological analysis argues that scholarship on early modern millennialism has been dominated by an unrevised Marxism, and quotes the first edition of this book to prove the point (pp. 3-4). It is possible, however, that Jue's concern to argue for a non-revolutionary millennialism fails to account for its discussion of the example of James Ussher.

Anglican Apocalypse in Restoration England' (2004), have demonstrated that eschatological tropes survived the eclipse of the puritan movement within the establishment itself.

Despite this wealth of information and variety of approach, however, much of the secondary literature fails in its purpose. Historians and literary critics alike have not always taken advantage of the theological vocabulary designed for the very purpose of discussing eschatology; indeed, it is often the case that the most basic of terms are used with various - and conflicting - meanings. Even the definitions of 'puritan' and 'millenarian' are contested.

In 1938 Woodhouse argued against a simplistic definition of 'puritanism': we should, he suggested, look instead for continuity, rather than a unity, in puritan identity.[7] In 1964 Hill observed that the term 'is an admirable refuge from clarity of thought.'[8] In 1983 Michael Finlayson noted that even in its own day the term 'served many purposes and was used with remarkable absence of precision'.[9] Ellwood Johnson similarly pushed into the foreground its semantic fluidity: 'the word changes in meaning from period to period: "Precisionism" in the interpretation of the Bible in the late sixteenth century; a struggle to change church polity to approximately 1620; the support of the rights of the middle class to the beginnings of the Civil War; a struggle with its more radical exponents during the Interregnum'.[10] As recently as 1997 Martyn Bennett was noting that 'defining a Puritan is very much like looking into a kaleidoscope; one slight movement of the mirrors or of the eyeline changes the image entirely, one twist of the end creates a completely new picture to study.'[11]

For the purpose of this thesis, nevertheless, there is some utility in retaining 'puritan', despite its ambiguity.[12] Each of the writers examined

---

[7] A.S.P. Woodhouse (ed.), *Puritanism and Liberty: Being the Army Debates (1647-9) from the Clarke Manuscripts with Supplementary Documents* (1938; rpr. London: Dent, 1992), p. [37].

[8] Christopher Hill, *Society and Puritanism in Pre-Revolutionary England* (1964; rpr. Harmondsworth: Penguin, 1991), p. 15.

[9] Michael Finlayson, *Historians, Puritanism, and the English Revolution: The Religious Factor in English Politics before and after the Interregnum* (Toronto: University of Toronto Press, 1983), p. 4.

[10] Ellwood Johnson, *The Pursuit of Power: Studies in the Vocabulary of Puritanism* (New York: Peter Lang, 1995), pp. 5-6.

[11] Martyn Bennett, *The Civil Wars in Britain and Ireland, 1638-1651* (Oxford: Blackwell, 1997), p. 74.

[12] Following the usage of Patrick Collinson, the term 'puritan' will be used without capitalisation to indicate its status as an adjective, referring to an ecclesiological trend, rather than as a proper noun, referring to a discrete

in this thesis could be recognised as puritans, though they did not all subscribe to the same extensive theology. Although most were opposed to prelacy, Ussher defended the Episcopal hierarchy. While most were keen to accommodate dissenting parties within one overarching ecclesiastical structure, Gillespie would tolerate none but Presbyterians. While most were 'experimental Calvinists', Milton was re-examining the foundations of this theology as *Areopagitica* went to press. Although most were defenders of ecclesiastical paternalism, Rogers defended the public ministry of women on an eschatological basis. In essence, the 'puritanism' of this selection of authors extends no further than their desire for further reformation of the protestant church within the three kingdoms - hence the identification of 'puritanism' with an ecclesiological trend.

But the problem of definition extends also to millennialism. 'Was John Foxe a millenarian?' Palle Olsen has asked, and answered: 'It is all a matter of definition.'[13] Much of the difficulty lies in the fact that the three major eschatological traditions which Christian theologians have developed - a-, pre- and postmillennialism - all found expression within the puritan movement. As we will see in our discussion of eschatological sources in the next chapter, the description of the 'millennium' in Revelation 20 eventually resulted in three different (though not mutually exclusive) interpretations. Amillennialists did not believe in a future millennium. Premillennialists did, and argued that Christ would return at its beginning. Postmillennialists also did, but argued that Christ would return at its end. But other positions were also represented – and some, like Brightman and Ussher, denied the principal assumption of the a-, pre- and postmillennial paradigms, that Revelation 20 referred to only one period of one thousand years. As the new appendix to this volume suggests, historians and theologians of competing parties have repeatedly misrepresented the dominant eschatology of the puritan period.

The debate over the eschatology of the Westminster Confession of Faith (1646) illuminates this confusion. Modern theologians have cited the Westminster Confession in support of their preferred eschatology. Peter Toon found 'no suggestion of a period of latter-day glory or of a millennium connected with the conversion of the Jews' and argued that the Confession is 'clearly' amillennial.[14] LeRoy Froom, whose four-

---

ecclesiological party. The typography of 'baptist' and 'independent' will vary insofar as they are used to refer to trends or parties.

[13] Palle J. Olsen, 'Was John Foxe a Millenarian?', *Journal of Ecclesiastical History* 45:4 (1994), p. 622.

[14] R. G. Clouse, 'The Rebirth of Millenarianism', in Peter Toon (ed.), *Puritans, the Millennium, and the Future of Israel* (Cambridge: James Clarke, 1970), p. 60.

volume *Prophetic Faith of our Fathers* (1948) supplies in bulk what it lacks in objectivity, disagrees and argues instead that the Confession is 'the strongest premillennialist symbol of Protestantism'.[15] James de Jong, on the other hand, rubbishes Froom's claim, alleging that 'Westminster's formulation must be seen as a deliberate choice of mild, unsystemized, postmillennial expectations.'[16] The dispute over the Westminster eschatology typifies the general confusion of the secondary material.

Puritan studies, in this respect, is peculiarly the victim of confessional bias. Even the *Milton Encyclopaedia*'s definition of millenarianism reflects that work's American background. In defining millenarianism as 'the active belief in the thousand-year reign of the saints on earth with Christ' they are opting for a premillennial norm; in reporting that millennialism is 'a matter of faith in most churches' and a 'conventional element of traditional eschatology', they are equating American fundamentalist teaching with the historic orthodoxy of the Christian church.[17] Marina Benjamin has reported that such millenarianism 'virtually is the mainline religion' in America.[18] Nevertheless, as we will see, countless confessional documents before and after the reformation outlawed those millenarian ideas beyond orthodoxy.[19] Opposition to millennialism has been the consistent norm of the Christian church.

Similarly, the teachings of that most textual of millenarian alliances - those radical puritans known as Fifth Monarchists - have been the subject of much confusion. Capp's study argued that the group were generally postmillennialists; he pointed to dissension in its ranks when John Simpson, a prominent leader, suggested a premillenarian eschatology and faced exclusion from the party.[20] Richard Greaves agreed, equating Fifth Monarchism with a distinctly postmillennial

---

[15] L. E. Froom, *The Prophetic Faith of Our Fathers: The Historical Development of Prophetic Interpretation* (Washington: Review and Herald, 1948), ii. 553.

[16] James de Jong, *As the Waters Cover the Sea: Millennial Expectations in the Rise of Anglo-American Missions 1640-1810* (Kampen: Kok, 1970), p. 38 n. 11.

[17] W.B. Hunter (gen. ed.), *A Milton Encyclopaedia* (London: Associated University Presses, 1978-80), v. 132.

[18] Quoted in Elaine Showalter, 'Apocalypse now and then, please', *The Times* April 16 1998, p. 38.

[19] On the regularly-repeated claim that millennialism was outlawed by the Council of Ephesus in AD 431, see Michael J. Svigel, 'The phantom heresy: Did the council of Ephesus (431) condemn Chiliasm?', *Trinity Journal* 24 n.s. (2003), pp. 105-12.

[20] B.S. Capp, *The Fifth Monarchy Men: A Study in Seventeenth-Century Millenarianism* (London: Faber and Faber, 1972), p. 192; R.L. Greaves, *Saints and Rebels: Seven Nonconformists in Stuart England* (Macon: Mercer University Press, 1985), pp. 99-132.

eschatology.[21] Nevertheless, we are informed by Capp that most of the Fifth Monarchist divines began their careers under the senior pastorship of William Bridge. If, as Murray claims, Bridge was a premillennialist - and his sermons certainly suggest that he was - such a combination sounds at best unlikely. Again, the secondary literature of puritan eschatology does not fall neatly into place.[22]

Perhaps because of these competing definitions, secondary studies have regularly brought their own parameters to bear on source documents. Toon's evaluation abandoned pre-, post- and amillennial categories in favour of descriptions of 'conservative' and 'extreme' millennialism. If his main concern was to impose distinctions based on the *political* implications of each system of eschatology, perhaps imagining that puritans were more interested in the implications of ideas than in the ideas themselves, he failed to do justice to the division in the ranks of the Fifth Monarchists caused by Simpson's premillennialism, as we noted above. This division was engendered purely by theological differences, and Simpson's allegiance to Fifth Monarchist socio-political ambitions seems to have remained intact.

Hill's parameters, for similar reasons, are unhelpful. *The English Bible and the Seventeenth Century Revolution* (1993), for example, probes no deeper than a differentiation between 'political' and 'apocalyptic' eschatologies - as if these were mutually exclusive schemes.[23] From other sources we learn that 'apocalyptic' millenarians could be entirely passive, pinning their hopes on an imminent advent, or alternatively they could set themselves up as the saints who would judge the world, like those Fifth Monarchists who periodically rose in armed insurrections. Hill also notes that 'so far as the printed record tells us, active revolutionary millenarianism fades out after 1661; Christ's coming is put into the distant future.'[24] The opposition at the heart of this statement - between revolutionary millenarianism and a far distant second advent - must also be qualified. It fails to take account of the theological nuances within puritan eschatology. Those Fifth Monarchists who were postmillennial, for example, had always

---

[21] Greaves, *Saints and Rebels*, pp. 132, 163.

[22] Capp, *The Fifth Monarchy Men*, p. 79; Iain H. Murray, *The Puritan Hope: Revival and the Interpretation of Prophecy* (Edinburgh: Banner of Truth, 1971), p. 53.

[23] Christopher Hill, *The English Bible and Seventeenth-Century Revolution* (Harmondsworth: Allen Lane 1993), pp. 304-5; cf. Geoffrey F. Nuttall, *The Holy Spirit in Puritan Faith and Experience* (1946; rpr. Chicago: University of Chicago Press, 1992), p. 111.

[24] Christopher Hill, *A Nation of Change and Novelty: Radical Politics, Religion and Literature in Seventeenth-Century England* (London and New York: Routledge, 1990), p. 231.

regarded Christ's return as reserved for the 'distant future' - yet this did not prevent them from advocating one of the period's most radical political agendas. Hill also notes that his analysis is based on extant literature. This would seem to ignore the crippling effect of the Restoration's re-imposition of censorship, and fails to explain the apparent continuity in millenarian activity in the later decades of the century.

Modern scholars would do well to understand the differences among puritans in the same terms as puritans themselves did. Reports from the Scottish Commissioners of the Westminster Assembly demonstrate that divisions there were theological, cutting along the lines of those who believed in a future millennium and those who did not. The most basic political implication of puritan eschatology - the objective of a godly nation under a godly leader - was common to each eschatological party. Even distinct literary implications, as we shall see, were shared between writers of the various schools. Modern scholarship would do well to take note.

Hill's terms are therefore too vague to be useful and, as Murray points out, they give the impression that 'far from being characterized by hope' the radical puritans 'expected the imminent end of the world'.[25] Paradoxically, it tended to be the orthodox, cautious amillennialists who expected the imminent end of the world; these men, like Richard Baxter, had no interest in speculating about an impending millennial reign of Christ.[26] It was the more radical of the brethren – among them recognisable pre- and postmillennialists - who were tending to forestall the second advent with radical political agendas. Perhaps Hill's penchant for radical thought caused him to read his preferences into his sources.

Debate also exists about the consummation of the puritan eschatological tradition. Neil Keeble's definitive study of *The Literary Culture of Nonconformity* (1987) argues that the millenarian disappointments of the mid-seventeenth century paved the way for the timidity (and, perhaps, the pessimism) of Restoration nonconformity, constructing the foil against which canonical writers - like Bunyan and Milton - were to react. Noting the growing quietism of the post-Restoration era, Keeble argues that 'militant millenarianism died with Venner'.[27] He emphasises, as does Geoffrey Nuttall, the spread of Quaker beliefs and the beginnings of a 'realised eschatology', in which

---

[25] Murray, *The Puritan Hope*, p. xxiii.

[26] William M. Lamont, *Godly Rule: Politics and Religion, 1603-60* (London: Macmillan, 1969), p. 55.

[27] N.H. Keeble, *The Literary Culture of Nonconformity in Later Seventeenth-Century England* (Leicester: Leicester University Press, 1987), pp. 24, 191.

the traditional elements of Christian eschatology were redefined into metaphors of Christian experience in the present world.[28] Hill also pointed to the centrality of the failed Fifth Monarchist risings in effecting such a sea-change in popular millenarianism: 'some Anglicans, including bishops and Isaac Newton, retained an academic interest in dating the Second Coming; but as a fighting creed millenarianism died when Venner's failures in 1657 and 1661 were followed by the year 1666, which produced national catastrophes but not the end of the world'.[29]

This emphasis on the development of 'realised eschatology' should not obscure the continuity of puritanism's revolutionary potential. Some evidence suggests that puritan apocalypticism retained its revolutionary potency as it evolved into eighteenth-century postmillennialism.[30] John Owen, we have noticed, retreated from his early literalism to project the Second Advent into the indefinite future; but his interest in radical politics remained. His involvement in anti-Richard Cromwell coup attempts in the late 1650s and the Rye House Plot in 1683 merits a great deal of further investigation. His relationship with the outlawed Covenanter groups, to whom he was linked by Robert Ferguson, has never been explored.[31] Richard Greaves has pointed to the discovery of several cases of pistols in Owen's home and the repeated allegations of his involvement with radical plots.[32] As Restoration persecution propelled the radical saints into an unusual degree of communality, the millenarian vision of godly rule became again the basis of the unity of the Scottish Covenanters and the English Fifth Monarchists - the three kingdoms' radical remnant. Burrage notes Fifth Monarchist activity as late as 1670,[33] and the continued millenarian speculation of the later period, implicitly loaded with political repercussions, is highlighted in William Lamont's study of *Richard Baxter and the Millennium* (1979), as well as Warren Johnson's more recent work. Nor indeed was the apocalyptic enthusiasm engendered by the Glorious Revolution entirely devoid of political expression, as the work of Hanserd Knollys and his fellow baptists would demonstrate. In the post-Restoration era,

---

[28] Keeble, *The Literary Culture of Nonconformity*, p. 204.

[29] Christopher Hill, *A Tinker and a Poor Man: John Bunyan and his Church 1628-1688* (New York: Albert A. Knopf, 1989), p. 343.

[30] Murray, *The Puritan Hope*, p. 271.

[31] R.L. Greaves, 'The Rye House Plotting, Nonconformist Clergy, and Calvin's Resistance Theory', in W. Fred Graham (ed.), *Later Calvinism: International Perspectives* (Kirksville: Sixteenth Century Journal Publishers, 1994), p. 507.

[32] R.L. Greaves, *Deliver Us from Evil: The Radical Underground in Britain, 1660-1663* (Oxford: Oxford University Press, 1986), p. 54.

[33] C. Burrage, 'The Fifth Monarchy Insurrections', *English Historical Review* 25 (1910), p. 746.

millenarianism and radical politics were not necessarily mutually exclusive interests. Perhaps the historiographical tradition of segmenting the period into discrete periods called 'Civil War' and 'Restoration' has contributed to this lack of panorama.

Nevertheless, faced with the conflicting paradigms of competing political and religious interpretations of puritanism, we need to recognise, as Roger Pooley warns us, 'that many of these critical arguments are themselves political; the hostility of Samuel Johnson, or T.S. Eliot to Milton's republican Nonconformity is echoed in as much subsequent Milton criticism as the desire to emphasise and appropriate it is in Blake or Christopher Hill.'[34] The political utility of the competing parameters within puritan studies can often be less clear than the overt partisanship of the occasional Marxist or Seventh-Day Adventist. Nevertheless, we might do worse than follow the advice given by William York Tindall, the first modern biographer of Bunyan: 'In an investigation of the godly men of the seventeenth century it is advisable to approach with caution the partisan records of sectarian history; and in a study of Bunyan, it is well to ignore, until one is familiar with the character of his work and with that of his contemporaries, the often partial or improper conclusions of his biographers and critics.'[35] So often has methodology obscured the meaning of the text.

Methodology

We might well wonder whether another study of the puritan apocalyptic tradition is necessary. Its history of ideas has been well covered, as the above selection of secondary sources would demonstrate. But despite the wealth and value of these sources, as Howard Hotson has noted, 'no sustained attention has been given to the complex nexus of exegetical, theological, philosophical, and historiographical problems' which such millenarianism raised.[36] Writers documenting the development of the puritan apocalyptic tradition have repeatedly set puritan ideologies in a vacuum, failing to recognise that eschatology was not something puritans studied so much as something in which they believed themselves to be involved, for the implications

---

[34] Roger Pooley, *English Prose of the Seventeenth Century, 1590-1700* (London: Longman, 1992), p. 146.

[35] William York Tindall, *John Bunyan, Mechanick Preacher* (1934; rpr. New York: Russell and Russell, 1964), p. xi.

[36] Howard Hotson, 'The Historiographical Origins of Calvinist Millenarianism', in Bruce Gordon (ed.), *Protestant Identity and History in Sixteenth-century Europe* (Brookfield: Scolar Press, 1996), p. 160.

of their eschatology were not purely theoretical. So too a contemporary analysis might also benefit from an application of the current philosophical interest in endings. Much of modern philosophy has been exploring notions of 'ending' and has itself advanced in an apocalyptic tenor.[37] This investigation of philosophy and eschatology has been particularised in *Apocalypse Theory* (1995), a collection of essays edited by Malcolm Bull, which juxtaposed digressions on subjects as diverse as classical music and historiographical models to insert the study of puritan eschatology within a larger, and more theoretical, framework.

Thus the millenarian texts of puritanism, with all their ambivalence and complexity, would seem to be ideal candidates in a reflection on the construction of a puritan poetics. Acutely concerned with the nexus of mimesis and transcendence, their Calvinistic millenarianism invoked an end-closed narrative which none of their works were able to deliver. This ideological involvement - and apparent aesthetic failure - signals that these texts are likely to prove interesting to several contemporary interpretive communities. Because of this type of ambivalence, recent critics, particularly among the New Historicists and Cultural Materialists, have come to view Renaissance texts as offering particularly rich readings. Although Stephen Greenblatt's work has reinstated aspects of Renaissance religion as crucial social phenomena, New Historicist critics have by-passed Renaissance texts with a strong theological bias. Debora Shuger, in *The Renaissance Bible* (1994), is an important exception. Overall, it would appear that the aesthetics of the cardinal's hat - celebrated by Greenblatt - are more important than those books which destroyed the ideology which upheld it. As Richard Strier has admitted, 'religion ... is something of a problem for New Historicism, which tends - unlike Renaissance English culture - to have a radically secular focus.'[38]

Nevertheless, any approach to the Renaissance which recognises the centrality of religious discourse is to be welcomed. Religious ideas permeated seventeenth-century society throughout the three kingdoms, and puritanism, with its strong textual bias, affords a rich mine for study. When puritan ideas are considered seriously, and their bearing on texts analysed, they can be seen to offer important insights into the practice of reading and writing in the early modern period and the construction of a distinctly Reformed metaphysics. Patricia Parker argues that in our own post-Derridean world, 'Renaissance texts indeed appear, with greater and lesser consciousness on the part of their

---

[37] Jacques Derrida, 'Of an Apocalyptic Tone Recently Adopted in Philosophy' *Semeia* 23 (1982), p. 63.
[38] Richard Strier, *Resistant Structures: Particularity, Radicalism, and Renaissance Texts* (Berkeley: University of California Press, 1995), p. 73.

writers, to share and even dramatise many of the same concerns post-structuralism raises about tropological and linguistic structures that generate not too little but too much meaning'.[39] Parker's comment only rephrases a staple of Reformation ideology: *finitum non est capax infiniti* - the finite cannot contain the infinite.

This maxim - the 'extra Calvinisticum' - was first expressed in the Eucharistic-Christological debates in the immediate post-Reformation decades.[40] Lutheran and Calvinistic theologians disputed the relationships between the two natures and the one person of the incarnate Son of God, with the Calvinists claiming that Christ's human and divine natures did not limit each other - for the finite could not contain the infinite. This motto became the basis of Calvinism's iconoclastic temper, and its textual implications are the evidence of the proto-deconstruction which contemporary readers find in puritan texts.[41] Puritanism's theology of idolatry compelled its adherents to posit the dismantling of the idol-image, that which, as John Knox defined, 'has the form and appearance, but lacks the virtue and strength which the name and proportion do resemble and promise.'[42] This thinking was soon applied to written texts. Richard Sibbes, for example, warned against men who 'idolise any discourse in books'.[43]

In *War Against the Idols* (1986), Carlos Eire argued that the basis of the Reformed movement was the application of this metaphysic of transcendence to Roman Catholic patterns of worship.[44] Reformers protested against the Roman doctrine of transubstantiation, arguing that it closed the transcendent God in a wafer. They opposed the cult of images, for the iconic power of the image drew the worshipper's attention to itself, rather than to what it represented. The literary strategy of puritanism applied the same doctrine to textual patterns. Puritans refused to close the infinite God within a finite text. As a consequence, the exploitation of poststructuralist concerns in the puritan apocalyptic tradition would appear to be a dramatisation of their theology. Puritan texts subvert their status as verbal icons,

---

[39] Patricia Parker and David Quint, *Literary Theory/Renaissance Texts* (Baltimore: John Hopkins University Press, 1986), p. 11.

[40] G. C. Berkouwer, *Studies in Dogmatics: The Person of Christ*, trans. John Vriend (Grand Rapids, MI: Eermans, 1954), pp. 274, 282-9.

[41] Heiko Oberman, 'The 'Extra' Dimension in the Theology of Calvin', *Journal of Ecclesiastical History* 21 (1970), pp. 60-62.

[42] John Knox, *The First Blast of the Trumpet against the Monstrous Regiment of Women* (1558; rpr. Dallas: Presbyterian Heritage Publications, 1993), p. 46.

[43] Richard Sibbes, *The Complete Works of Richard Sibbes*, ed. A.B. Grosart (Edinburgh: James Nichol, 1862-64), iii. 51.

[44] Carlos Eire, *War Against the Idols: The Reformation of Worship from Erasmus to Calvin* (Cambridge: Cambridge University Press, 1986), p. 3.

foregrounding their transitory nature only to point the reader past themselves towards a 'transcendental signifier'. Despite the claims of Stanley Fish, puritan texts are not 'self-sufficient' - building readers' confidence by constructing an argument they can follow - but are instead 'self-consuming'. Their language, in other words, calls 'attention to the insufficiency of its own procedures, calls into question the sufficiency of the minds it unsettles.'[45] Such strategy was basic to the plain Calvinistic aesthetic.

Thus Linda Gregerson, in *The Reformation of the Subject: Spenser, Milton, and the English Protestant Epic* (1995), traces the development of self-conscious puritan theorising of the text as a 'sign', and argues that, for puritans,

> the difference between signs and idols was thought to reside in a single, pivotal distinction: the one maintained a transitive or referential status and pointed beyond itself, ultimately to the transcendent. The other solicited attention or pleasure or belief on its own behalf, continuing to exist "for its own sake". . . In Reformation England, the verbal image was often thought to be as dangerous in its potential as the visual. Words, like pictures or statuary, were suspect for the very reason that they were powerful, capable of shaping and thus of waylaying the human imagination. Francis Bacon, who tried to conceive of a new epistemology under the new religion, thought that words could be "idols" too, and cautioned that "to fall in love with then is all one as to fall in love with a picture." The Puritan Richard Baxter denounced the "painted obscured sermons" of the Anglican preachers as no better than "the Painted Glass in the Windows that keep out the Light." It was incumbent upon the verbal artefact in this period to register and guard its own referential status and its correlative *in*utility for idolatrous purposes.[46]

Though Gregerson's interest is primarily in poetry, her remarks hold true for other aspects of puritan culture. A distinctive hermeneutic was at the centre of puritan - and protestant - identity.

For puritan authors, reading and writing were never ends in themselves; if, in the words of the Westminster divines, man's chief end was to glorify God and enjoy him forever, puritan literature was compelled to point past itself to its ultimate reason for existence. If puritan writing was to be true to its theological base, it was required to question the sufficiency of the human mind, of post-Fall epistemological patterns. Puritan literature existed to let men know God; this strategy

---

[45] Stanley Fish, *Self-Consuming Artefacts: the Experience of Literature in the Seventeenth Century* (Berkeley: University of California Press, 1972), p. 378.
[46] Linda Gregerson, *The Reformation of the Subject: Spenser, Milton and the English Protestant Epic* (Cambridge: Cambridge University Press, 1995), p. 2.

could only be successful as they undermined the authority of their own words and pointed instead towards the eternal *logos*.

Within apocalyptic puritanism, then, the parallel between God's providential closure of history and the textual closure of form became deeply imbued with iconoclastic theory. Thus, Parker's project balances the historical and textual notions of teleology in a manner John Foxe (at least) would earlier have applauded. Parker explicates the Latin 'dilato', itself etymologically linked to 'differo', the Latin root of Derrida's coined term 'différance'. Her results include various verbs and 'cultural assumptions' which signify 'the specific rhetorical technique of extending a discourse at length, the evangelical spread and imperial expansion of Christianity before the Last Judgement, and finally a process of delay that, in its juridical context, aims at the putting-off or suspension of judgement'.[47] Thus, with the etymology of the contemporary philosophical debate confirming the theory and theology of early modern puritans, contemporary readers can shake off 'more anxious modern theories of textuality', understanding the evidence behind such claims to merely be indicative of puritanism's biblically justified literary practice. David Jasper, a professor of theology at the University of Glasgow, is typical in his concerns about the Derridean assault on Christian thought; its 'cold, arresting and absurd logic challenges the presumption, critical or theological, of a centre or fixed principle; the notion of solid foundations or a formal structure built upon them. Relativities, deferment, *différance* - the death of certainty, the death, even of God.'[48] But puritans could hardly have intended that the textual excess of their work would demand such a conclusion.

Instead, in the core texts of the Reformation's literary heritage, the metaphysical deferral inherent to puritan literature simply enacts the theology it describes. Its lack of closure points both to the text's artificiality, its lack of iconic power, and also dramatises puritanism's apocalyptic interests - the deferral of the apocalypse and the world-wide expansion of Christ's kingdom. As Parker argues, 'the combination of temporal deferral and spatial extension ... crucially defines the self-reflexive strategies of a wide range of Renaissance texts', and it is certainly typical of those texts forming part of the puritan eschatological tradition. Parker continues to note that 'similarities between the recurrent figures of contemporary critical discourse and the characteristic terms of particular Renaissance texts have informed much of recent speculation on the potential application of this [post-structuralist] theory to a rereading of the Renaissance, not the least of

---

[47] Parker and Quint, *Literary Theory/Renaissance Texts*, pp. 11-12.
[48] David Jasper, *The Study of Literature and Religion* (London: Macmillan, 1989; 2nd ed. 1992), p. 111.

which has been the questioning of whether an ultimately Derridean reading of deferral in these texts is finally historically justified.'[49] The argument of this book is that it need not be. In a context which, like that of the puritans, is 'harassed (if not obsessed) by epistemological problems',[50] hermeneutical integrity can also be achieved through readings which are alive to the theology each text presents. As we will see, the apocalyptic aesthetic was puritan – not Derridean.

Thus the argument of this chapter and those which follow will embrace many of the insights raised by Derridean analysis of ambiguities and indeterminancies, but will also argue that such theoretically-informed readings in themselves do not go far enough. It will advance a reading sensitive to 'cultural poetics' to argue that the literary culture of early puritanism adopted the trope of textual excess to produce texts which teach, which employ their form to enact their theology. Situating the ambivalences of puritan texts within their authorial context demonstrates that they are involved in deliberate textual strategies, attempting to 'convert' the reader through the operations of the text. In John Bunyan's *Grace Abounding* and the conversion narratives of John Rogers, for example, the act and implications of reading inhabit a crucial centre in puritan discourses of conversion. The unclosed foreground of the puritan apocalypse was intended to effect the same change in the reader. There was so much more to puritan aesthetics than mere 'plain style'.

Thus the chapters following this introduction chart the theological development and literary implications of the puritan apocalypse from the 1550s to the 1680s. In one form or another, the aesthetics of apocalypse and the possibility of closure are pushed into the foreground and interrogated in each of the texts and contexts I examine. This alternative canon highlights the literary implications of the puritan apocalypse through snapshots taken at representative stages of its development. Thus each 'slice or cross-section of history'[51] demonstrates that the *topos* of the millennium was applied variously to universal history, the church government debates of the 1640s, and the social and psychological ferment of the 1650s. We will notice that the definition of Antichrist is always building, from Ussher's hostility to Rome, to Gillespie's hostility to Anglicanism and Rome, to Milton's hostility to

---

[49] Parker and Quint, *Literary Theory/Renaissance Texts*, pp. 182-3.

[50] John M. Steadman, *The Hill and the Labyrinth: Discourse and Certitude in Milton and his Near-Contemporaries* (Berkeley: University of California Press, 1984), p. 1.

[51] Howard Felperin, "Cultural poetics' versus 'cultural materialism': The two New Historicisms in Renaissance studies', in Francis Barker et al (eds), *Uses of History: Marxism, Postmodernism and the Renaissance* (Manchester: Manchester University Press, 1991), p. 86.

Presbyterianism and Anglicanism and Rome, to the later Rogers' hostility to Independency, Presbyterianism, Anglicanism and Rome. We will notice the multiple hermeneutical strategies within puritanism's 'literal' readings. We will trace a movement toward metaphor, as the puritan apocalypse is transferred from being a construction of the past to become an anticipation of the future and finally an investigation of the self in the present. We will document how apocalyptic historiography created a national sense of a past while the Long Parliament publications of the early 1640s constructed an alternative vision of collective identity based on a common future. We will notice how the godly readers constructed by the Geneva Bible increasingly questioned the integrity of the text, and finally, by invoking the realised eschatology of the radical sectaries, satirised the constructions of radical selfhood through the encoding of unstable narrative elements within *The Holy War*. At the edge of the promises, liminality is textual and psychological, as well as prophetic; the boundaries of confusion are literary and individual, as well as between this world and the next.

It must be emphasised that the 'canon' this thesis presents is only one trajectory through a massive matrix of controversial divinity. Previous studies have been organised around various schemes of interpretation. Some authors, like Christianson, have employed a 'history of ideas' approach to chart the evolution of the doctrine through its principal exponents; Liu, on the other hand, has traced the ebb of apocalypticism through puritanism's competing ecclesiological groupings. Others have focused on individual themes within this overarching puritan eschatology: Lamont's *Godly Rule* highlighted the links between millenarianism and theonomic rule, Hill has expounded the various definitions of *Antichrist in Seventeenth-Century England*, Rodney Peterson analysed *Preaching in the Last Days: The Theme of 'Two Witnesses' in the Sixteenth and Seventeenth Centuries* (1993), and Paul Brady has accounted for the various ascriptions of '666'. Although this thesis does not adopt any one of these approaches, it is hoped, nevertheless, that a sense of theological evolution will appear, and that the reader's appreciation of canonical texts such as those by Milton and Bunyan will only increase by seeing them within the context of which their authors were most aware. It is hoped that the reader will realise that it is impossible to understand the discourses of the civil wars without some knowledge of their evolution in the century beforehand; similarly it is hoped that the reader will sense the continuity of puritanism after the Restoration, noting that many of the familiar qualities of canonical writers are only the salient features of a century of apocalyptic investigation reaching a logical culmination. The tradition of puritan millenarianism produced texts which demonstrate 'an extraordinary sensitive register of the complex struggles and harmonies of culture' - and are therefore, in the terms of Stephen Greenblatt, 'great art', poised at the edge of the promises.[52]

---

[52] Stephen Greenblatt, *Renaissance Self-Fashioning: From More to Shakespeare* (Chicago: University of Chicago Press, 1980), p. 5.

CHAPTER 2

The Development of the Puritan Apocalypse

Writing at the edge of the promises was a sustained, if difficult, occupation. Norman Cohn noted the popularity of apocalyptic themes throughout medieval societies in *The Pursuit of the Millennium* (1957), and extended his analysis back into pre-New Testament cultures in *Cosmos, Chaos and the World to Come* (1993). From ancient Egypt to the rise and fall of Communism, he would argue, millenarian thinking has underpinned a variety of social negotiations. Cohn avoided an analysis of Renaissance culture within the three kingdoms, but hinted, in an appendix on the Ranters in *The Pursuit of the Millennium*, that there was a millenarian component to the ferment of the English puritan revolution. It is unfortunate that Cohn missed the eschatological explosion caused by the publication of the first English-language New Testament in 1525. With his grounding in pre-Christian and medieval apocalyptic material, he would have noted that the millenarianism underpinning the puritan revolution was not always entirely Biblocentric.

Contrary to popular belief, puritans did *not* restrict themselves to 'the Bible only' in their attempts to chart the predicted future. Jewish and classical texts were regularly culled for apocalyptic source material, and the popular press was quick to republish native prophecies - texts purporting to be authored by figures such as King Arthur's Merlin and others deriving from the ecstatic ramblings of radical enthusiasts. One modern historian, Katherine Firth, has cautioned against a reading of puritan millenarianism which simply reflects 'the bewildering array of ideas that make up the matrix of European thought during this period'. She warns that 'the intellectual history of the period is no less complicated than the political ... The interplay between such streams of thought as Christian Cabala, Hermeticism, angelology, and alchemy helped to drive an engine of thought in directions compatible with a brand of apocalypticism.'[1]

---

[1] Christopher Hill, *The World Turned Upside Down: Radical Ideas During the English Revolution* (1972; rpr. Harmondsworth: Penguin, 1991), p. 90; Capp, *The Fifth Monarchy Men*, p. 187; Katherine Firth, *The Apocalyptic Tradition in Reformation Britain, 1530-1645* (Oxford: Oxford University Press, 1979), pp. 204-5.

The most influential sources, nevertheless, came from a small and fairly discrete canon and were repeated endlessly throughout the puritan apocalyptic tradition. The popular idea of a six-thousand-year span of universal history, for example, derived from the *House of Elias*, a third century Hebrew midrash:[2]

> The world is to last six millennia;
> the first two millennia are to be an age of *tohu* (chaos),
> the next two millennia – an age of Torah,
> the next two millennia – the age of the Messiah.[3]

While the idea was more often repudiated than invoked, we can hardly assume that every puritan who alluded to a six-thousand-year schema of universal history was necessarily acquainted with Hebrew midrash. John Bunyan, for example, disparaged scholastic language study but was nevertheless able to argue that 'as God was six days in the works of creation, and rested the seventh; so in six thousand years he will perfect his works and providences that concern this world.'[4] Doubtless, echoes of the abstruse and arcane entered the popular imagination and lingered there long after their original source was forgotten. But some overt references to Elias continued to appear - in, for example, Johann Heinrich Alsted's *The Beloved City* (1643).[5]

Other writers foregrounded their debts to sources outwith the Judaeo-Christian tradition. John Napier, Lord of Merchiston and inventor of logarithms, appended quotations from the Sibylline oracles to his *Plaine Discovery of the Whole Revelation* (1593). Reflecting the ambivalence of puritanism's attitude to extra-Biblical sources of truth, Napier commented that the oracles were neither 'so authentik, that hitherto wee coulde cite any of them, in maters of Scriptures, neither so prophane that altogether we could omit them'.[6] Other ideas popular in the period have been traced to Merlin and Nostradamus, Paracelsus and Mother Shipton.

But not every puritan shared this fascination with non-Biblical apocalyptic. Thomas Hayne's exposition of *Christs Kingdom on Earth*

---

[2] Firth, *The Apocalyptic Tradition in Reformation Britain*, p. 5.

[3] Saul Leeman, 'Was Bishop Ussher's Chronology Influenced by a Midrash?' *Semeia* 8 (1977), p. 127.

[4] John Bunyan, *The Works of John Bunyan*, ed. George Offor (Glasgow: Blackie and Son, 1860), ii. 424.

[5] For a recent study of Alsted, see Howard Hotson, *Johann Heinrich Alsted, 1588-1638: Between Renaissance, Reformation, and Universal Reform* (Oxford: Oxford University Press, 2000).

[6] John Napier, *A Plaine Discovery of the Whole Revelation* (London, 1593; 2nd ed. 1611), p. 367.

(1645) anticipated that its readers needed to be warned off the 'senseless' teaching of 'Rabbi Elias'.[7] Similarly, Thomas Hall, author of *A Confutation of the Millenarian Opinion* (1657), rebuked the excessive credulity of some towards the eschatologies of 'Jewish Targums and Talmuds, Sibylline Oracles, the Koran, and astronomy'.[8] We can with more certainty assume that the apocalyptic source documents which Hall preferred - found in Scripture - were those with which most puritans would have been most familiar.

Certainly, in the puritan apocalyptic tradition, few terms were more evocative than 'Antichrist'. While the existence of this character was proof positive that the end was at hand, his importance in puritan thought disguises his rather infrequent appearances in Scripture. Antichrist is mentioned by name in only three passages:

> Little children, it is the last time, and as yee have heard that Antichrist shall come, even now there are many Antichrists: whereby we know that it is the last time ... Who is a liar, but he that denieth that Jesus is that Christ? the same is that Antichrist that denieth the Father and the Sonne. (*1 John* 2:18, 22)

> And every spirit that confesseth not that Jesus Christ is come in the flesh, is not of God: but this is the spirit of Antichrist (*1 John* 4:3)

> For many deceivers are entred into this world, which confesse not that Jesus Christ is come in the flesh. Hee that is such one, is a deceiver and an Antichrist. (*2 John* 7)

The Geneva Bible's decision to capitalise 'Antichrist' - a typographical decision which the Authorised Version did not maintain - is a hint of its more polemical apocalyptic agenda, as we shall later see.

The Reformed tradition, which the Geneva Bible buttressed, was not unique in asserting that Antichrist was the Pope. Around A.D. 600, Pope Gregory I had taught that the man who assumed the title of 'universal priest' would be Antichrist's forerunner; Joachim of Fiore, in the twelfth century, and Wycliffe, in the fourteenth, made a similar identification. Seventeenth-century exposition would prove that the puritans had no shortage of apocalyptic enemies, as Antichrist crept from the Vatican into the most Reformed of congregations. Archbishop

---

[7] Thomas Hayne, *Christs Kingdom on Earth* (1645), pp. 61-2.
[8] A. R. Dallison, 'Contemporary Criticism of Millenarianism', in Peter Toon (ed.), *Puritans, the Millennium, and the Future of Israel* (Cambridge: James Clarke, 1970), p. 111.

Ussher would complain that nothing was 'so familiar now a days, as to father upon Antichrist, whatsoever in church matters we do not find to suite with our own humours'.[9] His identification of the Pope as Antichrist was axiomatic for puritans; but subsequent writers added their own observations to the claims which they inherited from Ussher. George Gillespie added the Church of England to the Church of Rome; John Milton added the Presbyterians to the Anglicans and Roman Catholics; John Rogers added the leading Independents in the Cromwell circle to all those whom Milton had identified. Throughout the seventeenth century, Antichrist's influence was perceived to increase as his identification was pursued by an increasingly radical minority.

The apostle John's prophecies of Antichrist had long been read in parallel with the other passages describing a great eschatological enemy for the people of God. Passages like *2 Thessalonians* 2 provided further insights into this 'man of sin':

> Now wee beseech you, brethren, by the comming of our Lord Jesus Christ, and by our assembling unto him, That yee bee not suddenly mooved from your minde, nor troubled neither by spirit, nor by worde, nor by letter, as it were from us, as though the day of Christ were at hand. Let no man deceive you by any meanes: for that day shall not come, except there come a departing first, and that that man of sinne be disclosed, even the sonne of perdition, Which is an adversarie, and exalteth himselfe against all that is called God, or that is worshipped: so that he doeth sit as God in the Temple of God, shewing himselfe that he is God. (*2 Thessalonians* 2:1-4)

This chapter was something of a problem passage for puritans. In their hostility to Rome they were anxious to deny that the Pope had jurisdiction over genuine churches, but were faced with the problem that Antichrist had to be found in the 'Temple of God' - the visible Christian church. 'There is no head of the Church but the Lord Jesus Christ', the Westminster Confession would teach; 'nor can the Pope of Rome, in any sense, be head thereof: but is that Antichrist, that man of sin, and son of perdition, that exalteth himself, in the Church, against Christ and all that is called God.'[10] George Gillespie, a formulator of the confession, argued that the Pope's churches were consequently true churches: 'if there was not a true church when Popery and Antichristianism had most universally spread itself, why is it said that

---

[9] James Ussher, *The Whole Works of James Ussher*, eds C.R. Elrington and J.R. Todd (Dublin, 1847-64), vii. 45.
[10] *WCF* xxv. vi.

Antichrist sitteth in the temple of God?'[11] The English Presbyterian Thomas Manton later confirmed that 'the place wherein Antichrist shall arise is the visible Christian church.'[12]

Other writers alluded to similar tropes within biblical apocalyptic, describing the Pope as the 'beast', whose mark was necessary for buying and selling in his dominion. The 'mark of the beast' was 666 (*Revelation* 13:18). One writer who opposed the Scottish Covenant made the significant charge that it was composed of six hundred and sixty-six words.[13]

After the disclosure of the Antichrist's identity, the interpretation of the 'millennium' passage in *Revelation* 20 was of such defining importance that one's reading of it regularly determined one's ecclesiastical affiliation. This chapter describes a period of one thousand years when the Devil would be bound and Christ would rule with the saints. In his vision, the apostle John

> saw an Angel come downe from heaven, having the key of the bottomlesse pit, and a great chaine in his hand. And he tooke the dragon that olde serpent, which is the devill and Satan, and hee bound him a thousand yeeres: And cast him into the bottomlesse pit, and hee shut him up, and sealed the doore upon him, that hee should deceive the people no more, till the thousand yeres were fulfilled: for after that he muste be loosed for a little season. And I saw seates: and they sate upon them, and judgment was given unto them, and I saw the soules of them that were beheaded for the witnesse of Jesus, and for the word of God, and which did not worship the beast, neither his image, neither had taken his marke upon their foreheads or on their hands: and they lived, and reigned with Christ a thousand yeere. But the rest of the dead men shall not live againe untill the thousand yeeres bee finished: this is the first resurrection. Blessed and holy is hee, that hath part in the first resurrection: for on such the second death hath no power: but they shall bee the Priests of God and of Christ, and shall reigne with him a thousand yeere. And when the thousand yeeres are expired, Satan shall be loosed out of his prison. (*Revelation* 20:1-7)

This period of the thousand years was referred to by its Latin name, 'millennium', or the Greek term 'chiliad'. These two terms gave rise to a huge diversity of descriptive terms - 'millenarian', 'millennialist' and

---

[11] George Gillespie, *A Treatise of Miscellany Questions* (1649), in *The Works of George Gillespie: The Presbyterian's Armoury*, ed. W.M. Hetherington (Edinburgh: Robert Ogle, and Oliver & Boyd, 1846), p. 27.

[12] Thomas Manton, *The Complete Works of Thomas Manton* (London: James Nisbet, 1870-75), iii. 40.

[13] Christopher Hill, *Antichrist in Seventeenth-Century England* (London: Oxford University Press, 1971), p. 91.

'chiliast' being the most common. The place of the millennium in an individual's eschatology became a defining factor. Non-millennialists, as their name suggests, did not believe that the thousand-year reign was in the future. With Augustine, they either suggested that the period described in *Revelation* 20 was a symbol of the church age *in toto* - 'signifying the entirety of time by a perfect number'[14] - or merely a metaphorical description of the first thousand years of Christian history. John Foxe and the annotations of the Geneva Bible advanced this latter view. This type of millennium was not a golden age, as such; Calvin had already characterised the millennium as a period of persecution rather than of bliss. This was evidenced when non-millennialists paralleled the thousand years with the beginnings of Antichrist's rule.

Millennialists or chiliasts, on the other hand, maintained that the period described in *Revelation* 20 was a clear description of a future golden age. There were significant disagreements on detail. The saints would reign with Christ, some believed, visibly from his throne in Jerusalem. Others argued that godliness would pervade every avenue of socio-political life as entire communities would be brought under the jurisdiction of Old Testament law. The persecuted saints would be raised as the judges of the peoples; they would witness the earth's reversion to an Edenic state. The latter-day glory would encompass a great revival of evangelical Christianity while the deserts would blossom like roses, carnivores would become herbivores, and little children would play in safety beside asps' nests. As we shall later see, the millenarian school of interpretation grew in popularity and influence in the middle decades of the seventeenth century, finding a focus in the Independent and Presbyterian churches, but split into competing factions roughly aligned with England's various ecclesiastical groupings. George Gillespie, John Rogers and John Bunyan each evidenced distinctive features of millennialist belief. As eschatology engaged with the debate about Biblical church government, each side came to argue that their distinctives were to be associated with the pure church of the future millennial reign.

Some of the trends which featured in the millenarian movement would later be distinguished in pre- and postmillennial eschatologies. The premillennialists, we have noticed, argued that Christ would return *before* the millennium and often added that he would reign in person with his Church during the thousand years; they perceived the relation between this age and the millennium as one of radical disjunction. The postmillennialists, on the other hand, generally argued for continuity between this age and the next, that Christ's rule would be symbolic and

---

[14] Augustine, *Concerning the City of God Against the Pagans* (1467; rpr. trans. Henry Bettenson, Harmondsworth: Penguin, 1972), p. 908.

gradual, expressed in the increasing influence of Old Testament law over reformed societies, and that Christ's coming would *succeed* the millennium.

In practise, many premillennialists were really referring to three comings of Christ - two of which could be described as his 'second' coming. Their interpreters were slow to recognise this difficulty. Only fringe radicals like John Archer were prepared to admit to - and capitalise upon - this highly contentious deviation from traditional orthodoxy. 'Christ hath three commings', he declared; 'The first was when he came to take our nature, and make satisfaction for sin. The second is, when hee comes to receive his Kingdome; ... A third is, that when hee comes to judge all, and end the world: the latter commings are two distinct comings.'[15]

Many modern historians have missed the nuances of these competing positions and have assumed that 'the millennium' and 'the end of the world' are equivalent terms; John Archer, and other millennialists with him, contended that they were instead one thousand years apart. Recognising the distinctions within the millennialist school would caution us against making claims that millenarians expected the imminent return of Christ - although they often expected the millennium to commence in the near future, they anticipated waiting a least one thousand years for Christ's coming (if they were postmillennialists) or for the end of the world (if they were premillennialists).

Contemporary theologians might also seek to categorise puritan expositors according to their interpretation of the 'first resurrection' which was to precede the thousand-year reign in *Revelation* 20:5. Modern eschatologies generally divide themselves between 'literalists' and 'symbolists' at this point. Only modern premillennialists would understand the first resurrection to refer to a physical resurrection of the body; amillennialists and postmillennialists, by contrast, tend to see it as a metaphor of the individual's conversion, his passing from spiritual death to life. Conversion in the New Testament is regularly figured as resurrection: 'And you hath he quickened, who were dead in trespasses and sins' (*Ephesians* 2:1, AV). Unfortunately, this is not a helpful paradigm to apply to the puritan context. There the situation is less clear-cut. Premillennialists did tend to understand the first resurrection to be a literal, physical resurrection, and non-millennialists did tend to interpret it as an allegory of conversion. Postmillennialists, however, oscillated between the two positions. John Alsted's *The Beloved City* (1643) advanced a postmillennial reading of *Revelation* which included a physical first resurrection. John Cotton's *The Churches Resurrection* (1642)

---

[15] John Archer, *The Personall Reign of Chist upon Earth* (London, 1643), p. 15.

was also a postmillennial apologetic, but advanced an allegorical reading of the first resurrection: 'the first Resurrection was the rising of men from spirituall death to spirituall life.'[16]

Most millennialists were in agreement in their hopes of a 'fifth monarchy', the socio-political expression of the eschatological reign of the saints. This idea derived from the Old Testament apocalyptic book of *Daniel*. This prophet's vision of five great world empires was broader in scope, and gave puritans the parameters in which to interpret universal history:

> These great beasts which are foure, [are] foure Kings, which shall arise out of the earth, and they shal take ye kingdome of the Sainctes of the moste high, and possesse the kingdome for ever, even for ever and ever. After this, I wolde [knowe] the trueth of the fourth beast, which was so unlike to al the others, very feareful, whose teeth were of yron & his nailes of brasse: [wc] devoured, brake in pieces, and stamped the residue under his fete. Also to [knowe] of the ten hornes that were in his head, & of the other which came up, before whome thre fell, and of the horne that had eyes, & of the mouth that spake presumpteous things, whose loke was more stout then his felowes. I beheld, & the same horne made battel against the Sainctes, yea and prevailed against them, Until the Ancient of daies came, & judgement was given to the Saintes of the most high: and the time approched, that the Sainctes possessed the kingdome. (*Daniel* 7:17-22)

It was a concentration upon the chronology of this passage which gave the Fifth Monarchists their name. They were the saints, they believed, who would 'posses the kingdom'; but the same ambition was shared by most millenarians.

Another feature of Daniel's prophecy which excited attention was his scheme of seventy 'weeks'. These were periods of time which corresponded to the history of Israel: 'Seventie weeks are determined upon thy people, and upon thine holy citie to finish the wickednesse, and to seal up their sinnes, to reconcile the iniquitie, and to bring in everlasting righteousnesse, and to seal up the vision and prophesie, and to anoint the most Holy' (*Daniel* 9:24). When scholars like Joseph Mede attempted to formulate a universal chronology of the future, they regularly alluded to this providential time-clock as a basis for their calculations. James Ussher's letters regularly refer to the latest explanations of the seventy weeks.

Unfortunately, it is extremely hazardous to make any more concrete observations about the differences between the various eschatological schools within the puritan movement. Apocalyptic beliefs remained in a state of flux throughout the seventeenth century and each writer must

---

[16] John Cotton, *The Churches Resurrection* (London, 1642), p. 9.

be read in his or her own right without bringing to bear upon him or her the eschatological expectations which the succeeding centuries have accumulated. It is never enough simply to claim of an individual that he or she was a member of a particular eschatological party. There was a great deal of latitude both *between* and *within* each apocalyptic discourse, and the contemporary distinctions between a-, pre- and postmillennialism simply do not account for the varieties of puritan belief. It is unfortunate, as we will see, that modern scholars and historians have not maintained this caution.

The History of Puritan Interpretations

Although we have already discussed recent interpretations of the puritan millenarian tradition, it is, in some senses, impossible to effectively separate primary and secondary sources in a study of the history of the doctrine. The primary sources in the tradition were themselves written as secondary criticism, interpreting previous commentaries as much as interpreting Scripture: thus Thomas Hayne's *Christs Kingdom on Earth* (1645), for example, was subtitled as an examination of *What Mr. Th. Brightman, Dr. J. Alsted, Mr. J. Mede, Mr. H. Archer, The Glimpse of Sions Glory, and such as concurre in opinion with them, hold concerning the thousand years of the Saints Reign with Christ, And of Satans binding*. Simultaneously, some of the more recent scholarly evaluations of the puritan apocalyptic tradition were written self-consciously as a part of its legacy. Iain Murray's study of *The Puritan Hope* (1971), for example, appears to have been written both to document puritan eschatologies and to encourage the revival of postmillennialism amongst evangelical Christians. B.W. Ball's *The English Connection: The Puritan Roots of Seventh-day Adventist Belief* (1981) re-read puritan sources to advance his own premillennial denominational agenda. Both studies included valuable historical surveys alongside their didactic theological arguments, and effectively demonstrated the blur on both sides of the primary-secondary literature divide. For our purposes, the primary sources of apocalyptic puritanism are those studies published before the beginning of the eighteenth century.

Historical analysis is further complicated by those secondary works which explicate a vast body of puritan commentary but do not always agree on its most important figures. The centrality of Brightman and Mede, for example, has at times been eclipsed in a survey of more minor figures, while many of the sources cited by major expositors like Thomas Goodwin have never appeared in any discussion of the puritan apocalyptic tradition. Goodwin, in *An Exposition of the Book of Revelation* (1639), refers to Theodore Beza, Thomas Brightman, Joseph Mede, and

John Foxe, all of whom are well-documented figures; but he also refers
to the less well-known figures of the apocalyptic context - Patrick
Forbes, James Ussher, Matthew Parker, Franciscus Junius, Pareus,
William Ames, and John Napier.[17] Modern scholarship is more likely to
reconstruct the puritan apocalyptic tradition with accuracy when it pays
attention to the expositors its subjects regarded as important. It is for
this reason that this thesis discusses some individuals whose
apocalyptic teachings have not previously been subject to academic
analysis - the thesis will not ignore the significance which well-placed
contemporaries recognised. This is not an attempt to define a canon in
retrospect, but to elucidate various expressions of puritan
millenarianism which contemporary readers would have recognised as
existing within its tradition, as that tradition grew increasingly radical.

Nevertheless, as a background to the better understanding of the
selected works, some acquaintance with the overall development of the
puritan apocalyptic tradition is necessary. Its origins stretch back
further than we might imagine. After the rapid decay of the early
church, puritanism has its roots in the theology of St. Augustine, bishop
of Hippo (354-430), as Richard Muller noted in *Christ and the Decree*
(1986): 'Reformed theology appears not as a monolithic structure - not,
in short, as "Calvinism" - but as a form of Augustinian theology and
piety capable of considerable variation in its form and presentation.'[18]
Many elements of Augustine's thought remained paradigmatic in the
sixteenth and seventeenth centuries. His *City of God*, for example, was
the first catalyst of puritanism's eschatological innovations.

Augustine prepared his *City of God* in the years between 413 and 426.
The text was intended to combat the influence of the radical heretics of
his day; thus, after spending some chapters defending Christian
orthodoxy against pantheism, Augustine turned his attention to the
future prospects of the Church. Augustine revealed that even in his own
day 'some people have assumed, in view of this passage [*Revelation* 20],
that the first resurrection will be a bodily resurrection. They have been
particularly excited, among other reasons, by the actual number of a
thousand years, taking it as appropriate that there should be a kind of
Sabbath for the saints for all that time, a holy rest, that is, after the
labours of the six thousand years since man's creation ... I also
entertained this notion at one time.'[19] As we have already noted,
Augustine had come to refer the millennium either to the first thousand

---

[17] Thomas Goodwin, *The Works of Thomas Goodwin* (Edinburgh: James Nichol,
1861-66), iii. 4; 3; 36; 88; 61; 87-8; 103-4; 178; 180; 181; 194.
[18] Richard A. Muller, *Christ and the Decree: Christology and Predestination in
Reformed Theology from Calvin to Perkins* (Durham: Labyrinth, 1986), p. 176.
[19] Augustine, *City of God*, pp. 906-7.

years of the church age, or to universal history in its entirety, but did not pretend to offer a complete systemisation of apocalyptic teaching: of one part of Scriptural eschatology, he was prepared to admit that 'the meaning of this completely escapes me.'[20] Nevertheless, his antipathy towards millenarianism was hugely influential.[21]

Augustine's teaching exercised phenomenal influence in succeeding centuries, but the fact that Reformation confessions needed to reiterate his rejection of millennial belief demonstrates its perennial popularity. One of the most influential Reformation documents was the Augsburg Confession, a statement of faith drafted by Melancthon and published with the approval of Luther in 1530. The early protestant communities this confession represented explicitly condemned those 'Anabaptists' who denied the reality of eternal punishment along with others 'which spread abroad Jewish opinions, that, before the resurrection of the dead, the godly shall get the sovereignty in the world, and the wicked shall be brought under in every place'.[22] Similarly, in 1566, the second Helvetic Confession condemned 'the Jewish dreams, that before the day of judgement there shall be a golden world in the earth; and that the godly shall possess the kingdoms of the world, their wicked enemies being trodden under foot'.[23] This statement represented a multinational protestant front as the Reformed churches in Scotland, Hungary, Poland and Geneva all subscribed their assent. Between 1530 and 1566, then, nothing had happened to dampen the Reformed's hostility to millenarian ideas; instead, they had witnessed an event which was to acquire deep and lasting resonance for succeeding centuries, an event which had evidenced the fluidity and volatility of the early protestant identity.

This event was shocking in the extreme. The German town of Münster had declared itself Lutheran in the early 1530s, but quickly attracted the attention of neighbouring Anabaptist preachers. These were disciples of Melchior Hoffmann, a wandering preacher who had predicted that the millennium would commence in 1533. When the millenarian preachers arrived in the town they quickly gained dominance of the 'poorer classes', teaching the Christian's duty to share goods and cancel debts in preparation for the coming millennial kingdom. News of the town's reformation spread, and propertiless vagrants were attracted from miles around. A change in the leadership

---

20 Augustine, *City of God*, p. 933.
21 See Svigel, 'The phantom heresy: Did the Council of Ephesus (431) condemn chiliasm?', pp. 105-12.
22 Peter Hall (ed.), *Harmony of the Protestant Confessions* (1842; rpr. Edmonton: Still Waters Revival Books, 1992), p. 106.
23 Hall (ed.), *Harmony of the Protestant Confessions*, p. 88.

of the Anabaptists radicalised their apocalyptic tenor while the propertied classes grew alarmed by their increasing influence in local government. Eventually the radicals held unchallenged ascendancy. Those Lutherans and Roman Catholics who had not already withdrawn from the town were expelled by the Anabaptists; all who remained in the town were to be re-baptised upon pain of death. Münster, proclaiming itself the New Jerusalem, was immediately besieged by Roman Catholic forces; its links with the outside world were severed, sending it spiralling further into a primitivist and communist frenzy. A full theocracy was established; all books and manuscripts, except the Bible, were burned in a great bonfire in the cathedral's square. Slander and quarrelling were made capital offences, and polygamy was established, with one leader quickly gaining fifteen wives. The situation deteriorated into unfettered promiscuity while the constantly evolving leadership established itself in a very non-communist luxury. Food reserves dwindled; rats and hedgehogs were quickly replaced by human corpses as necessary foodstuffs for the starving townspeople. Those who eventually escaped after eight weeks of famine were refused passage through the besiegers' lines and were left to beg the soldiers to kill them as they starved slowly to death in no-man's-land. The several hundred Anabaptists who remained in Münster surrendered on the promise of safe conduct but were mercilessly massacred, as the authorities attempted to purge their land of this destabilising apocalyptic hope.[24]

The Reformers were sobered by the news: in putting vernacular Bibles in the hands of the unlearned, they had prised from the church the power of interpretation, and were compelled to recognise the twin threats of the totalitarianism of Rome and the danger of sectarian frenzy. They responded with ambivalence. Zwingli denied that *Revelation* was canonical; Luther only slowly overcame his initial hostility to its contents.[25] Such was the general lack of interest in the book that, as Irena Backus notes, 'Roman Catholic theologians persisted in thinking mistakenly that one of the hallmarks of the Protestant heresy was its rejection of the book of Revelation.'[26] Others exploited its contents to construct polemic against their twin enemies.

This was the context in which the pre-eminent theologian of the protestant Reformation, John Calvin (1509-62), cited *2 Thessalonians* 2 to buttress his arguments against both Rome and the Anabaptists. In his

---

[24] Cohn, *The Pursuit of the Millennium*, pp. 278-306.
[25] Firth, *The Apocalyptic Tradition in Reformation Britain*, p. 9.
[26] Irena Backus, 'The Church Fathers and the Canonicity of the Apocalypse in the Sixteenth Century: Erasmus, Frans Titelmans, and Theodore Beza', *Sixteenth Century Journal* 29 (1998), p. 662.

commentary on that book, first published in 1540, he noted Paul's reference to the final resurrection in a previous letter and conjectured that the apostle's warning was necessitated by 'some overcurious individuals' who, like the disciples of Melchior Hoffmann, 'seized this inappropriate moment to begin a discussion concerning the time of this day'. Calvin described this as the first of a series of eschatological attacks engineered by Satan: 'since he could not openly destroy the hope of the resurrection, he promised that the day was close and would soon be at hand, in order to undermine it by stealth ... Even at the present day he continually makes use of the same means of attack.'[27] Against Rome Calvin was more cautious. While he argued that the Pope was the 'man of sin', he conversely admitted that the Roman communion was not to be un-churched - Antichrist, as we have noticed, was required to sit in the true Temple of God. Calvin believed that 'anyone who has learned from Scripture what are the things that belong particularly to God, and who on the other hand considers well what the Pope usurps for himself, will not have much difficulty in recognising Antichrist, even though he were a ten-year-old boy.'[28]

Calvin's *Institutes* (1559) continued this twin attack. Referring to the millenarians as 'too childish either to need or to be worth a refutation', he found them advocates of gross error: 'those who assign the children of God a thousand years in which to enjoy the inheritance of the life to come do not realise how much reproach they are casting upon Christ and his Kingdom.'[29] Simultaneously, he claimed that since 'it is clear that the Roman pontiff has shamelessly transferred to himself what belonged to God alone and especially to Christ, we should have no doubt that he is the leader and standard-bearer of that impious and hateful kingdom.'[30]

Calvin's exegesis of *Revelation* 20 was less certain. His *Institutes* did not discuss it any further than to claim that the number one thousand 'does not apply to the eternal blessedness of the church but only to the various disturbances that awaited the church, while still toiling on earth'[31] - it was, after all, a prediction of martyrdom, and martyrdoms presupposed the existence of persecution. But that brief statement

---

[27] John Calvin, *Calvin's Commentaries: The Epistles of Paul the Apostle to the Romans and to the Thessalonians*, trans. Ross Mackenzie (Edinburgh: St. Andrew Press, 1972), p. 396.

[28] John Calvin, *The Epistles of Paul the Apostle to the Romans and to the Thessalonians*, p. 401.

[29] John Calvin, *Institutes of the Christian Religion*, eds J.T. McNeill and F.L. Battles (1559; rpr. London: SCM, 1960), iii. xxv. 5.

[30] Calvin, *Institutes*, iv. vii. 25.

[31] Calvin, *Institutes*, iii. xxv. 5.

appears to be Calvin's only reference to the millennium; his otherwise complete commentary on the New Testament passed over *Revelation* in silence. At the very least, we can say, its twentieth chapter did not play a pivotal role in his understanding of Christian history; nevertheless, the salient points of his eschatology seem clear.

This type of Augustinian reading was imported to the British Isles by the hundreds of protestant exiles who fled to the Continent from the persecution of Queen Mary in the 1550s. As we shall see in our discussion of John Foxe and the Geneva Bible, these Marian exiles were hugely influenced by the scholars they met in cities like Geneva. The ideology shared by John Foxe and the Geneva Bible's annotations reaffirmed the millennium to be a past event, and guarded resolutely against the type of popular millenarianism which had outraged the Reformers at Münster. They propagated their Reformed ideology through a massive publishing campaign involving everything from short tracts and dramas to general histories over twice as long as the Bible.

As a friend of John Foxe and as a colleague in exile, the Irish bishop John Bale (1495-1563) typified the concerns of the Marian exiles. In 1547 he published *The Image of Both Churches*, a verse-by-verse commentary on *Revelation* which advanced a distinctively protestant historiography within the familiar Augustinian eschatology. His preface argued for the critical importance of his subject-matter: 'he that knoweth not this book, knoweth not what the church is whereof he is a member.' *Revelation*, Bale thought, described both the 'true christian church, which is the meek spouse of the Lamb without spot ... and the sinful synagogue of Satan, in her just proportion depainted, to the merciful forewarning of the Lord's elect.' Bale's exposition of *Revelation* foregrounded its historical value, as a map of the church 'from Christ's ascension to the end of the world', and highlighted his indebtedness to Augustine: 'after the true opinion of St. Austin,' he claimed, 'either we are citizens in the new Jerusalem with Jesus Christ, or else in the old superstitious Babylon with antichrist the vicar of Satan.'[32]

Bale applied the thousand years of *Revelation* 20 to the first ten centuries of church history: 'mark ... the time from the ascension of Christ unto the days of Sylvester, the second bishop of Rome of that name; and ye shall find that it was from Christ's nativity a complete thousand.'[33] Satan, Bale claims, was set free by that Pope when he initiated his wicked liturgical innovations: 'when Christ shut [Satan] up, he took idolatry from the people; the pope hath restored it unto them

---

[32] Bale, *The Image of Both Churches* (1547), in *Select Works of John Bale*, ed. Henry Christmas (Cambridge: University Press, 1849), pp. 251-2.
[33] Bale, *The Image of Both Churches*, pp. 559-560.

again.'[34] The thousand-year binding prevented the rise of the false prophets, Mohammed and the Pope, prefigured in Scripture as Gog and Magog. 'Search the chronicles,' he encouraged his readers, 'and ye shall see that their beginnings were base, and their estate simple, before the thousand years were finished. But after that they grew up so high by their feigned simplicity and simulated holiness, that they became the two chief monarchs of the earth, and so in process ruled the universal world.'[35] The *Image* was a warning to those Christians who had retained their allegiance to the Bishop of Rome to flee his jurisdiction and the impending judgement of God.

But with this sharp delineation of the false church and the true came the first signs of a growing realisation that not all of elect England shared the saints' hope. Bale worried that his 'worldly-wise brethren ... which are neither hot nor cold' would resent the publication of the *Image*.[36] (Certainly a nineteenth-century *DNB* article would describe the *Image* as 'the best example of Bale's polemical power, showing his learning, his rude vigour of expression, and his want of tact and moderation'.[37]) Bale's allusion was to *Revelation* 3:15-16, where Christ warned the church at Laodicea that 'because thou art luke warme and neither cold nor hote, it will come to passe, that I shall spue thee out of my mouth.' Bale's *Image* began the pessimism which would later engulf puritans within the established church of England, fighting valiantly but unsuccessfully for further reform; it would transform such puritans into separatists, sending others to America to look for the New Jerusalem there, and would ultimately prise the millennium free from past history to catapult it into the future as a golden age of imagined social harmony and ecclesiastical purity. The seeds of the collapse of the puritan apocalypse were to be found in its defining texts. Nevertheless, Bale's Augustinian non-millennialism would remain virtually unchallenged in the popular puritanism of the 'three kingdoms' until the breakdown of government censorship and the first cracks in the Calvinist consensus at the end of 1640.

After the Marian exiles returned to find Elizabeth establishing England as at least a semi-reformed nation, the most influential representative of their school was William Perkins (1558-1602). Perkins exercised an important ministry in Cambridge, where his preaching was vital in the conversion of many future puritan leaders. Although he remained in the established church throughout his life, he helped popularise a worldview which would later be a vital catalyst in the

---

[34] Bale, *The Image of Both Churches*, p. 562.
[35] Bale, *The Image of Both Churches*, p. 571.
[36] Bale, *The Image of Both Churches*, p. 259.
[37] *DNB*, *s.v.* 'Bale, John'.

separatist trend within puritanism. Bale's comparison of England to the lukewarm Laodicean church was developed by Perkins, who expounded the significance of the Laodicean church for the contemporary English situation in his *Godly and Learned Exposition of the three first Chapters in the Revelation* (1595).

But Perkins never wrote anything to compare to Bale's *Image*. The *DNB* notes more favourably of him that his 'sound judgement is shown by the manner in which he kept clear of the all-absorbing millenarian controversy'.[38] Perkins, unlike many of his colleagues, rarely considered eschatological themes; his assumptions can, however, be traced in a variety of texts. *A Digest or Harmonie of the bookes of the old and new Testament*[39] lists in chronological order various biblical events and their historical situations. From this Perkins' understanding of the millennium becomes clear: Satan was bound in 295, he believed, and released in 1195. Between these two events, the seals of divine judgement began to open in 795, and the four horsemen of the apocalypse were released in 895. Still to come were the saints' conquest, their defeat of the beast and the Babylonian whore, the first resurrection, and the last judgement.[40] Perkins' thinking is elusive - he appears to endorse the Augustinian reading of *Revelation* 20 by endorsing a past millennium, but seems also to anticipate a *first* resurrection in the future. In contemporary terms, this would be to straddle uncomfortably both pre- and amillennialism; yet, paradoxically, Perkins is also often seen as a founding father of postmillennial thought. The danger of imposing reductionistic theological parameters could not be clearer.

Perkins' postmillennial importance is evidenced in the optimism of an early work entitled *A Fruitfull Dialogue Concerning the Ende of the World*.[41] This text participated in puritanism's genre of godly dialogue, in which the conversation of two characters (or more) was annotated for didactic effect. As in the most famous of this genre's titles, Bunyan's *Pilgrim's Progress* (1676), Perkins names his protagonist 'Christian'. Perkins' Christian castigates Worldling - his less spiritual foil - for his free market ideology and his pessimistic belief that the world would end in 1588:

> *Worldl.* ... I am sure you knowe as much as I: they say every where, that the next yeare eightie eight Doomes day will be.
> *Christ.* They are flying tales.

---

[38] *DNB, s.v.* 'Perkins, William'.
[39] This book does not have an entry in the STC.
[40] William Perkins, *The Workes of ... Mr. William Perkins* (London, 1612), ii. 817.
[41] This book does not have an entry in the STC.

> *Worldl.* Nay, I promise you: I have some skill, and I have read bookes of
> it that are printed; and talke goes, that there be olde prophecies of this
> yeare found in olde stone walls.
> *Christ.* I tell you plainely they are very lies...
> *Worldl.* ... *When after Christs birth there be expired,*
> > *of hundreds fiveteene, yeares eightie eight,*
> > *Then comes the time of dangers to be feared,*
> > *and all mankind with dolors it shall freight,*
> > *For if the world in that yeare doe not fall,*
> > *if sea and land then perish ne decay:*
> > *Yet Empires all, and kingdomes alter shall,*
> > *and man to ease himselfe shall have no way.*
> *Christ.* For my part I make as little accompt of these verses as of Merlins
> drunken prophecies, or of the tales of Robinhood[42]

Significantly, Christian goes on to find himself confronted with citations
from Elias and other 'Anabaptisticall revelations'. But, he warns, 'all
prophecies are not of God, and from his spirit: many are from the
phantasies of wicked men, and from the suggestion of the Devill.'[43]
Wordling nevertheless catalogues the harbingers of eschatological
doom:

> All the signes of the comming of Christ are past; Oh, what earthquakes
> have there been? what famine? what warres and hurliburlies among men?
> what signes in the Sunne and Moone? what flashing in the ayre? what
> blasing starres? surely, surely, the world can not last long: there is some
> cause that so many men so long agoe have spoken of these times, and
> speciallie of the next yeare.[44]

But the signs are *not* all past, Christian replies. He lists several which
await fulfilment, and includes in their number a most significant item -
'the conversion of the Jewes unto that religion which now they hate: as
appeareth in the 11. to the Romanes'.[45] The future, Christian was
arguing, was not entirely bleak - nor could the apocalypse be imminent.
There were better times ahead. There was yet the calling of the Jews to
be expected.

This latter-day conversion of the Jews to the Christian faith was to
become a staple component of subsequent puritan eschatology, but is an
expectation absent from the writings of the earlier Reformers. Calvin's
understanding was that the passage which appeared to teach the latter-

---

42 Perkins, *Workes*, iii. 467.
43 Perkins, *Workes*, iii. 468.
44 Perkins, *Workes*, iii. 470.
45 Perkins, *Workes*, iii. 470.

day conversion of the Jews - *Romans* 9-11 - only referred to 'spiritual Israel', not Jews but the elect of all ages, places, and nationalities. While several divines maintained this tradition, the massive dissemination of the Geneva Bible ensured that Perkins' teaching - mirrored in Beza's annotations on *Romans* in the margins of the Genevan New Testament - was firmly consolidated among English-speaking puritans. Perkins' own influence in the University of Cambridge was reflected in the number of subsequent puritan leaders who studied there and themselves came to advocate the 'conversion of the Jews' motif - among them Richard Sibbes and Thomas Goodwin. Robert Bolton (1572-1631), though a graduate of Oxford, recorded his interpretation of the New Jerusalem (*Revelation* 21) as a figure of 'the glory of the church here on earth, when both Jews and Gentiles shall be happily united into one christian body and brotherhood, before Christ's second coming'. This millenarian blessing was not to be seen as perfection in itself, he cautioned: 'If there be such excellency upon earth, what may we expect in the heaven of heavens!'[46]

But, with its inveterate anti-Catholicism, its Augustinian understanding of the millennium, and its belief in a end-times conversion of the Jews, the bulk of puritan eschatological teaching in the first three decades of the seventeenth century refused to go any further than Sibbes' remark that 'we are fallen into the latter end of the world'.[47] After Münster, the prospects of an earthly golden age were regarded with deep suspicion. John Preston was typical in his 1630 repudiation of those men who 'looke at some other advantages, when they looke at an earthy Kingdome, (as many of the Disciples did) when they looke for great matters by Christ in this world'.[48]

The Augustinian alternative, while emphasising the millennium's roots in the past, was nevertheless prepared to offer contemporary kingdoms an important role in the last days drama. The Christian monarch, the Genevans claimed, had a crucial role to play in the destruction of Antichrist. It was on this basis that the Marian exiles, prefacing the Geneva Bible, described Queen Elizabeth as the new Zerubbabel, the latter-day restorer of God's broken church. The Epistle Dedicatory prefacing the Authorised Version, in 1611, similarly praised James as the English Church's 'most tender and loving nursing Father', the agent of national reformation and the focus of international hostility against Antichrist. Since John Foxe, English protestants of all schools had associated individual monarchs with the predicted revolt against

---

[46] Robert Bolton, *The Four Last Things: Death, Judgement, Hell and Heaven* (1830; rpr. Pittsburgh: Soli Deo Gloria, 1994), pp. 99-100.
[47] Sibbes, *Works*, iv. 43.
[48] John Preston, *The Breastplate of Faith and Love* (London, 1630), p. 131.

the Babylonian harlot by those kings who had formerly been her slaves (*Revelation* 17:16). The Scottish eschatology of John Napier, Lord of Merchiston (1550-1617), directly challenged that claim.

In 1593 Napier published *A Plaine Discovery of the Whole Revelation* which explicitly acknowledged his direct debt to the Marian exiles. As a student at St Andrews, Napier had come under the influence of 'that worthie man of God, Maister Christopher Goodman', who had been preaching on the *Revelation*.[49] Goodman, as we will later see, had worked with John Knox in an attempt to push the Marian exiles into a position more radical than they were prepared to accept. Goodman's ideology shared the same basis as that adopted by others of the Reformed, but he was never shy of criticising existing authorities. This independent spirit was evidenced in his followers.

As a result of Goodman's influence, Napier had been directed into a life-long study of the apocalypse, adopting from his teacher many of the essential features of the Genevan eschatology. 'The thousand yeares that Satan was bound', Napier wrote, 'began in An. Christi 300. or thereabout', at exactly the same point as 'Antichrists universall raigne over Christians' began. Napier, significantly, had pushed back Antichrist's reign to coincide with the accession of Constantine, the emperor whose identification of church and state the Anglicans had promoted. The criticism of England's establishment was implicit. Constantine 'maintained Christianisme, to the abolishing of Sathans publicke kingdome', but simultaneously created a situation in which Antichrist could flourish. The millennium, for Napier, was not to be understood as a golden age but rather as the absence of 'universall warres among the nations'.[50]

Although Napier had dedicated his book to King James, his cool assessment of the Emperor Constantine initiated something of a re-evaluation of the role of the 'godly prince' in apocalyptic warfare. While Napier prefaced his first edition with a call for James to reform his household and his nation in preparation for such an apocalyptic role, the second edition of the *Plaine Discovery*, published in 1611, omitted any reference to the king's duties. James, in the interim, had taken possession of the English throne and had demonstrated a commitment to repudiate his Scottish Presbyterian childhood. In 1611, the translators of the Authorised Version had designedly bolstered the Episcopalian settlement; William Laud's election to the presidency of St. John's College, Oxford, in the same year, made evident the first signs of James' later Arminianism. His actions seem to have prompted a revaluation of the 'godly prince' ideology. Napier, no doubt concerned by James' new

---

[49] Napier, *A Plaine Discovery of the Whole Revelation*, sig. A2r.
[50] Napier, *A Plaine Discovery of the Whole Revelation*, pp. 82-3, 85.

direction, passed over his earlier monarchism in silence.

Napier's other significant contribution to the puritan apocalyptic tradition was his introduction of mathematics and his consequent transformation of the author from historical exegete to prophetical speculator. Napier's fame in history rests upon his discovery of logarithms, which he imposed upon the existing Genevan teaching to produce a strict chronological framework for his eschatological narrative. Napier calculated that each of *Revelation's* seven seals of judgement (*Revelation* 6:1-8:1) lasted seven years. Noting that the first seal presented a rider on a white horse, wearing a crown and commissioned to conquer, Napier argued that it characterised Christ: 'this behooved onely to beginne at that time that Christ was baptized, and began to preach and open up the sealed doctrine of our salvation, which was in the end of the 29. yeare of the age of Christ.'[51] The subsequent seals covered the events of the succeeding years, covering the first persecutions, heresies, and the writing of the four gospels, culminating in 71 A.D. when the last seal was opened and the Roman armies destroyed Jerusalem.[52] He reckoned that this year was also the beginning of the seven trumpets of divine judgement (*Revelation* 8:1-11:19), which each represented a period of 245 years. According to these figures, the second trumpet sounded in 316, the third in 561, the fourth in 806, and so on. This schema exactly corresponded to history, he believed: 'the starre and locusts of the fifth trumpet, are not the great Antichrist and his Cleargie, but the Dominator of the Turkes and his armie, who began their dominion in anno Christi 1051.'[53] Extrapolating from these figures, Napier concluded that the seventh trumpet, initiating God's final dealings with the earth, had sounded in 1541, and would complete its influence by 1786. The figures were further refined to expect the end of prophetic chronology between 1688 and 1700.[54] Through Napier, the puritan expositor moved from being a chronicler of the past to a predictor of the future.

These methodological revisions met with an enthusiastic response from a former Fellow of Queen's College, Cambridge, the English Presbyterian Thomas Brightman (1562-1607). In many ways Brightman's thinking was also characterised by a growing disenchantment with the reforms of the English church - so much so that his work was banned until the 1640s. Echoing Perkins' earlier comparison of England to the Laodicean church, Brightman claimed that 'Christ preferreth a blind Papist, or no Religion at all before this

---

[51] Napier, *A Plaine Discovery of the Whole Revelation*, p. 13.
[52] Napier, *A Plaine Discovery of the Whole Revelation*, pp. 140-44.
[53] Napier, *A Plaine Discovery of the Whole Revelation*, p. 4.
[54] Napier, *A Plaine Discovery of the Whole Revelation*, p. 26.

hoch pot luckwarmnesse.' The bishops 'love riches and honor so dearely, that they content themselvs with the losse of a full Reformation; yet that they might not seem to prefer any thing before the truth and good of the Church; they do with swelling words blazon the happiness of this Church thus governed as it is.'[55]

Brightman continued Napier's revision of the Genevan eschatology, prising it further from its implicit support of the Anglican establishment, and investing the apocalypse with a mathematical agenda which would revolutionise the puritan tradition. His conclusions were published after his death. In 1609 and 1610, *Apocalypsis Apocalypseos* and *Antichristum Ponteficiorum monstrum fictitum esse* were launched into the eschatological debate.[56] In 1615, in Amsterdam, *Apocalypsis Apocalypseos* was translated into English as *A Revelation of the Revelation*.

Like every other puritan commentary of the period, *A Revelation of the Revelation* traced God's dealings with the church throughout the ages. Thus the first thousand years of *Revelation* 20 ended in 1300, when Satan was released to incite the Islamic invasions of Europe in the fourteenth century. But - critically - Brightman's understanding of the European Reformation perceived a *second* millennium, after the 'first resurrection' signalled the Reformers' revival of Biblical theology. The Reformation had commenced the period of the saints' rule with Christ and would proceed into the destruction of the church's enemies and the culmination of the ages in the year 2300. In projecting a millennial reign after 1300, Brightman had made a breathtaking advance.

Like Napier, Brightman calculated that the latter part of the seventeenth century would witness great apocalyptic changes. Turkish power would begin to fall in 1650, the same year in which the Jews would be converted and Rome's power would begin to be destroyed. Then would prevail 'a most happy tranquillity ... the joy will be so much that it will be strange and unexpected: for in place of former troubles, there will be perpetual peace, & then Kings and Queens will be nursing fathers, and nursing mothers unto the Christian Churches.'[57]

Brightman constructed his interpretation on an exegetical collage: 'although therefore thou doe sometime doubtingly read over the Revelation of John, and the Song of Salomon, for the newnesse and strangenesse of the matter, yet, when by Daniels comming in, such an admirable consent of Scripture, giveth such cleer light to confirme the

---

55 [Anon.], *Reverend Mr. Brightmans Judgement* (1642), sig. A2v-A3r.
56 Hill, *Antichrist in Seventeenth-Century England*, p. 26.
57 [Anon.], *Reverend Mr. Brightmans Judgement*, sig. A4r.

matter in hand, feare not to embrace the truth.'[58] Thus much of his eschatology was worked out in his commentaries on *Daniel* and *Song of Solomon*, which were published together in 1635. Nevertheless, with the Laudian control of English presses, his work only found a sizeable native audience in the 1640s. Brightman became, in the words of a later translator, 'an English Prophet'[59] who counted it quite unnecessary to 'stick in mens great names'.[60]

Another Cambridge scholar, Joseph Mede (1586-1638), experienced similar suffering under the Laudian regime. In many ways he contrasted with Brightman. Mede was a diminutive, conforming Anglican who believed that the vision of heaven in *Revelation* 4 underscored God's preference for Episcopalian order: the twenty-four elders described in that chapter, he thought, 'represent the Bishops, and prelates of the churches'.[61] Although his work was banned under the Laudian hegemony, Mede was able to correspond on apocalyptic subjects with men like William Twisse and James Ussher. His apocalyptic studies only came into prominence after the Long Parliament had his works translated into English in the early 1640s. It is paradoxical that Mede, as an Anglican, should have been refused the right to publish his works in English until Parliament, coming to his rescue, impeached the Archbishop of Canterbury; and paradoxical too that his influence was greatest upon those puritans who abandoned the national church in a way that he could never countenance.

Mede's *Key of the Revelation* appeared as a translation of his Latin commentary, *Clavis Apocalyptica* (1627; second, enlarged, edition 1632). Reflecting his earlier training in mathematics, Mede's method initially ignored historical applications, instead identifying synchronisms within the text and assuming that similarities such as equivalent lengths of time were, in fact, identities: 'by the characters of Synchronismes is every interpretation to be tryed as it were by a square and plumb-rule.'[62] Thus his initial observations were entirely concerned with the letter of the text, rather than its application.

Mede followed the literary approach outlined in the later editions of the Geneva Bible by dividing *Revelation* into two 'books', the first consisting of material from chapters one to ten, and the second from chapters eleven to twenty-two. 'The first prophecie of the seales,' he

---

[58] Thomas Brightman, *A Most Comfortable Exposition of ... Daniel* (Amsterdam, 1635; rpr. 1644), p. 893.

[59] Brightman, *A Most Comfortable Exposition of ... Daniel*, p. 895.

[60] Brightman, *A Most Comfortable Exposition of ... Daniel*, p. 956.

[61] Joseph Mede, *The Key of the Revelation* (London, 1643), i. 35.

[62] Hill, *Antichrist in Seventeenth-Century England*, p. 27; Mede, *The Key of the Revelation*, i. 27.

claimed, was a part of the first book which 'comprehendeth the destinies of the Empire. The other of the little book, the destinies of the Church or of christian religion.'[63] The seven seals, described in the first book, represent the afflictions of the Empire in the years immediately after Christ, with the sixth seal beginning in 311. Mede understood the shaking of heaven and earth to represent 'that wonderfull change and subversion of the State of Rome heathen, by Constantine the great and his Successours, the Standard-bearers of the Lamb ... whereby suppose all the heathen gods shaken out of their heaven, the Bishops and priests degraded, dejected, and deprived of their revenewes for ever.'[64] The seventh seal contained the seven trumpets, which traced the history of the Empire from 395 until its apocalyptic culmination. Although the Empire split into ten kingdoms in 456, the apocalyptic judgements continued to be poured out upon their political successors. Thus the sixth trumpet was still in operation when Mede first published.

Unlike some other of his contemporaries, Mede was cautious about being too specific: 'we shall therefore enquire in vaine of those things which God would have kept secret and to be reserved for their owne times.'[65] Neither was he always concerned to find exact applications: 'it is not fit for the interpreter every where to keep the same order as the Historian doth.'[66] Thus recognising that God would give greater interpretative insight as the last days approached, Mede's exposition of the second 'book' - those chapters after *Revelation* 11 which dealt with the destiny of the church - shows a greater tendency towards allegory. Some events he refers to 'warre and slaughter ... yet to come', while recognising that 'our Brightman' had considered those parts of the prophecy to have been already fulfilled. But Mede writes with pastoral sensitivity: 'who would not much rather that so lamentable an accident to the Church were past, then to feare it to be yet to come?' Yet the pessimism his teaching engendered was always the true object of eschatological exposition: 'the expectation of a future calamity conduceth more to piety, then an over-credulous security thereof, as if it were already past.'[67]

Nevertheless the prophetic future was not entirely dark. Mede was certain that the thousand years of the millennium, although 'the most abstruse of all the propheticall Scripture', represented the future reign of the saints with Christ.[68] He did not follow Brightman in claiming that

---

[63] Mede, *The Key of the Revelation*, i. 38.
[64] Mede, *The Key of the Revelation*, i. 54.
[65] Mede, *The Key of the Revelation*, i. 121.
[66] Mede, *The Key of the Revelation*, ii. 107.
[67] Mede, *The Key of the Revelation*, ii. 13.
[68] Mede, *The Key of the Revelation*, ii. 121.

it was already one-third over. Mede identified the millennium with the future seventh trumpet and the day of judgement, both of which, he argued, would last one thousand years. It was a systematic repudiation of the Reformers' Augustinianism, and, for the paradoxical Anglican, far more thoroughgoing than Presbyterian Brightman's twin-millennial *via media*.

In the Preface to *The Key of the Revelation*, William Twisse, first Prolocutor of the Westminster Assembly, made this clear: 'Austin [relinquished] the doctrine of Christs Kingdome here on earth, which formerely hee embraced, as himself professeth in one of his works *De civitate Dei* [*The City of God*], where he treats thereof ... Yet Mr. Mede hath (in my judgement) exceeded in merit all others that went before him in this argument.'[69] Nevertheless, although Mede himself felt carried away - 'whither goe I? let us cease to be (as happily hitherto we have been) too curious'[70] - his exposition of the millennium was brief and cautious. His translator recognised the difficulties this exposition had presented, and indicated that fear of a hostile reception had prevented Mede from a more explicit treatment of the millennium in the 'Larger Commentarie, which I am perswaded he hath written'. The translator informed his readers that his exposition of the millennium was 'the pretended cause of restraint of his further progresse': 'howsoever it be not received by many as Orthodox, yet is delivered with that moderation and subjection to the censure of the Church, that it can displease no man.'[71] Mede's pattern of silence and self-censorship would be widely repeated among his friends in the first part of the seventeenth century - most notably, for our interests, by James Ussher. Nevertheless, however brief in exegesis, Mede's *Key* went on to exercise tremendous influence in the puritan apocalyptic tradition. Citing the annotations of Beza alongside texts by Brightman, Mede was positioning himself within the mainstream of English puritan thought and, as Milton's tutor at Cambridge, his texts seem to have influenced the theology of *De Doctrina* and the allusively apocalyptic rhetoric of *Areopagitica*.[72]

By 1642, texts by Mede and Brightman had come to acquire far-reaching political implications. After the political abuses of Charles' personal rule and the ascendancy of the Arminians within the English church, many puritans felt that the faith in king and bishop which Foxe's eschatology had encouraged was no longer tenable. Those texts

---

[69] Mede, *The Key of the Revelation*, sig. av.
[70] Mede, *The Key of the Revelation*, ii. 105.
[71] Mede, *The Key of the Revelation*, sig. a4v.
[72] See essays in Juliet Cummins (ed.), *Milton and the ends of time* (Cambridge: Cambridge University Press, 2003), for extensive discussions of this theme.

which the Long Parliament published - by Mede, Brightman, and the more radical brethren - were deliberately designed to provide puritans with an eschatological alternative to fuse with the more recent developments in the native tradition. These developments had recently been smuggled in from a second group of puritan exiles.

Many of the most influential expositors of the civil war era had been involved in groups which had been forced into exile by their refusal to conform to the Laudian innovations in the 1630s. Thomas Goodwin (1600-1680) resigned his Cambridge University preferments in 1634 and, as persecution of the puritan party intensified, he fled to Holland in 1639 to became pastor of an independent congregation in Arnheim. There Goodwin preached the sermons which were to be published as *An Exposition of the Book of Revelation* (1639). As a sympathiser of those puritans demanding further reformation in the English church, Goodwin did not share Mede's vision of an Episcopalian heaven. Instead, he claimed, the apostolic visions in *Revelation* 4 and 5 portrayed a system of church government which answered exactly to the one the Independents defended: 'such a pattern is given forth here as the only true pattern, into which all should be cast; and God sets forth his church as it should be in all ages, and as it was in John's time.'[73]

Despite this dramatic reinterpretation, Goodwin did, nevertheless, refer back to the previous giants of the puritan apocalyptic tradition. We have already noticed the breadth of his reading, his references to Beza, Foxe, Brightman and Mede alongside lesser-known apocalyptic expositors like Junius, Ussher, Forbes and Ames. Nevertheless, none of the previous commentators were prepared, as he was, to displace heaven. Goodwin was the first to claim that the 'kingdom of Christ on earth to come is a far more glorious condition for the saints than what their souls have now in heaven.'[74] Goodwin was staking a claim for the millennial kingdom far beyond Mede's conservative caution.

But between the ecclesiology of the primitive church and the glorious prospect of the future kingdom, Goodwin understood that *Revelation* contained a pictorial history 'from John's time to the world's end', an 'exact chronology of ... the world's monarchies'.[75] While he rejected the rabbinical idea of a six-thousand-year span of universal history, he did maintain that *Revelation* included sufficient data for believers to calculate their own chronology of the end. This, in fact, was the apostle's purpose, 'the thing herein principally aimed at.'[76]

Thus, observing the church's eschatological enemies in the paganism

---

[73] Goodwin, *Works*, iii. 3.
[74] Goodwin, *Works*, iii. 15.
[75] Goodwin, *Works*, iii. 1, 22.
[76] Goodwin, *Works*, iii. 73, 122.

of Islam and the idolatry of Rome, Goodwin contended that the Jews, whom he expected to be converted by 1656, would ally themselves with the church to defeat the Pope by 1666, and witness the beginning of the millennium by 1700.[77] Christian churches would increasingly align themselves with the ecclesiastical order of the Independents: 'the western churches, that have borne the heat of antichristian persecution, and overcome Antichrist ... shall in the end perfect their victory, and ... set up temples, increasingly more and more in light and glory, even until the New Jerusalem.'[78] The qualification was, of course, that it all 'may fall out sooner than we are aware of'.[79]

The advantage of Goodwin's reading was that he was able to separate the golden age of the millennium from the first - rather tarnished - ten centuries of Christian history. He was able to write it off completely as the age in which Antichrist gained pre-eminence over the visible church and instituted the tyranny which continued in the jurisdictions of Rome and Canterbury: the 'new refined Popery' of the Laudians, he claimed, has 'an intention and conspiracy in the end to make way for the beast'.[80] Ussher would later agree.

Although it was only subsequently systematised in the *Apologeticall Narration* (1644), embryonic Independent ecclesiology had abandoned any notion of apostolic succession in an ideological revolution which tore at the very heart of England's Anglican settlement. The Independent system of church government confirmed the power of ordination to rest in individual congregations - which Anglicanism and Presbyterianism strenuously denied. Consequently, its exponents no longer needed to trace a line of ordained ministers back to the apostles - nor did they need to retain the validity of the first ten centuries of the Christian church. The Independents freed themselves from history, and from the burden of attempting to find anything praiseworthy in the church's past. Exposition was so much simpler when the millennium was a future period of peace and prosperity for the church and saint alike. History could simply be written off.

Thus for Goodwin and his fellow Independents, ecclesiastical history evolved into a sharp dichotomy between the darkness of this age and the triumph of the next. But the saints were not to complacently presume upon the power of providence. Things were not likely to improve in the immediate short term:

---

[77] Goodwin, *Works*, iii. 158, 198.
[78] Goodwin, *Works*, iii. 62.
[79] Goodwin, *Works*, iii. 205.
[80] Goodwin, *Works*, iii. 71.

though we may think this dismal and black hour of temptation not likely to come so soon, seeing the clouds rise not fast enough so suddenly to overcast the face of the sky with darkness, yet we are to consider that we live now in the extremity of times, when motions and alterations, being so near the centre, become quickest and speediest; and we are at the verge, and, as it were, within the whirl of that great mystery of Christ's kingdom, which will, as a gulf swallow up all time; and so, the nearer we are unto it, the greater and more sudden changes will Christ make, now hastening to make a full end of all.[81]

Nevertheless Goodwin's exposition of *Revelation* passed over the thousand-year reign in comparative silence. His expositions of *Ephesians* (published posthumously in 1681), by contrast, lingered on the theme. He noted that 'many divines' expected a 'state of glory, of a glorious church on earth' which would 'continue for a thousand years, during which time the Jews shall have it, and the Gentiles together with them'. But Goodwin was conscious that his own millenarianism went beyond this Perkins-influenced postmillennial optimism. He understood this thousand years to be a special world created for Christ, 'between this world and the end of the day of judgement'. Not that Christ would descend and rule from Jerusalem - 'that is the old error of some' - but 'part of heaven shall come down and rule this world, to make the glory of it so much the more complete, to put down Adam's world.' He recognised that his millennialism was not beyond criticism: 'I have spoken these things unto you rather as that which hath a great show of truth in it, than as if I could answer all objections that might be made against it.'[82]

Goodwin was altogether within the Perkins tradition, however, in wondering how many of the English saints were ready for the apocalyptic changes which were shortly to shake their church. The situation among the godly was still like that of the church at Laodicea, he believed: 'of Protestants not one of a hundred are true worshippers.'[83] There was cause for alarm in the islands which 'God hath made the eminent seat of the church in these latter days.'[84] But the saints were not to distrust their promise of final victory. 'Fear not the cause of God in England', Goodwin declared in foreboding terms; although 'there is a battle to be fought', it is certain that 'Christ will not be foiled.'[85]

Goodwin's vivid image of England at the edge of a vast whirlpool of

---

[81] Goodwin, *Works*, iii. 204.
[82] Goodwin, *Works*, i. 521, 506, 525.
[83] Goodwin, *Works*, iii. 127.
[84] Goodwin, *Works*, iii. 178.
[85] Goodwin, *Works*, iii. 35.

the 'extremity of times' might well describe the sudden explosion in millenarian publications during the ominous middle decades of the seventeenth century. This acute awareness of imminence was also the basis of *A Glimpse of Sions Glory*, a sermon preached at the inauguration of an independent church in Holland in 1641. This has been described as 'an original Independent manifesto' which 'represented the thinking of a most influential group of Puritan divines in the English Revolution - a group which was to become the nucleus of the leadership of Independency'.[86] It is certainly the case that its sentiments were widely shared. Such was the ideological affinity of Goodwin and the other exiles - Jeremiah Burroughs, Philip Nye, William Bridge, Sidrach Simpson and John Archer - that scholars continue to debate the authorship of this text. Nathaniel Holmes, in *The Resurrection Revealed* (1653), claimed it was the work of Jeremiah Burroughs. The 'common report' that Goodwin was behind the text was cited in Robert Baillie's *A Dissuasive from the Errors of the Times* (1645) and seems more likely to be correct.[87] This debate has continued until recent times.[88]

In the *Glimpse*, Goodwin's voice had noticeably matured. This was itself confirmation of his apocalyptic claims: 'the neerer the Time comes, the more clearly these things shall bee revealed. And because they begin to be revealed so much as they doe now, we have cause to hope the Time is at hand ... Doth God begin to open this Booke? Know that the time is at hand.'[89] Goodwin's understanding of church government was more radical: 'Independency is a beginning, or at least a near antecedent of Christs Kingdome upon Earth.'[90] Consequently, Goodwin's appeal was to the common people to be the agents of God's cataclysmic judgement on the apostate churches: 'give God no rest, till he sets up Jerusalem as the praise of the whole World. Blessed is he that dasheth the Brats of Babylon against the stones: Blessed is hee that hath any hand in pulling downe Babylon.'[91] There is no place for any godly prince in this radical eschatology. 'You that are of the meaner rank, common People, be not discouraged', Goodwin exhorted; 'God intends to make use of the common People in the great Worke of proclaiming the Kingdome of his Sonne.'[92] The exiles would be exalted to positions

---

[86] Tai Liu, *Discord In Zion: The Puritan Divines and the Puritan Revolution* (The Hague: Martinus Nijhoff, 1973), p. 4.

[87] Robert Baillie, *A Dissuasive from the Errors of the Times* (London, 1645), p. 80.

[88] A.R. Dallison, 'The Authorship of 'A Glimpse of Syons Glory'', in Peter Toon (ed.), *Puritans, the Millennium, and the Future of Israel* (Cambridge: James Clarke, 1970). The STC attributes the tract to Goodwin.

[89] [Thomas Goodwin], *A Glimpse of Sions Glory* (London, 1641), p. 31.

[90] Baillie, *A Dissausive from the Errors of the Times*, p. 80.

[91] [Goodwin], *A Glimpse of Sions Glory*, p. 2.

[92] [Goodwin], *A Glimpse of Sions Glory*, p. 5.

of the greatest authority: 'Though the Governours of Judah have counted them factious, and Schismaticks, and Puritanes; there is a Time comming, when the Governours of Judah shall be convinced of the Excellency of Gods people.'[93]

The millenarianism of *A Glimpse* was decidedly futuristic. As Goodwin argued, if Christ himself had never yet reigned outwardly, his reign must never have begun: indeed, from outward appearances, it seemed, 'the Divell himselfe is a greater King.'[94] Citing church fathers and the Sibylline oracles in his defence, Goodwin maintained that the Independent churches with which he was associated were the temporal anticipations of the thousand-year reign. It would be a period marked by massive numbers of conversions. He expected 'a wonderfull Confluence of People to this Church, both Jew and Gentile shall joyne together to flow to the Beautifulnes of the Lord.'[95] These millennial congregations would enjoy unprecedented spiritual experiences: 'that is such a glorious presence of Christ, as shall so instruct them, as if they had not need to take heed to the Word of Prophesie ... the presence of Christ shall be there, and supply all kind of Ordinances.'[96] And it was all so very imminent. Echoing the calculations of 'that worthy Instrument of God Mr. Brightman', Goodwin determined that the apocalyptic judgements would begin in 1650 and would culminate in the millennial rule, which would begin in 1695.[97] Of course, such radical rhetoric had huge implications for England. Laudian censorship had meant that believers there had not been instructed in these ways: 'it is the Antichristian yoke that doth hide this Truth. Men dare not whisper of any truth, but of such as are held in the Church of Rome: But when there comes to be liberty of Churches, and that men may freely search into this truth, knowledge will be increased.'[98]

Time would prove his calculations wrong, but Goodwin's expositions retained the admiration of many puritans. As late as 1690 Increase Mather was still able to recommend his apocalyptic texts to Richard Baxter.[99] Goodwin's apocalyptic thought seems to have taken a firm grip of the New England puritans like Mather who shared his Independent ecclesiology. Goodwin had, for example, written a preface to *The Keys of the Kingdom of Heaven* (1644), a book on Congregational

---

93 [Goodwin], *A Glimpse of Sions Glory*, p. 26.

94 [Goodwin], *A Glimpse of Sions Glory*, p. 10.

95 [Goodwin], *A Glimpse of Sions Glory*, p. 21.

96 [Goodwin], *A Glimpse of Sions Glory*, p. 27.

97 [Goodwin], *A Glimpse of Sions Glory*, p. 32.

98 [Goodwin], *A Glimpse of Sions Glory*, p. 16.

99 Richard Baxter, *Calendar of the Correspondence of Richard Baxter*, eds N.H. Keeble and Geoffrey F. Nuttall (Oxford: Clarendon Press, 1991), ii. 309.

church polity authored by John Cotton (1584-1652) and intended as a contribution to the Westminster Assembly's discussions of church government. Cotton, like Goodwin, had fled Anglicanism's demands for conformity in the early 1630s. Establishing himself in the New World, he set about publishing a series of texts attacking the semi-reformed Anglican settlement, and calling for further reformation 'without tarrying'. Eschatological arguments played a critical role in his demands for the continuing revision of church government.

Cotton published *The Churches Resurrection* in 1642, an exposition of *Revelation* 20:5-6 which directly challenged accepted understandings of the millennium. Noting that the millennium was to be marked by the rule of the saints, he argued that if readers 'take any of these times, wherein this period of a thousand yeares is wont to be assigned, it will not hold true that the Saints had a time of Rule and Judicature after it; take a thousand yeares from Christ, or Constantine, or Theodosius, though a thousand yeares from that be expired long agoe, yet hitherto it is not given to the Saints to Rule.'[100] Cotton imagined the millennium to be a period when Satan's emissaries would be bound by proper discipline thoroughly enforced in church and state: 'if [ecclesiastical offenders] be Church members [the saints] will bind them in chaines of the Ordinances of God, as Admonition, and Excommunication ... and partly also from punishment from Civil Magistrates as need shall be.'[101] Cotton denied that the first resurrection would be a resurrection of bodies; he conceived of it as spiritual, as a revival of independent church polity among the saints. This was to be occasioned by the fall of the Pope and the consequent conversion of the Jews - for 'hitherto popery hath bin the great stumbling block that hindered the communion of the Jewes.'[102]

But within his fairly conventional expectation of the fall of Antichrist and the conversion of the Jews, Cotton launched an unprecedented attack on the Anglicans, implicating their church settlement with the horrors of Antichrist: 'you will finde little difference betweene Episcopacy and Popery, for they are governed by Popish Canons.'[103] In a sense his reaction epitomised the quiet concerns of the Calvinistic bishops throughout the 1620s and 1630s. This period had witnessed the gradual rise to prominence of William Laud (1573-1645), who had gained many enemies by patronising the proponents of what its enemies perceived to be Arminian theology and by imposing liturgical innovations. After his appointment as Archbishop of Canterbury in

---

[100] Cotton, *The Churches Resurrection*, p. 5.
[101] Cotton, *The Churches Resurrection*, p. 6.
[102] Cotton, *The Churches Resurrection*, p. 13.
[103] Cotton, *The Churches Resurrection*, p. 19.

1633, the English church no longer formally proclaimed the Pope to be Antichrist. Books like Foxe's *Acts and Monuments* were no longer published.[104] Puritan elements within the Anglican Church - men like James Ussher - were immediately suspicious. Rumours abounded that Laud had been offered a cardinal's hat, that he was leading the Church of England back to Rome. The more radical of the brethren had long considered the possibility that Antichrist's dominion extended even to the established church - but it was only after the collapse of censorship, and Laud's impeachment for treason in 1640, that they could say so in public.

No-one could have imagined the consequences. When the mood of the radical reformation found a public voice, there could be no stopping the eschatological spiral. The Long Parliament, as we have seen, ordered the translation and publication of works by Brightman and Mede, and other saints were more than eager to take advantage of its relaxation of book licensing. For the first time individual commentators found themselves addressing a literate and interested audience, as readers aligned themselves around the various publishing parties. One of the most influential of such 'interpretative communities' were the Fifth Monarchists, an amorphous group of radical millenarians who participated in joint activities across the denominational boundaries of the Independent and Baptist churches from which they were drawn. Although they only achieved prominence in the early 1650s, the essential ideas of Fifth Monarchism were disseminated throughout the 1640s in a series of important and influential texts. It was a movement driven by the printing press.

One of its embryonic exponents was John Archer (d. 1642), whose discourse of *The Personall Reigne of Christ upon Earth* was published in 1643. Archer's treatise highlights the salient features of the later movement, such as a concern for legal reform and the imposition of Old Testament law in place of England's hated Norman heritage. The Fifth Monarchists were interested in legal reform as an expression of Christ's impending millennial reign. Its beginning was imminent, Archer believed: 'it is likely, that Christs comming from heaven, and raising the dead and beginning his Kingdom, and the thousand yeeres will be about the yeere of our Lord 1700.'[105] This was not the end of the world, however. We have already noted that Archer believed that there would be *three* comings of Christ: one incarnation, one coming to set up his millennial kingdom, and one to institute the final judgement of the world. It was a simple matter, then, to work out when the world would end: 'now having found out when Christs Kingdome, or the thousand

---

[104] Hill, *The World Turned Upside Down*, p. 96.
[105] Archer, *The Personall Reign of Chist upon Earth*, p. 49.

yeers shall begin it is easie to guesse when the time of the last generall Judgement and the world end shall be.'[106] It would be, by implication, around the year 2700. If his dating of the second coming emphasised imminence, his understanding of the end of the world did not. Archer's eschatology was typical of the Fifth Monarchists in everything except his premillennial adventism.

Archer did not characterise the thousand year reign in any detail. After his initial descent, Archer expected, Christ would immediately withdraw again to heaven, leaving the continuing government of the earth to those saints who had died before 1700. They would be raised at this middle coming, 'and live immortall Lives and rule the World'. Other saints who witnessed the beginning of the Kingdom while still alive 'shall live but mortall lives, and under the Government of the other Saints'.[107] The believers in the millennium would enjoy 'immediate fellowship with God ... and not by Ordinances, but by God and the Lambe'.[108] All ordinances - every sacramental means of mediating the human and divine - would cease. This doctrine would achieve prominence and would exercise a highly intriguing influence on the literature of the Fifth Monarchist party, who, eager to begin the millennial reign, took up their pens to expedite their dominion of the world.

Another important text to be published in 1643 was *The Beloved City: Or, the Saints Reign on Earth a Thousand Yeares*, by Johann Alsted (1588-1638).[109] Alsted was a major European scholar, a native of Hesse-Nassau, in modern Germany, whose theological erudition was such that he was invited to attend the Synod of Dort in 1618. His reputation had been established by his teaching at Herborn, where he had taught Comenius, and by his *Encyclopaedia septem tomis distincta* (1630), a Ramist text used in Cambridge University and the infant Harvard College. Alsted had initially advocated the traditional Genevan eschatology, but gradually abandoned its Augustinianism in a series of eschatological studies which culminated in his *Diatribe de mille annis Apocalypticis* (1627) - the text translated by William Burton in 1643 as *The Beloved City*. Remarkably, Alsted echoed many of Archer's conclusions, with the only major exception being the 'middle' coming of Christ. Like Archer, he imagined that the future millennial rule of Christ would be initiated by a physical resurrection of the martyrs, and that their government would be the visible manifestation of Christ's sovereign rule. Alsted seems to have based his calculations on the chronologies of

---

[106] Archer, *The Personall Reign of Chist upon Earth*, p. 50.
[107] Archer, *The Personall Reign of Chist upon Earth*, p. 22.
[108] Archer, *The Personall Reign of Chist upon Earth*, pp. 28-9.
[109] On Alsted, see Hotson, *Johann Heinrich Alsted, 1588-1638*.

'that incomparable Magazine of all Learning and Piety, Dr. Usher'. It was on this basis, though the mathematics are obscured, that Alsted expected the millennium to begin in 1694 - 'or sooner'.[110]

The emphasis on Biblical chronology was continued in the other pamphlets of the period. In 1651, James Frese published *A Packet of Newes* in which he described the increasing imminence of the radical hope. Frese declared that England had six years to repent: 'according to the time and number of days, or yeers, answering the number of yeers from the Creation of the World, to the end of Noah's Flood, which was 1657. yeers; and thus answerably from the second Adam's work of Redemption, to the time of his coming in Glory, decked with eternal salvation and royal Majesty, shall be the like number of yeers, or days of time, 1657. as doth plainly appear by Christs own words in Mat. 24.'[111] Theological exclusivism was coming to deny salvation to any but the radical millennialists: 'if this plain demonstration of the truth ... be still hid, it is hid to them whose mindes are blinded by the God of this world.'[112] But the blindness of his critics could not extinguish Frese's hope:

> This reall truth of Christs eternall Reigne
> With all his Saints in Judah land againe.
> Oxford and Cambridge with their Philosophy,
> Their subtil Logick, and cunning Sophistry,
> Their learned quirks, and their Scholastique tricks,
> Though backt by Egypts Art, though fetch'd from Styx,
> Shall nere this truth obscure, for now this light
> Breaks forth most clear to many Christians sight[113]

Frese never achieved prominence among puritans; he was never recognised as a great poet or preacher. Nevertheless, his writing presents the radical hope in the manner in which most of its supporters would have encountered it - in a populist pamphlet mixing a variety of genres and making wildly extravagant claims. It was precisely the type of enthusiasm the critics of millenarianism relished to encounter.

And critics did exist. Between 1644 and 1646, several brethren maintaining an older resistance to millennialism published texts deeply hostile to the prevailing eschatological mood. Alexander Petrie (1594-1662) was a Scottish Presbyterian minister who had been active in the early Covenanting movement. In 1643 he had moved to Rotterdam to

---

[110] John Alsted, *The Beloved City* (London, 1643), p. 34, 57.
[111] James Frese, *A Packet of Newes* (London, 1651), pp. 7-8.
[112] Frese, *A Packet of Newes*, p. 36.
[113] Frese, *A Packet of Newes*, p. 58.

pastor a church composed of Scottish exiles, founded the previous year. He published *Chiliasto-mastix* in 1644, launching a vitriolic attack on the millenarianism sweeping through his native islands. Describing it as 'an old Jewish fancie and Cerinthian fable', he admonished his readers to forbear any association with such false teaching: 'old erroures ar lyke old whoores, that is, the more to be abhorred.' Petrie had no doubt as to the origins of this teaching, and suspected that it was engineered to advance the socio-ecclesiastical challenge which the Independents, in their *Apologeticall Narration*, had outlined at the Westminster Assembly in January 1644: 'you have heard this errour preached instead of the doctrine of Christ ... by some of the Authores of the Apologeticall narration for Independencie, who hade in their congregations not only Millenaries, but grosse Anabaptistes.'[114]

There can be no doubt that Petrie had grounds for his suspicion. No doubt his observations were drawn from his experience of working in the same Dutch cities in which the English Independents had formerly met. He would have been shocked to have witnessed the eschatological optimism displayed by the Commissioners which his Church of Scotland had delegated to attend the Westminster Assembly; the sermon George Gillespie would preach in March 1644 was as optimistic as anything the Independents could produce - and was equally keen to use apocalyptic rhetoric to further distinct socio-ecclesiastical ambitions. One wonders whether such information would have softened Petrie's approach: 'Mee thinkes', he said of his opponents, 'you speak nonsense.'[115]

Petrie's text encouraged puritans to revert to the very beginnings of their apocalyptic tradition, abandoning the concept of a future millennium and with it any hope of the national conversion of the Jews: 'the promises made unto the children of Abraham, Isaak and Jacob ar not to be restricted unto the Jewes according to the flesh ... bot of the faithfull ... [I]t is a great mistaking of the prophecies, if we shall still make an opposition betwixt Jewes and gentiles: believing gentiles are true Jewes.'[116] Petrie was echoing the conclusions of Calvin. But it was no surprise, he thought, that millenarians could find evidence for their teaching: 'any who hes the jaundies findes everie thing yallow.'[117]

Among the English, Thomas Hayne (1582-1645) was one of the few theologians to oppose the explosion of millenarian interest. In *Christs Kingdom on Earth* (1644) he catalogued competing views and refuted their arguments one by one. 'Divers are the Causes of Error in Religion',

---

[114] Alexander Petrie, *Chiliasto-mastix* (Rotterdam, 1644), n.p. [Preface, p. 3].
[115] Petrie, *Chiliasto-mastix*, p. 3.
[116] Petrie, *Chiliasto-mastix*, p. 9.
[117] Petrie, *Chiliasto-mastix*, p. 2.

he complained. 'Dr. Alstede was a man of vast comprehension, but had many Irons in the fire; Mr. Brightman ... pretending to give us a Revelation of the Revelation hee hath set forth an Obscuration thereof. Mr. Mede was my worthy and learned friend, but not to bee preferred before truth. Mr. Archer was held to bee a pious and good Christian ... Who should bee the penman of the Glympse I know not.'[118] Hayne invoked Foxe to buttress his reversion to the old Genevan amillennialism of the Marian exiles: 'for the space of a thousand yeares after Christs time, many were called in several Nations, and in every part of that thousand yeeres, many lived and reigned with Christ.'[119]

He situates his text as a debating chamber for the various apocalyptic voices, setting texts in contention amongst themselves: 'Dr. Alstede, who hath laboured most earnestly in his proofs about this point of the thousand years, never makes any conclusion for Christs visible and personall comming down again to earth. ... The Glimps. is unresolved, pag. 13., Mr. Cotton denies it, p. 4. Mr. Mede most modestly and ingenuously (as in his other writings, so in his Comment on the Apocalyps) lashes out not so far: but keeps to generall termes. Onely Mr. Archer is bold, as to wrest some other Scriptures, so here: and to make Christ visibly come from, and return to Heaven according to his fancy, rather then any text well understood.'[120] The millenarians 'mistake in placing the thousand yeares of the Saints reigning with Christ, the Churches puritie and happinesse, in the fag end of the world, and dregs of time', he argues. In all likelihood, the latter times will be 'worse and worse, as was the old world in Noah's time'.[121]

In a survey of the development of the puritan apocalyptic tradition, Hayne's work is of value not because he is a major or influential expositor but because he signals the most popular exponents of eschatological thought. His list bears a similarity to that drawn up by another English anti-millenarian, Thomas Edwards (1599-1647). Edwards must have been one of very few ex-Cambridge students who went into print against the millenarianism so many of his former university colleagues advocated. His *Gangræna* (1646) attacked the influence of the 'whirlegig spirits' inciting revolution throughout the land.[122] Their doctrines had been well established by this stage: they taught that 'Christ shall come again and live upon the earth, for a Thousand years reign', that 'Christians shall live without sin, without

---

[118] Hayne, *Christs Kingdom on Earth*, sig. A2r-A2v.

[119] Hayne, *Christs Kingdom on Earth*, p. 16.

[120] Hayne, *Christs Kingdom on Earth*, p. 18.

[121] Hayne, *Christs Kingdom on Earth*, pp. 47-8.

[122] Thomas Edwards, *Gangræna* (1646; rpr. *The Rota* and the University of Exeter, 1977), sig. A4v.

the Word, Sacraments or any Ordinance.'[123] Millenarian ideas had taken such a hold, he feared, that England 'is already in many places a Chaos, a Babel, another Amsterdam, yea, worse; we are beyond that, and in the highway to Munster.'[124]

Edwards' commitment to the Westminster Assembly and its Scottish representatives compelled his admiration for the works of Thomas Brightman, who, as we will see, grounded his eschatological hope on England's apocalyptic union with Scotland. Edwards praised Brightman as 'a man of propheticall spirit' and eulogised Ussher as a 'learned and godly Divine'.[125] It was the Independents and their 'misshaped Basterd-monster of a Toleration', he believed, who were responsible for the nation's woes.[126] Again, the radical Independents were blamed as the source of the millenarian frenzy; and again, their eschatology was portrayed as a part of their ecclesiastical package.

Edwards' concerns were mirrored in *A Dissuasive from the Errors of the Time* (1645), a text produced by one of the Scottish Commissioners at the Westminster Assembly, Robert Baillie (1599-1662). Although Baillie's work was a systematic refutation of contemporary errors - among them millenarianism and Independency - it presented a refutation founded upon the apocalyptic vision of the Scottish Covenanters, as his dedicatory preface notes: 'though now that brightnesse be much eclipsed, and over clouded,' he lamented, 'yet we are expecting with passionate desires, and confident hopes, the dissolution of these clouds, and the dispelling of the present darknesse, by the strength of the Beames of his ancient and undeserved kindnesse, towards that now suffering and much distressed Nation.'[127]

Baillie seems to have been well aware of the pedigree of the Independents' apocalypse: 'Alstedius Heterodox Writings were not long abroad, when Mr. Meade at Cambridge was gained to follow him: yet both these Divines were farre from dreaming of any personall raigne of Christ upon earth: Onely Mr. Archer, and his Colleague T.G. [Thomas Goodwin] at Arnheim, were bold to set up the whole Fabrick of Chiliasm.'[128] Baillie reported that, during this millennium, the Independents expected to 'live without any disturbance from any enemy, either without or within; all Christians then shall live without sinne, without the Word and Sacraments or any Ordinance: they shall

---

[123] Edwards, *Gangræna*, i. 23.

[124] Edwards, *Gangræna*, i. 120.

[125] Edwards, *Gangræna*, ii. 193; iii. 87.

[126] Edwards, *Gangræna*, i. 166.

[127] Baillie, *A Dissausive from the Errors of the Times*, Dedicatory Preface.

[128] Baillie, *A Dissausive from the Errors of the Times*, p. 224.

passe these thousands yeares in great worldly delights.'[129] That there should be a time when the Jewish nation would 'be converted to the fayth of Christ; and that the fullnesse of the Gentiles is to come in with them to the Christian Church.' Baillie agreed; but he denied that 'converted Jewes shall returne to Canaan to build Jerusalem; That Christ shall come from the heaven to reigne among them for a thousand yeares, there is no such thing in the scriptures'.[130] Baillie's alternative eschatology was strongly Genevan: citing Augustine's *City of God* and the annotations of the Geneva Bible, he refuted the Independents' appeal for church purity by invoking the Presbyterian order: 'Scripture makes the Church of God so long as it is upon the earth to be a mixed multitude, of Elect and Reprobate.'[131] As far as Baillie was concerned, to attack the Independent ecclesiology was to undermine their eschatology.

Again, Baillie pointed to the 'Liberty of Conscience, and Toleration' propounded by some of the radicals as the root cause of England's problems - 'so prodigious an impiety'.[132] But the literary expression of this toleration - the new leniency of state censorship - was to prove a decided embarrassment to the leaders of the more conservative puritan groups. By the beginnings of the 1650s the interpretative communities which had read the radical pamphlets had organised themselves into movements with shared agendas. As we have already noted, the Fifth Monarchist party aligned itself around preachers from various Baptist and Independent congregations who advocated a radical social and political programme in preparation for the millennial rule of the saints. The leaders of Independency grew quickly cautious of elements within their movement which were suddenly more radical than the movement's leaders. In the early 1650s the Independent leaders - like John Owen and Thomas Goodwin - began to distance themselves from the Fifth Monarchists, but the radicals were quick to point to their inconsistency. The earlier literalism of Owen and Goodwin had done more than merely predict civil conflict.

But despite the best efforts of the puritan leaders, the flux at the heart of the radical eschatology quickly evolved into discourses yet further removed from Genevan orthodoxy. The new Quaker movement, for example, was launched at the height of the millenarian agitation of the early 1650s. Its critics understood the movement's leaders to teach that Christ's second coming would not be visible and personal, but rather 'realised'. In essence, this 'realised eschatology' taught that Biblical

---

[129] Baillie, *A Dissausive from the Errors of the Times*, p. 225.
[130] Baillie, *A Dissausive from the Errors of the Times*, p. 243.
[131] Baillie, *A Dissausive from the Errors of the Times*, pp. 244, 251, 230.
[132] Baillie, *A Dissausive from the Errors of the Times*, Dedicatory Preface.

eschatology was no more than a series of allegories depicting the spiritual experience of an individual believer. Thus Christ's second coming represented death; the millennium represented any triumph over evil. As we will later see, this type of teaching, although publicly repudiated, came to exercise an intense grip upon the mature puritan imagination. Its essential elements were widely disseminated in the flood-tide of Quaker publication: one recent calculation recounts some 2939 Quaker titles published between 1660 and 1699.[133] Quaker theory was essentially millenarian. In denying the contemporary need for baptism and the Lord's supper, and in elevating the inner light above Scripture, they were claiming for themselves the imminent, immediate communion with Christ which Goodwin had predicted for millennial saints in *A Glimpse of Sions Glory*.

Other millenarians abandoned formal theologising to initiate social and political attempts to hasten the golden age. The Digger movement, for example, hoped to reassert an Edenic lifestyle in the communal ownership of rural property. The Levellers maintained a powerful presence in the Army and profoundly influenced Parliament in a series of petitions full of apocalyptic invective. There were also many less organised attempts to invoke the millennium. From the chaos of the unrestrained individualism of the civil wars there have survived accounts of crucifixions, self-proclaimed messiahs, attempts at miracles, and the discovery of strange and foreboding monsters. The conservative leaders of puritanism would have been horrified by such excesses; but, according to Thomas Hobbes, even they 'were the enemies which rose ... from the private interpretation of the Scripture'.[134]

It was in this individualistic confusion that the puritan apocalyptic tradition reached its logical conclusion. The Geneva Bible had transformed the godly into critical readers whose manipulation of apocalyptic ideas became ever more self-reflexive and self-aware. Puritan expositors had re-written their apocalypse from a metanarrative of universal history to a micronarrative of 'realised eschatology' within the conversion experience of an individual. They had prised from the apocalypse its external controls - the role of the godly king, or the historicity of the thousand-year reign - and had found themselves confronted with texts which interrogated the Calvinist aesthetic maxim and utterly defied closure. Nevertheless, despite its innumerable redefinitions, the dream of the golden age remained attractive to succeeding generations of puritans. But it had moved a long way from its origins, in the Geneva Bible and John Foxe, and the thought of the Marian exiles.

---

[133] Keeble, *Literary Culture of Nonconformity*, p. 129.

[134] Thomas Hobbes, *Behemoth* (1679; rpr. New York: Burt Franklin, 1975), p. 5.

CHAPTER 3

The Marian Exiles and the Construction of the Tradition

After the death of the young King Edward VI in 1553, the conditions of peace which English protestants had enjoyed were suddenly reversed. Mary, the new queen, had inherited an intense hatred of the Reformed faith from her mother, Catherine of Aragón, the first wife of Henry VIII. The character of Mary's reign was marked by her single-minded attempts to restore the former Roman Catholic settlement. Her government was responsible for the burning of two hundred and eighty-eight protestants between 1555 and 1558 - among them one archbishop, four bishops and almost sixty women and children. The martyrs would have been more numerous had not eight hundred English protestants - including five bishops - fled abroad at Mary's accession.

When these exiles fled to the Continent, they were engaging with a tradition which stretched back over two thousand years. Apocalyptic interest had always seemed to thrive when the godly were both persecuted and geographically estranged. The place of exile, like the Biblical wilderness, was a topography loaded with spiritual significance. Daniel had received his prophecy while in Babylonian exile, and John had documented *Revelation* while in banishment 'for the word of God and for the testimony of Jesus Christ' (*Revelation* 1:9). The puritan counterparts of these biblical heroes were to exercise a similar impact: Katharine Firth has claimed that 'no six years were more important than those from 1553 to 1559' in the development of the native apocalyptic tradition, and Jane Dawson has similarly noted that the Marian exile was 'of crucial importance' for British eschatological thought.[1] The cultural products of the exile's embryonic puritans were to be central in the development of protestant millennialist discourses throughout the succeeding centuries.

The flight of Mary's exiles took place less than two decades after the

---

[1] Firth, *The Apocalyptic Tradition in Reformation Britain*, p. 69; Jane E.A. Dawson, 'The Apocalyptic Thinking of the Marian Exiles', in Michael *Prophecy and Eschatology: Studies in Church History, Subsidia 10* (Oxford: Blackwell, 1994), p. 75.

events at Münster, and millenarianism was still deeply suspect. Nevertheless, these exiled communities became the laboratories of a new ideology which would inject an exegetical shock into the conventional Augustinian eschatology. History would be rewritten as a polemical exposition of *Revelation*, and the imminent climax of the ages would be postponed to allow for an increasingly optimistic eschatology involving massive numbers of conversions of Jews and unbelieving Gentiles into the Christian church. Textual integrity would be problematised as puritans grappled to theorise the aesthetics of apocalypse and enforce closure on texts representing unclosed history. Although their alternative apocalypse would be superseded, the distinctively protestant poetics it had engendered would be reflected in texts throughout the puritan period. In literary theorising and historical reconstruction, the exegesis of *Revelation* was the single most significant feature of the exiles' rhetorical project and the basis of the most enduring texts of mid-sixteenth-century protestantism - the annotations of the Geneva Bible and the historical studies of John Foxe.

The culture of the exiles was intensely literary. Building upon Bale's study of *The Image of Both Churches* (1547), the exiles grounded their anti-Marian polemic in apocalyptic themes. Bale, as we have seen, used the text of *Revelation* as a basis for his explication of church history, finding confirmations of his own anti-Catholic sentiments in John's description of eschatological turmoil. The exiles followed his example. John Olde translated Rudolf Gualter's *Antichrist* in 1556 and added his own *Short Description of Antichrist* one year later. Also in 1557 were published Bartholomew Traheron's lectures on *Revelation* 4 and Robert Pownall's *Admonition to the Towne of Callys*, invoking imminent apocalyptic judgement upon the English town.[2] Identical apocalyptic themes can be found in virtually every text the exiles produced: they saw themselves as the remnant who, as the preface to the first Geneva Bible suggested, 'love the comming of Christ Jesus our Lord'.[3]

Despite this common fascination with *Revelation*, however, deep divisions existed within the refugee ranks. The group which gathered in Frankfurt involved most of the exiles but struggled to contain the competing interests of early puritanism. These exiles never shared an ideology; they differed in the extent of their allegiance to the English government, the English church, the Genevan theology, and, most crucially, over the type of liturgy best suited to a Reformed congregation. One of the leaders, John Knox, preferred a prayer book similar to that used by Calvin in Geneva, while the chief of his pro-Anglican opponents, Thomas Lever, preferred the Book of Common

---

[2] Dawson, 'The Apocalyptic Thinking of the Marian Exiles', p. 77.
[3] *Geneva Bible* (1560), sig. iii[v].

Prayer instituted by the English church under Edward. For a while the situation was balanced, and relative peace prevailed, but with the arrival of Richard Coxe conservative conformists exercised increasing influence. Knox was ostracised by the conformists and found himself driven from Frankfurt. A few months later, in August 1555, some twenty of his followers failed to win concessions from the majority and, in September, they scattered. Calvin invited Knox and his followers to Geneva.

John Foxe

John Foxe (1516-1587) found himself torn between the conflicting parties and determined to pursue a more independent path.[4] He separated from the rest of the exiles and settled eventually in Basel, where he devoted himself to writing. It is likely that his work was designed, at least in part, to call attention to the common history of both groups, promoting a unity which would transcend the liturgical differences amongst the Reformed. The methodology which he had inherited from the Reformers emphasised that history was 'essentially ambiguous', but Foxe was quite prepared to move beyond their caution.[5] Recognising the polemical utility of finding patterns in history, he explicated *Revelation* to prove that the puritan refugees, disconsolate and divided, were vital members of history's winning side and were part of the tradition of dissent which characterised the truest English Christianity. As Stephen Greenblatt notes, 'it would take Foxe's massive rewriting of history ... to establish a "tradition" of resistance to illegitimate spiritual authority.'[6] Foxe's work was certainly optimistic and robustly eschatological, but its millenarian basis has remained a subject of debate, as we have seen. 'Was Foxe a millenarian?' Olsen has asked, and answered: 'It is all a matter of definition.'[7]

In the resulting 'Book of Martyrs', the *Acts and Monuments* (1563), Foxe signalled the linearity of history as a trail of blood from the apostles to the Marian exiles. It was an historical text twice as long as the Bible - by its own admission, 'set forth at Large' - but its reception demonstrated why Bale had been correct to argue that the reconstruction of history was the most important protestant objective

---

[4] For a sample of recent work on Foxe, see Christopher Highley and John N. King (eds), *John Foxe and his World*, St Andrews Studies in Reformation History (Aldershot: Ashgate, 2002).

[5] T.F. Torrance, 'The Eschatology of the Reformation', *Eschatology: Scottish Journal of Theology Occasional Papers* 2 (1953), p. 40.

[6] Greenblatt, *Renaissance Self-Fashioning*, p. 93.

[7] Olsen, 'Was John Foxe a Millenarian?', p. 622.

after the vernacular translation of Scripture.[8] The *Acts and Monuments* was a tremendously successful project whose popularity consolidated the pro-reforming narratives of 'the Bloody Times, Horrible Troubles, and Great Persecutions against the true MARTYRS of Christ'. Advancing a robustly protestant apologetic, it explained to the exiles and their supporters why they found themselves and their world as they did. It unpacked their identity under the framework of the continual opposition of truth and error, the unending war between Christ and Antichrist. False prophets and conniving prelates were hell's agents against the elect.

Foxe's narratives are certainly exciting reading: his heroes were carefully positioned to illustrate the series of historical crises true Christians had faced. He presented the first believers resisting Nero, the aged Polycarp defying Roman demands to offer incense to Caesar, and Anasthasius alone defending the Trinity. But the apocalyptic justification of his selection has been often overlooked. The 1570 edition of the text included among the 'principal Writers and Preachers' of the English church both John Gower (c.1330-1408) and Geoffrey Chaucer (c.1340-1400) – rather surprising representatives of England's millenarian remnant. Later editions included among the latter-day heroes both Dante and Petrarch, 'who called Rome the Whore of Babylon'.[9]

Foxe's martyrology was unpacked within a distinctly eschatological outline of church history. His prefaces detailed the methodologies he would adopt. Although his historiographical model evolved through the early editions of his work, Foxe ultimately decided on a five-fold division of providence in the 1570 edition of his *Acts and Monuments*.[10] The first division was the 'suffering time' of the first three hundred years after the apostles - the first persecution of the church. This period synchronised the prophetic types of the forty-two months of the Gentile trampling of the temple of God (*Revelation* 11:2) and the forty-two months of the domination of the beast from the sea (*Revelation* 13:5). This 'synchronism' was simply explained as a period of 294 years after the crucifixion of Christ. After this, 'according to the preordinate Council of God', divine mercy was outstretched 'to bind up Satan the old Serpent, according to the twentieth Chapter of the Revelation, for the space of a thousand years'.

Thus began the most significant feature of Foxe's historiography - his exposition of the millennium. Although Satan's power was constrained by Christ's death, the millennium itself did not begin until the

---

[8] Firth, *The Apocalyptic Tradition in Reformation Britain*, p. 60.

[9] Foxe, *Acts and Monuments* (1570), p. 5; 9th ed. (1684), i. a3v; i. a4r.

[10] Olsen, 'Was John Foxe a Millenarian?', p. 613.

persecutions of the early church had ceased - with the accession of Constantine. Beginning in 324, when 'the great Dragon the Devil [was] tied short for a thousand years after', it would last until 'the time of John Wickliffe and John Husse' and signified the increasing apostasy of the Roman church.[11] This millennium was not a glorious affair of the uninterrupted harmony of the rule of the saints, but a period when the visible church experienced increasing lethargy and intruding error. It began with a 'flourishing time', Foxe's second division of three hundred years' duration, when Constantine formally adopted the Christian faith on behalf of the Roman Empire, but its degeneration quickly followed.

The third division of church history began six hundred years after the apostles, and was described as a 'declining or backsliding time'. This period also lasted three hundred years, and brought Foxe's history up to the end of A.D. 1000. In this period the church grew in ambition and pomp, and was 'much altered from the simple sincerity of the Primitive Time'. Foxe lamented that while 'in outward profession of Doctrine and Religion, it was something tolerable, and had some face of a Church: ... some corruption of Doctrine, with Superstition and Hypocrisie was then also crept in.' This was a characterisation of the millennium which would find few echoes in the optimism of later puritan thought. Foxe's binding of Satan could not prevent the spread of heresy. The result of this, in the fourth division, was that the church's 'Doctrine and sincerity of Life was utterly almost extinguished.'

After 1080, under the leadership of Gregory VII (also known as Hildebrand, Pope between 1073-85) and Innocent III (Pope between 1198-1216), the church was 'turned upside downe, all order broken, discipline dissolved, true doctrine defaced, Christian Faith extinguished ... Then was the clere sunne shine of Gods word overshadowed, with mists and darknes, appearyng like sackcloth to the people, which neyther could understand that they read, nor yet Permitted to read that they coulde understand.'[12] Thus continued the middle ages, 'duryng which space, the true church of Christ, although it durst not openly appeare in the face of the world, oppressed by tyranny: yet neyther was it so invisible or unknowne, but by the providence of the Lord, some remnaunt alwayes remained, from tyme to tyme, whiche not onely shewed secret good affection to sincere doctrine, but also stood in open defence of truth agaynst the disordered Church of Rome.'[13] The true church - once an Empire - had become a remnant outside the visible sacramental continuum of the 'disordered Church of Rome'.

Antichrist's four hundred years of unchallenged rule of the Roman

---

[11] Foxe, *Acts and Monuments* (1563; 9th ed. 1684), i. 111.
[12] Foxe, *Acts and Monuments* (1570), Preface, p. 4.
[13] Foxe, *Acts and Monuments* (1570), Preface, p. 4.

church was brought to an end in 'the time of John Wickliffe and John Huss'. Satan's loosing in 1324 had resulted in the persecution of the first reformers, and the struggle between the true and false churches had continued ever since for, as Foxe put it, 'the true Church of God goeth not lightly alone, but is accompanied with some other Church or Chappell of the devill to deface and maligne the same'.[14] This fifth period, in which Foxe was writing, 'followeth the reformation and purging of the Church of God, wherein Antichrist beginneth to be revealed, and to appear in his colour, and his Antichristian Doctrine to be detected, and the number of the true Church increasing'. This fifth period had lasted almost three hundred years - 'and how long it shall continue more, the Lord and Governor of all times, he only knoweth.'[15] Tudor puritans could expect an imminent apocalypse: *Revelation* 20:3 noted that there was only to be 'a little season' between Satan's loosing and the end of all things.

Thus the suffering of the native church in the English Reformation was the grand crescendo of the *Acts and Monuments*. Queen Mary's persecution had brought to a focus the universal movements of providence. Her new regime heralded Europe's hope of deliverance. The exiles were sure Catholic Babylon was soon to fall. Frequently citing Wycliffe as the 'morning star of the reformation', they pointed to England's special role in Antichrist's destruction.

It was easy for this apocalyptic foregrounding of England to gain social and political credibility. After the accession of Elizabeth, England was the only major power to enjoy a protestant hegemony, as a besieged island outpost of the Reformation. Opposition to the Papal Antichrist was the basis of Elizabeth's foreign policy and of arguments over the royal dynasty. It provided central themes for the literary culture surrounding Edmund Spenser's *Faerie Queene* (1590), in which the English 'godly prince' was to take the leading role in the final cosmic drama. Foxian rhetoric was purposely designed to establish bishop and king.

The 'theoretical respectability' of such sentiment led to its massive dissemination.[16] After the exiles returned, pulpits rang to the sound of the exile's historiography, as English protestants listened to a theologically-justified analysis of the sufferings of the elect. Fuelled by fear of 'Romanists under the bed', England embraced Foxe's interpretation of history, and an estimated ten thousand copies of the *Acts and Monuments* were circulating by the end of the seventeenth century. This figure cannot account for the number of unacknowledged

---

[14] Foxe, *Acts and Monuments* (1570), Preface, p. 3.
[15] Foxe, *Acts and Monuments* (1563; 9th ed. 1684), i. 1.
[16] Hill, *Antichrist in Seventeenth-Century England*, p. 13.

quotations of Foxe's work in larger works, and the many abridgements and imitations which popular presses produced.[17] Christopher Hill has noted *The Theatre of God's Judgements* (1597), by Oliver Cromwell's schoolteacher, Thomas Beard, which similarly portrayed world history as 'a struggle between God and the powers of darkness, in which the elect fight for God and are certain of victory in so far as they obey his laws'.[18]

Not content with only signalling the importance of his country, Foxe went on to make dramatic claims about his text. Bale had earlier argued that Scripture was 'a light to the chronicles and not the chronicles to the text'[19] - implying the lesser importance of the historical record of providence - but Foxe claimed that Scripture and history were of equal usefulness in furthering the cause of Reformation. As 'we see what light and profit cometh to the Church by Histories in old times set forth', he claimed, 'so likewise may it redound to no small use in the Church, to know the Actes of Christes Martyrs now since the time of the Apostles'.[20] For Foxe, Scripture and the *Acts and Monuments* were interrelated because his history was an hermeneutical prerequisite. As 'the Book of Revelation ... containeth a Prophetical History of the Church', he argued, 'so likewise it requireth by Histories to be opened.'[21] Certainly the publishers of a 1684 edition advised their readers that the *Acts and Monuments* was 'justly to be esteemed (as the learned confess) the next of all human penn'd Books to the sacred Bible.'[22]

Nevertheless, despite the massive dissemination of his book, certain aspects of Foxe's ideology remain obscure. Debate continues as to the extent to which the *Acts and Monuments* encouraged the belief in England's elect status as a nation divinely appointed for a unique end-times role. This idea was a seventeenth century commonplace but, as Patrick Collinson has recently noted, can be traced with certainty as far back as the fourteenth century.[23] Matthew Parker, archbishop of Canterbury between 1559 and 1575, invoked the trope to claim that

[17] William Haller, *Foxe's Book of Martyrs and the Elect Nation* (London: Jonathan Cape, 1963), p. 14.

[18] Christopher Hill, *God's Englishman: Oliver Cromwell and the English Revolution* (1970; rpr. Harmondsworth: Penguin, 1990), p. 37.

[19] Bale, *The Image of Both Churches*, p. 253.

[20] Foxe, *Acts and Monuments* (1570), Preface, p. 10.

[21] Foxe, *Acts and Monuments* (1563; 9th ed. 1684), i. a6ᵛ.

[22] Foxe, *Acts and Monuments* (1684), i. [a]ʳ.

[23] Patrick Collinson, 'Biblical rhetoric: the English nation and national sentiment in the prophetic mode', in Claire McEachern and Debra Shuger (eds), *Religion and Culture in Renaissance England* (Cambridge: Cambridge University Press, 1997), p. 21.

England should support reform, and, as a consequence, the cause of England would always be the cause of God. John Aylmer, in *An Harborowe for Faithfull and Trewe Subjects* (1559), argued that God, in fact, was English. Thus, later puritans would argue, divine mercy was expressed in the accession of godly Queen Elizabeth, allowing the elect a respite after the Counter-Reformation brutalities of her sister; in 1588, 'the year of our Redemption', only the breath of God could have been responsible for the winds which destroyed the Armada;[24] and the discovery of the Gunpowder Plot in 1605 demonstrated the divine defence against Catholic assaults on the foundations of English political life.[25]

Modern historians disagree as to whether this powerfully nationalistic ideology was really rooted in Foxe. William Haller, in 1963, was the first to claim that it was. John Spencer Hill confirmed this interpretation: 'undoubtedly the most important assertion of national vocation in Elizabethan England is John Foxe's *Acts and Monuments*.'[26] Other scholars have disagreed. Neville Williams and Richard Bauckham have portrayed a Foxe more interested in protestant internationalism than in England's status as an 'elect nation'. In 1990 David Loewenstein discovered 'little sense of any messianic national destiny' in Foxe's work.[27] William Lamont has argued that while later puritans did read the 'elect nation' idea in their copies of Foxe, they were deliberately underplaying the text's 'intended European dimension'.[28]

The debate centres around the polar concepts of the 'faithful remnant' and the 'reformed nation'. Both expressions represented ideologies which became increasingly incompatible as the scholarly defence of the Elizabethan settlement developed. The reformed nation concept highlighted the role of the godly prince, who was to be responsible for national reformation and the waging of eschatological warfare against the Pope. The faithful remnant idea, on the other hand, expressed a fear that the godly would always be a minority, and that establishment hierarchies - whether of church or state - were often handicaps in the quest for godly reformation. Both ideas can be found in the *Acts and Monuments*, as Dawson has noted, but the evolving political

---

[24] Foxe, *Acts and Monuments* (1563; 9th ed. 1684), i. c2v.

[25] John Spencer Hill, *John Milton: Poet, Priest and Prophet: A Study of Divine Vocation in Milton's Poetry and Prose* (London: Macmillan, 1979), p. 86.

[26] Hill, *John Milton*, p. 88.

[27] David Loewenstein, *Milton and the Drama of History: Historical Vision, Iconoclasm, and the Literary Imagination* (Cambridge: Cambridge University Press, 1990), p. 10.

[28] William Lamont, *Richard Baxter and the Millennium: Protestant Imperialism and the English Revolution* (London: Croom Helm, 1979), p. 14.

situation engendered increasing support for the concept of the elect nation: 'the idea of the True Church as a suffering and persecuted minority of the faithful was obviously inappropriate to describe a comprehensive national church. Instead, the English Protestants seized upon the alternative language of the People of God in covenant relationship with God.'[29] After the exiled pessimism of Bale - recasting, as we have seen, the English church as a half-reformed Laodicea which God would soon abandon - the ideology of the Marian exiles evolved into a rhetoric of nationalistic optimism. As David Loades has argued, Elizabethan puritans regarded the reforming Tudors as 'agents of divine providence in a special sense.'[30] We shall see that the changing annotations of the Geneva Bible would later reflect puritanism's reversion to the pessimistic idea of the remnant. Certainly Elizabeth capitalised upon the political utility of the *Acts and Monuments*. Through her support Foxe's ideology was incorporated into the essential cultural capital of the age with the result that, as Haller has noted, the 'work had an influence on the English mind second only to that of the English Bible'.[31]

But Foxe's writings disseminated more than crude pro-government propaganda. Less well-known than his 'Book of Martyrs' is his interest in drama. His major play, *Christus Triumphans* (1556), was written while Foxe was compiling the historical source material for the *Acts and Monuments* and, perhaps as a consequence, was an extended reflection on the nature of his historiographical and theological method. In *Acts and Monuments* Foxe used *Revelation* to pattern history. In *Christus Triumphans* he used *Revelation* to question the very possibility of writing history.

Contrary to the stereotypes of history, plays were regarded as a legitimate tools for the inculcation of protestant positions during the first Reformation.[32] Many of these were neo-Latin academic dramas rarely intended for performance - Beza had written a drama called *Abraham's Sacrifice* (1550) and Bucer had recommended biblical histories as eminently suitable material for tragedies. Other dramas were clearly written with performance in mind. Anti-reformation parliaments

[29] Dawson, 'The Apocalyptic Thinking of the Marian Exiles', p. 84.

[30] Loades, 'John Foxe and the Traitors: The Politics of the Marian Persecution', in Diana Wood (ed.), *Martyrs and Martyrologies: Papers read at the 1992 Summer Meeting and the 1993 Winter Meeting of the Ecclesiastical History Society* (Oxford: Blackwell, 1993), p. 244.

[31] Leonard J. Trinterud (ed.), *Elizabethan Puritanism* (New York: Oxford University Press, 1971), p. 41.

[32] Andrew Pettegree, *Reformation and the culture of persuasion* (Cambridge: Cambridge University Press, 2005), pp. 76-101.

attacked the 'preachers and scaffold players of this new religion', as pulpits and stages united to advance a militantly reformist agenda.[33] Eire has noted that protestant ideology was regularly enacted in public, 'announced on the stage through dramatic poems or plays, which often combined sharp satire with theological argumentation'.[34] In *Christus Triumphans* Foxe was working within a well established tradition, and successfully calculated the mood of the pro-Anglican exiles he hoped to please: there is no evidence, for example, that Thomas Lever, leader of the anti-Knox group of exiles, ever repudiated drama when he was appointed archdeacon in Coventry after the exile - and this despite his reputed 'puritanism'.

Foxe's play certainly indicates a conciliatory purpose. Published one year after the division of the exiles, and dedicated to those English merchants who had remained with Lever's Anglicans in Frankfurt, it seems likely that its composition was a deliberate attempt to heal the rift between the two rival groups. Like the *Acts and Monuments*, its subject matter - the history of the invisible and pure church of Christ - was designed to unite the aspirations of exiles on both sides of their liturgical divide.

Largely overlooked by scholars in favour of his larger works, Foxe's Latin drama constituted an allegorical representation of the sweep of church history from Adam to Armageddon. Its stated aim was to portray human history as an exposition of *Revelation*, but, as in Milton's treatment of *Genesis*, Foxe used the dramatisation of Scripture to situate the discourse of a larger philosophy. Advertising itself as a *comoedia apocalyptica*, the play conflated time, letting Eve converse with Mary, and juxtaposed such scenes of fantasy with a hard-edged social critique. Everywhere 'Ecclesia', the Greek word translated as 'church', was the heroine; representing variously the church of the Old Testament, the New Testament and finally the Church of England, Foxe dramatised her timeless struggle with Antichrist.

There is no doubt that Foxe was keen to explore the concurrence of play and history, of sign and thing signified. The *Acts and Monuments* had divided church history into 'five sundry diversities of times'. *Christus Triumphans* seemed to anticipate and mirror this structure in its five-act division of its theme. This identification of the form of text and providence was problematised and interrogated in the play's content.

The Prologue seemed highly conscious of the play's innovative style: 'our matter is totally sacred and totally apocalyptic, what has been

---

[33] Patrick Collinson, *From Iconoclasm to Iconophobia: The Cultural Impact of the Second English Reformation* (Reading: University of Reading, 1986), pp. 11-12.
[34] Eire, *War Against the Idols*, p. 100.

heard of by many but never seen before.'[35] Foxe was playing on the etymology of 'apocalypse', the Greek root of which is equivalent to the English 'revelation' or 'revealing'. In portraying what was 'never seen before', then, *Christus Triumphans* both described the apocalypse and became an apocalypse. The play was claiming to mix what it was and what it represented, collapsing the distinctions between the signified and the signifier, between fact and form.

The play's conclusion brought this theme to its focus. There was an initial attempt to parallel the twin closures of text and history:

> And I think we should prepare all the more quickly since it seems that all the parts of the play have been acted out and that the scene of this world is rushing to that final "Farewell, and applaud." Thus, with the catastrophe of everything imminent and the prophecies completely fulfilled, nothing seems to remain except that apocalyptic voice soon to be heard from heaven, "It is finished."[36]

Foxe could not offer that apocalyptic voice. He could attempt to close his text, but never the history his text described:

> Nothing remains except the bridegroom himself, who will bring the final catastrophe to our stage. When that will happen none will say for sure. The poet had shown what he could. And he earnestly advises you not to be unprepared, lest the bridegroom, when he comes, reject you as you sleep. The time is perhaps not long. We see the marvellous preludes: how Satan battles against Christ with all his forces everywhere in the world today, as hard as he did of yore. But the lamb will prevail, triumphant at last, and the bride of the lamb.[37]

Foxe would seem to have been figuring history as a 'stage' whose

---

[35] Foxe, *Christus Triumphans*, in John Hazel Smith (trans.), *Two Latin Comedies by John Foxe the Martyrologist: Titus et Gesippus, Christus Triumphans* (London: Cornell University Press, 1973), p. 229: Res tota sacra est totaque Apocalyptica: / Audita quae multis, nunquam at uisa est prius.

[36] Foxe, *Christus Triumphans*, p. 207: Tantoque id maturius nobis agendum arbitror quod, expletis iam omnibus fabulae partibus, mundi huius scena properare uidetur ad supremum illud "Valete et plaudite"; sicque imminente rerum omnium catastropha emensisque prorsus uaticiniis ut nil restare uideatur nisi uox illa Apocalyptica, de coelo mox audienda, "Factvm est."

[37] Foxe, *Christus Triumphans*, p. 371: Restat nihil, ipse / Nisi paranymphus summam qui scenae imponat / Catastrophen. Id quum fiet certum nemo / Dicet. Poeta, quod possit, praestitit. Ipse ac / Monet sedulo imparati ne sitis, sponsus / Cum ueniet uos ne dormitantes excludat. / Tempus fortasse haud longum est. Mira uidemus / Rerum praeludia: Sathan cum Christo totis / Vt pugnat copiis, ubique terrarum / Hodie, ut cum alias, maxime. Agnus at uincet / Triumphans tandem agnique sponsa.

performance Christ alone could end. *Christus Triumphans* reached out beyond the stage to grasp for an a-historical transcendence, blurring the opposition of reality and its representation. This refusal to 'close' the text, by arguing even at its end that it represented only a beginning, signalled a refusal to 'close' history. A concern for true mimesis prevented Foxe from offering a closure which his subject matter did not allow. There could be no closure in texts which claimed to represent history. Thus Foxe took advantage of the confusion of sign and thing signified to deny that the play could ever really describe the end; all it could provide was a prelude to a history which, for the reader-audience, patently continued. The rest of history was the unwritten appendix to Foxe's text.

Nevertheless, as an apocalypse and a representation of the apocalypse, the play invested itself with scriptural authority and simultaneously yearned for its own dissolution. The Prologue expressly hoped that 'perhaps it will not be long before stage representations will lie neglected; then indeed we will see all with our own eyes, when God sends in actual fact what he now only promises.'[38] In desiring the negation of stage plays - and, by implication, the Scriptural exegesis they recounted - *Christus Triumphans* was desiring the negation of itself. Millenarian iconoclasm was being wrapped up in textual annihilation. It would become a standard feature of puritan apocalyptic texts, imagining an eschatological world where the mediating ordinances of texts, sacraments and Scripture were no longer necessary in the immediate presence of God. As the Reformers pained themselves to establish the authority of Scripture alone over the traditions of the Roman Catholic Church, Foxe's play was envisaging and anticipating the extermination of that sole authority.

Yet this foregrounding of textual weakness, of the text's inability to encapsulate its subject, would be repeated throughout the puritan apocalyptic tradition. *Christus Triumphans* was signalling its referential status and highlighting to its audience that its protestant poetics could never claim completion. After all, *finitum non est capax infiniti*. Foxe's drama was a sign, not an icon: very literally, it pointed past itself to 'the bridegroom himself, who will bring the final catastrophe to our stage'. The deconstruction of the authority of the text was deliberate - the didactic function of *Christus Triumphans* was to register the limits of human rhetoric. Its evangelistic impetus was to question the epistemology of a fallen humanity.

Collinson has argued for the existence of a radical disjunction in

---

[38] Foxe, *Christus Triumphans*, p. 229: Forsan nec diu / Id erit ludi quum iacebunt scenici. / Quippe oculis tum ipsi cuncta contuebimur, / Re quum ipsa mittit nunc quae promittit Deus.

puritan aesthetics, claiming the emerging puritan movement ditched its initial cultural baggage around 1580. These early and uncomfortable links with Catholic forms of the play, the ballad and the image, he claims, were replaced by a distinctly Reformed aesthetic.[39] *Christus Triumphans*, however, demonstrates the *continuity* of Foxe and his seventeenth-century puritan successors, and evidences that the theme of millenarian textual iconoclasm was being explored well within the boundaries of the first century of reformation. Nevertheless the play's complication of form is its most important feature; its innovative and iconoclastic style challenges the centuries of neglect which it has suffered.

The Geneva Bibles

The various Bibles which the exiles produced picked up on Foxe's concerns and enlarged upon his historical and theoretical reading of *Revelation* through self-interpreting texts designed to consolidate and guard the teachings of the Reformers.[40] The early protestant communities were faced with demands for literalistic exegesis from two fronts. The Roman Catholic church, insisting that Jesus Christ was sacrificially offered in the mass, compelled protestants to choose between 'transubstantiation or a trope'.[41] Catholic hermeneutic was supported by the might of a monolithic inquisitional structure. The Anabaptist millenarians, on the other hand, insisted that *Revelation* 20 described a utopian period which could be anticipated by revolutionary ferment. The events at Münster had warned protestants of the danger of this type of totally unlegislated reading.

The interpretative debate was of vital importance: within the Reformation's hermeneutical arguments, the eternal destiny of souls and the temporal destiny of kingdoms turned on the correct interpretation of one single phrase. The protestant leaders, in providing vernacular Scripture, opened the door to a raging individualism which they struggled to control, but they were faced also with dissension among the ideologues. Foxe's initial historicising was repudiated as uncertainty about when the millennium had begun led to fundamental

---

39 See Collinson, *From Iconoclasm to Iconophobia*.

40 For recent discussions of the Geneva Bibles, see David Daniell, *The Bible in English: Its History and Influence* (New Haven: Yale University Press, 2003) and Joel Swann, 'Reading Revelation in the English Geneva Bibles' (unpublished BSc dissertation, University of Manchester, 2006).

41 Stephen Greenblatt, 'Remnants of the sacred in Early Modern England', in Margarita de Grazia et al (eds), *Subject and Object in Renaissance Culture* (Cambridge: Cambridge University Press, 1996), pp. 340-2.

doubt as to *whether* it had ever begun, as we shall later see. Nevertheless, the Geneva Bibles' provision of marginal annotations was intended to offer the interpretative guidelines required by those protestants concerned to support the social and religious *status quo*.

For several decades the Geneva Bible strategy was highly successful. After the Marian exiles returned, the Geneva translation quickly established a firm foothold in English church life. One hundred and forty editions of its most popular version were printed between 1560 and 1644. Between 1575 and 1618 at least one new edition of the Geneva Bible appeared each year. Between 1560 and 1611, when the Authorised (King James) Version was produced, only five editions of Tyndale's New Testament, seven editions of the Great Bible, and twenty-two editions of the Bishop's Bible had been published, despite the fact that the latter two translations were both church-sponsored. In the same period over one hundred and twenty editions of the Geneva translation were produced as a Bible designed for the common reader.[42] With their innovative and convenient size, roman type and innovative verse divisions, Geneva Bibles were 'used and pored over by three generations of English Protestants before the Civil War', according to Christopher Hill.[43] Even after 1611 the allegiance of protestant Bible readers took time to transfer. The Authorised Version translators quoted the Geneva text in their preface to the new work. Over sixty editions of the Geneva translation (some of the New Testament only) were published after the Authorised Version first appeared.[44] Geneva Bibles were published until the 1640s and their interpretative notes were included in some editions of the Authorised Version well into the next century.

But the singular description of the 'Geneva Bible' is actually a misnomer. There were *four* different versions of Scripture which emanated from the exiles and were known collectively as the 'Geneva' translation. These editions indicate in themselves the evolution of puritan thought and demonstrate one aspect of the Reformation's hermeneutical ferment. In 1557 Calvin's brother-in-law, William Whittingham, printed the first English New Testament to include verse divisions.[45] It annotations were sparse; those on *Revelation* were the epitome of caution and moderation. Only four annotations out of the total one hundred and forty (excluding Scripture references) linked the Roman Catholic church with Antichristianism. Establishing the

---

[42] *Historical Catalogue of Printed Editions of the English Bible 1525-1961* (1903; 2nd. ed. rev. A.S. Herbert) (London: British and Foreign Bible Society, 1968), *passim*.

[43] Hill, *Antichrist in Seventeenth-Century England*, pp. 3-4.

[44] *Historical Catalogue of Printed Editions of the English Bible*, passim.

[45] *Hist. Cat.* number 106; STC 2871.

tradition of editorial annotations which the later editions would follow, this testament's notes were exegetical rather than doctrinal, focusing on problems of text over theology. The second Scripture which the exiles printed was the first full Geneva Bible (1560), the result of scholarly collaboration between William Whittingham, Miles Coverdale and Christopher Goodman.[46] This was the most popular of the Geneva Bibles. Its title page was loaded with symbolic imagery: it presented a woodcut of the children of Israel, bounded on one side by the advancing Egyptian army and on the other by the apparently unpassable Red Sea with the pillar of cloud - denoting God's presence - high in the sky above. Above and underneath the woodcut were arranged excerpts from the narrative of the Red Sea crossing: 'Feare ye not, stand stil, and beholde the salvacion of the Lord, which he wil shewe to you this day ... The Lord shal fight for you: therefore holde your peace' (*Exodus* 14:13-4). Around the sides of the woodcut were the words of *Psalm* 34:19: 'Great are the troubles of the righteous: but the Lord delivereth them out of all.' The project's polemical agenda and political utility could not have been made clearer.

As we noted, the 1560 Bible described its readers as 'them that love the comming of Christ Jesus our Lord'.[47] Its entire ethos was bathed in the apocalyptic atmosphere of the exiled communities. The preface to Queen Elizabeth was robustly millenarian, alluding to the description of Satan in *Revelation* 20 and the paradigm of the five monarchies of *Daniel*:

> God wil fight from heaven against this great dragon, the ancient serpent, which is called the devil and Satan, til he have accomplished the whole worke and made his Churche glorious to him selfe, without spot and wrincle. For albeit all other kingdomes and monarchies, as the Babylonians, Persians, Grecians & Romains have fallen & taken end: yet the Churche of Christ even under the Crosse hath from the begynning of the worlde bene victorious, and shalbe everlastingly.[48]

Reflecting this mood, the annotations on *Revelation* showed a great deal of development from those adopted in the earlier New Testament. Expanding in size to number some four hundred, they called upon their audience to 'Read diligently: judge soberly, and call earnestly to God for the true understanding hereof',[49] but sought to protect the imagined 'simple reader' from the exegetical excesses of his age.[50]

There was less doubt now that the Pope and his church were the

---

[46] *Hist. Cat.* number 107; STC 2093.

[47] *Geneva Bible* (1560), sig. iii[v].

[48] *Geneva Bible* (1560), sig. iii[v].

[49] *Geneva Bible* (1560), 'Argument' of *Revelation*.

[50] *Geneva Bible* (1560), sig. iiii[v].

enemies of God - but the attempts to combat the exponents of radical reformation were equally intense. The new annotations explained the 'depnes of Satan' in *Revelation* 2:24 as a reference to the 'monstruous errors and blasphemies' of 'Anabaptists, Libertines, Papists, Arians, &c.' *Revelation* 21:24 was explained as a confirmation that 'Kings and Princes (contrarie to that wicked opinion of ye Anabaptists) are partakers of the heavenlie glorie, if they rule in ye feare of the Lord.' This confirmation of England's establishment would find fewer echoes in succeeding editions of puritan Scriptures.

One theme introduced in the 1560 Bible which would find widespread acceptance, however, was its teaching of a future period of unparalleled peace and prosperity for the church. This was not explicated from *Revelation* 20, as in later postmillennialism and the Münster theology, but found its roots in the annotations on *Romans* 11. These notes suggested that the elect Gentiles were to be called into the church for the duration of the time when the Jews had been blinded by God to the truths of Christianity, but that when the 'fulnes of the Gentiles' had entered the church, grace would again be extended to the Jews and that their conversion *en masse* to Christian faith would encourage yet greater revival amongst the Gentiles. 'The Jewes now remaine, as it were, in death for lacke of the Gospel: but when they & the Gentiles shal embrace Christ, ye world shalbe restored to a newe life.'[51] It was a doctrine with a powerfully optimistic eschatological twist: 'the time shal come that the whole nation of ye Jewes ... shalbe joyned to the Church of Christ.'[52] Once adopted by Perkins, this teaching would go on to influence the major puritan expositors throughout the evolution of the movement and remain a staple of mainstream protestant eschatology for the ensuing centuries. In this respect, at least, the 1560 Bible was correct to imagine the finality of its interpretations. Annotating *Revelation* 10:4, where John was commanded to 'seale up' the things he has heard, '& write them not', the Genevan editors exhorted readers to 'beleve that that is written: for there is no nede to write more for the understanding of Gods children.'

The appearance in 1576 of a third Genevan *Revelation* must have disappointed this hope of interpretative finality.[53] This new production was part of a fresh translation of the New Testament prepared from Beza's Latin text by Laurence Tomson, an English puritan M.P. Marginal references and annotations on *Revelation* were reduced to eighty-eight in number, and only two of these identified the eschatological importance of Roman Catholicism. The Geneva/Tomson

---

[51] *Geneva Bible* (1560), note on *Romans* 11:15.
[52] *Geneva Bible* (1560), note on *Romans* 11:26.
[53] *Hist. Cat.* number 146; STC 2878.

New Testament seemed to capture the public imagination, being reprinted separately some twenty-seven times and being included in twelve editions of the complete Bible between its first appearance and the introduction of the fourth Genevan *Revelation* in 1599.[54] This edition accounted for over half the Geneva Bibles ever published, and in Scotland, where it was known as the 'Bassandyne Bible', it retained a monopoly until 1610 as the only Bible to be printed there. Tomson's New Testament featured annotations heavily influenced by Beza's ultra-predestinarian theology, combined with the original Genevan Old Testament. It has been noted that Beza's annotations were designed to educate their readers into Calvinism and supply them with answers to challenges to it.[55] John McNeill has argued that in some instances the notes actually went beyond Calvin's theology.[56] Beza's notes on *Revelation* were so brief, however, that another edition was called for as puritan polemics intensified in the 1580s.

Thus in 1599 a fourth major edition was printed, combining Tomson's New Testament with new annotations on *Revelation*, taken from the work of the Huguenot scholar François Du Jon (1545-1602).[57] Better known by his Latin name, Franciscus Junius was a French Reformed minister who served various refugee congregations before accepting posts to teach theology in the universities of Neustadt, Heidelberg and Leiden, where he was to die of the plague. He had published an extensive bibliography of Biblical commentaries and had been called upon to negotiate between conflicting parties among the English exiles.[58] Although a towering academic figure, his public reputation was only established by the contributions he made to the definitive protestant Latin Bible, which he had translated with Immanuel Tremellius.

Junius was highly interested in apocalyptic thought. In 1589 he had published a Latin work entitled *Notae in Apocalypsim* which was followed three years later by a longer French *Exposition de l'Apocalypse* (1592). Both texts were translated into English, and the shorter work -

---

[54] Lewis Lupton, *A History of the Geneva Bible* (London: Fauconberg Press, 1966-81), vii. 157-163; Historical Catalogue of Printed Editions of the English Bible, passim.

[55] Dan G. Danner, 'The Later English Calvinists and the Geneva Bible', in W. Fred Graham (ed.), *Later Calvinism: International Perspectives* (Kirksville: Sixteenth Century Journal Publishers, 1994), p. 497.

[56] John T. McNeill, *The History and Character of Calvinism* (Oxford: Oxford University Press, 1967), p. 312.

[57] *Hist. Cat.* number 248; STC 2174.

[58] C. de Jonge, 'Franciscus Junius (1545-1602) and the English Separatists at Amsterdam', in Derek Baker (ed.), *Reform and Reformation: England and the Continent c.1500-c.1750* (Oxford: Blackwell, 1979), p. 167.

now entitled *Apocalypsis, a Brief and Learned Commentarie upon the Revelation of St. John* (1592) - was adapted to become the marginal annotations on *Revelation* in the last Geneva Bible. As we shall see, these annotations advanced the most historicised reading of John's visions within the exile tradition, but opened themselves and their text in a manner entirely unsuited to its articulation of teleological closure.

Junius' most basic problem was his need to negotiate an interpretative space in a text which he denied allowed that possibility. He was compelled to conciliate established readers while promoting new readings which advanced towards closure and denied interpretative ambiguity. The Geneva Bible, as the flagship text of English reform, was designed to counter one and a half thousand years of established interpretations and argue that protestant exegesis was history's best. It was vital for the Reformation project that this argument was enforced. Nevertheless, within this overarching aim, Junius was simultaneously forced into a re-reading of the Reformation's central document which he had to publish without drawing attention to his hermeneutical manoeuvrings. Yes, protestant readings were best; but his protestant reading was the best of all. It was highly ironic that Junius' ending was the fourth attempt to close history within the Geneva Bible tradition.

Whatever the methodological difficulties, the resulting volume was intensely popular. Gerald Sheppard has noted that the annotations of this edition were 'indicative of the climate of opinion among puritans in the first half of the seventeenth century' on both sides of the Atlantic.[59] Its pan-European production and pan-Atlantic impact maximised the influences it represented and developed. The resulting Geneva/ Tomson/Junius New Testament passed through three separate printings but appeared as part of a complete Bible in twenty-four different editions. This chapter will focus upon a 1602 issue of the 1599 New Testament which incorporated the most contemporary theological innovations in its annotations, and represented some of puritanism's most systematic explorations of historical application and textual integrity in the first years of the seventeenth century.[60]

The first thing a reader would notice as he turned to *Revelation* was a table of dates and historical events, describing itself as 'the order of time whereunto the contents of this booke are to be referred.'[61] This table summarised the annotator's notes, and indicated Junius' attempt to provide a comprehensive explication of the text which was sensitive to *Revelation*'s authorial context. It was an attempt at justification by

---

[59] *Geneva Bible* (1602), p. 1.
[60] *Hist. Cat.* number 272; STC 2902.
[61] *Geneva Bible* (1602), p. 124v.

history alone which would lead to a confusion of genres, investing futuristic speculation with the weight of proven fact. The similarity with Foxe's method is immediately apparent, but despite their common historical project, the notes of the Geneva Bible offered a far more sophisticated and extensive reading of *Revelation* than did Foxe's *Acts and Monuments*. They also extended into the future in a way that Foxe never imagined: Junius was unable to give dates for the church's victory over the harlot, the two beasts, the dragon, or death, but his editor included the events in the chronological table leaving the date-column blank for the reader to fill in the appropriate data. One significant omission from the chronological table was the expectation of a latter-day conversion of the Jews, though this doctrine remained in outline in the 1599 Bible's notes on *Romans*. The silences between the various layers of discourse within the Geneva annotations stands in sharp contrast to the thematic integrity of Foxe's single-authored production.

Perhaps the most obvious difference between Foxe and Junius was their dating of the millennium. Both writers agreed that it was to be applied to the past, but while Junius placed the binding of Satan as a period of martyrdom after A.D. 70, the Roman sacking of Jerusalem, Foxe situated it as a period of initial glory which began with the accession of the archetypal 'Christian emperor' Constantine in A.D. 324. This explication was bound up with the competing political ideologies of the Genevan texts. Junius was much less interested than Foxe in the theology of the 'godly prince'.

Elizabeth, as we have seen, was extremely sensitive to the political utility of Foxe's text, but her successor was openly hostile to the Geneva Bible - he described it, in 1604, as 'the worst of all Bibles'.[62] James' ire was apparently raised by several annotations which he regarded as positively seditious. These were the marginalia which argued that disobedience to royal edicts could be 'lawful' (note on *Exodus* 1:19) and that the violent deposition of Jezebel represented 'Gods judgements to all tyrants' (note on *2 Kings* 9:33). Knox's radical political theology was perhaps too clearly explained. Junius' undermining of England's eschatological monarchy would be echoed by subsequent puritan expositors as the reform party was pushed increasingly into separatism and dissent. By 1599, the puritans whom Foxe had regarded as an 'elect nation' were returning to a vision of themselves as a 'faithful remnant'.

But there was much more to Junius' exposition of apocalyptic historiography than an anti-monarchical exegesis of *Revelation* 20. He was more concerned than Foxe to ground his commentary in the historical detail which he found throughout *Revelation*. This explication commenced detailing the historical context of the seven Asian churches

---

[62] Quoted in Trinterud (ed.), *Elizabethan Puritanism*, p. 206.

addressed in a series of letters in *Revelation* chapters two and three: 'now because Saint John wrote this book in the ende of Domitian the Emperour his reigne, as Justinius and Ireneus doe witnesse, it is altogether necessary that this should be referred unto that persecution which was done by the authority of the Emperour Traian: who began to make havocke of the Christian Church in the tenth yeere of his reigne, as the Historiographers doe write' (note on 2:10). The rest of *Revelation* he divided into two sections, 'one common unto the whole world, unto the 9. Chapter: and another singular of the Church of God, thence unto the 22 chapter' (note on 4:1). The two sections are themselves the contents of two heavenly books: 'these histories are sayd to be described in severall bookes, Chap. 5.1. and 10.2.' Within this second 'book' - the history of the church - Junius again found two divisions. The 'state of the Church conflicting with temptations' was recounted in chapters 10 to 16, and the 'state of the same Church obtaining victory' was then documented until the end of the twentieth chapter (note on 11:1). His exegetical outline would be mirrored in several important seventeenth-century expositions - Mede, Brightman and Goodwin, for example, would all follow this pattern.

This future influence was made possible by the success and popularity of the Geneva/Tomson/Junius Bible. From 1560, Geneva Bibles had always encouraged their audience to 'read diligently: judge soberly, and call earnestly to God for the true understanding hereof.'[63] In Junius' edition the processes which encouraged 'diligent reading' were highlighted as the text educated the reader away from the more extreme forms of millenarian activism. Perhaps appropriately, in a volume which included Petrarch and Dante as part of the elect remnant (note on 14:6), the radical eschatologies were dismantled by means of the introduction of literary-critical terms.

The Renaissance had reinvigorated the study of rhetoric, the means by which a text could be encoded with persuasive powers; but with the Reformation, and the creation of a private and independent reader of Scripture, increasing emphasis came to be laid upon the decoding of texts. Aristotle's *Rhetoric* gave way to more modern aids to interpretation which foregrounded their theological application. Thus the title-page of Henry Peacham's *The Garden of Eloquence* (1577) claimed the book 'helpeth much for the better understanding of the holy Scriptures', and the title-page of Dudley Fenner's *Artes of Logick and Rethoricke* (1584) similarly advertised its 'opening of certaine parts of Scripture, according to the same'.[64] Though Debora Shuger has claimed

---

[63] *Geneva Bible* (1560), 'Argument' of *Revelation*.
[64] Quoted in Linda Gregerson, *The Reformation of the Subject: Spenser, Milton and the English Protestant Epic* (Cambridge: Cambridge University Press, 1995), p. 5n.

that the introduction of this new vocabulary of criticism was intended to preserve the flexibility of reference permitted by the old medieval allegorical method, it is clear that the Geneva Bible's project ostensibly intended the opposite, closing down on hermeneutical variance.[65] Culling interpretative techniques from Elizabethan literary handbooks, the Geneva Bible constructed the universal priesthood of believers into a critically-aware interpretative community.

These techniques were propelled into increasing importance as the Reformers replaced an infallible church with an infallible book. The first protestant Reformers had wrestled to establish the principle of *sola Scriptura* - the authority of the Bible alone - over a millennium of Roman Catholic ecclesiastical tradition which had equated as the word of God the unwritten tradition of the church and Scripture. It was perhaps appropriate, then, that the metaphor of the book achieved such prominence in the text of *Revelation:* 'I saw in the right hand of him that sat upon the throne, a book written within, and on the back side sealed with seven seals ... And no man in heaven nor in earth, neither under the earth, was able to open the book, neither to look thereon' (5:1-2). The self-reflexive prominence of this metaphor sourced the Genevan presumption that the writing of God was inherently authoritative. One annotation argued that 'authority is given unto this Revelation, by these things: first, by [Christ's] appearing from heaven in this habit and countenance, strong, ready, glorious, surveying all things by his providence, and governing them all by his omnipotence, verse 1. Secondly, that he brought not by chance, but out of a book, this open Revelation' (note on 10:1).

Thus infatuated with the permanence of the printed word, Junius traced the authority of the Geneva Bible to its source, God's book, in God's hand. In the annotation on 10:1, quoted above, God's revelations through the written and incarnate Word were paralleled, and *Revelation* was made at once inside and outside of itself, figuring as an object inside its own story. Thus it became, in the hands of the reader, an object of incarnation in itself, straddling the contexts of heaven, first-century Patmos and sixteenth-century England. The godly reader was holding in his own hands the 'little book open' (10:2) that Christ himself had used. Junius was claiming that *Revelation* was the a-historical transcendent signifier which Foxe had attempted to invoke. The *Acts and Monuments* had described the course of human history; but for its puritan readers, Junius' notes claimed, the Bible was the book which governed it.

It was another millenarian fusion of form and content: John had

---

[65] Debora Kuller Shuger, *The Renaissance Bible: Scholarship, Sacrifice and Subjectivity* (Berkeley: University of California Press, 1994), p. 5.

described a book sealed, with the writing unseen on the inside; his narrative had detailed the opening of the seals and the consequent unfolding of the scroll. The Geneva notes were performing a similar function, but in their 'opening' they would tease themselves until eventually their continuity was undermined. The infallible, divine authority the Reformers needed to invest in the printed word was problematised by an awareness that their language, human language, could never enforce God's extra-historical closure. *Finitum non est capax infiniti.* God cannot be bound in time.

Nevertheless Junius' attempts to educate his readers into the proper use of critical and rhetorical terms sought to minimise the dissonance of this reading. The description of the black horse of *Revelation* 6:5, he argued, indicated that 'God will destroy the world with famine, withdrawing all provision: which is by the figure Synecdoche comprehended in wheat, barley, wine, and oyle' (note on 6:5). In 16:17, Junius prevented his readers from imagining a speaking seat when he glossed the 'loude voice out of the Temple of heaven from the throne' as coming 'from him that sitteth on the throne, by the figure called Metonymia'. Neither was the river of blood flowing from the winepress of the wrath of God to be understood literally, as being as high as a horse's bridle: 'That is, it overflowed very deepe, and very farre and wide: the speech is hyperbolicall or excessive, to signifie the greatnesse of the slaughter' of Armageddon (note on 14:20). Enallage was used to make plural the 'image of the beast' in 13:14; by claiming that the beast has many images, Junius provided himself a ready excuse to attack the Catholic practice of the adoration of images of saints. So too the terms hypallage (17:1), parenthesis (16:15), and antithesis (17:12) were all used and subsequently explained for the help of the 'simple reader' so usefully described by Michael Jensen.[66]

This then, according to Franciscus Junius, was what it took to 'read diligently'. Only with a proper knowledge of rhetorical criticism could the godly understand the mysteries of apocalypse. Left to itself, it appears, the *Revelation* was singularly un-revealing. In addition to this, the aid of the Holy Spirit was also required. If 'no prophecy of the Scripture is of any private interpretation', the reader must 'ask of God the gift of interpretation, for he that is the author of the writings of the Prophets, is also the interpreter of them' (*2 Peter* 1:20, and note). But because the Holy Spirit's witness was ultimately couched in subjectivity, the Geneva editors themselves sought to be the final arbiters of meaning, closing the lid on the hermeneutical ferment; even the layout of notes on the page required the reader to see each chapter

---

66 Michael Jensen, '"Simply" Reading the Geneva Bible: The Geneva Bible and its Readers', *Literature and Theology* 9 (1995), pp. 30-45.

as self-enclosed, firmly surrounded by the apparatus of interpretation. At times this closure is excessive - at the end of *Revelation* chapter four, there is an explanatory note with no corresponding reference in the text.

This foregrounding of the transitory nature of the Biblical commentary as 'sign' enhanced and supplemented the textual ambivalence elsewhere apparent - the interpretative competition, for example, between the various editions of the Geneva Bible. This paradox was highlighted in Junius' discussion of the symbolic number '666' (13:18) - the dialogue motif at once constructed the reader and challenged the received orthodoxy of Genevan puritanism:

> How great and of what denomination this number of the beast is by the which the beast accounteth his wisdom, Saint John declareth in these words, Dost thou demand how great it is? it is so great, that it occupieth the whole man: he is alway learning, and never commeth to the knowledge thereof.[67]

Junius was portraying this excess knowledge as an educational drive which would never be satisfied, which could never attain completeness or closure: 'ever learning, and are never able to come to the acknowledging of the trueth' (*2 Timothy* 3:7). And knowledge that defied closure, he claimed, was devilish; such a pursuit was allegorically represented by the number of the beast. The gloss on *1 Corinthians* 1:20 made a related point: 'where art thou, O thou learned fellow, and thou that spendest thy days in turning thy books?' It is not simply that accumulated learning could never earn salvation; learning which never ceased was enough to hurtle 'the disputer of this world' into hell. But Junius' assertion was immediately problematised in his open admission of variations within the parameters of even Reformed scholarship. The 1560 Geneva Bible had claimed that '666' stood for the numerological representation of the Greek word 'Latinus' (with its obvious Roman Catholic reference), while at the same time allowing for the idea that the Pope 'began to be manifest in the worlde' 666 years after the *Revelation* was communicated. Junius acknowledged the debate, but protested that he was not ignorant of 'the common sort of interpreters' or the 'other interpretations ... brought upon this place: but I thought it my duty, with the good favour of all, and without the offence of any, to propound mine opinion on this point.'[68] Hill is aware of 'at least nine different ways in which the letters of the Pope's name or titles can be added' to result in the figure 666.[69] Nevertheless, Junius was silent on the implications of this stance and the negotiation with

---

[67] *Geneva Bible* (1602), note on *Revelation* 13:18.
[68] *Geneva Bible* (1602), note on *Revelation* 13:18.
[69] Hill, *Antichrist in Seventeenth-Century England*, p. 4.

earlier readings it involved. More radical revisions were introduced without comment. John, for example, had described a star which fell from heaven and received the keys of the bottomless pit (9:1). The 1560 notes had argued that 'This authoritie chiefly is committed to the Pope in signe whereof he beareth the keyes in his armes.' Junius' contention that it was either Christ or 'some inferior Angel' could hardly have advanced a more diverse interpretation.

But, as Junius' revision of 9:1 indicates, confusion was not restricted to differences between versions. In providing an alternative reading for his audience - that the star applied to one of two identities - he was admitting differences within the same edition. It was a useful enterprise, allowing an interpretative aperture within which his reader could be controlled, providing an illusion of hermeneutical freedom. A similar method was adopted in Junius' exposition of the 'Temple of God' which John was commanded to measure. It was 'either that of Jerusalem, which was a figure of the Church of Christ, or that heavenly exemplar' (note on 11:1).

This type of uncertainty was, according to the notes, only a concession to humanity's fallen nature. While the Church triumphant 'trod under feet mutability and changableness' (note on 12:1), the Church militant was still subject to ambiguity. Although 'the wheat is mingled with the chaff, and the good fish with that which is evil', the apocalyptic wrath of God would bring all to definition (note on 12:4). Nevertheless, this plurality and ambivalence manifested that the Geneva Bible was itself within the grasp of Antichrist, whom it imagined would 'persecute most cruelly the holy men, and put them to death, and shall wound and pierce through with cursings, both their names and writings' (note on 11:12). In challenging their own interpretations, the Genevan annotations demonstrated that the jurisdiction of Antichrist was larger than they thought.

Perhaps this admission of interpretative confusion precipitated the doctrine of progressive revelation which underpinned the Genevan textual products and which would be basic to the radical philosophy of the later decades. While the elect were now enjoying gradual enlightenment in the things of God, their difficulties would be solved only at the second coming: 'now I know in part; but then shall I know even as I am known' (*1 Corinthians* 13:12). Side-stepping the explication of '666', this quest for ultimate knowledge was made legitimate when the individual was aware that attainable knowledge was limited - this was a sure sign that he had God's favour. The pursuit of God's secrets, on the other hand, was a sure sign of reprobation.

There were implications also for the dating of the second coming. Unlike many later puritan expositors, the Genevan editors contended that it was 'sufficient for us to know that God hath appointed a latter day for the restoring of all things, but when it shall be, it is hidden from us all, for our profit, that we may be so much the more watchful, that we be not taken, as they were in old time in the flood' (note on *Matthew* 24:36). This explanation and exploitation of uncertainty essentially prepared the reader for the final disclosure of the ultimate purpose of *Revelation*, wrestling the meaning of the book away from its audience altogether:

> But there will be some that will abuse this occasion until evil, and will wrest this Scripture unto their own destruction, as Peter saith. What then? saith the Angel, the mysteries of God must not therefore be concealed, which it hath pleased him to communicate unto us. Let them be hurtful to others, let such be more and more vile in themselves, whom this Scripture doth not please: yet others shall be further conformed thereby unto righteousness, and true holiness ... Also (saith God by the Angel) though there should be no use of this book unto men: yet it shall be of this use unto me, that it is a witness of my truth unto my glory, who will come shortly, to give and execute just judgement.[70]

Almost the last words of the Geneva Bible, it is appropriate that God was speaking in the margins, outside Scripture and in the narrative that properly belongs to men. 'And that Word ... dwelt among us' (*John* 1:14). Paralleling the incarnation, God's voicing within the realm of human discourse clouded the unassailable divide between the human and divine - even here the form of the text undermines its didactic purpose. Thomas Aquinas had envisaged a gradated path to heaven, a 'chain of being' between humankind and their God.[71] The Reformers had balanced this immanence with transcendence. Junius' notes pursued this middle path, maintaining immanence and transcendence in unspoken tension.

Like the concluding couplet of a sonnet, these lines turned on its head the foregoing body of accumulated scholarship. If, as these notes claim, the final purpose of the Bible is to witness to the glory of God in those parts which could not be understood as much as in those which could, then there is no need for any interpretation at all. *Revelation*, it seems, could be successful even when it was least a revelation - it achieved its purpose even when it failed to communicate. *Revelation* 'worked' no matter its result: metaphysical meaning could be found in the scriptural text precisely because no semantic meaning could be perceived. Ultimately, as the above quotation demonstrates, *Revelation* existed not for the sake of readers who sought to understand it, but for the glory of the God 'who will come shortly'.

---

[70] *Geneva Bible* (1602), notes on *Revelation* 22:10-11.
[71] Eire, *War against the Idols*, p. 3.

The annotators' failure to contain or 'close' the transcendent voice of God between the marginalia simply enacted the central thesis of the European Calvinist movement. Eire has claimed that the foundation stone of reformation was the new understanding of the metaphysical relationship between the spiritual and the material, with the arguments primarily finding a locus in worship. The reformers adhered to a third principle after *sola fides* and *sola scriptura* to emphasise the transcendence of God and of the spiritual realm: *finitum non est capax infiniti* - the finite cannot contain the infinite.[72] Eire has claimed that it was a recognition of the transcendence of God - his very lack of containment or closure - which became the driving force behind reform. Junius' notes transfer this doctrine of worship to the context of literary production: 'of necessity the words must be attempred unto the mysteries, and not the mysteries corrupted or impaired by the words' (note on *Revelation* 1:4). His concern for accuracy overrode his desire to 'contain' his subject; his text foregrounded its own weaknesses to point the reader back beyond itself, testifying to the glory of the Bible's subject, rising far above the words on the page.

Thus human interpretation must always be insufficient for the fullness of the divine narrative. In the face of such mystery, form and content could agree: the returning Saviour would have 'a name written, that no man knew but himself' (19:12). The notes' description of Christ here foiled that unclosed learning of '666': 'he is... in this verse, searching out all things, ruling over all, to be searched out of none' (note on 19:12). He would contain all things, but could not himself be contained; and if the Word of God could be 'searched out of none', the entire enterprise of the Geneva Bible - and indeed the Christian faith itself - was surely in some difficulty. Yet Junius was prepared to cut the Gordian knot and claim that understanding of Scripture was ultimately unnecessary for the successful communication of its ideas - whether or not it is 'searched out', it would always declare the glory of God. Junius thus explained the unexplainable; and in explaining the reasons why his subject could not be shown, he undermined the entire exile enterprise. Such was the culmination of the textual negation *Christus Triumphans* had originally suggested.

Recent theorists have provided contexts within which this interpretation of the Geneva Bible's didacticism is confirmed. Thomas Greene has noted how the typical Renaissance text

> will never overcome the incompleteness of our humanity. It will never achieve absolute closure, freedom from deferral, perfect finality, those unreal dreams of the twentieth-century mind. But it may still attain a

---

[72] Eire, *War against the Idols*, p. 3.

distinction of conative energy and refinement ... A textual construct like a cultural construct is a leaning tower, artificial and precarious, that draws our eyes.[73]

But the cultural products of Geneva do more than this, highlighting for the reader their self-reflexive artificiality, their transitory nature and muddled reasoning, drawing the eyes of the reader not to but past themselves. The cultural products of Geneva are signs, not icons. They symbolise the culture which produced them, iconoclastic and divided.

John Foxe and the Geneva Bible both attempted to 'regulate cultural tensions and harmonise dissonances'; Foxe aimed to patch over the divisions amongst the exiles, and the historical project shared by each of these works attempted to construct a pan-European protestant hegemony based on the explication of history. Thus these texts further enact Greene's theories, as they

reproduce those activities of assimilation and rejection, moral discrimination, mythic fabrication, symbolic reordering, that cultures typically perform. The text can be read as an idealised miniature culture, whether or not it allows the idealisation to be perceived as a critique. But it plays this role only at a risk: it may fail to harmonise its dissonances but only succeed in exposing them; its mythic constructs may collapse; the tensions it wants to regulate may explode.[74]

As we have seen, in their worries over closure, John Foxe and Franciscus Junius situate a wider discussion. Highlighting their concerns, it seems, the Geneva Bible and Foxe's drama invoke these mythic fabrications precisely because of the dissonances they entail. The textual products of Geneva capitalise on their exposed cracks; indeed the very exposition of such weaknesses was basic to their protestant poetics of the 'sign'. If the annotations were 'spectacles', as one contemporary described them, they had also to be transparent.[75] But Greene's comparison of texts and cultures is apt in other ways too: the massive dissemination of the literature of the one hundred or so Marian exiles in Geneva defined and constructed another culture, of 'nationhood' and divine vocation, in the islands they had earlier been forced to abandon.

As part of the twentieth-century Scottish diaspora, the literary critic Edwin Muir noted that 'people who lose their nationality create a

---

[73] Thomas M. Greene, *The Vulnerable Text: Essays on Renaissance Literature* (New York: Columbia University Press, 1986), p. xiii.

[74] Greene, *The Vulnerable Text*, p. xiii.

[75] Quoted in Lloyd E. Berry, *The Geneva Bible: A facsimile of the 1560 edition* (Madison: University of Madison Press, 1969), p. 23.

legend to take its place.'[76] In sixteenth-century Geneva, the fabricated legend of lost nationality turned in upon itself, celebrating its own weaknesses, and returned to the motherland as the basis for the official policy of that government which had formerly burned its supporters. The Genevan Bibles and Foxe's historiography foregrounded the weaknesses which were basic to their status as protestant 'signs' but, in so doing, necessarily deferred closure and a definitive exposition of *Revelation*. In developing the poetics of the 'sign', Foxe had failed to close the past and Junius had failed to close the future. The ensuing decades of the seventeenth century would witness the consolidation of their poetics and the crisis of their theology as the movement of which they were a part began its collapse. Scripture underwrote, then Scripture undercut; as puritans had read for generations, 'The hope that is differred, is the fainting of the heart' (*Proverbs* 13:12).

---

[76] Quoted in Murray G.H. Pittock, *The Invention of Scotland: The Stuart Myth and the Scottish Identity, 1638 to the Present* (London: Routledge, 1991), p. 1.

CHAPTER 4

James Ussher and the Collapse of the Genevan Worldview

The life and career of James Ussher (1581-1656) stand as fascinating case studies of the initial impact and ultimate collapse of the eschatology produced by Foxe and the Geneva Bibles. Bridging the first and third generations of post-exile puritanism, Ussher retained the exiles' early priorities, negotiating the polarities of the 'faithful remnant' and the 'godly nation' as competing bases for the Irish protestant identity. During the 1620s, as Ussher increased in influence in the Stuart court, England's changing ecclesiastical climate compelled him to conceal his millenarian interests and to re-evaluate his identification of Antichrist. Paradoxically, his retention of the Marian exiles' ideology - so basic to his theological defence of the Irish church - distanced him from those English puritans with whom he had most theological sympathy. As the century progressed, the increasing dichotomy in puritan ideology reversed his initial ecclesiastical inclusiveness and precluded his participation in the century's most defining Calvinistic synod - the Westminster Assembly.

Ussher was born in January 1581, and entered Trinity College, Dublin in 1593, one year after its opening. The theological atmosphere of the new institution was both a cause and a consequence of the ecclesiastical policy of the Irish reformed church. Two of the college's first five fellows were men who had been Ussher's schoolteachers, the Scottish Calvinistic exiles James Fullerton and James Hamilton. They were joined by two refugee English Presbyterians, Walter Travers, who was also a fellow, and Humphrey Fenn.[1] The college fellows educated their students into the pan-European Reformed orthodoxy required for mission work in Ireland. Ussher was a good student. He gained his B.A.

---

[1] Norman Sykes, 'James Ussher as Churchman' *Theology* 60 (1957), p. 56; Alan Ford 'The Church of Ireland, 1558-1641: A puritan church?', in Alan Ford et al (eds), *As by Law Established: The Church of Ireland since the Reformation* (Dublin: Lilliput Press, 1995), p. 55. A full intellectual biography will be provided in Ford's *James Ussher: Theology, History and Identity in early-modern Britain and Ireland* (Oxford: Oxford University Press, 2007).

in 1598, his M.A. in 1601, and two years later he was appointed Chancellor of St. Patrick's Cathedral in Dublin. In 1607 he was awarded a B.D. and was appointed Professor of Divinity in Trinity College. In 1613 he gained a D.D. and was appointed as Vice-Chancellor the next year. Subsequent promotions propelled Ussher into the social and political arena. He became Bishop of Meath in 1621, a member of the Irish Privy Council in 1623, and finally, in a patent signed by King James only days before his death in 1625, Archbishop of Armagh. It was the climax of his meteoric rise, and a position Ussher maintained until his death in March 1656.[2]

There can be no doubt that Ussher's Irish situation revolutionised the implications of an already radical ideology. Unlike their counterparts in England or Geneva, where state legislation kept reasonably tight control of religious dissent, Irish Catholics were not curiosities which could be held safely at arm's length. Ussher was driven to grapple with the consequences of living so close to Antichristians and consequently his apocalyptic hostility to Rome became the most basic feature of his worldview. As Phil Kilroy has noted, Ussher's 'fascination with history, chronology and the ages of Satan, the Beast ... was no mere academic study; rather it was an effort to justify the reformation movement on a historical-theological basis.'[3]

Following the teaching of the Marian exiles and the Reformers, Ussher identified the harlot of *Revelation* 17 as 'the particular Church of Rome, the city-church; which they call the mother-church, the Holy Ghost stileth "the mother of harlots and abominations of the earth."'[4] His posthumously published tract exploring *What is Understood by Babylon* argued that 'Rome (whose faith was once renowned throughout all the world) [had] become "Babylon the mother of whoredoms and abominations of the earth".' Nor were the protestants to hope for further reformation within the Roman church: 'Rome is not to cease from being Babylon, till her last destruction shall come upon her; and that unto her last gasp she is to continue in her spiritual fornications, alluring all nations unto her superstition and idolatry.'[5] Consequently, the Pope was not a spiritual leader whose influence should be courted: 'for all his holiness', Ussher argued, he 'is that wicked one of whom the

[2] *Alumni Dublinenses* (1935), s.v. 'Ussher, James'; Alan Ford, 'James Ussher and the creation of an Irish protestant identity', in Brendan Bradshaw and Peter Roberts (eds), *British Consciousness and Identity: The Making of Britain, 1533-1707* (Cambridge: Cambridge University Press, 1998), p. 199.

[3] Phil Kilroy, 'Sermon and Pamphlet Literature in the Irish Reformed Church, 1613-34', *Archivium Hibernicum* 33 (1975), p. 117.

[4] Ussher, *Works*, ii. 477.

[5] Ussher, *Works*, xii. 542-3.

apostle prophesied'.[6] Article 80 of the Irish Articles - the confessional basis of the Irish church - clearly stated that the Pope was the 'man of sin' predicted by Paul in 2 *Thessalonians*.

Unlike his fellow puritans in London, however, Ussher was surrounded by the adherents of this false church. Irish protestants existed as a besieged remnant, a faithful elect in a nation which retained a superstitious allegiance to Rome. The reality of this situation dramatised the Irish protestant identity and was the basis for the unity of its reformed church. Following the protestant ecumenical policy of Trinity College, Ussher extended 'the right hand of Brotherly fellowship' to any who would 'joyne against the Common and grand adversary in the Romish Babylon'.[7] Apocalyptic hostility to Rome - wherever its insidious influence was perceived - was the ideological glue holding together a very diverse spectrum of protestant interests.

Members of the Irish reformed church were acutely aware of the dangers of Roman Catholic resurgence. For them, Antichrist's threat was militaristic as much as it was theological. On the day Ussher was ordained, in 1601, an attempted Spanish invasion was rebutted at Kinsale as Continental Catholics again sought a back door into England.[8] No doubt they had calculated on the implicit sympathy of the native Irish: their common faith had made great strides towards instituting a shadow hierarchy, a Roman bishop in every diocese, and protestants had never recovered the ground lost in the 1550s by Queen Mary's re-establishment of the Catholic faith. But Irish protestants recognised that the real source of this hostility was not the Vatican. In 1617, a correspondent described to Ussher how 'mass was said in Kilkenny very lately by one, to an assembly of women (and one boy, that by chance fell in among them, by whom also the matter was discovered), that when it was ended transformed himself into the likeness of a he goat, with some other unmannerly pranks, which I had rather he should do, than I relate.'[9] The sulphur smell of lecherous devilry consolidated the protestants' apocalyptic hostility to Rome. In opposing the Pope, they were engaged to fight against the Devil himself.

Ussher's response to this danger occupied his writings. Whether in scholarly pursuit of the details of esoteric chronology, or in providing

---

[6] Ussher, *Works*, xii. 543.

[7] James Ussher, *Confessions and Proofes of Protestant Divines of Reformed Churches, That Episcopacy is in respect of the Office according to the word of God, and in respect of the Use of the Best* (Oxford, 1644), pp. A2v-A3ʳ.

[8] Graham Parry, *The Trophies of Time: English Antiquarians of the Seventeenth Century* (Oxford: Oxford University Press, 1995), p. 132.

[9] Ussher, *Works*, xvi. 342-3.

theological ammunition to counter Jesuit claims, Ussher's work was infused with his hatred and fear of the Antichrist who sat in the Vatican. Apocalyptic hostility to Rome informed his entire worldview.

Ussher and Chronology

It is rather ironic, then, that Ussher's system of universal Biblical chronology - an attainment for which he is deservedly famous - should have found its way into the margins of the Douai-Rheims translation, the standard English Catholic Bible. For generations, English-language Bible readers have been informed by Ussher's calculations that the world was made in October 4004 B.C. Nevertheless, although the texts in which Ussher developed this argument were the results of a lifetime of his study, his reputation as a chronologist was gained only latterly, the product of his later years spent in scholarly seclusion in England. The *Annales Veteris et Novi Testamenti* appeared toward the end of his life, in 1650, and its English translation, *The Annales of the World*, was published two years after his death, in 1658. Ussher's definitive chronology, the *Chronologica Sacra*, was also published posthumously, and the inclusion of his dates in margins of the Authorised Version, the most widely disseminated source of his thinking, only began in 1701. Ussher's life, nevertheless, was immersed in negotiations with Biblical chronology.

His contemporary reputation had a quite different basis, however. The *Answer to a Challenge Made by a Jesuit* (1625) was the Ussher text most frequently reprinted in the seventeenth century, and commentators have underplayed the extent to which this type of polemical research in theology and history was underpinned by his eschatological and chronological studies. By the age of fifteen he had dated the Old Testament narratives until the demise of the Hebrew monarchies. In his Doctor of Divinity oration in 1614, he expounded Daniel's seventy weeks, a pivotal chronological and millenarian passage.[10] 'I remember that some three or four years since,' he wrote in 1618, 'having occasion, in a public lecture in the college, to speak of the beginning of Daniel's Seventies: I laboured to prove that Artaxerxes Longimanns began his reign toward the end of the third year of the seventy-seventh Olympiad.'[11]

This often silent dependence upon a scheme of eschatologically justified universal history has confused some critics. Hugh Trevor-Roper has noted that the utility of his chronological study 'consisted partly in the support that it gave to that historical (or meta-historical)

---

[10] Ussher, *Works*, i. 321.
[11] Ussher, *Works*, xv. 108.

philosophy which Ussher, throughout his life, sought to prove.'[12] Along with Saul Leeman, Trevor-Roper has contended - without direct quotation - that this meta-historical philosophy was in essence the paradigm established by the third-century rabbinical midrash entitled *Elias*. As we have seen, *Elias* claimed that human history could be divided into three periods, each of two thousand years' duration. The first two millennia were an age of chaos, the second two millennia were the age of Jewish law, and the last two millennia were to be the age of the Messiah.[13] Noting that *Elias* and Ussher both envisaged that the Messiah would be born four thousand years after Creation, Trevor-Roper paralleled the two sources, and implied that Ussher adopted the rest of the midrash's paradigm, consequently imagining history's closure in its six thousandth year. This error was also the basis of recent newspaper reports that Ussher predicted that the world would end in October 1996 or 1997. Leeman's curiosity as to whether Ussher was even aware of the midrash typifies the extent to which this argument has been based on ignorance of the sources. Ussher's letters demonstrate quite clearly that his book-agent, in 1655, was consulting with Rabbi Menasseh Ben Israel over 'marginal readings' in the prophecy.[14]

Nevertheless, the Trevor-Roper/Leeman thesis is unsupported by the sources. Ussher and *Elias* found chronological concurrence only on the dating of the Messiah's birth in the year 4000 *Anno Mundi*. Differences between the systems were significant. According to Ussher's chronology, the Israelites' exodus from Egypt and the giving of the law took place in 2513 A.M., half a millennium too late for *Elias'* scheme.[15] The only symbolism in Ussher's system appears to be the completion of Solomon's Temple, in 3000 A.M., and the birth of Christ - whom the Temple foreshadowed - exactly one thousand years later. This repudiation of *Elias* was typical of mainstream puritanism. John Bunyan was one of very few puritans to adopt the idea that the history of the world was based upon six or seven thousand-year epochs.

Although Biblical chronology was a respectable hobby for Renaissance gentlemen, interesting individuals as diverse as Hugh Broughton, William Perkins, Heinrich Bullinger, Bellarmine, Kepler,

---

[12] Hugh Trevor-Roper, *Catholics, Anglicans and Puritans* (1987; rpt. London: Fontana, 1989), p. 160.

[13] Saul Leeman, 'Was Bishop Ussher's Chronology Influenced by a Midrash?' *Semeia* 8 (1977), p. 127.

[14] Ussher, *Works*, xvi. 360.

[15] James Barr, 'Why the World was Created in 4004 B.C.: Archbishop Ussher and Biblical Chronology', *Bulletin of the John Rylands University Library of Manchester* 67 (1985), p. 607.

Luther, and Sir Walter Ralegh, it was replete with polemical utility.[16] Ussher used his chronological framework to situate his pro-reform historical narratives. His histories of the *Antiquities of the British Churches* (1639), *A Discourse of the Religion Anciently Professed by the Irish and British* (1631), and *Gravissimae Quaestionis de Christianiarum Ecclesiarum in occidentis praesertim partibus ... Historica Explicatio* (1613) were each based upon the calculations he was continuing to make into the universal span of history. Reprints of these works were bound with Ussher's most systematic historico-eschatological explication. As this *Gravissimae Quaestionis* would demonstrate, Ussher's eschatology was far more complex than a simple adherence to *Elias* would allow.

Ussher and the Millennium

The most defining components in Ussher's apocalyptic worldview were the textual products of the Marian exiles. Ussher had been educated into their ideology during his undergraduate days in Trinity College. Its library contained texts which exercised intense influence over his subsequent scholarly investigations. By 1608, the university's library contained multiple expositions of *Revelation* as well as works by Thomas Brightman, Franciscus Junius and Hugh Broughton, who had published commentaries on Daniel and Revelation. Also in the catalogue were Johannes Lichtenberger's *Prognosticatio*, which was a compendium of millenarian prophecies, and the sole English translation of the Scriptures was a 1601 edition of the Geneva Bible. These texts shaped Ussher's eschatological understanding. Perhaps the most seminal influence on Ussher's historical thought was Trinity's copy of *De Quatuor Summis Imperiis* (1556) by Johannes Sleidanus. Ussher's historical awareness was constructed through his complex response to this text's representation 'Of the Four Great Empires'. Sleidanus' view of history was based on his exposition of *Daniel's* five monarchies. Civilisation, he thought, would cycle through four great earthly empires - Assyria, Persia, Greece, and Rome - culminating in the 'fifth monarchy' of Christ's direct rule on earth. Sleidanus' history was distinctly millennial, understanding the fifth monarchy as the thousand-year period described in *Revelation* 20. Elizabethanne Boran notes the popularity of commentaries on *Revelation* in Ussher's library. These volumes exercised a profound influence on the development of Ussher's thought.[17]

---

[16] C.A. Patrides, *Premises and Motifs in Renaissance Thought and Literature* (Princeton: Princeton University Press, 1982), pp. 55-7.

[17] Elizabethanne Boran, 'The Libraries of Luke Challoner and James Ussher, 1595-1608', in Helga Robinson-Hammerstein (ed.), *European Universities in the*

A similar eschatological exposition of history was the basis of Ussher's first published text, the *Gravissimae Quaestionis de Christianarum Ecclesiarum Successione et Statu* (1613). This text was a chronicle of the Christian church from its earliest ages to the twelfth century explicated through detailed analysis of *Revelation* 20. It built, self-consciously, on the thought of the Marian exiles - Ussher repeatedly cites the commentary of 'Francis du John'.[18] Though published in Latin, an English translation was made by Ussher's brother, Ambrose, and remains unpublished in the manuscript collection of Trinity College, Dublin.[19] Its existence provides an intimate glimpse into the puritan atmosphere of early modern Irish protestantism.

Gravissimae Quaestionis was a pro-Reformation apologetic defending the repeatedly-questioned roots of the protestant faith: 'Where was your church before Luther?' was a question 'rife in the mouth' of Ussher's adversaries.[20] Its dedication began with a reference to *Revelation* 13:3 - where 'all the world wondered after the beast' - and Ussher stated his purpose to challenge the success of the 'Roman boast' and turn it on its head. He cited their claim that 'there was no mortal man in the whole world before Martin Luther, that is before the year of our Lord 1517, that held that faith which the disciples of Luther, Calvin and other awoke heretics (as they name them) profess.'[21] Ussher set himself the task of demonstrating the Romanists' error.

Ussher's response to the protestant inability to point to visible ecclesiastical continuity from the apostles was to adopt Foxe's ideology of the faithful remnant. The 'remnant' was a series of amorphous groups who each maintained that the ecclesiastical defence of 'integritie of doctrine'[22] was of greater consequence than episcopal succession. Ussher approved of their approach: 'if there be anie church that ... possesseth not the foundations of the apostolicall teaching,' he argued,

---

Age of Reformation and Counter-Reformation (Dublin: Four Courts, 1998), pp. 98-102.

[18] Ussher, *Works*, ii. 1, for example.

[19] TCD Ms. 2940. Quotations are taken from this source, and referencing conventions cite Ambrose's original pagination.

[20] Ussher, *Works*, ii. 493.

[21] TCD Ms. 2940, p. 1; Ussher, *Works*, ii. iii: '"neminem toto orbe mortalium ante Martinum Lutherum, hoc est ante annum Domini Christi 1517. extitisse, qui eam fidem teneret, quam Lutheri, Calvini, aut aliorum hæresiarchum" quos appellant "discipuli, profitentur."'

[22] TCD Ms. 2940, p. 1; Ussher, *Works*, ii. iii: 'maximi antiquæ fidei Defensoris dignum patrocinio.'

'it is to be forsaken.'[23] Instead the believer was to search for a church which conformed 'not in all small questions of Gods law, but onlie, truely especialy in ye rule of faith.'[24]

The situation of the Irish church allowed Ussher a degree of rhetorical space which the historiographers among the Marian exiles had not enjoyed. In Ireland, until the time of the civil wars, Rome was the only threat to the fragile Reformation settlement. Ussher then could lean rather more to the 'left' than Foxe; he could afford to be rather more celebratory in his descriptions of the radical reformers. As a consequence, *Gravissimae Quaestionis* devoted space to detailed defences of the Waldensians and Albigensians, and untangled Rome's etymological assault upon the Cathars. Roman Catholic writers had claimed the latter were called after cats - 'because they kisse the taile of a cat, in the shew whereoff, as they say, Lucifer appeareth to them'. But, 'more soberlie', others contended that the Cathars earned their name because 'they said them selves were pure and cleane'.[25] His creedal bias was never obscured, always foregrounding that 'heretical' doctrine 'not much differing from that w[hi]ch this day the protestants embrace'.[26] As an important part of the godly remnant, the Cathars were 'puritans' almost in name.

The English translation of *Gravissimae Quaestionis*, prepared in manuscript by Ussher's brother Ambrose, consequently described these radical reformers as 'puritans' whose underground gatherings were 'conventicles'. This choice of terminology was surely significant. Ambrose's use of 'puritan' in the English translation may have been designed to connote the proto-Presbyterian ideas promoted by William Bradshawe in his *English Puritanisme* (1605). Bradshawe had contended that Calvinistic doctrine and eschatological animosity to Rome were the essence of English puritanism. His title was significant: although the term 'puritan' retained its original opprobrium, the 'hotter sort of protestants' were beginning to appropriate it for their own ends. In this theological atmosphere, *Gravissimae Quaestionis* was a defining text, an

---

[23] TCD Ms. 2940, p. 11; Ussher, *Works*, ii. 24: 'siqua est Ecclesia quæ fidem respuat, nec Apostolicæ prædicationis fundamenta possideat; ne quam latem perfidiæ possit aspergere, deserenda est.'

[24] TCD Ms. 2940, p. 12; Ussher, *Works*, ii. 25: 'quando ille non nisi in præcipuis et quæ maximi sunt momenti religionis capitibus præstari possit, in regula fidei præcipue.'

[25] TCD Ms. 2940, p. 194; Ussher, *Works*, ii. 248: '"quia obsculantur posteriora catti, in cujus specie, ut dicunt, appareret eis Lucifer:" magis vero sobrie alii, Catharorum nomen eis inditum existimant, vel quod puros se et mundos dixisse.'

[26] TCD Ms. 2940, p. 181; Ussher, *Works*, ii. 231: 'doctrinam suam, ab ea quam hodie Protestantes amplectuntur parum differentem.'

historical description of a continued and distinctly puritan tendency throughout church history. It was also a rallying point for Irish protestants; as we will see, the theological agenda governing Ussher's selection of heroes would also define the pan-Calvinist ecumenism of the Irish reformed church.

Ussher's history, like Foxe's, depended upon eschatological themes. While Foxe's *Acts and Monuments* began with an exposition of its historical parameters, Ussher began his treatise with a history of the various expositions of *Revelation* 20. John's teaching of the thousand-year binding of Satan was the cornerstone of Ussher's historical inquiry, the 'most received interpretation of the prophecie delivered in the twentieth ch. of the revelation'.[27]

The binding of Satan was described as that period when 'he is restrained [from] procuring the universal seduction.'[28] Like Junius, Ussher reported that this millennium was variously dated from the birth or death of Christ, or from the destruction of Jerusalem in A.D. 70, though he was certain that it 'endured for the space of a thousand years'.[29] Ussher followed Junius in his caution against literalistic exegesis: 'Christ tied ye devil, not with bodilie chaines, but with ye chaines of his mightie power.'[30] Satan, though bound, 'remained the god of this world, and wrought in ye children of disobedience, among whom he also has his throne; but always walketh about as a roaring lyon, seeking whom he may devoure'.[31]

Applying this exegesis to church history, Ussher discovered that in the first six ages of the Christian church apostolic purity was largely retained, despite the persecutions of Huns, Goths, Alans, Vandals, and Persians. Ussher explained that 'also after Constantine ye great and before Mahomet ye lawgiver, Sathan was indeed so much loose, not only to vex ye churches and christian people, but also to take away and waste their provinces and kingdoms: as may be seen in ye persecutions.'[32] Like Calvin, Ussher imagined this millennium as being

---

27 TCD Ms. 2940, p. 3; Ussher, *Works*, ii. ix: 'Prophetiæ in 20. Apocalypseos capitulo traditæ maxime recepta interpretatio proponitur.'

28 Ussher, *Works*, ii. ix: 'ligatum dici Satanum, quando ab universali seductione procuranda est cohibitus.'

29 Ussher, *Works*, ii. ix: 'per mille annorum spatium duravisse.'

30 Ussher, *Works*, ii. 4: 'Religavit enim Christus Diabolum non vinculis corporeis, sed vinculis potestatis suæ immensæ.'

31 TCD Ms. 2940, p. 3; Ussher, *Works*, ii. 5: 'Nam et "Deus hujus seculi" mansit, et "egit in hominibus contumacibus," inter quos et thronum suum habuit, semperque "obambulat tanquam leo rugiens, quærens quem devoret."'

32 Ussher, *Works*, ii. 6: 'Satanum ligatum asserit, ne persecutionibus amplius noceret Ecclesiæ: a Constantini videlicet Imperatoris temporibus, a quo sublatæ

marked chiefly by tribulations: 'where the state of that thousand where Sathan was bound is described, there is mention made of those who were smitten for the testimony of Jesus, and for ye word of God.'[33] The church's experience of tribulation, rather than their control of the Empire, was the mark of the millennium. Ussher recorded that the faithful remnant 'grew by persecutions, and was crowned by martyrdomes'.[34] Their first bishops 'were content with ye holie laurels of martyrdom, which they esteemed better than anie diadem or scepter'. Their 'glorie was ignominie; majestie humilitie; happiness, tyrants anger; rest, punishment; life, death itself'.[35] But increasing wealth, nevertheless, stifled their initial virtue.

The end of the millennium was signalled as the Church gained temporal power. Antichrist's power was reaching its zenith when the bishops began to claim the powers of temporal kings. Satan was 'newly loosed' during the reigns of the Holy Roman Emperors Henry III (1046-56) and Henry IV (1084-1105) and the Popes Gregory VII (1073-85) and Paschal II (1099-1118).[36] The name of Hildebrand, as Gregory VII was also known, recurs in accounts of this period. The reforms which he instituted directly challenged lay investiture - the right claimed by monarchs to oversee ecclesiastical appointments within their temporal jurisdiction. Henry IV, when king of Germany, understood Hildebrand's threat and deposed him. Hildebrand responded by excommunicating the king. On his accession as Holy Roman Emperor in 1084, Henry sacked Rome and drove Hildebrand into exile. The ensuing civil wars resulted in the widespread acceptance of Rome's assertion of her ecclesiastical power over civil jurisdictions, but Ussher noted with some pleasure Hildebrand's deathbed confession, 'that he had greatly sinned in his pastorall cure, which was committed him to govern, and by the persuasion of the Devill, had stirred up hatred and wrath against

---

persecutiones, usque ad annum Domini 1300. quo Turcicum imperium in Ottomanno coepit.'

[33] TCD Ms. 2940, p. 3; Ussher, *Works*, ii. 6: 'ubi status Millenarii illius, in quo vinctus erat Satanas, describitur, expressa mentio fit eorum qui securi percussi sunt propter testimonium Jesu, et propter sermonem Dei.'

[34] TCD Ms. 2940, p. 16; Ussher, *Works*, ii. 32: 'Christi Ecclesia nata fuit et adulta, persecutionibus creverit, Martyriis coronata sit.'

[35] TCD Ms. 2940, p. 16; Ussher, *Works*, ii. 33: 'pontifices martyrii sacra laurea contentos fuisse, quam omni diademate et sceptro potiorem habebant, reliquisque ornamentis ducebant superiorem, nemo ignorat. Prima illa ætate, gloria eorum erat ignominia; majestas, humilitas; felicitas, tyrannorum ira; quies, supplicium; vita, mors ipsa.'

[36] Ussher, *Works*, xi. 417.

mankind'.[37] The true church - once more a faithful remnant - fled underground to escape persecution: 'The whole church of the saints shall be hid, for in such sort the elect of God shall have their wisdom as in such sort that they shall keape their wisdom to themselves; as notwithstanding darkness prevailing, they ... dare not preach publickly.'[38]

Ussher's conception of the millennium was unusual in Anglican historiography. He understood the danger of church-state proximity, and certainly opened *Revelation* to demonise Rome's claims to temporal power. Of course this problematised some bases of Anglicanism's establishment, but did not prevent Ussher appealing for the king's protection of Reformed religion, as we will later see. Rome's claims were confuted and Ussher's analysis demonstrated his suspicion of statist pretensions. Foxe saw the church's gaining of temporal power as the beginning of her golden age, but Ussher saw it as Satan's fiercest attack. For him, the golden age remained firmly in the future.

But Ussher did little more than hint at his optimistic expectations. The third part of *Gravissimae Quaestionis*, covering the period from 1370 to 1513, never appeared, though the contents page gave some indication of Ussher's initial intentions: 'The third part, God willing, shall follow; in w[hi]ch is handled of the state of things from the beginning of the popedom of Gregorie the XI. unto the beginning of the popedom of Leo the X. ... Also: of the new binding of Satan, by the restoring of the gospel, begune to be about the midle of the 2d. thousand.'[39]

The most tantalising feature of this projected continuation is not its description of the British reformation after 1370 - Foxe would supply much of that information - but Ussher's reference to a second millennium which had begun around that time - 'the new binding of Satan'. This was utterly revolutionary by the standards of the early seventeenth century. Ussher was one of the first European divines to capitalise on the appearance of Brightman's *Apocalypsis Apocalypseos* in 1609. Johannes Piscator was also arguing for a future millennium by

---

[37] TCD Ms. 2940, p. 119; Ussher, *Works*, ii. 157: '"valde peccaverit in pastorali cura, quæ ei ad regendum commissa erat, et suadente Diabolo contra humanum genus odium et iram concitaverit."'

[38] TCD Ms. 2940, p. 123; Ussher, *Works*, ii. 163-4: 'Universa sanctorum abscondetur Ecclesia. Ha enim electi Dei sapient sibi ipsis id, quod sapient; ut tamen prædicare publice (prævalentibus tenebris) non præsumant. Non quod animare fideles et secretius exhortari desistant, sed quod prædicare publice non audebunt.'

[39] Ussher, *Works*, ii. xi: 'Pars tertia, deo volente, subsequeter: in qua agendum de statu rerum ab initio pontificatus Gregorii XI. usque ad initium pontificatus Leonis X. id est ... De nova ligatione Satanæ per Evangelii restaurationem sub medium secundi millenari exiguo tempore fieri coepta.'

1613, the first of the Continental Calvinists willing to broach the doctrine their confessions described as a 'Jewish error'.[40] Ussher was writing at the heart of the century's most profound theological development, the translation of the millennium from the past to the future.

Brightman, whose work was represented in Trinity's libraries, had outlined his belief that *Revelation* 20 referred to two millennia. The first, stretching from A.D. 300 to 1300, would correspond to the binding of Satan (*Revelation* 20:2), while the second, between 1300 and 2300, corresponded to the reign of the martyrs (*Revelation* 20:5). Brightman's apocalyptic commentary is correctly cited as one of the most influential of the seventeenth century, but his work is generally understood to have sprung from an eschatological vacuum, the absence of millennialist ideas. Ussher's *Gravissimae Quaestionis* demonstrates that the Irish theologian was quick to capitalise on Brightman's novel exegesis. Ussher's treatise should be recognised as one of the most important in the puritan apocalyptic tradition and a fascinating demonstration of his commitment to radical theology and to unqualified negotiation with his Genevan heritage.

But the third part of his history, offering its discussion of 'the new binding of Satan', never appeared. This was not the result of a sudden loss of interest, for the two Latin orations which Ussher delivered for his D.D. in 1613 were also on millennialist themes. One of these orations, as we have noticed, was on the subject of *Daniel's* seventy weeks; the other was on the subject of the reign of the saints in *Revelation* 20. What Ussher said we can only conjecture: neither treatise is extant. Their importance is in demonstrating the prominence of apocalyptic themes in Ussher's thinking at this time.[41]

Nevertheless, as Ussher's puritan friends lamented his failure to capitalise on the success of *Gravissimae Quaestionis*, Ussher was forced to explain why the third part never appeared. Writing to Thomas Lydyat in 1619, he explained that the reason the final part went unpublished was because he wanted to answer the allegations made against the earlier sections by his uncle, the Jesuit apologist Richard Stanyhurst. Although Stanyhurst had died the year before, Ussher expected that his criticisms would still be published:

> I purpose to publish the whole work together much augmented; but do first expect the publication of my uncle Stanihurst's answer to the former, which I hear since his death is sent to Paris to be there printed. I am advertised also, that even now there is come out, at Antwerp, a treatise of

---

[40] Hotson, 'The Historiographical Origins of Calvinist Millenarianism', p. 159.
[41] Ussher, *Works*, i. 321.

my country-man Christopher de Sacro-Bosco, De verae Ecclesiae investigatione, wherein he hath some dealing with me. Both these I would willingly see, before I set out my book anew: that if they have justly found fault with any thing, I may amend it; if unjustly, I may defend it.[42]

Ussher's position - which had already been criticised in Stanyhurst's *Brevis praemunitio pro futura concertatione cum Jacobo Usserio* (Douai, 1615) - received no further posthumous interrogation. Years passed and Stanyhurst's expected publication failed to materialise - while Ussher's final section failed to appear.

It appears that Ussher's research for *Gravissimae Quaestionis* had resumed but was being hampered by a more serious problem. Events at court were conspiring to silence his revolutionary voice. James died in 1625, after initiating the movements towards his son's engagement to the French Catholic princess, Henrietta Maria. Puritans were stunned. Their godly monarch was contemplating an allegiance with the subjects of Antichrist, and the ecclesiastical atmosphere of the court was darkening accordingly. It seems that Ussher's agents in England were noticing the difference. Dr. Thomas James, Ussher's book-finder, wrote in February 1625: 'I am encouraged by your lordship's letters to go on chearfully in my intended course and discovery ... I have written to his grace by his chaplains for helps necessary for the forwarding so great work, as the visibility and perpetual succession of the Church [as *Gravissimae Quaestionis* was also known] but what can I poor weak man do, unless my lord of Canterbury command help, and command books and all things necessary to so great and requisite a work?'[43] George Abbot, Archbishop of Canterbury, had shared Ussher's apocalyptic-Calvinistic worldview, and had opposed the alleged Arminianism of Richard Montagu's *New Gagg* (1624), which was England's first printed attack on the doctrine that the Pope was Antichrist.[44] Nevertheless the latter years of Abbot's term as the English metropolitan were marked by Arminianism's creeping through his clergy. Abbot had fallen from court favour after accidentally shooting a servant while hunting and was now quite unable to exercise any influence in support of Ussher's project and in defence of the old Reformed theology.[45] In his fall from grace, Abbot had become complicit in the stifling of anti-Roman polemic, and was a signal reminder to Ussher of the danger of losing face with the King. In

---

[42] Ussher, *Works*, xv. 148.
[43] Ussher, *Works*, xv. 264.
[44] Anthony Milton, *Catholic and Reformed: The Roman and Protestant Churches in English Protestant Thought 1600-1640* (Cambridge, Cambridge University Press, 1995), p. 112.
[45] Kenneth Fincham and Peter Lake, 'The ecclesiastical policy of James I', *Journal of British Studies* 34:2 (1985), pp. 194-207.

Abbot's enforced silences, puritans understood that the dull sleep of apostasy was sweeping over the leader of England's protestant church.

Nevertheless, even as he moved from academia into the political sphere, Ussher's educational involvement highlighted his millenarian interests. Ussher twice attempted to have Joseph Mede appointed as Provost of Trinity College. Mede's international reputation had been established by his *Clavis Apocalyptica*, first published in Latin in 1627 and later translated for the benefit of an English-speaking audience by order of Parliament in 1643. Mede's letters to Ussher confirmed that he sent multiple copies of his *Clavis* to Ussher in 1628, with a covering note flaunting his radical eschatology: 'I had no intent or thought, nor yet have, to avow that old conceit of the Chiliasts, That the world should as it were labour 6000. years, and in the seventh thousand should be that glorious sabbath of the reign of Christ, (I inclined to think it much nearer:).' In fact, the letter claims, Mede was expecting the end in 1736, 'the very year when the 1260. years of the beast's reign will expire'.[46] We have already noted Ussher's distaste for this type of extrapolation from *Elias*.

Nevertheless, Ussher's reply expressed his approval of Mede's book. It was, Ussher claimed, a 'most accurate explication' which he 'cannot sufficiently commend', but it may be that this was not only on the basis of Mede's radical millennialism.[47] We have already noted Mede's claim in his *Clavis* that the ordering of heaven - as described in *Revelation 4* - reflected an episcopalian hierarchy. Consequently, in 1644, Ussher referred to this passage to invoke Mede's credibility among the radical saints to bolster his plans for the union of English Calvinists in a modified episcopalian settlement. The *Clavis*, Ussher claimed, 'doth unlock unto us his judgement in behalf of Episcopacy, to be so fully according to the Word of God'.[48] But Mede was no uncritical Anglican. He was perplexed by the rise of the Arminians, and voiced his concerns to Ussher: 'we know not here in what case we stand; strange things have come to pass since your grace was with us.'[49]

Ussher's appropriation of Mede was matched by Mede's attempt within English millenarian circles to appropriate the reputation of Ussher. Ussher's system of eschatology was the subject of several letters between Mede and the influential English premillennialist William Twisse. In 1637 Twisse inquired of Mede whether Ussher 'doth retract

[46] Ussher, *Works*, xv. 407.

[47] Ussher, *Works*, xv. 561; Clouse, 'The Rebirth of Millenarianism' (1970), p. 60.

[48] Ussher, *Works*, (1644), p. 41.

[49] Ussher, *Works*, xvi. 456. Jeff Jue claims Mede was sympathetic to the Laudians, though he retained the identification of the Pope as Antichrist; *Heaven upon Earth*, pp. 19-64.

his former opinion touching the Binding of Satan, which in his Book De successione Ecclesiae [as *Gravissimae Quaestionis* was also known] he conceives to have been in the days of Constantine'.[50] Mede was uncertain:

> What my Lord of Armagh's opinion is of the Millennium, I know not, save onely that I have not observed him, neither when I gave him my Synchronisms, nor in discourse thereabout after he had considered them, to discover any opposition or aversation to the Notion I represented thereabout. The like Mr. Wood told me of him, after he had read his papers; nay that he used this complement to him at their parting, I hope we shall meet together in Resurrectione prima [the first resurrection]. But my Lord is a great man, and thinks it not fit (whatever his opinion be) to declare himself for a Paradox; yet the speeches I observed to fall from him were no wise discouraging. He told me once he had a brother (si bene memini) who would say, He could never believe but the 1000 years were still to come.[51]

Perhaps that was why Ambrose translated his brother's millenarian text. Mede's remark supports the suggestion that Ussher was concealing his radical inclinations for preferment at court. At the very least it demonstrates that it was possible for Ussher's contemporaries to suspect him of investing in this type of radical discourse.

As one might expect, then, Ussher's early millenarianism was largely abandoned in his later public pronouncements. His concern to promote the sanctifying effects of the hope of the second advent remained: 'God's children long for the coming of Christ: it is made a mark of those that shall be saved.'[52] Nevertheless, in his later writings, the idea of an earthly golden age before the coming of Christ is consistently repudiated: 'And yet were the Pagans so mistaken herein that, "When they heard the Christians did expect a kingdom, they undiscreetly supposed that they meant a worldly one, not that which hereafter they should have with God," at the second coming of our Saviour.'[53] Again, he claimed, 'They that preach, "The saints shall reign upon the earth," did not learn it from God; "for our kingdom is not of this world".'[54]

Such conservative non-millennialism could not allow for a literal understanding of the 'first resurrection' of *Revelation* 20. Although Mede's contact had suggested that Ussher believed the first resurrection was in the future, and involved a raising of the body, Ussher's recorded

---

[50] Mede, *Works*, ii. 1036.
[51] Mede, *Works*, ii. 1044.
[52] Ussher, *Works*, xiii. 295.
[53] Ussher, *Works*, xi. 391.
[54] Ussher, *Works*, xiii. 363.

pronouncements repeatedly invoked the established Augustinian reading of *Revelation* 20. The 'Resurrectione prima' was 'a rising from sin', and conversion was 'a resurrection before a resurrection'.[55] Ussher's position would be reflected in the writings of later millennialists, as we have seen, who were able to hold to a future millennium while understanding that the first resurrection was spiritual conversion. Ussher's withdrawals from radical discourses could not disguise that he anticipated - and perhaps initiated - later developments in the evolution of the puritan millennium.

Arminianism and the Identity of Antichrist

The Arminian clamp-down on Genevan ideology was, for many puritans, an immediate signal of their ecclesiastical intentions. As Arminians dominated church preferments after the 1620s, public discussion of the doctrines of election and reprobation was prohibited to all but the most eminent churchmen. The annotation-less Authorised Version was slowly but surely taking the place of the Genevan translation as the nation's most popular Bible. Ussher's *Gravissimae Quaestionis* was forced to remain unfinished; no editions of Foxe's *Acts and Monuments* were printed during Laud's time as Archbishop of Canterbury; and no English-language edition of any commentary on Daniel or Revelation by Brightman, Pareus, Alsted or Mede was published in England until 1640.[56] Ussher and his correspondents began to wonder whether Antichrist was revealing himself within the Anglican communion.

A flurry of letters to and from Samuel Ward of Cambridge highlighted God's providential warnings: in 1626, when the King's prohibition of the public discussion of Calvinist themes was renewed, Ussher advised Ward that 'all men's hearts [were] failing them for fear, and for looking after those things which are coming on the land. The Lord prepare us for the day of our visitation, and then let his blessed will be done. There is a proclamation to be presently set out for the stopping of those contentions in points of religion, which I send you herewith.'[57] Ussher's anxiety was couched in an extended allusion to *Luke* 21:25-7: 'And there shall be signs in the sun, and in the moon, and in the stars; and upon the earth distress of nations, with perplexity ... Men's hearts failing them for fear, and for looking after those things which are coming on the earth ... then shall they see the Son of Man coming in a cloud with power and great glory.' Ussher was making a

[55] Ussher, *Works*, xiii. 93, 503.

[56] Hill, *Antichrist in Seventeenth-Century England*, p. 37.

[57] Ussher, *Works*, xv. 339.

direct link between the changing ecclesiastical preferences of the English court and the final tribulation of the elect.

Ward's reply related a fascinating incident:

> There was last week a cod-fish brought from Colchester to our market to be sold; in the cutting up which, there was found in the maw of the fish, a thing which was hard; which proved to be a book of a large 16⁰. which had been bound in parchment, the leaves were glewed together with a gelly. And being taken out, did much smell at the first; but after washing of it, Mr. Mead did look into it. It was printed; and he found a table of the contents. The book was entitled, A preparation to the cross, (it may be a special admonition to us at Cambridge).[58]

Ussher was sagely aware of the portent's significance: 'The accident is not lightly to be passed over, which, I fear me, bringeth with it too true prophecy of the state to come; and to you of Cambridge, as you write, it may well be a special admonition, which should not be neglected.'[59] Ward's next letter confirmed his awareness of the 'danger' of the 'Arminian faction'.[60]

In 1629, with the beginnings of the 'eleven years' tyranny' of Charles I's personal rule, Ussher was confined to Ireland by royal command - ostensibly to ensure proper dedication to his ecclesiastical calling instead of his scholarly perambulations around the libraries of Europe. The reality of the situation was clear. Religious opposition was being stifled everywhere within the established church. Although he was already under Laud's suspicion, Ussher's attempts to nominate the millenarian Joseph Mede and the Calvinistic Richard Sibbes as Provosts of Trinity College seemed deliberately calculated to offend the dominant church party.

It would be hard to overestimate the seriousness of the situation the Calvinistic Anglicans saw developing. As Christopher Hill put it, 'in an age when every Englishman was automatically a member of the state church, when uniformity in religion was regarded as essential to the unity of the state, it was thus no laughing matter to see Antichrist not safely distanced in Rome, but in Canterbury and indeed in every parish in the country.'[61] The rise of what its opponents perceived to be Arminianism within the established church forced Ussher into adopting a critical distance from his own communion. When Antichrist could sign the Thirty-nine Articles it was increasingly necessary to suspect the very institutions which had been England's defence in her battle to

---

[58] Ussher, *Works*, xv. 344-5.
[59] Ussher, *Works*, xv. 346.
[60] Ussher, *Works*, xv. 347.
[61] Hill, *Antichrist in Seventeenth-Century England*, p. 51.

establish the protestant faith. Ussher was witnessing a phenomenal paradigm shift: after Laud's accession to the Canterbury see, the English church no longer proclaimed the Pope to be Antichrist. No wonder puritan hearts were failing them for fear.

Surviving evidence would seem to suggest that Ussher attempted to bolster the pan-Calvinist front. In December 1625, only months after his appointment to Armagh, Ussher and John Preston preached at Barrington Hall, in the heartland of the Essex puritan movement, in what has been described as 'a sort of regional synod of the godly, preparing their struggle against the Arminians'.[62] In 1631 he demonstrated the antipathy he felt towards Laud when he sent him a presentation copy of a Latin history of Gottschalk - a character well known for his vocal defence of predestinarian theology.

But the godly were not as resolute as Ussher had hoped. In 1635 Ussher complained to Samuel Ward about the publication of the *Five Pious and Learned Discourses* by Robert Shelford, a noted Laudian: 'while we strive here to maintain the purity of our ancient truth, how cometh it to pass that you in Cambridge do cast such stumbling blocks in our way?'[63] Ussher's opposition to the *Discourses* was not only due to their promotion of what was perceived as a neo-Roman sacramentalism, but more dangerously, their attack upon the reformed eschatological consensus. Shelford advocated a 'futuristic' reading of *Revelation* which the Jesuits had first conceived to parry protestant claims that the Roman church was apocalyptic Babylon and her leader the man of sin. According to this interpretation, Antichrist would be an apostate Jew and would not be revealed until the last few years of history. It was an astounding theological development which would be rebuffed by protestants of almost all persuasions until the beginning of the nineteenth century. Shelford's claims echoed the themes of Richard Montagu's *New Gagg* (1624) - which had outraged Archbishop Abbot - and posed a profound difficulty for Anglican coherence. How could the established church oppose Antichrist when it could not agree on his identity? Gradually a pattern emerged in the Laudians' behaviour. They would not concede that the reformation was a struggle between Christ and Antichrist and consequently they closed down on any text which suggested it was.

Ussher's eschatological worldview, we have seen, was the basis of his history, and his understanding of the polarities of history - Christ's war

---

[62] Elizabethanne Boran, 'An Early Friendship Network of James Ussher, Archbishop of Armagh, 1626-1656', in Helga Robinson-Hammerstein (ed.), *European Universities in the Age of Reformation and Counter-Reformation* (Dublin: Four Courts, 1998), p. 126.

[63] Ussher, *Works*, xvi. 9.

against Antichrist - was the basis of his church's unity. The Arminian suppression of Genevan historiography, consequently, shook the ideological foundations of his church. In 1635 Laud's henchmen Wentworth and Bramhall begun the process of expelling the Ulster Presbyterians from the Church of Ireland. Ussher watched as the English establishment undermined the basis of his anti-Catholic alliance in Ireland and, in Wentworth's apparent promise of the Graces, appeared to actively reward Catholic dissent. Perceval-Maxwell has neatly summarised the reaction to this situation: 'the members of the reformed church felt they had a duty to destroy the church of Rome in Ireland ... And when Charles I held out the Graces to Irish Catholics in 1628, then the last days had come.'[64]

Ussher understood it all in millenarian terms, and rose to the defence of this most seminal of doctrines. He wrote to Laud in January 1636 - three years after Laud's appointment as Archbishop of Canterbury - to confirm that he stood 'fully convicted in my Conscience That the Pope is Antichrist and so if I should be so mad as to worship the Beast, or to receive the mark of his Name, I must be αυτοκατακριτος ['self-condemned'], and justly expect the Vengeance threatned against such.'[65]

It was an extremely high-risk strategy. Charles' marriage to Henrietta Maria ensured Antichrist's influence in the royal court, and profession of Roman Catholic faith became fashionable as noble ladies fawned upon the attentions of the French princess. Arminian historians reflected these new interests in their sudden concern to repudiate the 'faithful remnant' ideology of Foxe and Ussher in order to align themselves more clearly with the visible succession of church unity through the unreformed church in the middle ages to the church fathers. The consequent debate about historiographical methods was founded upon the historians' eschatological predilections; Laud's clamp-down on the publication of Foxe attempted to regulate the traditional Genevan view. Antichrist could not be the Pope when the English hierarchy wanted to trace their roots through the Pope's church.

Ussher's confidence in the Anglican hegemony was sorely shaken. In the years remaining until his death, he positioned himself closer and closer to the King, endeavouring to educate him back into the privileges and responsibilities of the godly prince. His attempts were met by disappointment: the manner of Charles I's reign made untenable the trust in king and bishop on which the Marian exiles' eschatology had

---

[64] M. Perceval-Maxwell, 'Strafford, the Ulster-Scots and the covenanters' *Irish Historical Studies* 18:72 (1973), p. 525; Kilroy, 'Sermon and Pamphlet Literature in the Irish Reformed Church, 1613-34', p. 119.

[65] Alan Ford, 'Correspondence between Archbishops Ussher and Laud' *Archivium Hibernicum* 46 (1991-2), p. 18.

been based.[66] Consequently, the Genevan inheritance was not ruined by the success of Laudian revisionism - for most puritans retained the traditional ascriptions of Antichrist - but rather it was ruined by the fact of Laudian revisionism. Puritans could not support an establishment when the establishment repudiated the platform on which that support was to have been based.

When the apocalyptic basis of Ussher's work was undermined, the Reformation project he advanced became untenable. The imagined 'rise of Arminianism' brought a new history, a new ecclesiology, a new role for the king, a new Antichrist, and a new attitude to Rome. Irish protestants could not afford to compromise on any of these issues.

Ussher and the Godly Prince

Ussher's attitude to the rise of Arminianism was bound up with his relationship to the king. Part of the 'package' he had inherited from the Marian exiles included a political ideology which foregrounded the 'godly prince' motif. Martin Bucer's *De Regno Christi* (1550) had addressed the young Edward VI, teaching him that 'it is certainly the duty of all kings and princes who recognise that God has put them over his people that they follow most studiously his own method of punishing evildoers. ... Accordingly, in every state sanctified to God capital punishment must be ordered for all who have dared to injure religion.'[67] The 1559 edition of Calvin's *Institutes of the Christian Religion*, to cite another example, taught that the supreme magistrate was responsible to enforce the individual's duties to God as well as to his neighbour: 'This proves the folly of those who would neglect the concern for God and would give attention only to rendering justice among men. As if God appointed rulers in his name to decide earthly controversies but overlooked what was of far greater importance - that he himself should be purely worshipped according to the prescription of his law.'[68]

The Marian exiles similarly theorised this possibility, documenting the role of the 'godly prince' as the nation's representative in furthering reformation. In the marginalia of the Geneva Bible, and in texts like John Knox's *First Blast Against the Monstrous Regiment of Women* (1558), they had pointed to a series of Old Testament precedents for monarchs taking the initiative for religious reform and compelling subjects to concur with royal judgements. The Geneva Bible observed that the law

---

[66] Lamont, *Godly Rule*, p. 25.
[67] Jack Sawyer, 'Introduction to Bucer's *De Regno Christi*', *Journal of Christian Reconstruction* 5 (1978-9), p. 11.
[68] Calvin, *Institutes*, iv. xx. 9.

of God was a king's 'chief charge and whereby onely his throne is established' (on 2 *Kings* 11:12) and that 'God wolde have his servants preserved, and idolaters destroyed: as in his Lawe he giveth expresse commandment' (on 2 *Kings* 10:23). The 1566 Confession of Helvetia, which was officially approved by the Church of Scotland, taught that the 'chiefest duty' of the civil magistrate was to 'advance the preaching of the truth, and the pure and sincere faith, and shall root out lies, and all superstition, with all impiety and idolatry, and shall defend the church of God. For indeed we teach that the care of religion doth chiefly appertain to the holy magistrate.'[69] The ideal of 'godly rule' itself only ceased to be axiomatic in the 1640s - John Milton, as we shall later see, was one of its first critics.

As a consequence of this popularity, this ideology spilled over into reformation rhetoric, as successive English monarchs were described as Josiahs and Zerubbabels, as the proper agents of state-sponsored iconoclasm to ensure the reconstruction of the Biblical church. Although the claims were intended to refute the Vatican's invocation of world-wide jurisdiction, a significant millenarian impulse informed this teaching. The enduring European topos of the 'Emperor of the Last Days' has been unpacked in Norman Cohn's *Pursuit of the Millennium* (1957) - a wide variety of groups were each expecting an apocalyptic hero who would lead the forces of good against the personification of evil. As the Reformation geared the last battle as a struggle between Christ and the Roman Antichrist, the latter-day Christian monarch was understood to have the duty of destroying papal superstition - especially in England, which the dedicatory preface to the Authorised Version described as 'our Sion'.

In Ireland, a pragmatic recognition of Rome's combination of spiritual and military threats led many to support the church-state settlement which the Marian exiles had outlined. The Irish Reformed recognised that the legislative power of central government could effectively bolster their socio-political isolation as a vulnerable minority in an ungodly land and consequently they vigorously adopted the 'godly prince' doctrine. They attempted to fuse the defensive ideology of Foxe's 'faithful remnant' with the aggressive demands for millenarian theocracy they found in the annotations of their Geneva Bibles. Irish puritans simply could not afford the luxury of Laodicean pessimism, for their Catholic counterparts were not simply complacent about reform - they were sometimes violently opposed to it. The vulnerability of the Irish church developed into eschatological theorising.

Like the English puritans, the Irish Reformed might have been encouraged by James' early interest in theology: he had been

---

[69] Hall (ed.), *Harmony of the Protestant Confessions*, p. 473.

Calvinistic, rigidly anti-Catholic, and profoundly millenarian. His *Fruitful Meditation on Revelation xx.* was published in 1588, the year of the Armada, as a platform for three important subsequent works discussing *Revelation* and, in *An Apologie for the Oath of Allegiance* (1609), the 'godly prince' ideology. In these texts James figured himself as a latter-day David, the ultimate international hero of the protestant cause. As a consequence, the Presbyterian minister Patrick Galloway even introduced James' *Meditatioun upon ... the XV Chap. of the first buke of the Chronicles of the Kingis* (1589) as being the work of a 'nuresing father to that flocke conquished by the blude of Christ and committed to his lieutenantrie within his awin boundis'[70] - explicitly investing the King with the aspirations and responsibilities of the eschatological monarch described in *Isaiah* 49:23, who should, according to the Geneva notes on that verse, 'bestowe their power and autoritie for the preservation of the Church.' George Buchanan, tutor of James Stuart, had educated the prince into an awareness of his theonomic responsibility to guard the law of God. The pro-Union rhetoric of 1603 had been grounded in Foxian-millenarian discourses. For puritans on both sides of the border, James seemed an ideal candidate for the latter-day godly prince.

Nevertheless, his move to London began a sea-change in his thought. After his accession to the English throne, James pursued a more secular millenarianism, promoting the myth of the Stuart golden age which Charles continued.[71] Advertising himself as Scotland's Apollo, James found himself enjoying in England the institutional security of a monarchy which had in Scotland been supported by theological discourse. He was suddenly freed from the inconvenience of pandering to the democratic threat of Presbyterianism, and, announcing 'no bishop, no king', he beat a public retreat from his earlier biblicism. James intended to turn 'clean contrary' to the 'high and profound mysteries' of *Revelation* - they were not required for him to enjoy success as a ruler of England.[72]

Steering a 'middle path' away from the preoccupations of his puritan childhood, James refused to 'Calvinise' the doctrinal basis of the Church of England in 1604. He refused to adopt as regulative for that church any of the possible Calvinistic alternatives to the Thirty-nine Articles - the Lambeth Articles, Ussher's Irish Articles, or even, later on, the

---

[70] Quoted in Arthur H. Williamson, *Scottish National Consciousness in the Age of James VI: The Apocalypse, the Union and the Shaping of Scotland's Public Culture* (Edinburgh: John Donald, 1979), p. 41.

[71] Graham Parry, *The Golden Age Restor'd: The Culture of the Stuart Court, 1603-42* (Manchester: Manchester University Press, 1981), p. x.

[72] Quoted in Williamson, *Scottish National Consciousness in the Age of James VI*, p. 32.

canons of the Synod of Dort, to which he would send an influential delegation to conciliate the varied Continental interests. Even his plan to replace the heavily annotated text of the Geneva Bible with the commentary-less Authorised Version of 1611 contributed to his larger design to prevent a proper debate of the doctrines of grace in the open pulpit and to promote the type of monarchy the Genevan notes attacked. His public lagged behind. The Authorised Version translators quoted the Genevan text in 'The Translators to the Reader'; Geneva Bibles were published until the 1640s and, we have noted, Amsterdam printers were publishing Authorised Bibles with the Genevan annotations well into the next century.

James was even abandoning the millenarian discourse upon which he had built his narrative of the godly prince to ensure the success of the 1603 union. In *A Meditation upon the Lord's Prayer*, for example, he forthrightly attacked Brightman's innovative exegesis: 'for let the vain chiliasts gape for that thousand yeares of Christs Kingdome to bee settled upon earth, and let Brightman bring downe that heavenly Jerusalem and settle it in this world, the Word of God assures us that the latter dayes shall prove the worst and most dangerous dayes.'[73] In 1621, the 'Jewish error' that Christ's kingdom would be temporal was confuted at court by Laud and John Prideaux, later bishop of York.[74] The atmosphere of James' court was demonstrably hardening against the type of millenarian and Calvinistic theology Ussher had advanced. Ussher's caution was therefore well-founded: this was still the age of ear-cropping, and clergy in the Church of England had supported the execution of millenarian Anabaptists as recently as 1612.[75] The anti-puritan sentiment of Jacobean court drama - like Ben Jonson's *Bartholomew Fair* (1614) - was the least of Ussher's worries.

This was the innate danger in James' totalising religious policy. In 1613, the year in which Ussher's first great history was published, James increased attempts to forge a common religious settlement throughout his three kingdoms, regularising the relationship between the Churches of England and Ireland as he had earlier insisted upon the harmonisation of the canons and practices of the Churches of England and Scotland. He was demanding the obedience required by Foxe's 'godly ruler' while undermining the puritan ideology upon which that authority was built. James was forgetting the apocalyptic interests of his youth, demanding his theonomic rights (the obedience due to a 'nursing

---

[73] James, *Works* (1616), p. 581.
[74] Hill, *Society and Puritanism in Pre-Revolutionary England*, p. 197; Steve Schlissel (ed.), *Hal Lindsey and the Restoration of the Jews* (Edmonton: Still Waters Revival Books, 1990), p. 84.
[75] Hill, *A Nation of Change and Novelty*, p. 256.

father of the church') without his eschatological responsibilities to impose Calvinism and oppose Rome.

Ussher used the example of the Hebrew king Josiah to situate the godly king's role: 'many are content to take upon them as little as may be. They will shift off the government of the Church unto others, and they think they have done well, if they have caused justice to be preserved and peace, when as the apostle, giving us a reason why we should pray for all in authority, he setteth down this, as one effect we shall have by our prayers, that we shall live by them a peaceable and a quiet life in all godliness and honesty ... both in the duties of the first, as also of the second table.'[76] He was clear that 'civil government is not to be restrained within the things which are in outward and civil government only, but it also must show itself in causes ecclesiastical ... the magistrate is bound with this civil authority to punish as well the faults committed against the first table as against the second.'[77]

Ussher responded to James' lethargy by advancing more strongly his 'godly prince' thought. The supremacy of the royal magistrate, and his duty to enforce God's law in the reconstruction of the church, were themes which recurred in Ussher's work: 'will a good prince say, shall I tolerate them who are abominable to the Lord my God?'[78] In the dedication of *An Answer to a Challenge Made by a Jesuit in Ireland* (1625), Ussher praised James that 'before you were twenty years of age, the Lord had taught your hands to fight against the man of sin, and your fingers to make battle against his Babel. Whereof your paraphrase upon the Revelation of St. John, is a memorable monument left to all posterity.'[79] Ussher could remember when the king had celebrated his eschatological role, when it had been appropriate for puritans to address James, as Ussher did in the dedication of *Gravissimae Quaestionis* (1613), as 'defender of the Catholic faith'. The later Ussher continued to link the king's role as destroyer of Romanism and harbinger of the second advent: 'when shall we see Popery go down? ... when the Lord putteth his spirit into the hearts of these princes to hate the whore with an unfeigned hatred.'[80] But far from hating the whore, James had married his son to one of her adherents - the French princess Henrietta Maria. For Ussher, the Stuarts' political machinations were all part of the same eschatological drama. Their failure to 'hate the whore with an unfeigned hatred' was delaying Christ's return and denying the imposition of godly rule in the present. In essence, James and Charles

---

[76] Ussher, *Works*, xiii. 570.

[77] Ussher, *Works*, xiii. 571-2.

[78] Ussher, *Works*, xiii. 573.

[79] Ussher, *Works*, iii. vi-vii.

[80] Ussher, *Works*, xiii. 576.

were personally deferring the second advent.

Charles' extension of the Graces to Irish Catholics in 1628 - his promise of a limited religious toleration - only continued the royal attack on Ussher's ideal of a godly king committed to the extirpation of popery. Although at this time Charles was at war with both France and Spain - Europe's Catholic superpowers - his favour towards Irish Catholics smacked of political expediency rather than apocalyptic principle. Ussher corresponded by playing the godly prince's eschatological responsibilities against Charles' self-interest in the chaos of the 1640s. If 'we would have our thrones established,' he reminded the king, 'we must labour that idolatry be suppressed.'[81]

Nevertheless, despite the rise of Arminianism and the failure of the Stuarts to reform the land, Ussher's Genevan heritage committed him to full support of the King. He maintained royal absolutism while regularly reminding the king of his responsibilities. His attitude was like that of Thomas Manton, whose *Exposition on the Epistle of Jude* (1658) advocated godly rule despite the possibility of 'calamities of the godly upon every change of the prince's mind ... If the Lord see persecution necessary for the church , we must endure it, and so we shall be gainers both by good princes and bad.'[82] Ultimately, however, the Laudians prevailed. Ussher's gamble, elevating the principle of theonomic rule above actual Calvinist control of the throne, had not paid off. With the rise of Arminianism, Ussher saw Antichrist influence the throne of the godly prince. His faithfulness to the eschatological and political ideology of the Marian exiles had undermined his theological influence.

Ussher and the Westminster Assembly

The sudden surge of puritan nonconformity in the 1640s further isolated Ussher's thinking. The Anglican hierarchy had abandoned truth; and the holders of truth had abandoned the hierarchy. Ussher was committed to the integration of both Calvinist truth and Episcopal government. Conforming puritans - like Ussher - were faced with the demands of mutually exclusive allegiances.

Behind Ussher's political and ecclesiastical manoeuvrings was a tenacious commitment to his Genevan heritage which drove him to isolation from his most natural allies in England. With several other Episcopalians, Ussher was invited to attend the meetings of the Westminster Assembly, an ecclesiastical synod whose proceedings were to prove the most influential of the seventeenth century. Ussher

---

[81] Ussher, *Works*, xiii. 575.
[82] Thomas Manton, *The Complete Works of Thomas Manton* (London: James Nisbet, 1870-75), v. 238.

undoubtedly sympathised with much of the thinking of the delegates - indeed, he had spent his life defending their Calvinism in the Irish church alongside some of the Presbyterians from Scotland who had organised the Assembly. But Ussher never attended the debates in Westminster Palace.

On the 22nd of June 1643, only days before the first meeting of the Assembly, Charles reacted against Parliament's initiative, forbidding the meeting and denying that any of its conclusions should be received by any of his subjects. Immediately, Ussher's worldview was thrown into turmoil. He was faced with a stark choice. He could achieve his lifetime goal, helping his puritan colleagues establish a Calvinistic confession for the Church of England; alternatively, he could obey his king. Ussher could not maintain the integrity of both aspects of his Genevan heritage. The decision must have been difficult, but ultimately Ussher was unable to prise Calvin's theology from the Genevan ideology of the godly prince. The English puritans had advanced beyond his uncomplicated adherence to the trends of sixteenth-century Anglicanism. Ussher's commitment to the thinking of the Marian exiles annulled any unity he might have enjoyed with the English Presbyterians.[83]

Thus Paul Christianson, in *Reformers and Babylon* (1978), erred in claiming that the Foxian tradition was torn apart by 'extremists', by those 'imbued with a lesser store of moderation'.[84] It was shattered by the effect of the inconsistencies which lay at its very heart, manipulated by a representative of the establishment Foxe had sought at all costs to maintain. The exiles' puritan consensus was undermined when its principal and foundational ideology - its sense of history as the fulfilment of a very literal apocalypse - unravelled beneath its feet. Almost everything Ussher believed was grounded upon his apocalyptic vision, but his worldview could not withstand the stress of a changing political paradigm.

Ussher conceded all he could to maintain the integrity of his Genevan worldview. His later studies moved away from his earlier apocalypticism, retreating into a chronological investigation stripped of its polemical utility. Nevertheless the execution of King Charles in 1649 exploded the heart of Ussher's notions of authority. After the shock of the regicide, Ussher continued his bibliographic and historical research, developing the ideas which would rock the establishment he knew.

---

[83] William Maxwell Hetherington, *History of the Westminster Assembly of Divines* (1856; rpt. Edmonton: Still Waters Revival Books, 1993), p. 111.

[84] Paul Christianson, *Reformers and Babylon: English Apocalyptic Visions from the Reformation to the Eve of the Civil War* (Toronto: University of Toronto Press, 1978), p. 45.

Once more in scholarly seclusion, Ussher's apocalyptic predilection seems to have revived. In November 1655, his book-agent Herbert Thorndike reported to the Archbishop that he was consulting Rabbi Menasseh Ben Israel over some 'marginal readings' in the prophecy of *Elias*.[85] Ussher's millenarian interests had remained until the months before his death, and did not wane as the events of the Interregnum, all apocalyptically justified, destroyed his Genevan consensus. His death, in 1656, was followed by Cromwell's ordering of a state funeral. Ussher, the arch-conservative, had won the respect of the radicals he deplored. Rewriting Foxe's past and the Geneva Bible's future, Ussher probably never realised that he was the source of the eschatological rage they were exploiting.

---

[85] Ussher, *Works*, xvi. 360.

CHAPTER 5

George Gillespie and the Scottish Revolution

Robert Blair and John Livingstone returned to Scotland in 1637, driven out of Ussher's reformed church by Wentworth's anti-Presbyterian policies. They found their homeland engulfed by a revolutionary apocalypticism caused by many of the same factors which had witnessed their expulsion from the Irish church earlier that year. James' campaign to 'Arminianise' the churches throughout his three kingdoms had produced dissatisfaction in Ireland, and the purging of nonconformist elements from the Irish church, but had failed to popularise there the eschatological optimism many Scots were beginning to adopt. After the union of the crowns in 1603, Scotland had been forced into a new subordination to her southern neighbour. Her king, now James I of Great Britain, returned to his native country only once, in 1617, in an attempt to coerce the Scottish church - already balancing bishop and presbytery - into accepting his proposals for increased uniformity with the English church. The Articles of Perth (1618), which encapsulated his ecclesiastical demands, provoked the hostility of Scotland's large Presbyterian party, who were offended by the Arminian theology and anglicization they claimed the innovations represented. The substance of these demands was, however, less important than the manner by which James hoped to impose them. His attempts to override the free courts of the Church of Scotland mounted a direct challenge to the 'crown rights of King Jesus'. It was an assertion of divine right over church as well as state - a claim for supremacy that Presbyterians condemned. James' campaign for an Arminian ecclesiology was a declaration of war between Scotland's temporal and spiritual jurisdictions.

Presbyterians were outraged. Perceiving that the innovations were nothings less than the dregs of Arminianism – if not outright popery – their response prompted a constitutional crisis. On 23 July 1637, at the first reading of the new prayer book in St Giles Cathedral, Edinburgh, Jenny Geddes hurled her stool at the presiding Dean. The ensuing riot, variously perceived with horror and delight, was easily assimilated into the dissenting worldview: God was stirring again to rebuild his ruined people. Scotland's Presbyterian resistance was an eschatological movement whose rhetorical structures and theological nuance would catalyse the developing puritan discourses of the end. In the thought of the Covenanters - and in particular in the preaching of George Gillespie - the millenarianism of the Scottish revolution built on Ussher's conclusions and precipitated the themes which England's most radical sectaries would expand. As John Coffey notes, 'once the rebellion got under way, the apocalyptic outlook that had been fostered by the Presbyterian preachers gave it great momentum.'[1]

Although the political narrative of the Scottish revolution has been mythologised in its telling and retelling, the ideological forces shaping the nation's dissent have suffered much neglect. With the signing of the Covenant in 1638, Scottish opposition voices consolidated their gains and presented their enemies with a single statement of grievance fusing their initial socio-political, economic, and religious discontents. The sources of grievance stretched back into the reign of James VI. When James acceded to his mother's throne in 1567, he inherited a country riven by its economic, cultural and religious commitments. Agricultural inefficiency was being balanced by a rising concern to make 'improvements'. Increasing numbers of single-owner estates amalgamaneted smaller interests, reinforcing class distinctions and making it more difficult for hard-working peasants to become land-owners. Attempts to eradicate a 'backward' Highland culture accelerated when it became clear that the Gaels were not only reluctant to abandon established patterns of industry, but were proving hostile to the dictates of central government and were maintaining crucial links with their fellow Roman Catholics in Ireland. The plantation of thrifty and disciplined Lowland protestants was intended to dispel the darkness of the Hebridean islanders.[2]

Fundamentally, however, the dissent was registered in the terms of a distinctly Scottish and Presbyterian faith. James had consistently worked towards an Episcopal government for the Scottish church. In 1572, in his minority, the Concordat of Leith began the practice of filling vacant bishoprics. Thereafter ensued a series of tussles between the ecclesiastical demands of king and parliament. Compromise was finally reached after 1612, when bishops were made permanent members of the presbyteries. But James continued to press for Episcopalian advance, and his 1618 Articles of Perth (confirmed by Parliament in 1621) seemed finally to promise the eclipse of the Scottish liturgical tradition.

However successful in winning the support of Parliament, James'

---

[1] John Coffey, *Politics, Religion and the British Revolutions: The mind of Samuel Rutherford* (Cambridge: Cambridge University Press, 1997), pp. 243-4.
[2] Martyn Bennet, *The Civil Wars in Britain and Ireland, 1638-1651* (Oxford: Blackwell, 1997), p. 10.

innovations were unpopular in the churches. Presbyterian townsfolk resented paying extra taxes to subsidise the detested Arminian impositions. The nobility were suspicious of the political power exercised by the new bishops, and felt threatened by Charles' plans to reclaim the old church lands which his father had given away. The entire social structure was groaning under the weight of reform in church and state. Millenarianism, among the leaders of the Scottish Presbyterians, became popular precisely because their old world was dying.

Consequently, the influence of millenarian ideas in the Scottish church cannot be overstated. An embryonic postmillennialism developed when individuals as diverse as anti-prelatical extremists (like Richard Cameron) and future archbishops (like Robert Leighton) agreed that the world would experience increasing gospel influences as the end of time approached. They were united with moderate Presbyterians in expecting an enlargement of Christ's kingdom 'by bringing all kingdoms and nations some way under his sceptre, that the prophecy of John the Divine, Rev. xi. 15, shall be acknowledged to be fulfilled: all the kingdoms of the earth are become the Lord's and his Son Christ's.'[3] So pervasive was this influence that the *Dictionary of Scottish Church History and Theology* notes that Alexander Petrie, the minister of a Scottish congregation in Holland, was 'almost a lone voice' in dissenting from the new eschatology.[4] Petrie's *Chiliasto-mastix* (1644), we have seen, interrogated fashionable millennialism. Nevertheless, as embryonic postmillennialism was embraced by ecclesiastical rivals for quite distinct ends, it was inevitable that its component parts would evolve.

The writings of Samuel Rutherford, one of the most prominent of the Covenanting brethren, typify this 'party' exploitation of apocalypse. Rutherford was extremely concerned with the 'new and strange leaven' which the Arminians were introducing into Scotland's 'fallen kirk', but wrote also of his longing for the time when he would 'see the beauty of the Lord in his house' and 'the woman travailing in birth, delivered of the man child of a blessed reformation'.[5] The apocalyptic child Rutherford expected was a fully-fledged Presbyterian system. Scotland's Christians, he implied, could oscillate between adherence to the woman of *Revelation* 12, 'clothed with the sun' and bringing the man-child to birth, or the scarlet woman of *Revelation* 17, drunk with the

[3] David Dickson, *A Commentary on the Psalms* (1653-5; rpt. Edinburgh: Banner of Truth, 1959), i. 440.

[4] Nigel Cameron et al (eds), *Dictionary of Scottish Church History and Theology* (Edinburgh: T&T Clark, 1993), p. 563, s.v. 'Millennialism'.

[5] Samuel Rutherford, *Letters of Samuel Rutherford*, ed. Andrew Bonar (1891; rpt. Edinburgh: Banner of Truth, 1984), pp. 438, 371.

blood of the saints. Their alignment with these archetypes depended entirely upon their view of the new prayer book. One of the longest of Rutherford's letters is addressed to his parishioners, warning them in no uncertain terms of the dangers of flirting with the scarlet whore: 'all the ceremonies that lie in Antichrist's foul womb, the wares of that great mother of fornications, the Kirk of Rome, are to be refused.'[6] Rutherford's letters were prising *Revelation* free of its accepted interpretations, figuring Scotland's church as the theatre in which the apocalyptic drama was to be enacted. Scriptures which were once safely historicised were being stripped of their interpretative shackles and applied to religious and political disputes on the tempestuous brink of civil war. Rutherford was reflecting the later puritan trend of making metaphors from apocalyptic Scripture - a tradition which, we will see, would find its logical conclusion among the Quakers.

The roots of this radical temper can be traced to Scotland's alternative eschatological heritage. William Lamont has claimed that after 1580 Scottish scholars concentrated their labours on developing a distinct ecclesiology while English theologians investigated eschatology - but this neat antithesis is not entirely justified.[7] Although the eschatological traditions of puritans in England and Scotland both descended from the Reformers through the same group of Marian exiles, the Scottish tradition was always more radical than the English and developed with a freedom which the English tradition was denied. The English tradition, as we observed in the experience of James Ussher, was hampered by its construction of the paradigm of the godly prince, the Christian monarch who would lead the church in the destruction of Antichrist. This theme tempered the revolutionary potential of English millenarianism and channelled its energy into consolidating the monarchical *status quo*. Knox's more rigorous theology - which many in the Scottish church adopted - did not foreground the monarch's latter-day role to quite the same extent. Millenarian ideas were launched without the controls necessary for them to support the established order.

This movement of attitudes to the godly prince is visible, we discovered, in the differences between the 1593 and 1611 editions of Napier's *Plaine Discovery of the Whole Revelation*. We have noticed that the later edition deliberately overlooked the apocalyptic role which, in the first edition, Napier had assigned to James. When the works of Brightman, in England, echoed the conclusions of Napier's second edition, they were immediately silenced by the Arminian clamp-down

---

6 Rutherford, *Letters*, p. 440.

7 William Lamont, *Puritanism and historical controversy* (London: U.C.L. Press, 1996), p. 145.

on theological speculation. Napier, on the other hand, had established a native audience and, as a consequence, Scottish puritans were able to negotiate with Genevan eschatology for several decades before the English Long Parliament republished the works of Brightman, Alsted and Mede for English readers in the early 1640s. This programme of publication seems to have been a deliberate attempt to foster the unfettered millenarianism which had by then already destroyed Episcopacy in Scotland. As a consequence, the anti-prelatical opinions of many English puritans were grounded in Brightman's exegesis - though they were coming late to a tradition which had long existed in Scotland. Far from discouraging eschatological inquiry, as Lamont implies, the Scottish context actively fostered the development of such new thinking.

Scottish opposition groups, then, had established a discourse within which they could voice their complaints of the Arminian impositions. When the ecclesiastical crisis came, in summer 1637, the Presbyterians knew exactly how best to attack the new liturgy. Richard Baxter remembered what he had heard of the first reading of the new prayer book: 'One woman ... cried out in the church, "Popery, popery," and threw her stool at the priest; and others imitated her presently, and drove him out of the church; and this little spark set all Scotland quickly in a flame.'[8] The echoes which resounded throughout St. Giles' Cathedral reverberated around Scotland as the prayer book controversy proved to be the catalyst for a wider revolt. It was, in a very real sense, the beginning of the revolution which was to rush through the three kingdoms; it began with a stool in the air and climaxed with the executioner's sword sweeping down upon King Charles. In imposing his Arminian reforms, James had sown the wind; he left his son to reap the whirlwind.

By autumn 1637, the apocalyptic register intensified as the tension between presbyter and bishop increased. 'I marvel not that Antichrist, in his slaves, is so busy,' Rutherford exclaimed, 'but our crowned King seeth and beholdeth, and will arise for Zion's safety.'[9] Rutherford's rhetorical slippage between Charles and Christ - with the latter being the church's true covenanted king - evidences the puritan suspicion that earthly monarchs could often act as impediments to reformation. As Charles' army marched north to counteract the Scottish threat, Rutherford's attention was turned to 'our Lord Jesus ... on horseback, hunting and pursuing the beast'. This reversal of identities - Christ as the latter-day godly prince and Charles as the beast he was hunting -

---

[8] Richard Baxter, *The Autobiography of Richard Baxter*, ed. N.H. Keeble (London: Dent, 1974), pp. 19-20.
[9] Rutherford, *Letters*, p. 471.

was an ominous glimpse of things to come. Foxe's pro-government propaganda could not have been more inverted.

Certainly this end-of-the-world view would have seemed plausible to the ministers and elders who had gathered together in Glasgow Cathedral in November 1638 as a General Assembly of the Scottish church. They mounted a radical programme to rebut the Arminian reforms. Abolishing bishops and challenging royal prerogative, the General Assembly met just in time to correspond with the fall of Babylon, which Napier had predicted for the subsequent year. Appropriately, their defiance was to end the old order. As T.C. Smout has noted, 'the fall of the Scottish bishops in 1638 was the first incident in a new revolutionary situation that eventually engulfed the whole of the British Isles in a raging storm of civil war.'[10] Yet their Presbyterian defiance was implicitly couched in apocalyptic thought. As Walter Makey has noted, the entire Covenanter enterprise was a 'groping for the millennium'.[11]

The Westminster Assembly and the Millennium

The millenarian spirit of puritans on both sides of the border was most clearly manifest in the build-up to and the meetings of the Westminster Assembly, an ecclesiastical conference called by Parliament without the King's permission to reform the confessional basis of the English church in 1643. Since the Reformation and the Marian exile, links between puritans in Scotland and England had always been strong. In the more recent past, individuals within each group had exercised ministries which transgressed national boundaries. John Livingstone, for example, left his native Scotland in the early 1630s to spend time in London before he began his ministry in north-east Ireland and attempted emigration to New England. In the English capital he met some of the pre-eminent London puritans - Richard Sibbes, William Twisse, Philip Nye, and Thomas Goodwin - along with his fellow Scot, Alexander Leighton, who was then imprisoned in the Fleet for his anti-prelatical sentiments. Livingstone would have enjoyed a good reception: English puritans were fascinated by developments in Scotland in the later 1630s, and certainly understood the Scottish revolution in the apocalyptic terms the Scots shared. John Bastwick's 1638 tract entitled *The Beast is Wounded. Or, Information from Scotland, concerning their Reformation* informed his English readership of the Scottish challenges to the

---

[10] T.C. Smout, *A History of the Scottish People 1560-1830* (London: Fontana, 1969), p. 61.

[11] Walter Makey, *The Church of Scotland 1637-1651: Revolution and Social Change in Scotland* (Edinburgh: John Donald, 1979), p. 57.

'Antichristian power' of prelacy and the 'Idol-booke' of Common Prayer.[12] For those groaning under the totalitarian yoke of prelacy, the Scottish destruction of Episcopacy seemed like the halcyon days of reformation come again.

It was this sense of working together against a common enemy which drew the puritan brethren from both sides of the border into an alliance. By the beginning of the 1640s the informal links which had existed between the various non-prelatical Calvinistic groups in Scotland and England were evolving into a 'puritan pact' intended to ally Presbyterians and Independents in both countries against their common enemy - the bishops. Events were moving at speed. In May 1641, the London puritan Stephen Marshall had been serving with Archbishop Ussher on a Long Parliament committee working towards a modified episcopacy; by September, Marshall was anticipating the fall of the bishops, breathlessly wondering 'whether GOD ever did such a thing for matter and manner, as he hath nowe done for these two unworthy Nations'.[13] Jeremiah Burroughs, Marshall's colleague, shared his excitement at the imminent collapse of Anglicanism. Both preachers understood the eschatological importance of the event, 'the great worke of the Lord that He is doing in this latter age of the world'.[14] Quoting Mede and Brightman, the prophets of the new apocalypse, Burroughs was advocating a new union of the nations, Scotland and England united in a covenanted crusade for Christ. For these English divines, the proceedings which led to the Westminster Assembly were grounded in the apocalyptic union of England and Scotland, an eschatological alliance against Episcopacy.

The Scots had long anticipated this type of thinking, although their interest also extended to Ireland. Rutherford had exploited apocalyptic images to consolidate his vision of an alternative union of the three kingdoms: 'England and Ireland shall be well-swept chambers for Christ and his righteousness to dwell in; for he hath opened our graves in Scotland, and the two dead and buried witnesses are risen again, and are prophesying.'[15] The necessary result of Scottish reform was the reform of the other Stuart kingdoms. Burroughs agreed on the three-kingdom concept, though he quietly pointed to England's pre-eminence in reformation. Although 'England was the first Kingdome in all the

---

[12] John Bastwick, *The Beast is Wounded* (London, 1638), pp. 4, 6.

[13] R.L. Greaves, *Saints and Rebels: Seven Nonconformists in Stuart England* (Macon: Mercer University Press, 1985), pp. 14-15; Stephen Marshall, *A Peace-Offering to God ... for the PEACE concluded between ENGLAND and SCOTLAND* (1641), p. 3.

[14] Jeremiah Burroughs, *Sions Joy ... For the PEACE concluded between ENGLAND and SCOTLAND* (1641), p. 2.

[15] Rutherford, *Letters*, p. 577.

worlde that received the Gospel with the countenance of supreame authority', he claimed, her future lay in a union with the Scots.[16] He justified his stance by appealing to the apocalyptic commentators: 'when God opens a doore, it shall not be shut againe ... Which Mr. Brightman above thirty yeares agoe applied to the Church of Scotland; God hath opened a doore unto them and to us, surely none shall be able to shut it; let men threaten, and plot, and endeavour what they can, God who hath brought to the birth will cause to bring forth.'[17] Burroughs had no doubt that the proposed union would settle the root and branch extirpation of bishops. Antichrist had been allowed to prevail, but 'this time God intends to ruine him. You come at the time of his downfall,' he told M.P.s, 'when he is falling, in Gods very day of recompencing vengeance for all the blood he hath shed, and all the mischiefe he hath done.'[18] This iconoclastic temper was set in a robustly apocalyptic context: 'that which God hath begun to doe amongst us, we hope is the beginning of that great worke that he intends to doe in this latter age of the world.'[19] The fall of the bishops in Scotland bred hope in England that the end of all things was near.

The Scots were quick to ally themselves with this anti-prelatical eschatology. Alexander Henderson described Episcopalianism as 'a stumbling block hindering Reformation, and ... a prejudice to the Civil State'.[20] Consequently, the alliance towards which these puritans had been working was formalised in November 1641, only months after the sermons by Marshall and Burroughs. Representatives from Scotland travelled to London to negotiate the alliance after the collapse of Ussher's scheme to settle the church on the basis of a modified episcopacy. The English puritans began to realise that England's shifting balance of power no longer demanded their uncomfortable co-operation with the more orthodox of the Anglican divines, and that an agreement between the pro-Independency and pro-Presbyterian parties among the puritans could quicken further reformation and achieve the total abolition of the bishops.

The Scots were keen to assist. In November, members of the three groups met in the London house of the prominent English Presbyterian Edward Calamy, where Calamy and the Independent leader Philip Nye agreed that '(for advancing of the publike Cause of a happy Reformation) neither side should Preach, Print, or dispute, or otherwise act against the other's way; And this to continue 'til both sides, in a full

---

[16] Burroughs, *Sions Joy*, p. 51.

[17] Burroughs, *Sions Joy*, p. 55.

[18] Burroughs, *Sions Joy*, p. 60.

[19] Burroughs, *Sions Joy*, p. 33.

[20] James Reid, *Memoirs of the Westminster Divines* (Paisley: Young, 1811), ii. 385.

meeting, did declare the contrary.'[21] Gaining the support of the English Independents, and Presbyterians on both sides of the border, the puritan pact was intended to carry the saints into the millennium.

As the civil war impacted upon domestic politics, the Scots came eventually to possess the casting vote in the wars between King and Parliament. After much debate, they opted to support the English Parliament and demanded that any promise of military help for the English Parliament must be matched by their attempts to introduce religious uniformity in England. As a result, the Scots were invited in August 1643 to contribute to the work of the Westminster Assembly, which, we have noted, had been convened by Parliament to reform the Thirty-nine Articles of the Church of England. Under Scottish influence, this original agenda was soon scrapped and the divines began work on an entirely new confession of faith and directory of congregational worship designed to unite the churches throughout the realm in the 'reformation and defence of religion, the honour and happiness of the King, and the peace and safety of the three kingdoms of Scotland, England, and Ireland.'[22]

The Scots quickly realised that their most natural allies in the Assembly were not their ecclesiological allies, the English Presbyterians, but rather the Independents, with whom they enjoyed an eschatological affinity. In December 1643, Robert Baillie, one of the Scottish Commissioners at the Assembly, observed that 'Goodwin, Burroughs, and Bridge, are men full, as it seems yet, of grace and modestie.'[23] The Scots and the English Independents shared two major common concerns. Firstly, both groups described their efforts to establish a pure church in the same terms. Rutherford, for example, described how the Westminster divines were 'debating, with much contention of disputes, for the just measures of the Lord's temple'.[24] Thomas Goodwin had already figured the Old Testament temple and tabernacle as 'types of the church to come'.[25] This temple-building rhetoric, with its roots in the ideology of the Marian exiles, was to exercise an important function in the development of a distinctively puritan poetics, as we will later see. The second major common theme of the two groups was their intense eschatological optimism. Christ's kingdom, they expected, would be extended through missionary effort and, some claimed, military

---

[21] Quoted in Greaves, *Saints and Rebels*, p. 15.
[22] Hetherington, *History of the Westminster Assembly of Divines*, p. 129.
[23] Iain H. Murray, 'The Scots at the Westminster Assembly' *Banner of Truth* 371-2 (1994), p. 14; Robert Baillie, *The Letters and Journals of Robert Baillie*, ed. David Laing (Edinburgh: Robert Ogle, 1841-2), ii. 111.
[24] Rutherford, *Letters*, p. 618.
[25] Goodwin, *Works*, iii. 2.

conquest. One of the most prominent themes in puritan writing of this period was the 'conversion of the Jews' motif, the doctrine that a massive influx of Jewish converts into the Christian church in the last days would herald an unprecedented revival of protestantism among the Gentiles. The various puritan commentators took great pains to include this as a feature in their chronologies. Iain Murray has noted that it was the English Independents and Scottish commissioners who were largely behind the introduction of this optimistic eschatology: 'ground for hopefulness in regard to the prospects of Christ's kingdom ... was introduced in sermons before Parliament or on other public occasions by William Strong, William Bridge, George Gillespie and Robert Baillie, to name but a few.'[26] These were the sentiments lying behind the Assembly's *Directory for Public Worship*; published later in 1644, it was, as we shall see, a good reflection of the mood inside the 'puritan pact'. In this handbook of congregational practice ministers were directed to pray for

> the conversion of the Jews, the fullness of the Gentiles, the fall of Antichrist, and the hastening of the second coming of our Lord; for the deliverance of the distressed churches abroad from the tyranny of the antichristian faction, and from the cruel oppressions and blasphemies of the Turk; for the blessing of God upon the reformed churches, especially upon the churches and kingdoms of Scotland, England, and Ireland, now more strictly and religiously united in the Solemn National League and Covenant.[27]

Thus concern for the well-being of the church in the three nations reached out also to other nations. The Covenant was submitted to foreign governments as the basis of a pan-European protestant league. It was sworn throughout the North American plantations. It inspired missionary work amongst the native Americans as the 'knowledge of the Lord' was indeed appearing to sweep over the earth 'as the waters cover the sea'. Even Baillie, normally so cautious and conservative, found enthusiasm in its pages: 'we are thinking of a new work overseas, if this church were settled,' he claimed; 'The outward providence of God seems to be disposing France, Spain, Italy, and Germany, for the receiving of the Gospel. When the curtains of the Lord's tabernacle are thus far, and much further enlarged, by the means which yet appear not, how shall our mouth be filled with laughter.'[28]

The more radical of the brethren did not look to prayer alone as the means of winning the world. The Earl of Leven was overheard alluding

---

[26] Murray, *The Puritan Hope*, p. 44.
[27] *Subordinate Standards*, p. 142.
[28] Baillie, *Letters and Journals*, ii. 192.

to the possibility of a Covenanting army overturning Rome and driving the Catholics out of Europe altogether.[29] His ebullience was shared by General Leslie, who was considering 'what glory it would be before God and man if we were to drive the Catholics out of England and follow them to France, and plant, either with consent or by force, our religion in Paris, and thence, go to Rome, drive out Antichrist, and burn the town.'[30] The Scottish Covenant invested its credibility in the future, as Philip Nye admitted on the day England's Parliament swore to uphold its claims: 'the effect of that oath you shall find to be this, that the kingdoms of the world become the kingdoms of the Lord and his Christ, and he shall reign for ever, Rev. xi.'[31] As Walter Makey has rightly emphasised, the National Covenant was working for 'a vast theocracy extending from Shetland to Munster and beyond.'[32]

But the unity of the puritan brotherhood was put under strain when these two major themes came into conflict. Puritans increasingly identified the establishment of the church's future prosperity with the inauguration of the most biblical form of church government. Goodwin's exposition of *Revelation* had first argued on this basis in 1639. Throughout the 1640s this concept entered the thinking of each of the competing ecclesiastical groups. In the 1650s John Owen claimed that the new heavens and earth would witness the establishment of the true 'way of gospel worship'.[33] This juxtaposition of ecclesiological and eschatological themes eventually undermined the puritan movement. Millenarianism could not remain an abstract as England entered what James de Jong has described as its 'vortex of history' in the 1640s.[34]

As the Assembly's divines turned their attentions to the thorny issue of church government, the centrifugal forces of competing eschatologies teased the saints apart. The Covenant had only required that its adherents pledge themselves to 'preserve' the reformed religion of the Church of Scotland and to support 'the reformation of religion in the kingdoms of England and Ireland, in doctrine, worship, discipline, and government, according to the word of GOD, and the example of the best reformed Churches'.[35] Both Independents and Presbyterians had eagerly subscribed to this oath, many of them in blood; but the ambiguity of

---

[29] Burrell, 'The Apocalyptic Vision of the Early Covenanters', p. 20.

[30] J.G. Fotheringham, *The Diplomatic Correspondence of Jean De Montereul and the Brothers De Bellievre French Ambassadors in England and Scotland 1645-48* (Edinburgh: Scottish Historical Society, 1898), i. xiv.

[31] Reid, *Memoirs of the Westminster Divines*, ii. 373-4.

[32] Makey, *The Church of Scotland 1637-1651*, p. 31.

[33] Owen, *Works*, viii. 337.

[34] de Jong, *As the Waters Cover the Sea*, p. 77.

[35] *Subordinate Standards*, pp. 224-5.

exactly which groups constituted the 'best reformed Churches' could not sustain the initial unity it had effected. Both Presbyterians and Independents were certain the appellation was theirs.

Much of the difficulty stemmed from the role which the Scots were forced to play. Had there been a greater ecclesiological consensus, they could have left much of the defence of Presbyterianism to others. In England, however, the Presbyterian system was still something of a novelty. In 1643, Baillie noted that 'a Presbyterie to this people is conceaved to be a strange monster.'[36] Years later, Richard Baxter remembered that 'Presbytery was not then known in England, except among a few studious scholars, nor well by them.'[37] Consequently, convinced that the Scottish pattern was the best example of reformed ecclesiology, the commissioners took upon themselves the mantle of its defence. In so doing they distanced themselves from their most natural allies. In December 1643 Baillie recorded the Scots' decision to 'eschew a publick rupture with the Independents, till we were more able for them'.[38] Nevertheless, by the beginning of February 1644 the Independent 'dissenting brethren' had published their *Apologeticall Narration* 'in a most slie and cunning way'.[39] Their publication took the Scots by surprise, and forestalled their attempts to 'avoid the premature determination of points disputed by the Independents'. The fissures underlying the puritan pact were increasingly evident.[40] On March 4th Rutherford reflected on his colleagues:

> There is nothing here but divisions in the Church and Assembly; for besides Brownists and Independents (who, of all that differ from us, come nearest to walkers with God), there are many other sects here, of Anabaptists, Libertines who are for all opinions in religion, fleshly and abominable Antinomians, and Seekers, who are for no church ordinances, but expect apostles to come and reform churches; and a world of others, all against the government of presbyteries.[41]

The Scots were beginning to recognise the fragility of their relationship with the English saints. By March 1644 the unity of the brotherhood – and the entire success of the puritan enterprise – was hanging in the balance.

---

[36] Baillie, *Letters and Journals*, ii. 117.
[37] Richard Baxter, *Reliquiae Baxterianae, or Mr. Richard Baxter's narrative of the most memorable passages of his life and times* (London, 1696), iii. 41.
[38] Baillie, *Letters and Journals*, ii. 117.
[39] Baillie, *Letters and Journals*, ii. 130.
[40] Hetherington, *History of the Westminster Assembly of Divines*, pp. 182-3.
[41] Rutherford, *Letters*, p. 619.

Gillespie and Eschatology

It was with the purpose of addressing this imminent collapse in puritan unity that the divines and M.P.s looked to George Gillespie (1613-1648). Gillespie had arrived at the Assembly in 1643 bringing with him his reputation as an outstanding defender of the Presbyterian cause in Scotland. His importance has been noted by Trevor-Roper, who described him as 'the youngest, most learned, most argumentative' of the Scottish commissioners.[42] In 1637, at the age of twenty-five, he had published *A Dispute Against the English Popish Ceremonies obtruded on the Church of Scotland*. The value of his treatise was recognised even by those who had little sympathy for his suggested ecclesiastical improvements. In 1638, at the revolutionary General Assembly, he preached on *Proverbs* 21:1 - 'the king's heart is in the hand of the LORD' - and was chided, even there, for its radical overtones. He had lost none of this verve by the time he arrived in London. Gillespie became the most frequent speaker in debates, confounding even the mighty Selden. Baillie was voluminous in his praise: 'none in all the companie did reason more, and more pertinentlie, than Mr. Gillespie ... We gett good help in our Assemblie debates of my Lord Warriston; but of none more than that noble youth Mr. Gillespie.'[43]

In the sermon he delivered to the Assembly divines and M.P.s on the 27th March 1644, Gillespie marked the final moments before the unity of the brotherhood utterly collapsed. His sermon was the climax of the Scottish revolution, exhibiting the momentum and the unity built upon its exuberant eschatological hopes. Gillespie expressed the themes and concerns of the puritan brotherhood, expounding the rhetorical strategies which would be refined and enlarged by the radical sectaries of the Commonwealth and beyond. His sermon is the key to understanding some of the most important events of mid-seventeenth-century history.

As Gillespie stepped into the pulpit of St. Margaret's Westminster he would have been well aware that in his audience were the M.P.s who had most opposed and obstructed the findings of the Westminster Assembly. He had few friends in the London establishment. As recently as 1638 his dissertation on *The English Popish Ceremonies* had been burned by the common hangman. More immediately, the Scottish Commissioners were frustrated by the reluctance of the Commons to consent to the principles already established by the Assembly. They seemed to be deliberately slow in institutionalising the attainments they

---

[42] Hugh Trevor-Roper, 'The Fast Sermons of the Long Parliament', in Hugh Trevor-Roper (ed.), *Essays in British History Presented to Sir Keith Fielding* (London: Macmillan, 1965), p. 116.
[43] Baillie, *Letters and Journals*, ii. 117, 140.

had promised in return for Scottish military aid. Gillespie was acutely conscious of the difficulties he faced. His opponents were 'resolved to give the worst name to the best thing which we can do'.[44]

As a consequence, Gillespie's strategy was twofold. He intended to carry with him in his argument as many as he could for as long as he could. By citing Brightman's exegesis Gillespie was deliberately attempting to build bridges with the English millenarian tradition and the expositions of the Independents before him.[45] Secondly, by publishing his sermon he was attempting to by-pass the Commons' hesitation and influence a wider audience above and beyond the confines of Parliament. To publish was to appeal to the people as the ultimate authority and to reflect the democratic strategy of the English revolution. Hence Gillespie's title-page highlighted the sermon's populist millenarian pulse: 'When the Lord shall build up Zion, he shall appear in his glory' (*Psalm* 102:16).

There is certainly an element of tub-thumping in his invocation of the most basic protestant fears. Gillespie recapitulated the concerns which had led to the Scottish involvement in the Westminster Assembly. His litany of dissent was a catena of Scottish grievance. It was the heir of their Reformation monarchs, Charles I, who, on the 9th of October 1643, declared the Solemn League and Covenant 'a traitorous and seditious combination against us and the established religion of this kingdom'.[46] It was a covenanted nobleman, Montrose, who turned malignant and led an army of Catholic Highlanders and Irishmen against the armies of the covenant - and this shortly after the incredible spectacle of the papal nuncio leading the Irish rebels.[47] Contemporary estimates put the number of protestants killed in the Irish rebellion at two hundred thousand.[48] The Scots had been profoundly shaken. Gillespie therefore berated the willingness of the 'malignants' to 'thirst after so much Protestant blood', 'to associate themselves with all the Papists at home and abroad whose assistance they can have', to court the assistance of 'those matchless monsters (they call them subjects) of Ireland', and their resolution to 'give the worst name to the best thing which we can do ... they have not been ashamed to call a religious and loyal covenant a traitorous and damnable covenant'.[49] The Scottish Parliament, in July

[44] Gillespie, *Works*, i. 11. Page references within the text are to Gillespie, 'A Sermon Preached ... March 27, 1644', in Gillespie, *Works*, i. 1-26.

[45] Gillespie, *Works*, i. 15.

[46] Hetherington, *History of the Westminster Assembly of Divines*, p. 128.

[47] David Stevenson, 'The Century of the Three Kingdoms', in Jenny Wormald (ed.), *Scotland Revisited* (London: Collins and Brown, 1991), p. 112.

[48] Baxter, *Autobiography*, p. 32.

[49] Gillespie, *Works*, i. 11.

1644, lamented the 'danger imminent to the true Protestant religion ... by the multitude of Papists and their adherents in arms in England and Scotland and Ireland'.[50] Royalist collusion with Roman Catholics presented a clear and present danger to the protestant cause in the three kingdoms. There is a basic stoking of fear at the heart of Gillespie's rhetoric.

This strategy was, however, entirely applicable to his subject-matter. Gillespie's sermon expounds and applies *Ezekiel* 43:11, in which the prophet is commanded to display to the Israelites the plans of the new temple which God had revealed to him - but only on the condition that the listeners were 'ashamed of all that they have done'. From this text Gillespie derived the twin aims of his sermon, attempting to bring 'humiliation' to his hearers and to outline God's demands for the establishment of the pure system of church government. This order reflected the puritan maxim to reform the individual before the institution: 'So should we measure, by the reed of the sanctuary, first the inner house of our hearts and minds, and then to measure out outer walls, and to judge of our profession and external performances.'[51]

The first difficulty Gillespie faced was to justify his drawing from an Old Testament prophecy the organisational principles of the New Testament church. Scottish attempts to establish a Presbyterian church in England regularly appealed to the Old Testament temple-building rhetoric because the Scots had become rather adept at applying the promises of Israel to themselves. This rival 'elect nation' was certain of its place in the final drama of history: 'now, O Scotland,' Rutherford declared, 'God be thanked, thy name is in the Bible.'[52] Similarly, some of the godly looked upon the work of church reformation as the New Testament equivalent of establishing Judaism among the idols: 'your high places', Gillespie told the Commons, are 'not yet taken away, many of your old superstitious ceremonies to this day remaining'. Gillespie reminded his listeners that the best arguments for Episcopacy - 'antiquity, custom, and other defences of that kind' - were the same arguments used for the 'high places of will worship' in the former dispensation.[53] This implicit criticism of the King, whose reforms he was attacking, would have been unthinkable under the old eschatology. 'I have no pleasure to take up these and other dunghills,' Gillespie claims; 'the text hath put this in my mouth which I have said.'[54] To the Scottish Commissioners, the *via media* strategies of James' conforming

[50] *Subordinate Standards*, p. 222.
[51] Gillespie, *Works*, i. 18.
[52] Quoted in Coffey, *Politics, Religion and the British Revolutions*, p. 228.
[53] Gillespie, *Works*, i. 5.
[54] Gillespie, *Works*, i. 11-12.

Anglicanism stood as condemned as the Canaanite fertility cults the Jews had to destroy. Coffey has noted Rutherford's similar repudiation of the godly prince ideology.[55]

This, then, was the theological and political basis for Gillespie's outlining of the four applications of the temple prophecy in *Ezekiel* from which he drew his subject-text. The first fulfilment Gillespie points to is the Jewish temple as it was rebuilt after the Babylonian exile - 'for though many things in the vision do not agree to that time, as hath been proved, yet some things do agree'. Secondly, Gillespie points the reader to the universal church, and quotes twice from the New Testament to evidence his claim that the apostles regarded the early church as the prophetic fulfilment of the Jewish temple. Thirdly, Gillespie claims that the prophecy has a particular application to the church as it enters the glory and prosperity of the 'last times' - for in his policy of consensus he omits the word 'millennium'. This theme of latter-day glory is the basis of the extended sermon as a whole. The institution of the proper form of biblical church government, Gillespie argued, was the 'happiness' which God 'reserved to the last times, to build a more excellent and glorious temple than former generations have seen'. Gillespie argues this case on the basis of the church's latter-day prosperity, 'the fullness both of Jews and Gentiles, which we wait for'.[56] The times of revival and reformation would be 'peaceable and quiet times to the church', when the princes of earth 'shall no more oppress the people of God' but will turn their attentions instead to precipitating the downfall of 'the whore (of Rome)'.[57] Gillespie argued that 'the church, the house of the living God, shall not lie desolate for ever, but shall be built again' when 'the kingdom of Antichrist shall come to an end'. His audience was to 'consider the great revolution and turning of things upside down in these our days'; certainly, he felt, 'the work is upon the wheel.'[58] The events of the Westminster Assembly could announce the end of the times symbolised by the wilderness exile of the apocalyptic woman of *Revelation* 12 - and the Presbyterian reformation-in-waiting, which Rutherford had already described, would be complete.

Perhaps it was because of this sense of imminence that Gillespie feared his sermon should take longer than necessary. He made 'haste to the several particulars contained in my text'.[59] His first major theme was the humiliation of his reader. The objective of humbling the reader was a common trope in seventeenth-century puritan literature - especially if

[55] Coffey, *Politics, Religion and the British Revolutions*, p. 233.
[56] Gillespie, *Works*, i. 7.
[57] Gillespie, *Works*, i. 8.
[58] Gillespie, *Works*, i. 9.
[59] Gillespie, *Works*, i. 9.

we are to believe Stanley Fish, who sees texts toying with their readership, encapsulating in their form the purpose of their argument. With the other puritan divines, Gillespie believed that the twin aims of Gospel preaching ought to be the listener's recognition of man's hopelessness and God's ability to bestow salvation. Related to this was the idea that 'conviction of sin' - awareness of one's condemnation and helplessness under God's moral law - should precede the application of God's remedy in the Gospel. This was a standard Calvinistic technique. John Owen, writing his treatise on *Justification* (1677), argued that Christ 'makes a difference between [men], offering the gospel unto some and not unto others, - but such as were convinced of sin, burdened with it, and sought after deliverance'.[60] On a similar basis, Gillespie highlights his determination to inculcate, as far as he can through literary means, 'a change upon our corrupt and wicked affections', a 'change upon our blind minds', and a 'change also upon our actions' - these are the three 'heads' of his sermon, the three points around which his discourse is organised.[61] To illustrate the need for repentance and humiliation, Gillespie launches into his first major point, a liturgy of England's failure: 'the land is not healed, no, not of its worst disease, which is corruption in religion.'[62] He calls upon the M.P.s to remember their past failings - the 'abominations' of episcopacy - and informs them that they will know nothing of the new plan of God until they evidence their humiliation for dallying with such abominable error.[63]

Following the traditional structure of the puritan sermon, Gillespie then makes 'applications' of his first doctrine. Variously applied to the malignant faction, the kingdom at large, to ministers and ordinary Christians, Gillespie reminds his audience of the persistence of their sinful ways. England's shame should stem from an awareness of the spiritual benefits she has lacked, for the outrages she has committed upon the godly, for her pride in the attainments of Episcopacy, and for her cold response to the mercies already shown her.

The second application of the doctrine of 'humiliation' deals with the national need to be cleansed of, and humbled for, sin: 'it is not enough to cleanse the house of the Lord, but you must be humbled for your former defilements wherewith it was polluted.'[64] Gillespie outlines 'four considerations which may make England ashamed and confounded before the Lord'.[65] First, he invokes the good that England has not

---

[60] Owen, *Works*, v. 76.
[61] Gillespie, *Works*, i. 9.
[62] Gillespie, *Works*, i. 5.
[63] Gillespie, *Works*, i. 9.
[64] Gillespie, *Works*, i. 12.
[65] Gillespie, *Works*, i. 13.

practised: 'the reformation of the church of England hath been exceedingly deficient, in government, discipline and worship'. Secondly, he invokes the idolatry of the 'prelatical clergy', and England's guilty complacence. Gillespie interrogates his audience with a barrage of some twenty questions:

> Hath not England harboured and entertained Papists, priests, and Jesuits in its bosom? Is it not just that now you feel the sting and poison of these vipers? Hath there not been a great compliance with the prelates, for peace's sake, even to the prejudice of truth? Doth not the Lord now justly punish that Episcopal peace with an Episcopal war?[66]

But God was not hearing the answers to these questions: 'The silencing, deposing, persecuting, imprisoning, and banishing of so many of the Lord's witnesses, of the most painful and powerful preachers, and the preferring of so many either dumb dogs or false teachers, maketh the voice of bloods to cry to heaven, even the blood of many thousands, yea, thousands of thousands of souls, which have been lost by the one, or might have been saved by the other.'[67] If Irish rebels had slain their 'hundred thousands', the Episcopal innovations had accounted for 'thousands of thousands of souls'.[68] Gillespie had no doubts about the seriousness of the Arminian threat.

Gillespie's third criticism - for that is what his applications amount to - is of the pride of the Anglican church. Instead of mourning its sin and inadequacy, he feels, it has been 'proud of its clergy, learning, great revenues, peace, plenty, wealth, and abundance of all things'. Consequently, the divine programme of reformation could not be accomplished without the help of the Scots. The Scots were necessary because the English church made 'an idol of this Parliament, and trusted to its own strength and armies, which hath provoked God so much, that he hath sometimes almost blasted your hopes that way, and hath made you to feel your weakness even when you thought yourselves strongest'. As Burroughs and Marshall had already said, England could not hope to accomplish the divine programme without the covenanted armies of the Lord. This was a union based explicitly on an exegetical tradition: as we have noted, Burroughs, Marshall and Gillespie each quote Brightman. Gillespie's rhetoric demands that both nations combine to head off God's iconoclastic fury: 'God would not have England say, "Mine own hand hath saved me," Judg. vii. 2; neither will he have Scotland to say. "My hand hath done it:" but he will have both to say, His hand hath done it, when we were lost in our own

---

[66] Gillespie, *Works*, i. 14.
[67] Gillespie, *Works*, i. 14.
[68] Gillespie, *Works*, i. 11.

eyes'.[69]

The fourth aspect for England's humbling returns the reader to the discourse of England's national election on the purposes of God. As a covenanted country she had, like ancient Israel, become the 'bride of Jehovah'. As a result of her failure to impose Presbyterianism - which Gillespie regarded as covenant-breaking - 'England deserved no more but to get a bill of divorce, and that God should have said in his wrath, Away from me, I have no pleasure in you.' But grace had prevailed. God 'hath received you into the bond of his covenant, he rejoiceth over you to do you good, and to dwell among you; his banner over you is love'.[70] Nevertheless, Gillespie laments that a nation which has enjoyed so much grace should squander its rapidly diminishing resources.

After thus cataloguing the sins of the kingdom at large, Gillespie narrows his application to ministers, where he reasserts the primacy of the lower clergy in the late reformation, and calls upon the clergy to lead the nation's penitence. The fourth and final target for his 'humiliating' is the individual believer, irrespective of his station. Gillespie claims that his text 'teacheth us a difference betwixt a presumptuous and a truly humbled sinner; the one is ashamed of his sins, the other not'.[71] The preacher's discreet chiasmus disorientates the reader and compels him to abdicate his independence and critical distance as Gillespie touches upon the most important and most frequent topic in puritan devotional literature - the certainty of the salvation of the individual soul.

Gillespie's analysis of the differences between temporary and true faith place him squarely within the tradition of English puritanism. Following Richard Sibbes, English puritan divines had identified a state known as 'temporary faith', in which one who was not truly regenerate could display many external signs typical of a regenerate state. This idea seemed to blur the distinction between the elect and the reprobate. Gillespie's invocation of the fear of false hope could certainly be seen as a device to stoke up the most basic fears, fears which lay at the very heart of the puritan movement, in an effort to make his audience even more malleable. 'By this mark,' he says, 'let every one of us try himself this day.' At the same time, however, Gillespie's Calvinism required him to admit that he and his listeners were ultimately powerless to effect 'humiliation': 'if the Lord do not open their eyes to see their shame, their end will be destruction.'[72] Such an admission of inadequacy and his inability to accomplish his sermon's purpose -

---

[69] Gillespie, *Works*, i. 15.
[70] Gillespie, *Works*, i. 15-16.
[71] Gillespie, *Works*, i. 16.
[72] Gillespie, *Works*, i. 11.

though perfectly orthodox theologically - forces a recognition of Gillespie's inability to 'close' his text. His arguments were ultimately unable to 'humiliate' his reader. His text represents his 'desires' but could not enforce his will. It was a theme he would explore in his poetics, as we will later see.

Gillespie and Millenarian Ecclesiology

Having attempted to humble his audience, Gillespie turned to his second theme, outlining 'the form of the house' of the proposed millenarian settlement. Gillespie was clear that the Presbyterian system represented an ideal ecclesiological order. He highlighted the unity of the temple - as one building it typifies the unity which all God's people would enjoy in the last days, when it will no longer be 'temple against temple, and altar against altar'.[73] In the last days there would not be a plurality of churches (as Independency would have it) but only a single Presbyterian church, within which would be contained the 'great increase' expected in those days. Gillespie here adopts God's iconoclastic fury to represent world-wide revival in the latter days: 'the gospel will prove a second flood, which will overthrow the whole earth, though not to destroy it (as Noah's did), but to make it glad; "For the earth shall be filled with the knowledge of the glory of the Lord, as the waters cover the sea," Hab. ii. 14; Isa. xi. 9.'[74]

Gillespie's defence of the Presbyterian order was grounded in his recognition that the Bible does not close every discussion it offers. Emphasising the sufficiency of Scripture even in those areas where it seemed insufficient, Gillespie became involved in a robust defence of the finality of the biblical instructions for the church's witness and practise. Certain circumstances, he argues, 'are not determined by the word of God'. Anglicanism had attempted to compel adherents to observe commands which Scripture had not included - observations of the feast days of the liturgical year, for example. Gillespie contests their claim; it is crucial to his project that he defend the Bible as it is, denying Anglicanism's attempts to offer an illegitimate imposition of closure on those areas of silence: 'neither kings, nor parliaments, nor synods, nor any power on earth, may impose or continue the least ceremony upon the consciences of God's people, which Christ hath not imposed.'[75] This recognition of interpretative space would be a central feature of the rhetorical method of Gillespie and - in future decades - the radical sectaries.

---

[73] Gillespie, *Works*, i. 20.
[74] Gillespie, *Works*, i. 21.
[75] Gillespie, *Works*, i. 19.

The sermon foregrounds its parallels with the Bible by retaining its most apocalyptic moments to its end. The millennium Gillespie presents seems to stand between the conservative millenarianism of Ussher - which was conservative only because he did not pinpoint dates within his own lifetime - and its more radical developments during the revolution. Gillespie carefully avoids the term 'millennium', but foregrounds his own adherence to many of the ideas later groups would highlight and enlarge upon. He was, nevertheless, keen not to be mistaken as a supporter of their more radical cause. Safeguarding his comments from the manipulation of some of the emerging premillennialists, he argues that his exegesis has 'no affinity with the opinion of an earthly or temporal kingdom of Christ, or of the Jews' building again of Jerusalem and the material temple, and their obtaining a dominion above all other nations'. Gillespie held that these were 'good grounds of hope to make us think that this new temple is not far off; and (for your part) that Christ is to make a new face of a church in this kingdom'. God, indeed, 'is even now about the work'. There were six reason why Gillespie knew the time was near.

The first of these reasons was that 'the Jews ... have of late come more into remembrance, and have been more thought of, and more prayed for, than they were in former generations.'[76] This was of course largely the result of the Geneva Bible's notes on *Romans* 11, as we have seen. It was also an emphasis which would be institutionalised in the documents of the Westminster Assembly. The *Larger Catechism* (1647) explains 'Thy kingdom come' as a prayer 'that the kingdom of sin and Satan may be destroyed, the gospel propagated throughout the world , the Jews called, the fullness of the Gentiles brought in; ... that Christ would rule in our hearts here, and hasten the time of his second coming, and our reigning with him forever.'[77] The *Directory for Public Worship* (1644), as we have noted, echoed these sentiments.

Gillespie points to the Westminster divines as being called together 'for such a time as this'. They were 'Zorobabels, and Jehoshuas, and Haggais, and Zechariahs' whose job it was to build the new temple of the Lord. This was a remarkable development, appropriating the language which the Marian exiles had addressed to Queen Elizabeth, and using it to refer to the M.P.s. But the Commons were called to action in a way that Elizabeth had not: 'is not the old rubbish of ceremonies daily more and more shovelled away, that there may be a clean ground? and is not the Lord by all this affliction humbling you, that there may be a deep and a sure foundation laid?'

The third reason why Gillespie felt the latter-day glory was near was

---

[76] Gillespie, *Works*, i. 22.
[77] *Subordinate Standards*, p. 109.

because the work has already enjoyed partial success in Scotland. Echoing the claims of John Bastwick and other English puritans, he argued that 'Christ hath put Antichrist from his outerworks in Scotland, and he is now come to put him from his innerworks in England.' God, having begun the work, would surely bring it to completion.

The last three of the reasons pointed to the role of the Westminster divines in the apocalyptic drama. They were themselves the fulfilment of *Revelation* 11:1: 'and there was given unto me a reed like unto a rod: and the angel stood, saying, Rise, and measure the temple of God, and the altar, and them that worship therein.' The Westminster divines had this reed in their hands, as they measured and defined the nature and government of the pure church, and the Commons, whom Gillespie addresses, enjoyed the use of the governmental rod. Doomsday too was being pre-empted as the separation of the truly godly from those who were merely adopting a pragmatic policy of least resistance to the second reformation indicated that God was isolating his sheep from the goats: 'God doth so alienate and separate betwixt you and them.'

Gillespie's final reason is that the 'time seemeth to answer fitly'. Though the Presbyterians had always proved the doyens of caution, the closing moments of Gillespie's sermon seem to indicate that a millenarian fervour was affecting even the conservative Scots:

> The new temple is built when the forty-two months of the beast's reign, and of the treading down of the holy city (that is, by the best interpretation, twelve hundred and sixty years) come to an end. ... I cannot pitch upon a likelier time than the year 383, at which time (according to the common calculation) a general Council at Constantinople (though Baronius and some others reckon that Council in the year 381) did acknowledge the primacy of the bishop of Rome ... Did not then the beast receive much power.[78]

Gillespie's appeal for joint action with the Independents invoked the common protestant historical interpretation of the *Revelation*, added to it a chronology based on fact, and arrived an explanation which he hoped would confound the dissenting brethren and the obstruction of the M.P.s. The year 1643 – 1260 years after 383 – had become loaded with eschatological significance. In 1643, the year in which the Westminster Assembly began its deliberations, the reign of the beast would end.

This was a radical rewrite of protestant history. No longer was the conversion of Constantine the beginning of a golden age for the church; rather it marked the beginnings of the usurpation of Antichrist. Echoes of this could be found in Napier's work. Napier had pointed to the year 300 as the beginning of the 1260-year reign of the beast, making the end

---

[78] Gillespie, *Works*, i. 23.

of his reign concurrent with the beginnings of native reformation in 1560. Gillespie brings the beast's fall into his own seventeenth century, illustrating his fear that the official conversion of the three kingdoms to the reformed faith had not extirpated Antichrist's influence. The beast had continued to reign through the bishops. Presbyterianism was stamping its own identity on the apocalypse. Nevertheless, Gillespie argued, God was actually now waiting in the wings to intervene in England, as events would subsequently show: 'God's work will, ere it be long, make a clearer commentary upon his word.' The preacher did caution his audience that the latter-day glory would not necessarily follow immediately upon the beast's fall - when Antichrist's time is ended 'he makes war against the witnesses, yea, overcometh and killeth them.' But the victory of evil is short-lived, for the two witnesses rise again after three and a half days. His readers were to take heart: 'assuredly, the acceptable year of Israel's jubilee, and the day of vengeance upon Antichrist, is coming, and is not far off.'[79]

Thus, perhaps surprisingly, Gillespie actually mentions 'presbyterial government' only in his last paragraph. Seeking to carry his audience with him as far as he can, he spends page after page outlining the common ground on which they can proceed, invoking the shared foundations of the protestant mythology and the paranoia of apocalypse to show finally - and decisively - that the ecclesiology of the Scottish Commissioners, rooted in the traditions of historic protestantism, was the only form of church government pure enough for the millennium. 'Give me leave, therefore, to quicken you to this part of the work, that, with all diligence and without delay, some presbyteries be associated and erected (in such places as yourselves in your wisdom shall judge fittest), with power to ordain ministers with the consent of the congregations ... "Arise therefore, and be doing, and the Lord be with thee".'[80]

This demand for collective action challenges any attempt to regard his sermon as a 'closed' text. 'Reformation ends not in contemplation, but in action.'[81] Closure then is taken from the sermon, as Gillespie moves beyond the text and requires closure in his audience. They become implicated in his text and are denied the autonomy of critical distance. Gillespie's theology, in other words, enacts his poetics of apocalypse.

---

[79] Gillespie, *Works*, i. 24.
[80] Gillespie, *Works*, i. 25.
[81] Gillespie, *Works*, i. 24.

Gillespie and the Poetics of Apocalypse

In both form and content, Gillespie's sermon was a model of millenarian exposition. Many of the rhetorical techniques which later writers would feature were here first explored. The Calvinistic emphasis on 'humbling' the reader, for example, is dramatised in Gillespie's rhetoric. His hermeneutics spiral as he argues that God is glorified in human incapacity: 'we must be confounded, that God may be glorified', he claimed. But he also warned that our hermeneutical incapacity may also be the result of divine curse: 'what wonder that they who receive not the love of the truth be given over to "strong delusion, that they should believe a lie?"'[82] Like the Geneva Bible's annotations, Gillespie argues that aspects of the gospel are revealed even when its message is not understood. God works in the gospel both for the salvation of the elect and the blinding of the reprobate. Ignorance is a result of God's judgement. Gillespie's argument does all it can to clarify his message, in turn threatening and cajoling, calling to remembrance the past blessings and invoking imminent apocalypse, in a desperate bid to influence public opinion before God's judgement is poured out on the land. But awareness of the reader's inability to impose closure on the sermon is not always negative. The form of Gillespie's rhetoric, which invites the reader to acknowledge his incapacity, constructs a lack of closure into a positive Christian hermeneutic. Gillespie advances a deliberate exploitation of Calvin's iconoclastic ideology: *finitum non est capax infiniti.*

Throughout his sermon, Gillespie pursues this attempt to humble his reader. His opening section, which justifies his comparison of Old Testament temple and New Testament church, outlines his hermeneutic strategy, and seeks to educate the reader into the proper method of interpretation. It also engages him in a circular method which is ultimately highly self-referential. At times Gillespie seems intent on maintaining an active reader, encouraging his involvement in the text. One footnote, for example, advises the reader to 'compare' parallel passages in *Ezekiel* and *Revelation* to prove their similarity. Nevertheless, at the same time the reader's involvement in the text is vigorously policed. Gillespie's narrative invites the reader to share his point of view: 'we must needs hold with Jerome, Gregory, and other later interpreters.'[83] Gillespie allows an interactive aperture of audience dialogue - 'Now, if you ask how the several particulars in the vision may be particularly expounded ...'[84] He anticipates and demarcates the questions his reader can ask.

---

[82] Gillespie, *Works*, i. 10.
[83] Gillespie, *Works*, i. 6.
[84] Gillespie, *Works*, i. 7.

His strategy of 'humbling' the reader also involves educating him into a particular hermeneutical method - which is immediately problematised. Like Foxe, Gillespie highlights the importance of history in the puritan hermeneutic. Gillespie answers critics who claim that the temple prophecy can be understood only through mathematical calculations by arguing that the supreme need is not Napier-like geometry but rather 'ecclesiometry', by which he means the knowledge of 'the church in her length, or continuance through many generations; in her breadth, or spreading through many nations; her depth of humiliation, sorrows and sufferings; her height of faith, hope, joy, and comfort.' For Gillespie - as for Foxe - knowledge of church history is a necessary prerequisite to a proper understanding of Scriptural prophecy.

Nevertheless, the reader was also instructed to 'measure each part [of church history] according to this pattern here set before us' (p. 7). Just as the Bible was to be explained by history, Gillespie claims, church history was to be arranged and explained through the parameters established in the Bible. The Bible creates, organises, and verifies an external reality - a reality which must be recognised to understand the Bible's creative, organisational, and verifying power. The argument is circular, a significant challenge to the Reformers' appeal to the perspicuity and sufficiency of Scripture: Gillespie seems to suggest that the Bible could be understood only by reference to texts outside its canon. As he confesses, there is 'great mystery here which I cannot reach'.

Like Foxe, Gillespie acknowledges that in certain circumstances a lack of historical application in Scriptural prophecy can also yield meaning and instruction. Abandoning the specific details of Foxe's arguments, Gillespie maintains the principles of the exile's thought: 'what agreeth not to the type must be meant of the thing typified; and what is not fulfilled at one time must be fulfilled of the church at another time.' The argument is complex: Gillespie alludes to the familiar Biblical hermeneutical strategy of 'type' and 'antitype', where the type is the prediction and the antitype the reality to which the prediction points. Gillespie's sermon has taken the Old Testament temple as a type of the church; the temple, in a sense, is the sign, and the church is the thing signified. But Reformed theology denies that Old and New Testament believers form two separate bodies - they are all members of one church. Gillespie compels his reader to conclude that the church is a type of itself. Like the later radicals, he conflates the distinction between sign and thing signified.

This quotation also evidences flexibility in Gillespie's approach, allowing him to claim that an event is a fulfilment of prophecy even if it does not exactly fit the original prediction: 'what is not fulfilled at one time must be fulfilled of the church at another time.'[85] Those parts of the prophecy which cannot find application - the prophetic 'excess' Patricia Parker expected - can simply be held over until the next fulfilment is decided upon. Application and alleged fulfilment, then, are almost arbitrary.

This harmonises with his attempts to invoke the closure of the Biblical text to conceal its very *lack* of closure. If Gillespie's 'rule' of interpretation demands that 'what is not fulfilled at one time must be fulfilled of the church at another time' he allows for a totally arbitrary allocation of 'fulfilment' irrespective of how closely the historical fulfilment matches its alleged prediction. There is no need to find any extended correspondence when the most arbitrary common detail might suffice. Gillespie's hermeneutical strategy takes advantage of a lack of closure to indefinitely replicate its own authority: if certain details are to be carried over from this fulfilment to the next, this lack of closure works to maintain the expectation that the next fulfilment will be closed. To admit that a prophecy had been fulfilled was to admit that its authoritarian flexibility had ended. To point only to 'partial fulfilments' was to consolidate its authority and maintain the rhetorical space which allowed for new interpretations.

Such 'spaces' in the interpretative discourse were central in the evolving dialogue of post-Renaissance Biblical criticism: as Debora Shuger comments, 'mythic transformations were possible because in Renaissance practice the biblical narratives retained a certain (if limited) flexibility: not necessarily a theological flexibility but a sort of extradogmatic surplus of undetermined meaning - or rather meaning capable of being interpreted in various ways.'[86] Consequently, Gillespie's lack of closure could also work as a potent claim for textual authority. Gillespie's sermon was able to capitalise on its weakness to construct its most powerful claim for authority.

The presence of interpretative space left Gillespie with a trump card. The subject of his sermon - the Old Testament temple - had found its glory in its articulation as a site for the manifestation of the transcendent God. The 'greatest glory' of the old temple, Gillespie claims, was that '"the glory of the God of Israel" came into it.'[87] That temple was 'successful' because it could not even begin to attempt to 'close' the reality it contained. 'But will God indeed dwell on the earth? behold, the heaven and heaven of heavens cannot contain thee; how much less this house that I have builded?' (1 *Kings* 8:27). Gillespie, on this basis, attempts to capitalise upon his apparent weakness; after describing the

[85] Gillespie, *Works*, i. 7.
[86] Shuger, *The Renaissance Bible*, p. 5.
[87] Gillespie, *Works*, i. 22.

temple, Gillespie's sermon attempts to become one. Only the reader's awareness of Gillespie's 'failures' to close his text allows for the recognition that in its moment of apparent defeat it most closely resembles the Jewish temple as a site for the transcendence of God. Gillespie's text mimics the subject it describes. In allowing interpretative spaces, Gillespie is enacting his theology, and further conflating the distinction between form and content, between the sermon and its subject.

This is why Gillespie's sermon, though inviting reader-response criticism in its claim to shape a reader, must always subvert it. The ultimate way for Gillespie to ensure the humiliation of his readers is for him to ensure that they confront his transcendent God. His sermon becomes a catalyst for theophany, a site where the divine presence is manifest. Gillespie's sermon points past itself, invoking the transcendence of God and guarding its 'referential status'.[88] It is a sign, not an icon. Gillespie's rhetorical devices ensure that his reader is pointed to his *lack* of closure, and then *past* his lack of closure to the God whom that lack of closure describes. He capitalises on his inability to close the infinite.

Gillespie's ultimate concern, then, is more with representing God than manipulating his reader - though admittedly both ideas are closely associated in Calvinist thought. Calvin began his *Institutes* with the maxim that 'it is certain that man never achieves a clear knowledge of himself unless he has first looked upon God's face, and then descends from contemplating him to contemplating himself.'[89] In a sense, then, the initial worries over adequate humiliation are a trick, designed no doubt to intrigue the curious into reading on, before finally they come face to face with the hermeneutics of their fallen humanity. The transience of their interpretations, and the profundity of Gillespie's subject-matter, force them to acknowledge the limits of human perception. Such was the first step toward the knowledge of Gillespie's God.

Struggling with the problem of how human language could contain the infinite, Gillespie locates his sermon within the Reformed discourse of worship, the rediscovery of the transcendence of God and the human impossibility of adequately describing him. Calvin had argued that God's infinity 'ought to make us afraid to try to measure him by our own senses'.[90] As a consequence, Gillespie's sermon foregrounds its own lack of closure, pointing to the God who alone transcends the textual web. God is best described in the silences and through the

---

[88] Gregerson, *The Reformation of the Subject*, pp. 2-4.

[89] Calvin, *Institutes*, i. i. 2.

[90] Calvin, *Institutes*, i. xiii. 1.

difficulties of Gillespie's text. The poetics of his Covenanting millenarianism point to the God who transcends space and time.

The Aftermath of the Covenanter Millennium

Despite his employment of rhetorical structures, Gillespie's sermon failed to have the effect he had intended. As the summer of 1644 approached, the unity of the puritan brotherhood continued to crumble. At the end of May Rutherford was growing disconsolate about the success of his work: 'the truth is, we have at time grieved spirits with the work; and for my part, I often despair of the reformation of this land, which saw never anything but the high places of their fathers and the remnants of Babylon's pollutions.'[91]

That summer, the Scottish divines were decisively outflanked within the Assembly. The Independents were seconded into a committee with the Scots to prepare a preface to the *Directory for Public Worship*. This was a pretence to divert the Independents from further obstructing the Assembly's progress towards the introduction of Presbytery. Nevertheless this action brought together those parties representing the most consistent millenarian influences.[92] The text they prepared reflects their shared eschatology and sense of the importance of the historical moment, arguing that 'in these latter times ... God vouchsafeth to his people more and better means for the discovery of error and superstition, and for attaining of knowledge in the mysteries of godliness, and gifts in preaching and prayer.' Similarly, 'the gracious providence of God ... at this time calleth upon us for further reformation.'[93]

Nevertheless, the work of the Assembly drove the Presbyterians and the Independents increasingly apart. Baillie, always the least affable of the Scots, was the first to offer a reinterpretation of their alliance with the Independents. By April 1644, only weeks after Gillespie's sermon, he was privately acknowledging that 'likely ... we will be forced to deal with them as open enemies';[94] perhaps, like William Hetherington, two centuries later, he understood the *Apologeticall Narration* of the Independent brethren as a 'declaration of war'.[95] Elements on both sides determined to force a confrontation. In February the Five Dissenting Brethren - the leaders of the Independent faction at Westminster - had explicitly denied that it could ever 'enter into our hearts to judge'

---

[91] Rutherford, *Letters*, p. 618.
[92] See also Baillie, *Letters and Journals*, ii. 242.
[93] *Subordinate Standards*, pp. 136-7.
[94] Baillie, *Letters and Journals*, ii. 168.
[95] Hetherington, *History of the Westminster Assembly of Divines*, p. 189.

Presbyterianism as antichristian. But others did - Baillie records that allegations that the Westminster Assembly was 'ane Antichristian meeting, which did erect a Presbyterie worse than Bishops'.[96] Others calculated that the Solemn League and Covenant numbered 666 words.[97] By June, in a joint introduction to that seminal defence of the 'New England way', John Cotton's *The Keys of the Kingdom of Heaven* (1644), Thomas Goodwin and Philip Nye lamented the 'sharpest contentions' of 'these knowing times'.[98] Nevertheless, both sides seemed entrenched in their opposing ecclesiologies.

Soon others joined the debate. Following books like John Smyth's *The Character of the Beast* (1609), baptist sectaries attacked the paedobaptist position of Presbyter and Independent alike: in 1644 Christopher Blackwood led *The Storming of Antichrist in his two last and strongest Garrisons, Of Compulsion of Conscience and Infants Baptism*. Others argued against the Calvinistic basis of all the above groups, 'they are that great Antichrist ... who deny the general redemption of ... the whole creation.' John Milton described the demands of the new regime as 'worse than those of Trent' before clinching his famous motto: 'New Presbyter is but old Priest writ large.'[99]

Fearing the rise of the radical sectaries, the Presbyterians initiated the first of the Revolution's reactionary withdrawals. As the 1640s wore on, and the failure of the Westminster Assembly became evident, they began a slow retreat from millenarian engagement. Coffey notes that by November 1647, when Rutherford finally left the Assembly's debates, 'all his work to establish Presbyterian government in England seemed in danger of collapse.'[100] The sectaries, formerly represented by the mainstream Independents like Goodwin and Nye, had found a new champion in Oliver Cromwell, rising with his Ironsides after his victory at Marston Moor in June 1644.[101] Slowly but surely the puritan brethren were polarising into competing factions.

For some, these very divisions were a sign of the times. Archibald Johnston, the 'Fifth Monarchy Presbyterian',[102] advised the Westminster divines that 'until KING JESUS be set doun on his throne, with his scepter

---

[96] Lamont, *Godly Rule*, pp. 110-2; Baillie, *Letters and Journals*, ii. 145.

[97] Hill, *Antichrist in Seventeenth-Century England*, p. 91.

[98] Woodhouse (ed.), *Puritanism and Liberty*, p. 293.

[99] Milton, 'On the New Forcers of Conscience Under the Long Parliament', ll. 14, 20, in *The Works of John Milton*, gen. ed. Frank A. Patterson (New York: Columbia University Press, 1931-40), i.

[100] Coffey, *Politics, Religion and the British Revolutions*, p. 54.

[101] Hill, *God's Englishman*, p. 70.

[102] Christopher Hill, *The Experience of Defeat: Milton and Some Contemporaries* (London: Faber and Faber, 1984), p. 77.

in his hand, I do not expect God's peace, and so no solide peace from men in those kingdomes; but that soveraigne truth being established, a durable peace will be found to follow thereupon.'[103] The Independent leaders expressed their disappointment at the failure of theocracy by moving, for a short while, toward more extreme positions.[104] Thomas Goodwin lurched toward the left, moving from the relative safety of his 1639 commentary on *Revelation* and the 1641 *Glimpse* to become something of a hero among the Fifth Monarchists.

Others were less than enthusiastic. Thomas Hayne's *Christs Kingdom on Earth, Opened According to the Scriptures* (1645) blamed the Long Parliament's republication of *A Glimpse* and the works of Brightman, Alsted, Mede, and Archer for the eschatologically-(mis)informed tenor of the Civil War. Hayne was implicitly acknowledging the success of the Long Parliament's republishing campaign: as we have seen, with the exception of the works of Brightman, all these books had been first published, or at least translated into English, in only the preceding five years.

Baillie's *A Dissuasive from the Errors of the Times* (1645) continued to berate the Independents. Baillie - once their ally - condemned their hope that the Independent system of church government

> is a beginning, or at least a near antecedent of Christs Kingdome upon Earth. That within five years Christ is to come in the flesh; and by a Sword of Iron, to kill with his own hand the most of his enemies; and therefore to passe over a thousand years as a worldly Monarch with his Saints: Who shall live with him all that time in all sorts of fleshly delights. Mr. Archer they onely Pastor that ever they had, whose praises they sound forth so loud in their Apologetick, would persuade us of the same, and more grosse stories. Mr. Burrowes in his late Sermons upon Hosea, runs in the same way.[105]

He thundered against the millennialism of some Independents, complaining that such 'chiliasm' was condemned until 'the Anabaptists did draw it out of its grave':

> it was by all Protestants contemned; onely Alstedius, after his long abode in Transilvania, began in his last times to fall into likeing with some parts thereof, pretending some passages of Piscator for his incouragement. Alstedius Heterodox Writings were not long abroad, when Mr. Meade at Cambridge was gained to follow him: yet both these Divines were farre from dreaming of any personall raigne of Christ upon earth: Onely Mr. Archer, and his Colleague T[homas].G[oodwin]. at Arnheim, were bold to

---

[103] Quoted in Burrell, 'The Apocalyptic Vision of the Early Covenanters', p. 21.
[104] de Jong, *As the Waters Cover the Sea*, p. 41.
[105] Baillie, *A Dissausive from the Errors of the Times*, p. 80.

set up the whole Fabrick of Chiliasm, which necessary and most comfortable ground of Christian Religion, to be infused into the hearts of all children by the care of every parent at the Catechising of their family.[106]

Thus the disputes over church government were highlighting eschatology as a site containing profound implications for ecclesiology. Where the Scottish conservatives and the English radicals had earlier found common ground they now allowed no more than hostile suspicion.

Thus, in spring 1644, the puritan movement split between those who favoured Presbytery and those who preferred the establishment of Independent churches after the pattern of New England. Presbyterians stepped back from the brink of the millennium to work for a national church counting both elect and reprobate among its members; Independents pressed ahead in their determination to allow only the saints the privileges of the new age. Before 1644, Haller notes,

the independents and the separatists of all sorts remained relatively obscure and seemed unimportant. After that date, they suddenly came forward to oppose the majority in the Assembly, disrupt its plans, multiply sermons and pamphlets beyond number, fill Cromwell's army, push forward a revolution far more sweeping than any which the original Puritan reformers had conceived, and eventually to give the term Puritan the meaning it has to a large extent since retained.[107]

But, ironically, it was the Presbyterian withdrawal from apocalyptic warfare which allowed all that went after. The Scots had invested the revolution with a revisionist millenarian momentum, stripping it of the external controls which consolidated the status quo. As their new apocalyptic worldview evolved from being one war's symptom to another war's cause, they watched its development with fear.

---

[106] Baillie, *A Dissausive from the Errors of the Times*, p. 224.

[107] William Haller, *The Rise of Puritanism: or, the way to the New Jerusalem as set forth in pulpit and press from Thomas Cartwright to John Lilburne and John Milton, 1570-1643* (1938; rpt. New York: Columbia University Press, 1957), p. 174.

CHAPTER 6

John Milton and the Reaction to the Westminster Assembly

Some of the first responses to the theocratic claims of the Westminster Assembly were made by the self-appointed spokesman of the sectaries, John Milton (1608-74). Attacking Baillie and Rutherford in his sonnet 'On the new forcers of conscience' and satirising Gillespie in Sonnet XI ('A book was writ of late called *Tetrachordon*'), Milton's hostility towards the Scots was provoked by their influential attempts to impose a strict Presbyterian discipline on England. In 1644 the Westminster divines were outlining a system of book licensing which, Milton believed, would be absolutely antithetical to the progress of reformation. The eschatological tenor of their Covenanting programme was matched by Milton's equally eschatological rebuttal of their claims. The Westminster divines' attempts to safeguard the ecclesiology of their millennium were attacked in Milton's defence of the sole means by which his millennium might be attained. His defence of free inquiry built upon the Scots' investigation of apocalyptic rhetoric, but voiced a poised and reasoned interrogation of their assumptions.

Milton understood the Scots' attempts to control the press as a serious attack on reformation. In *Areopagitica* (1644), his extended analysis of the Presbyterian threat, he alluded to a Biblical passage describing the situation of a nation abandoned by God. God intended to 'send even a faintness' into the hearts of the exiled Israelites, 'and the sound of a leafe shaken shall chase them' (*Leviticus* 26:36). Milton threatened the Presbyterian theocrats with the vengeance of the God whose kingdom they believed they were establishing: under licensing, he punned, 'when God shakes a Kingdom', men would 'fear each book and the shaking of every leaf'.[1]

Milton's pun alluded to the Hebrew conception of the apocalyptic Day of the Lord, which was symbolised, in biblical register, by the 'shaking of an olive tree' (*Isaiah* 24:13). The threat to the leaves of trees

---

[1] Milton, *Works*, iv. 350, iv. 331. Unless otherwise noted, page numbers cite John Milton, *Areopagitica* (1644), in *The Works of John Milton*, gen. ed. Frank A. Patterson (New York: Columbia University Press, 1931-40), vol. iv.

(in Hebrew thought) and books (in Milton's thought) signalled this end. For some puritans writers, the apocalypse was becoming a curiously textual affair where the earth and its books would be subject to increasing tumult as the final days approached. It was becoming a test of textual authority as much as orthodoxy. A sign of its times, Milton's *Areopagitica* struggles at the edge of literary expression to contain the forces it describes. Literary critics have responded appropriately. Haller described *Areopagitica* as 'not a pamphlet but a poem';[2] Christopher Kendrick described how it 'responds to the exigencies of its political context more subtly and perhaps more comprehensively than any other of [Milton's] pamphlets'.[3] In *Areopagitica*, Milton's ideology crafted poetry from doctrine, and positioned itself at the forefront of God's new light.

Milton and Eschatology

Milton's self-conscious display of the Elizabethan roots of his eschatology marks his text as part of the canon of puritan millenarian literature. More so than the other writers we have already examined, Milton's creative mind defies systematic containment.[4] Throughout his writing life, his philosophy of history developed and evolved, shaping and being shaped by the turbulent events of those various civil wars throughout the three kingdoms. As David Loewenstein notes, individual tracts mirror the confusion of their times; they

> never offer a fully or consistently developed philosophy of history. Rather, they are occasional works in which Milton responds creatively to an immediate sense of historical drama ... Only in the great poems, and especially in Michael's prophecy concluding *Paradise Lost*, do we encounter a more sustained meditation on the uneven, turbulent course of postlapsarian history, with all its tribulations, tragic conflicts, and uncertainties.[5]

Ideas of any sort were rarely fixed for Milton; when 'all the windes of doctrine were let loose to play upon the earth', those which prevailed pushed him into ever increasing heresy.[6] Milton did compile his own

---

[2] Quoted in Edward le Comte, *Milton's Unchanging Mind: Three Essays* (Port Washington: Kennikat Press, 1973), p. 71.

[3] Christopher Kendrick, *Milton: A Study in Ideology and Form* (London: Methuen, 1986), p. 19.

[4] Cummins (ed.), *Milton and the ends of time*, contains several essays relevant to this discussion.

[5] Loewenstein, *Milton and the Drama of History*, p. 6.

[6] Milton, *Works*, iv. 347.

systematic theology, *De doctrina christiana*, begun in 1640 and unpublished at his death, but the lack of stasis in his thought prevents the modern reader from simply turning to this to read the fruit of his life's study back into his earlier work. Milton's theology evolved throughout his lifetime, and in his early years he publicly committed himself to ideas which, upon more deliberate reflection, he later abandoned. The invocation opening the closing prayer in *Of Reformation* (1641), for example, is an appeal to the 'Tri-personall GODHEAD' whose existence *De doctrina* famously denies.[7]

Similar forces are at work in Milton's eschatology. Some critics, among them John Spencer Hill, have projected a conservative Milton, espousing the postmillennial theology of mainstream puritanism. Others qualify this conservatism. Loewenstein's insightful studies have equated Milton's mature premillennialism with that of his Cambridge tutor, Joseph Mede.[8] The famous 'Samson' passage in *Areopagitica* certainly seems to betray the influence of the English translation of Mede's *Clavis* (1643). In 1644, Milton saw 'in my mind a noble and puissant Nation rousing herself like a strong man after sleep, and shaking her invincible locks'.[9] One year earlier, in the introduction to the *Clavis*, William Twisse described 'God awaking as it were out of a sleep, and like a gyant refreshed with wine: and the Lord Christ awaking, and stirring up his strength for the raising up of Jacob, and restoring the desolations of Israel, and blessing us with a resurrection of his Gospel, and discovering the man of sin, and blasting him with the breath of his mouth.'[10] But Milton seems in places to have surpassed even Mede's radical thought. Mede denied any personal reign of Christ upon earth, but Milton and the radical sectaries disagreed.

Based on the supposition that Milton's ideas were (or became) static, the paradigm within which the 'Miltonic worldview' debate is conducted is fraught with difficulty. Criticism of the sort which searches for or analyses a text in relation to a fixed 'Miltonic ideology' is ultimately inadequate. Accounts which seek to discuss the overall tenor of Milton's eschatology in words other than 'proximate' and 'imminent' are doomed to failure.[11] If Milton's eschatology was never fixed, or even if it only became fixed later in his life, the matured thinking he presents

---

[7] Milton, *Works*, iii. 76.

[8] Hill, *Milton and the English Revolution*, p. 393; A.L. Rowse, *Milton the Puritan: Portrait of a Mind* (London: Macmillan, 1977), p. 206; Loewenstein, *Milton and the Drama of History*, p. 12.

[9] Milton, *Works*, iv. 344.

[10] Mede, *The Key of the Revelation*, sig. b2.

[11] Michael Fixler, *Milton and the Kingdoms of God* (London: Faber and Faber, 1964), p. 213.

in *De doctrina* has little relevance to the composition of his earlier works
- unless the reader is interested in drawing a line of intellectual
development from his first known English verse, 'On the Death of a Fair
Infant' (1628), to his posthumously-published systematic theology
(1825). In the absence of any other evidence, Milton's evolving
eschatological understanding must be deduced in each case from the
internal evidence of individual texts, and here it is fortunate that his one
constant certainty - that his war was with Antichrist - demanded the
continual foregrounding of his shifting eschatological ideas.

Thus the younger Milton is several steps away from his later
literalism. 'On the Morning of Christ's Nativity' (1629), for example,
argues for the non-millennial commonplace that the incarnation of
Christ initiated the binding of Satan described in *Revelation* 20:

> ... from this happy day
> Th' old Dragon under ground
> In straiter limits bound,
> Not half so far casts his usurped sway[12]

Much of the early prose, at the same time, invokes the idea of an
imminent apocalypse. *Of Reformation* (1641) describes Christ as 'the
Eternall and shortly-expected King [who shall] open the Clouds to
judge the severall Kingdomes of the World'.[13] Understanding the
millennium to have been fulfilled in the past, the young Milton did not
apparently believe that any other prophecies were yet to be
accomplished before Christ could return. This reflects the early puritan
tradition of Bale and Foxe, before the Geneva Bible popularised the
'conversion of the Jews' motif.

This Augustinianism did not go long unchallenged. Milton
experienced an increasing disenchantment with the roots of this
Genevan ideology. It is certain that he admired and used the Geneva
translation of the Bible, but he increasingly qualified and finally
abandoned its annotations on *Revelation* and those espousing Calvinistic
orthodoxy.[14] His relationship with Foxe's martyrology is more
problematic, partly, as we have seen, because scholars still debate what
it was that Foxe believed.[15]

One concept which has been traced to the *Acts and Monuments* is that
of the 'elect nation'. This topos certainly features in Milton's prose. Early
in his career, for example, Milton had supported those Presbyterians

[12] Milton, 'On the Morning of Christ's Nativity', ll. 167-170, in Milton, *Works*, i.
[13] Milton, *Works*, iii. 5, 78.
[14] Hill, *Milton and the English Revolution*, p. 395.
[15] Olsen, 'Was John Foxe a Millenarian?', pp. 600-1.

who had collectively attacked Bishop Hall's defence of episcopacy. Under a pen-name created by the juxtaposition of their initials, SMECTYMNUUS, they had collectively endorsed a modification of the 'elect nation' idea, combining it with a sweeping attack on Episcopal offices. This type of ideology became common currency in the sermons before Parliament in the 1640s. *Of Reformation* echoed this sentiment, lauding England as 'the first Restorer of buried Truth'. *Areopagitica* confirmed England's special status in history: 'why else was this Nation chosen before any other, that out of her as out of Sion, should be proclam'd and sounded forth the first tidings and trumpet of Reformation to all Europ ... God is decreeing to begin some new and great period in his Church, ev'n to the reforming of Reformation it self: what does he then but reveal Himself to his servants, and as his manner is, first to his English men.'[16] Nevertheless, like Stephen Marshall and the other SMECTYMNUUS Presbyterians, Milton combined this 'elect nation' posturing with a swift indictment of the ideology by which Ussher and Foxe had consolidated the offices of bishop and king.[17] His anti-Episcopal tracts are among his first works to renegotiate the received Elizabethan commonplaces.

Of Reformation, for example, was quite explicit in its antipathy to Constantine, the original of the 'godly prince'. Milton could not understand why 'hee must needs bee the Load-starre of Reformation as some men clatter'; from Milton's point of view, Constantine's reign concurred with the time when 'Antichrist began first to put forth his horne'.[18] Some of this text's Latin verses deliberately aligned the emperor with the Church's last enemy:

> Impudent whoore, where hast thou plac'd thy hope?
> In thy Adulterers, or thy ill got wealth?
> Another Constantine comes not in hast.[19]

Milton transposed his historiographical revisionism into politically-loaded ecclesiology: 'there is just cause therefore that when the Prelates cry out Let the Church be reform'd according to Constantine, it should sound to a judicious eare no otherwise, than if they should say Make us rich, make us lofty, make us lawlesse.'[20]

Nevertheless, although Milton criticised the prelates for self-aggrandisement, his 'elect nation' ideology served to accentuate his own

---

[16] Milton, *Works*, iv. 340.
[17] Milton, *Works*, iii. 5.
[18] Milton, *Works*, iii. 23, 25.
[19] Milton, *Works*, iii. 27.
[20] Milton, *Works*, iii. 23, 25, 28.

status. Milton aspired to be England's greatest national poet and a peer of the classical writers. Consequently, he was highly interested in the cultural implications of England's election. Perhaps basing his thinking on the Renaissance *translatio studii* topos, which taught that virtue was moving steadily westward from Italy, Milton was scripting his own immortality when he imagined history stopping with England ascendant, and himself as the country's greatest literary figure. *Of Reformation* ends with his imagining the time 'when thou the Eternall and shortly-expected King shalt open the Clouds to judge the severall Kingdomes of the World'. Milton's thoughts were on his own millennial role: 'amidst the Hymns, and Halleluiahs of Saints some one may perhaps bee heard offering at high strains in new and lofty Measures to sing and celebrate thy divine Mercies, and marvelous Judgements in this Land throughout all AGES.'[21] Milton's construction of his identity as a prophet was feasible only as long as it could be interpreted within the paradigm of the nation's divine calling.

Aspects of this elect nation topos entered mainstream English political discourse. England was paralleled with Zion: Stephen Marshall claimed that Parliament was constituted by 'the chosen men of your Tribes',[22] and *Areopagitica's* puritan leaders were described by Milton as a Sanhedrin-like 'sev'nty Elders'.[23] Like Gillespie, Milton overlooks the reforming potential of the monarch and addresses his rhetoric to the Parliament. He also invokes the 'temple-building' topos, alluding as early as 1641 to the same passage that his Presbyterian rival would later employ: 'it cannot be wonder'd if that elegant and artful symmetry of the promised new temple in *Ezechiel*, and all those sumptuous things under the Law were made to signifie the inward beauty and splendour of the Christian Church thus govern'd.'[24] So pervasive in the puritan revolution, the metaphor of Jewish reconstruction was used to figure the continuing process of establishing a fully reformed church, whose projected pattern moved, in Milton, through Presbyterianism to Independency and beyond.

Similar combinations of apocalypticism and social critique can be found Milton's other productions from this period. Through his studies of the Biblical teaching on divorce, a treatise *Of Education*, and several more anti-Episcopalian pamphlets we can trace a growing disenchantment with the Presbyterian polity of the Westminster divines and an increasing sense that Milton's interest was less in 'The

---

[21] Milton, *Works*, iii. 78.
[22] Stephen Marshall, *A Sermon Preached before the Honourable House of Commons ... November 17. 1640* (1641), p. 29.
[23] Milton, *Works*, iv. 342.
[24] Milton, *Works*, iii. 191.

Reformation' as an historical event than as a continuing process - a process which would culminate only at the moment of eschatological triumph.

Paradoxically, Milton's growing expectation of the millennium was determined by his look to the past. *The Doctrine and Discipline of Divorce* (1643), for example, extrapolated ideal marriage practice from the example of Adam and Eve.[25] Similarly, the reforms described in *Of Education* (1644) were intended 'to repair the ruins of our first Parents by regaining to know God aright'.[26] Cotton Mather placed this type of Edenic millenarianism at the very heart of puritan identity: 'the First Age was the Golden Age: to return to That, will make a Man a Protestant, and I may add, a Puritan.'[27] Because his scheme of providential history moved in a great cycle from one Eden to another, Milton and his fellow puritans could look to the experience of their first parents to anticipate their own destiny. Salvation would restore to mankind all that their first parents lost. The struggle for the rights of the saints was in essence a struggle to regain the freedom their first parents had squandered in the Fall.

Puritans, in adopting this Eden-consciousness, became the prisoners of their times. As is well known, many Renaissance projects looked to the past for a programme of future action.[28] The etymology of 'revolution' and 'restoration' show the potency and immediacy of such historical awareness in the seventeenth century: both the regicide in 1649 and those events surrounding the Restoration of Charles II in 1660 were interpreted as returns to a better age, though by different people and for different reasons. Graham Parry has remarked that the 'very term 'Restoration' carried with it a religious connotation, associated with the idea of return to an original state of perfection', and Hill has made a similar point in claiming that the 'usage of 'revolution' follows the thought of those who originally looked to the distant past (the Garden of Eden, the primitive church, the free Anglo-Saxons) and then discovered that they were really looking to the future'.[29] There was a similar movement in linguistic investigation. Perhaps encouraged by the familiar Renaissance topos of a universal 'natural' language, Bunyan regarded Hebrew as the prelapsarian 'holy language'. Other puritans gave this topos an infusion of apocalypse: Richard Kidder urged Christians to study Hebrew to hasten the conversion of the Jews, while

---

[25] Milton, *Works*, iii. 396.
[26] Milton, *Works*, iv. 277.
[27] Quoted in Lamont, *Puritanism and Historical Controversy*, p. 132.
[28] Hill, *Milton and the English Revolution*, p. 346.
[29] Parry, *The Golden Age Restor'd*, p. 108; Hill, *A Nation of Change and Novelty*, p. 83.

the Fifth Monarchist William Aspinwall took the argument one step beyond, encouraging his brethren to learn Hebrew in preparation for the millennium, when all prelapsarian norms would be reinstated.[30]

This type of Eden-consciousness frames Milton's understanding of history. The moment of re-creation to which all history moves is the moment when the present dichotomy of material and spiritual finally gives way and the world finds itself back where it begun. As we shall see, John Rogers would later imagine Independent churches as nearing the stage when they would no longer need the mediating help of preachers, sacraments, or Bibles. The final moment he envisaged would be one of total inter-penetration, an everlasting moment when, as Milton imagined it,

> Earth be chang'd to Heav'n, & Heav'n to Earth,
> One Kingdom, Joy and Union without end.[31]

It was to be the eternal conflation of physical and spiritual realms, an imitation of the first Eden, itself a 'new-made world, another heaven', the nexus of two disparate realities.[32] Then would be the 'new heavens' and 'new earth, according to his promise, wherein dwelleth righteousnesse' (2 *Peter* 3:13). Then would return the 'golden days, fruitful of golden deeds'.[33] But, in his inter-Paradise parenthesis, Milton constructs meaning from a history *in medias res*. Conflating reality and its representation - history and mimesis - Milton's history was itself in epic form.

In *De doctrina* Milton's mature thought moved from the allegorical to the literal interpretation of Biblical eschatology. Certain of a sudden second advent, preceded by 'false prophets, false Christs, wars, earthquakes, persecutions, pestilence, famine, and the gradual decay of faith and charity',[34] he is aware that some of his puritan colleagues expect a general calling of the Jews, but cautiously reserves his own judgement on that matter. Surprisingly, he is less hesitant about the

---

30 Bunyan, *Works*, ii. 500; Paul J. Korshin, *Typologies in England* (Princeton: Princeton University Press, 1982), p. 333; J.F. Maclear, 'New England and the Fifth Monarchy: The Quest for the Millennium in Early American Puritanism', in Alden T. Vaughan and Francis J. Bremer (eds), *Puritan New England: Essays on Religion, Society and Culture* (New York: St. Martin's Press, 1977), p. 81; Nigel Smith, 'The Uses of Hebrew in the English Revolution', in Peter Burke and Roy Porter (eds), *Language, Self and Society: A Social History of Language* (Cambridge: Polity Press, 1991), *passim*.
31 *PL* vii. 160-1.
32 *PL* vii. 617.
33 *PL* iii. 337.
34 Milton, *Works*, xvii. 341.

millennium:

> beginning with [the Last Judgement's] commencement, and extending a
> little beyond its conclusion, will take place that glorious reign of Christ on
> earth with his saints, so often promised in Scripture, even until all his
> enemies shall be subdued. His kingdom of grace, indeed, which is also
> called "the kingdom of heaven", began with his first advent, when its
> beginning was proclaimed by John the Baptist, as appears from testimony
> of Scripture; but his kingdom of glory will not commence till his second
> advent.[35]

This is an unhesitating premillennial argument which, like Mede,
parallels the length of the Day of Judgement with the millennium, but
differs from the Cambridge scholar in asserting that Christ would
actually reign in person on earth, as we noted. Milton claims that 'the
"judgement" here spoken of will not be confined to a single day, but
will extend through a great space of time; and that the word is used to
denote, not so much a judicial inquiry properly so called, as an exercise
of dominion.'[36] Judicial sentencing is reserved until after the end of the
thousand years, when Satan is again unleashed to 'assail the church at
the head of an immense confederacy of its enemies; but will be
overthrown by fire from heaven, and condemned to everlasting
punishment'.[37] In chapter one, we noticed the inadequacy of the *Milton
Encyclopaedia*'s description of his 'millennialism' as 'conventional' and
'thoroughly neutral and devoid of immediacy'. This definition is a good
description of some aspects of the pietism of some varieties of
contemporary American fundamentalism, but is hardly sympathetic to
Milton's place amid the revolutionary nuances of seventeenth-century
England.[38] Milton was moving a long way from the millennial apathy of
the 'Nativity Ode'.

There were, nevertheless, aspects of the Genevan heritage which
Milton never abandoned. Hill describes Milton as a consistently 'radical
millenarian' who retained a Foxian 'vision of England as leader of an
international revolution'.[39] Although he rebutted Junius in *De doctrina*
and attacked Constantine in *Of Reformation*, Milton was always sound
on the identification of Antichrist and the existence of progressive
revelation.[40]

The very existence of progressive revelation, in fact, was central to

35 Milton, *Works*, xvii. 359.
36 Milton, *Works*, xvii. 359.
37 Milton, *Works*, xvii. 363.
38 Hunter (gen. ed.), *A Milton Encyclopaedia*, v. 132.
39 Hill, *Milton and the English Revolution*, p. 106.
40 Milton, *Works*, xvii. 359.

Milton's developing thought. The very fact that he abandoned many of his original intellectual positions demonstrated his sensitivity to the 'new light' shining in his day. But on this staple of the Genevan heritage Milton constructed an elaborate defence against the eschatological claims of the Westminster divines. Milton's obsession with progressive revelation developed into an eschatological epistemology which emphasised the progression of revelation, the continual out-breaking of new light. His eschatological epistemology emphasised that truth was continually being clarified, and that our seeing 'through a glass darkly' would soon be replaced by our seeing immediately, at the return of Christ. 'Now I know in part,' Paul wrote in the Geneva Bible, 'but then I shall know even as I am knowen' (*1 Corinthians* 13:12). Recognising that the Westminster divines' licensing bill would forbid the publication of whatever new thinking challenged the Presbyterian consensus, Milton worried that their eschatologically-justified theonomy was actually preventing the second advent. Once again, the puritan apocalypse was turning in upon itself, arguing that its former incarnation opposed its actual end. It is this tense ambivalence which fuels the potency of *Areopagitica*.

Areopagitica and the Westminster Assembly

Areopagitica, Milton's greatest exploration of the Presbyterian threat, is grounded in his developing eschatology. Its concept of national election is determinedly ambivalent. Despite Milton's profoundly historical consciousness, *Areopagitica* is more concerned with Italian history than English heroes. It pre-empts the paradox of *Paradise Lost*, whose initial design as a 'British' epic would be obscured in the significant omissions from its great summary of church history - where no mention of a native reformation would be made.[41] *Areopagitica* anticipates Milton's significant later reversals: after the pan-European Calvinist front collapsed with the condemnation of the 1649 regicide by the Dutch Republic, the French Huguenots, and the Scottish Presbyterians, Milton's own theological research took him away from his initial Genevan orthodoxy.[42] Forced to find a faithful remnant somewhere other than in the crescent sweeping from Geneva, his research into British history confirmed the existence of a perpetually faithful remnant. These were not the heroes of Foxe and Ussher, however; they were those groups espousing mortalism, anti-Trinitarianism, and the other heresies in which Milton was dabbling. *Areopagitica* anticipates this trend.

---

[41] *PL* xii. 502-43.
[42] Hill, *Milton and the English Revolution*, pp. 166-7.

Areopagitica demonstrates that even in the mid-1640s Milton feared that the Continental and English reformations could yet prove of little significance. There was ample opportunity for the puritan elite represented at the Westminster Assembly to effect no greater change than the identity of the tyrant. Thus Milton's description of a Christendom bound under papal bondage is very similar to his complaints in *Areopagitica* of those 'new forcers of conscience', who

> Spiritual Lawes by carnal power shall force
> On every conscience; Laws which none shall finde
> Left them inrould, or what the Spirit within
> Shall on the heart engrave. What will they then
> But force the Spirit of Grace it self, and binde
> His consort Libertie; what, but unbuild
> His living Temples, built by Faith to stand,
> Thir own Faith not anothers[43]

This is to criticise the Westminster divines for the same things for which Gillespie had criticised the Anglicans.

Consequently, Milton appears less concerned with tracing the ebb and flow of Catholic power than in mirroring the old priests and new presbyters. Both represent the same Antichristian tyranny of conscience. He 'could not give the Puritan Reformation any historical significance'[44] when

> Men whose Life, Learning, Faith and pure intent
>   Would have been held in high esteem with Paul
>   Must now be nam'd and printed Hereticks.[45]

Milton's history performs a related function: in *Areopagitica* history is a weapon to outline the repressive Catholic origins of licensing. Milton shows affinity with Rogers, who would argue that 'these Prelatical Presbyterians take the people by guile and craft, pretending Antiquity, and that they came from far, when indeed their Discipline came but from Rome, or the Councel of Trent, in a Novelty.'[46] It was not in defeat, but in 'the barrenness of victory', that the Independents were forced to re-evaluate the 'puritan pact'.

Narrating his Italian journey allows Milton to parallel the horrors of papal despotism with the Presbyterian licensing bill: 'it was as little in

---

[43] *PL* xii. 521-527.
[44] Trevor-Roper, *Catholics, Anglicans and Puritans*, p. 281.
[45] Milton, 'On the new forcers of conscience', ll. 10-12, in Milton, *Works*, i.
[46] Rogers, *Ohel*, p. 59.

my fear, that what words of complaint I heard among lerned men of
other parts utter'd against the Inquisition, the same I should hear by as
learned men at home utterd in time of Parlament ... [Licensing] will
soon put it out of controversie that Bishops and Presbyters are the same
to us both name and thing.'[47] Milton, it seems, was less concerned with
abstract truth than with the freedom to dissent from it. For Milton,
theocracy - the rule of God - meant the freedom to dissent.

In the 1640s, life in England's oasis of Reformed theology was far
from serene:

> I had hope
> When violence was ceas't, and Warr on Earth,
> All would have then gon well, peace would have crownd
> With length of happy dayes, the race of man;
> But I was farr deceav'd ...[48]

Written after the overtly millenarian hopes of the summer of 1641,
Areopagitica marks Milton's disappointment with his investment in the
puritan Long Parliament. For Milton, Trevor-Roper claims, 'the Long
Parliament was not, could not be, a mere political assembly. It was a
glorious band of heroes, a sodality of Arthurian knights under whose
leadership the world's great age was to begin anew.'[49]

But with the changing currents of the civil wars, Milton's evaluation
of this body changed. Their legislative programme, he would later
complain, was too much like 'that jealous haughtinesse of Prelates and
cabin Counsellours that usurpt of late';[50] like Satan in *Paradise Lost*,
whose impotence reduced him to merely fracturing God's rhetoric,
Milton recognised the futility of anti-Presbyterian political action and
turned from immediate millenarian engagement to the deconstruction
of the Presbyterian apocalypse, invoking and undermining their
inherited Elizabethan eschatology. The doctrine of progressive
revelation was his most powerful weapon.

It was possible to harness the *translatio studii* topos to explain why
England should be prominent in world affairs. In its original setting the
translatio studii idea had taught that English society was becoming
increasingly refined; this confirmed the puritan notion that God's
revelation was being increasingly revealed, that his purposes were
becoming clearer through the passing of the years. This idea of
'progressive revelation' was central to puritan discourse, especially as it

---

[47] Milton, *Works*, iv. 330-1.
[48] *PL* xi. 779-83.
[49] Trevor-Roper, *Catholics, Anglicans and Puritans*, p. 252.
[50] Milton, *Works*, iv. 295.

reached its most concentrated form in the revolutionary years; it argued that spiritual enlightenment did not come all at once but was rather gradually revealed through history. The Hebrew prophet Daniel, for example, had been commanded to 'shut up the wordes, and seale the boke til the end of the time [when] knowledge shalbe increased.'[51] The 1560 Geneva Bible annotation on this verse had informed puritans that they were the heirs of this increasing revelation: 'til the time that God hathe appointed for the ful revelation of these things: and then many shal runne to and fro to searche the knowledge of these mysteries, which things they obteine now.'

Attempting to counter any excessive apocalyptic excitement, Ussher, in 1627, had argued that 'Truth is the daughter of Time; wait therefore'.[52] But in *Of Prelatical Episcopacy* (1641), an extended critique of the Archbishop's view of history as a prerequisite for Biblical hermeneutics, Milton disagreed. For Milton, truth was 'the daughter not of Time, but of Heaven, only bred up heer below in Christian hearts, between two grave & holy nurses the Doctrine, and Discipline of the Gospel'.[53] It was not to be God's providence in history which was to reveal his outstanding mysteries, but rather immediate revelation imparting truth to the believer's conscience: 'time [is] the Midwife rather then the mother of Truth.'[54] He displaced Ussher's passive waiting for truth by arguing that true understanding is to be actively searched out in Scripture alone, without the patristic distractions of knowing who thought what and when. This is the 'new light sprung up and yet springing daily';[55] it is light to be actively sought.

But Milton followed the Geneva annotation in claiming that truth was exclusively the property of believers. Their access to this truth was grounded in the doctrine of regeneration, God's re-creation of fallen humanity in conversion. This was in line with the standard Calvinist view, expressed by John Owen; he saw the goal of the Christian life, begun in conversion, as the restoration of that 'image of God' lost at the Fall.[56] Other divines concurred. Stephen Charnock believed that 'regeneration is a universal change of the whole man'; Thomas Adams argued that as 'Adam was created after the image of God, and placed in Paradise; so the new man is confirmed to the image of Christ, and shall

---

[51] *Geneva Bible* (1560), Daniel 12:4.

[52] Ussher, *Works*, xiii. 350.

[53] Milton, *Works*, iii. 91.

[54] Milton, *Works*, iii. 370.

[55] Milton, *Works*, iv. 345.

[56] Sinclair B. Ferguson, *John Owen on the Christian Life* (Edinburgh: Banner of Truth, 1987), p. 55.

be reposed in the paradise of everlasting glory.'[57] Calvin, in *Institutes* iii. ii. 20, similarly argued that the elect 'behold God's glory with such effect that we are transformed into his very likeness.' In the *De doctrina* Milton argued that in conversion 'the intellect is to a very large extent restored to its very former [i.e. prelapsarian] state of enlightenment.'[58] Reversion to Edenic normality, then, was not simply to make its recipient a puritan, or protestant, as Mather had argued; it was to make him a genuine Christian, ready to receive God's outstanding truth.

Believers thus had a head start in progressive revelation, but they could never claim to be the holders of its finality, an impossible claim on a fallen earth where efforts at omniscience were doomed to frustration. Milton's eschatological epistemology achieved closure only at the final resurrection. Only in heaven shall 'God ... create us all doctors in a minute'.[59] Milton censures any contradiction of this - the people of God are still in the wilderness, still pitching their tents and seeing Canaan only from the Pisgah heights:

> he who thinks we are to pitch our tent here, and have attain'd the utmost prospect of reformation, that the mortall glasse wherein we contemplate, can shew us, till we come to the beatific vision, that man by this very opinion declares, that he is yet farre short of Truth.[60]

He mixes his allusions, nodding also to *1 Corinthians* 13:12, where the apostle sees 'through a glass darkly'. Again the apocalypse is in view - the day of unrestricted understanding is the day of the second coming.

This anticipation of increasing revelation was the basis of *Areopagitica*'s claim for limited freedom of the press. The pamphlet's great concern for 'truth' as the victor in the battle of books, as we will later see, demonstrated Milton's awareness that ultimate revelation - the totality of all revelation which would ever be revealed - could not be known on earth. Thus Milton quotes Selden - Ussher's friend and Gillespie's opponent - to the effect that 'all opinions, yea errors, known, read, and collated, are of main service & assistance toward the speedy attainment of what is truest.'[61] A surprising ally, Selden was an Erastian intent upon subjecting the church to state control. Milton would have had little sympathy with his larger programme. Nevertheless, Milton enacts his own argument, allowing an opponent space within his tract, demonstrating that even heretics had something to offer the elect.

---

[57] I.D.E. Thomas, *The Golden Treasury of Puritan Quotations* (Edinburgh: Banner of Truth, 1975), p. 235.

[58] Hill, *Milton and the English Revolution*, p. 148.

[59] Patrides, *Milton and the Christian Tradition*, p. 284.

[60] Milton, *Works*, iv. 337.

[61] Milton, *Works*, iv. 309.

Milton too was ready to allow that liberty of press should be extended to unbelievers - though, as he notes in passing, never to Catholics: 'I mean not tolerated Popery, and open superstition.'[62] Milton's 'rule of the saints' was not the imposition of an ecclesiology upon the nation so much as a careful guarding of the individual's capacity for spiritual change. Consequently, on a national scale, literary toleration was crucial for the continuation of God's progressive revelation.

But this doctrine of progressive revelation also allowed Milton to forcibly position his cause with that belonging to God. Toleration was vital for the future of progressive revelation as only the free interplay of ideas could generate Truth: 'for God sure esteems the growth and compleating of one vertuous person, more then the restraint of ten vitious';[63] and Cromwell, who 'would rather tolerate Mohammedanism than persecute one of the elect', agreed.[64] The Geneva Bible had argued that 'schismes and heresies ... turne to the profit of the elect.'[65] John Rogers would claim that 'errors are usefull, as well as truth, and it is expedient that they should be 1 Cor.11.19'.[66] In 1657 John Bunyan would write that 'it is very expedient that there should be heresies amongst us, that thereby those which are indeed of the truth might be made manifest.'[67] Milton's own argument, in Temple-building language, was that 'there must be many schisms and many dissections made in the quarry and in the timber, ere the house of God can be built.'[68] While still a Presbyterian, John Owen warned that heresies were to be expected in the latter days.[69] We have already noticed that the toleration of those groups dissenting from the Presbyterian settlement divided the Westminster divines; one nineteenth-century Presbyterian historian praised the majority for denying 'such a toleration, the real meaning of which was, civil, moral, and religious anarchy.'[70] But in dissenting from the views of the Scots Commissioners, the Independents' arguments for toleration were circular: because these were the last days, heresy should be tolerated to allow for further revelation, in fulfilment of the prophecy of *Daniel*; but at the same time, they claimed, the existence of those ideas themselves was a mark of the end.

---

[62] Milton, *Works*, iv. 349.
[63] Milton, *Works*, iv. 320.
[64] Hill, *Milton and the English Revolution*, p. 152.
[65] *Geneva Bible* (1602), note on 1 Corinthians 11:19.
[66] Rogers, *Ohel*, p. 206.
[67] Bunyan, *Works*, ii. 181.
[68] Milton, *Works*, iv. 342.
[69] Owen, *Works*, xiii. 51.
[70] Hetherington, *History of the Westminster Assembly of Divines*, p. 154.

Apocalyptic Aporia

The frequent use of aporia throughout *Areopagitica* demonstrates to the careful reader that its author was himself the recipient of increasing knowledge. The transitions of logic within Milton's tract mirror the transitions between his works, and demonstrate that even as he wrote the pamphlet he was receiving new light.

Areopagitica's exploitation of progressive revelation enacts Milton's prescription for the further reformation of puritanism: 'not only to look back and revise what hath bin taught heretofore, but to gain furder and goe on, some new enlighten'd steps in the discovery of truth'.[71] Thus Milton develops his sense of the historical moment by an appeal to the past. His 'Roman recovery' is usefully ambiguous, for the syntax obscures whether it is to be a recovery *to* or *from* Roman forms, whether it is advocating an espousal of classical virtue, or warning of Catholic danger.[72] Both possibilities could be confirmed by an appeal to other passages in the tract. But only by depicting the past can Milton demonstrate how crucial is the present, when danger is within and without: his England, like Bunyan's Mansoul, is 'a City ... besieg'd and blockt about, her navigable river infested, inrodes and incursions round, defiance and battell oft rumor'd to be marching up ev'n to her walls, and suburb trenches'.[73] The *Nativity Ode* had contrasted the futurity of judgement with the 'now' of bliss begun;[74] in *Areopagitica* Milton has an equally strong sense of the importance of the historical moment, again reinforced through the repetition of 'now':

> now, as our obdurat Clergy have with violence demean'd the matter, we are become hitherto the latest and backwardest Schollers, of whom God offer'd to have made us the teachers. Now once again by all concurrence of signs, ... God is decreeing to begin some new and great period in his Church ... Behold now this vast City ... a Nation of Prophets, of Sages, and of Worthies.[75]

This explains the urgency of the tract: Milton is writing when 'things are not yet constituted in Religion', before the Westminster Assembly submitted a finalised discussion of its results to Parliament in 1646. Now 'the time in special is', Milton claimed. 'God is decreeing to begin some new and great period in his Church, ev'n to the reforming of Reformation it self.'[76]

---

[71] Milton, *Works*, iv. 350.

[72] Milton, *Works*, iv. 294.

[73] Milton, *Works*, iv. 343.

[74] Milton, 'On the Morning of Christ's Nativity', l. 167, in Milton, *Works*, i.

[75] Milton, *Works*, iv. 340-41.

[76] Milton, *Works*, iv. 332, 340, 347.

But the Westminster divines were hazarding further light as they attempted to stamp out the possibility of future revelation. The urgency of *Areopagitica* is due to the threat posed to progressive revelation and continuing reformation, 'this light of the Gospel which is, and is to be'; the free press, Milton argues, 'was the peoples birthright and priviledge in time of Parliament, it was the breaking forth of light'.[77] November 1644 was one of the last chances for Milton to make his voice heard; the new legislation would silence *Areopagitica* before it came off the press.

This urgency finds expression in Milton's allusions: 'we reck'n more then five months yet to harvest; there need not be five weeks, had we but eyes to lift up, the fields are white already.'[78] Milton's Englishmen are markedly different from the Jewish audience addressed by Christ, who expected harvest in four months (*John* 4:35). Milton's allusion argues the apocalyptic complacency of his intended audience - a complacency which is, he implies, greater than the scriptures will warrant. Milton expects his apocalypse very much sooner than those of his contemporaries. Similarly the allusions to the 'parables of the kingdom' from *Matthew* 25 imply a strong apocalyptic expectation: 'it is not possible for man to sever the wheat from the tares, the good fish from the other frie; that must be the Angels Ministery at the end of mortall things.'[79] It was impossible to separate good books from bad, he was claiming; why even bother?

The change in tone throughout Milton's work during the early 1640s was critically influenced by the disappointment of his initial eschatological hopes. Milton had expected that the February 1642 exclusion of the bishops from the House of Lords would occasion the descent of the New Jerusalem - but the actions of the controlling Presbyterian party in the freshly constituted House of Commons distanced him from his initial reading of history and prophecy. His hesitation was not unique: the 1640s also witnessed a more general public rejection of millenarian theology as well as the withdrawal as a body of the Presbyterians from the millenarian brotherhood. In response, Milton deconstructs his earlier interests, in what Kendrick recognises as 'the moment of the revolution's solidarity with itself, the moment in which Milton betrays his closest affinity with the heretical class, and class factions without whose support the bourgeois could not have been instated.'[80] Loewenstein explains this: '*Areopagitica* does project a millennial vision of history where national regeneracy might be perfected in the near future', because it embodies 'the tension

---

[77] Milton, *Works*, iv. 329, 332.
[78] Milton, *Works*, iv. 341.
[79] Milton, *Works*, iv. 349.
[80] Kendrick, *Milton*, p. 47.

between Milton's sense of the extraordinary potential for social transformation, which accompanies his apocalyptic conception of history, and his sense of the tragic shortcomings of reformation in his age.'[81]

Thus *Areopagitica* serves as a 'Piatza' for the competing discourses in puritan apocalyptic thought.[82] Milton juxtaposes the rhetoric of the orthodox (which he criticises) and the radicals (upon which he bases his own argument), and attempts to police the contrast and didacticise the results. He narrates the amillennial eschatology of the Augustinian tradition and highlights its Catholic legacy. Criticising that licensing controlled by 'glutton Friers', he argues that 'they have a conceit, if he of the bottomlesse pit had not long since broke prison, that this quadruple exorcism would barre him down'.[83] This is a reference to the Catholic belief, shared by a number of protestant scholars, that the millennium had begun with or shortly after the incarnation and had ended around one thousand years later. Satirically, Milton recounts the claim of Catholicism that the Church's approval of any given text implies that the devil will be barred from that space. The immediate juxtaposition with Claudius' attempt to control flatulence shows Milton's evaluation of how likely he believes their attempts are to succeed. But in his criticism of ideas by their pedigrees, Milton implicitly involves his non-millennial puritan brethren, and certainly his characterisation of the *Imprimaturs* typify the dialogic element inherent in puritan millenarian texts.

> Sometimes 5 Imprimaturs are seen together dialogue-wise in the Piatza of one Title page, complementing and ducking each to other with their shav'n reverences, whether the Author, who stands by in perplexity at the foot of his Epistle, shall to the Presse or to the spunge.[84]

Milton situates the text as a 'piazza', a meeting place for competing discourses which are powerful enough to contain the possibility of 'the sponge' - aporia, self-annihilation - and which separate the author from the effects of his work.

But Milton holds resolutely to his authority as author. Instead of excessive textual activity, he aims for an holistic text, free from dialogue with itself, and contends that this can be accomplished in his native vernacular: 'our English, the language of men ever famous, and formost in the atchievements of liberty, will not easily find servile letters anow to spell such a dictatorie presumption.' Yet, as we shall see, Milton uses

---

[81] Loewenstein, *Milton and the Drama of History*, p. 39.
[82] Milton, *Works*, iv. 304.
[83] Milton, *Works*, iv. 303-4.
[84] Milton, *Works*, iv. 304.

this language to create a text bearing all the hallmarks of those he attacks - dialogue, self-negation, and the diminishment of the author. He has 'ript up' history, and 'drawn as lineally as any pedigree' the origin of book licensing. He has involved the church heroes of Foxe and Ussher in the effects of 'the most Antichristian Councel and the most tyrannous Inquisition that ever inquir'd'.[85] In deconstructing the licensing bill he has undermined the heritage of Elizabethan protestantism. He has done more than he imagined to 'dissect one by one the properties it has'.[86]

Reflecting its author's awareness of the continual revelation of 'new truth', *Areopagitica* is a transitional text. In its pages, Milton offers a variety of opinions and demonstrates, as we have seen, adherence to ideas he would later abandon. *Areopagitica* is a text in dialogue with itself. Thus, though arguing that 'Arminius was perverted', Milton refuses wholesale commitment to Calvin: the reforming party, he claims, have 'lookt so long upon the blaze that Zuinglius and Calvin have beacon'd up to us, that we are stark blind'.[87] Milton is not afraid of celebrating the 'grave and frugal' Unitarian protestants of Transylvania and the 'two Apollinarii', the younger of whom gave his name to the Church's first major Christological heresy.[88] There is retreat also from the immediately apocalyptic tone of the earlier anti-prelatical pamphlets; Milton is increasingly aware of Antichrist's encroachments into the puritan movement, as the Presbyterian faction struggled to keep a lid on the radical discourse of which his pamphlets were part.

But *Areopagitica* struggles to contain itself. The pamphlet is a powerful demonstration of Milton's insights into the power of language. Like George Gillespie, Milton hoped to displace Bishop Joseph Hall's *Humble Remonstrance* (1641) - intended to 'impaire [Parliament's] merits with a triviall and malignant Encomium' - with the 'plainest advice' Milton regarded as the best 'praising'.[89] His summary of his own strategy and that of his rival foregrounds the manipulation both texts intend. Milton's words do things, and it is to the praise of the Commons if they can tell true praise from false and align themselves so as to be influenced by the true. England 'shall observe yee in the midd'st of your Victories and successes more gently brooking writt'n exceptions against a voted Order, then other Courts'.[90] Fighting Antichrist, Milton's imagined or intended Parliamentary

---

[85] Milton, *Works*, iv. 305.
[86] Milton, *Works*, iv. 306.
[87] Milton, *Works*, iv. 313, 339.
[88] Milton, *Works*, iv. 307, 340.
[89] Milton, *Works*, iv. 294-5.
[90] Milton, *Works*, iv. 295.

readers would be huddled round his latest polemic, discussing his implied reader and adjusting themselves and their policies accordingly, just as the study of the 'polite wisdom and letters' of 'the old and elegant humanity of Greece' had kept the English of old from becoming 'Gothes and Jutlanders'.[91] Thus Milton's book tests his M.P.s, and it is *their* quality which is determined by *his* book - a rather inverted censorship. But the sentence involves the reader too: 'brooking' is slightly ambiguous, signifying either their active use of, or their mere toleration of, published dissent. The only use of this term in Milton's poetry - 'restraint she will not brook' - is in the context of Adam and Eve's 'mutual accusation', and their refusal to consider the criticism of the other.[92] This is exactly the sort of situation Milton wants to avoid, when opposites jar and the confusion is without profit. Divergences of opinion are useful only inasmuch as the result is not 'vain'.[93] Milton's manipulation of his reader is an attempt to promote dialogue. The reader's response is crucial to the success of his tract.

There are times when Milton's dialogue with his reader fuses purposefully with *Areopagitica*'s textual inconsistencies - its self-directed iconoclasm. Critics are wrong to understand such moments as 'inadequacy' or 'incompetence'.[94] Stanley Fish's provocative reading of the pamphlet has argued that these moments are pragmatic and deliberate, that Milton's intent is to make the reader a censor too, teasing out and separating good from bad, right from wrong. Both book and reader, in other words, censor each other. This challenges the dichotomy between the reader and the text: those M.P.s whom Milton imagines his tract is shaping, for example, would also be the readers learning the duties of appropriate censorship from his tract. Paradoxically, *Areopagitica* is teaching its censors how to read and is dignifying the censor's role. Such complexity is strategic in the poet's ostensible role as a defender of freedom - for Milton was also to serve for a year as an official censor of the press in 1649.[95]

Truth is fostered and its existence is confirmed in the imagination of the individual, and it is this process of education, rather than the freedom of the press or the freedom of speech, which is *Areopagitica*'s

---

[91] Milton, *Works*, iv. 295-6.

[92] *PL* ix. 1184, 1187.

[93] *PL* ix. 1189.

[94] Hugh M. Richmond, *The Christian Revolutionary: John Milton* (Berkeley: University of California Press, 1974), p. 115.

[95] Kendrick, *Milton*, p. 27; Richmond, *The Christian Revolutionary*, p. 113; Abbe Blum, 'The author's authority: *Areopagitica* and the labour of licensing', in Mary Nyquist and Margaret W. Ferguson (eds), *Re-membering Milton: Essays on the Text and Traditions* (London: Methuen, 1987), p. 74.

most basic burden. But Milton's position is complicated: his philosophy - that Truth is the result of the battle of books, not merely a contestant in it - forbids its own succinct statement - if it is indeed 'true'. If Milton was simply to state his doctrine, the reader could enjoy no certainty as to its present accuracy - reading it sometime after it was written. 'Truth', by this stage, could have progressed. Thus there are transitions even within *Areopagitica*. Constantly defying closure, Milton's 'truth' can only be crystallised beyond the text. It is the recognition of this which marks the 'fit reader', and ultimately frustrates the search for the 'Miltonic worldview'.

Thus, while Milton's role in the 1644 tract and the 1649 censorship are both replete with contradiction, they can be read as advancing a synthesised hermeneutical strategy. They are not aporia, but function to educate the reader - though of course a poor reading may well send the pamphlet 'to the sponge' on this basis of such apparent incoherence. *Areopagitica*'s philosophy claims that such contradictions are a source of strength, despite the dangers they imply. In the present, for example, truth is 'everywhere tottering and overcome';[96] but the future cannot be imagined because of the denial of closure such a philosophy demands. All that the reader is allowed to know is that the Church's search for Truth will continue 'till her Master's second coming'. Total knowledge can never be achieved and consequently the search for it is useless. It is difficult to know why Milton's reader should struggle to attain something which will never be achieved.

Milton side-stepped these difficulties by attacking the facile logic of the proposed licensing bill: 'ironically,' Fish claims, 'it is only by permitting what licensing would banish - the continual flow of opinions, arguments, reasons, agendas - that the end of licensing - the fostering of truth - can be accomplished.'[97] But Milton forgets his own attack is based on equally shaky ground. Far from ensuring liberty of press, it shows that such liberty is unnecessary.[98] Fish has pointed out that the argument against licensing (generally read as an argument for books) undermines itself. If books won't corrupt their readers, then neither will they edify them: potency must be denied in every direction, irrespective of its intentional effect. Similarly, when in the historical argument the only books Milton mentions are those which exercised a negative effect upon society, his only argument seems to be that pre-publication censorship - which he is attacking - has very little effect

---

[96] Milton, *Works*, xii. 195.
[97] Stanley Fish, 'Driving from the Letter: truth and indeterminacy in Milton's *Areopagitica*', in Mary Nyquist and Margaret W. Ferguson (eds), *Re-membering Milton: Essays on the Text and Traditions* (London: Methuen, 1987), p. 246.
[98] Fish, 'Driving from the Letter', p. 246.

anyway. In any case, there are in a sense no such things as bad books, since they can all do a little harm, and no such things as good books, since they do no real good: 'a fool will be a fool with the best book, yea or without book.'[99] If there is no real difference, if all books are imbrued with original sin, how can any of them represent Truth on the battlefield, never mind Truth as the result of history's epistemological struggle? Thus Milton stumbles to his first conclusion: 'if purity can be found neither in books, where it first seemed to reside, nor in naturally pure hearts, where the argument next seemed to place it, then it cannot be found anywhere.'[100] In form and content, then, ambivalences between tracts - and within them - are part of this war of truth.

Loewenstein has affirmed Milton's New Critical sensitivity in his prose pamphlets: his 'representations of history reveal his sensitivity to the contradictions and conflicts involved in historical and social processes, not a naïve and disengaged political sensibility, as is sometimes claimed.'[101] Thus

> Milton's vivid sense of historical crisis fuels their brilliant and disturbing rhetoric. He follows other millennialists in stressing the importance of divine actions in history; but ... he more self-consciously explores his own role in reshaping that dynamic process through his polemical texts, and thus reveals how deeply his historical vision and literary imagination are really one.[102]

Fixler and Fish agree with Loewenstein in seeing this holistic view of history as a strength; Rowse, however, condemns *Areopagitica* as being 'wholly rhetorical, its argument self-contradictory, its assumptions, as usual, illusory'.[103] Fish has remarked that the early pages of *Areopagitica* display 'a curious inability to settle down and to pursue unambiguously the line of argument that was so strongly promised when books were the object of an apparently unqualified praise'.[104] Georgia Christopher has seen 'spiritual adventure' in the mutability of Milton's text;[105] we have already noticed that Milton's doctrine of progressive revelation 'realises' his eschatology by constantly deferring final judgement. Milton fashions our reading as a microcosm of universal history. Fish argues that the reader, far from becoming a celebrant of texts, is

---

[99] Milton, *Works*, iv. 314.
[100] Fish, 'Driving from the Letter', p. 241.
[101] Loewenstein, *Milton and the Drama of History*, p. 3.
[102] Loewenstein, *Milton and the Drama of History*, p. 12.
[103] Rowse, *Milton the Puritan*, p. 95.
[104] Fish, 'Driving from the Letter', p. 240.
[105] Georgia B. Christopher, *Milton and the Science of the Saints* (Princeton: Princeton University Press, 1982), p. 21.

constantly 'being driven from the letter', first from books, then from that letter represented by the history of Athens and Rome.[106]

But Milton goes much further than Fish suggests. *Areopagitica* moves the argument away from the very text in which it is communicated. This is Milton's most radical withdrawal. Through its engagement with Milton's eschatological epistemology, *Areopagitica*'s argument is conducted in inference, destroying the boundary of its own existence and demanding a closure outwith its last page, articulated only in the mind of its reader. Advancing the philosophy that *finitum non est capax infiniti*, Milton has totally undercut the distinction between the reader and his book.

Milton's rejection of other utopian texts was based on their being too static: he 'mistrusts utopias precisely because they do *not* permit direct engagement and dialogue, the very activities on which the godly nation thrives'.[107] His *Areopagitica* avoids this precisely by becoming an image of the culture (and the reader) it projects, in which ideologies conflict to produce Truth. But does this Truth prevail? We have seen that Milton's method forbids him to even finally say what Truth is: to define is to negate. The tract can never say what it is about. It is continually discussing itself one step away from real description. Its arguments prevail not on paper, where they can never be posited, but in the inferences of the reader - and Milton can only hope the reader understands. *Areopagitica* embodies the deconstructionist claim that 'we cannot establish a determinate bound, or limit, to a textual work so as to differentiate what is "inside" from what is "outside" the work.'[108] There is no "outside" in the textual web: 'what ever thing we hear or see, sitting, walking, travelling, or conversing may be fitly call'd our book, and is of the same effect that writings are.'[109] In many ways the literature of seventeenth-century millenarians *requires* those implications which elude or exceed it: such excess is a necessary part of the text, and its existence must be signalled to the reader. Such 'shrewd books, with dangerous Frontispices' encapsulate the energy of the puritan apocalypse and the movement of European Calvinism at large.[110] Kendrick has observed this problematic closure: 'The book is a vial of concentrated energy possessed of its proper eschatology; it may erupt into new and comprehensive significance at any moment.'[111]

---

[106] Fish, 'Driving from the Letter', p. 243.

[107] Loewenstein, *Milton and the Drama of History*, p. 41.

[108] M.H. Abrams, *A Glossary of Literary Terms* (1957; 9th ed. London: Holt, Rinehard and Winston, 1988), p. 205.

[109] Milton, *Works*, iv. 320.

[110] Milton, *Works*, iv. 317.

[111] Kendrick, *Milton*, p. 29.

Milton would surely approve: 'books are not absolutely dead things, but do contain a potency of life'; as *Areopagitica* demonstrates, they are 'lively' and 'vigorously productive'.[112]

This would certainly appear to suggest the redundancy of the author. Milton's introduction to the tract informs his reader of the 'power' which refuses to recognise literary decorum; his 'passion' o'erleaps itself, and his self-reflexive memo highlights the extent to which he is continually in danger of moving beyond the structure he initially outlines: 'but I have first to finish, as was propounded.'[113] Later he finds himself anticipating subsequent argument: 'see the ingenuity of Truth, who when she gets a free and willing hand, opens her self faster, then the pace of method and discours can overtake her.'[114] His argument and its content are paralleled - truth 'is always running ahead of any attempt to apprehend it.'[115] Thus the uncertainty of apocalypse bears massive influence on his evasive and subtly-shifting style. Milton is so much at the cutting edge of truth that revelation progresses even as he writes: his argument isn't quite contained in the logical four-part structure he had initially outlined. In pointing his reader to Truth's attempt at evasion, Milton glosses his own style, commenting on his own method and legitimising the parallel arguments of form and content, demonstrating that Truth is greater, or at least quicker, than language, and necessitating his implicit claim that Truth will be realised finally beyond words and beyond his tract, not through literary mediation, but immediately in the sense of the reader. The 'choisest periods of exquisitest books' exist outside their covers.[116]

This argument beyond the book side-stepped the boundaries covered by the proposed legislation to still contest 'a second tyranny over learning'.[117] What Milton understood as the best way to avoid the proposed legislation Thomas Goodwin had already outlined as the manner in which the Holy Spirit would illumine believers during the millennial period. In *A Glimpse of Sions Glory* (1641), as we noticed in the Introduction, Goodwin argued that divine revelation in the millennium would be immediate, by-passing words to impact and manifest itself upon the believer's heart alone. There would be no remaining necessity for an author or for a book. In both accounts, by Milton and by Goodwin, Truth is communicated without any mediator. Even now, an author like Milton can impede Truth by remaining within an outlined

---

[112] Milton, *Works*, iv. 298.
[113] Milton, *Works*, iv. 306.
[114] Milton, *Works*, iv. 315.
[115] Fish, 'Driving from the Letter', p. 243.
[116] Milton, *Works*, iv. 327.
[117] Milton, *Works*, iv. 331.

structure: if new revelation always made the previous paragraph out of date, how could there be any future for publishing?

This harmony of God and the believer, of political pragmatism and spiritual revelation, finds expression also in Milton's view of the reconstruction of Truth. *Areopagitica* argues that full Truth came with Christ and will return again with him: 'Truth indeed came once into the world with her divine Master, and was a perfect shape most glorious to look on.'[118] Though she has since known desolation, Milton is aware that Truth's limbs will one day be reunited: 'we have not yet found them all, Lords and Commons, nor ever shall doe, till her Masters second comming; he shall bring together every joynt and member, and shall mould them into an immortall feature of lovelines and perfection.'[119] It is the responsibility of believers also to be 'searching what we know not, by what we know, still closing up truth to truth as we find it'.[120] The believer's responsibility in the present is the same as that belonging to Christ at his apocalypse.

Balachandra Rajan has linked Milton's disruption of the material-spiritual dichotomy with the puritan attempt at literary self-fashioning. The abandonment of the text's finality, Rajan argues, unleashes a centrifugal force which questions its own existence: 'the divine image and its presence and perfecting within us can no longer form the basis of correlation between outer reality and inner self-making. Divested of this safeguard, the poetry of self-formation will be driven to interrogate the status of its fictions, recognising them as possibly no more than fictions.'[121]

This is what *Areopagitica* does to the millenarian landscape of the Interregnum. Milton posits and questions, posits and questions, until the attack is as much upon textual authority and the utility of publishing as it is upon the eschatological foundations of contemporary puritan thought. But the retreat from the word has implications for the reading of the tract which teaches just that - and by staking his reputation as prophet within the credibility of his texts, Milton risks the dissolution of his own character in the constantly fluctuating typology of his tract. *Areopagitica*'s Milton is like Satan in *Paradise Lost*, who is denied the possibility of independent action and is reduced to fracturing God's rhetoric in an attempt to achieve significance: like Satan, Milton's actions are re-actions.

Nevertheless the author argues beyond the text, but then claims that

---

[118] Milton, *Works*, iv. 337.
[119] Milton, *Works*, iv. 338.
[120] Milton, *Works*, iv. 339.
[121] Balachandra Rajan, *The Form of the Unfinished: English Poetics from Spenser to Pound* (Princeton: Princeton University Press, 1985), p. 101.

very situation - of being 'beyond the text' - is impossible. Milton's philosophy of what constitutes a text seems to annul his modified closure: 'what ever thing we hear or see, sitting, walking, travelling, or conversing may be fitly call'd our book, and is of the same effect that writings are.'[122] This is not so much a subversion of closure as a frontal attack upon it.

Nevertheless, just as radical groups define themselves in opposition to a culture only to find themselves incorporated within it, so Milton's assault on the text is immediately institutionalised. Here, in form as much as content, *Areopagitica* corresponds most closely to Thomas Greene's theorisation of the typical Renaissance text: 'it tries to regulate cultural tensions and harmonise dissonances; it tries to reproduce those activities of assimilation and rejection, moral discrimination, mythic fabrication, symbolic reordering, that cultures typically perform. The text can be read as an idealised miniature culture, whether or not it allows the idealisation to be perceived as a critique. But it plays this role only at a risk: it may fail to harmonise its dissonances but only succeed in exposing them; its mythic constructs may collapse; the tensions it wants to regulate may explode.'[123] *Areopagitica*'s dissonances are exposed, its tensions do explode: consequently the tract has been read variously as an emblem of the culture war between court and country;[124] an image of time;[125] an image of class struggle;[126] and an emblem of its own message.[127] Trevor-Roper has described the 'explosive' mixture of classical learning and millenarianism,[128] and, as Fish claims, the pamphlet consumes itself in a series of fragmented discourses, consuming itself 'in a surfeit of its own passion'.[129] Blum has summarised the debate: '*Areopagitica*'s seeming contradictions have been interpreted as Milton's "manifesto for indeterminacy", a conversion of various factions' disagreements into a nonoppositional celebration of intellectual energy, and finally and quite differently, as the product of a self-validating, monistic ethos which registers the tensions deriving from a bourgeois problematic.'[130] Actually Milton

---

[122] Milton, *Works*, iv. 320.
[123] Greene, *The Vulnerable Text*, p. xiii.
[124] Hill, *Milton and the English Revolution*, p. 21.
[125] Kendrick, *Milton*, p. 25.
[126] Kendrick, *Milton*, p. 39.
[127] Fish, 'Driving from the Letter', p. 248.
[128] Trevor-Roper, *Catholics, Anglicans and Puritans*, p. 253.
[129] Kendrick, *Milton*, p. 73; Nigel Smith, '*Areopagitica*: voicing contexts, 1643-5', in David Loewenstein and James Grantham Turner (eds), *Politics, Poetics and Hermeneutics in Milton's Prose* (Cambridge: Cambridge University Press, 1990), p. 111.
[130] Blum, 'The author's authority', p. 77.

seems to be voicing these ideas to present a kind of synopsis of contemporary millenarianism which he immediately deconstructs. Some of his peers read the millennium as a synecdoche; others thought that types were giving way to literal reality, and that the execution of the king would herald the descent of the real Messiah. *Areopagitica* becomes a site where the literal and figurative pull equally strongly and equally consistently in opposite directions.

The resulting temper was a real assault on the Westminster orthodoxy. When seen in the context of the Geneva Bible tradition, *Areopagitica* is profoundly ambiguous: its ambivalent discourse is the product of dislocation, which is itself the principal aim of Antichristian persecution. When the beast makes war against the saints, Junius had written, 'he shall persecute most cruelly the holy men, and put them to death, and shall wound and pierce through with cursings, both their names and writings.'[131] Reflecting the prominence of the printing press in the successful spread of Reformation teaching, Junius identifies the fate of the martyrs with that of their books. He ignores the destructive energy of his own notes.

Milton adopts the same techniques to radically different ends - he harnesses this dislocation of a formal poetic as a means to convey his message, a means of preventing future persecution. Dislocation becomes crucial to the creation of a reader-censor, a 'fit audience', capable of interpreting and reading beyond the text. In stepping away from the text, the educated reader is moving closer to the Quaker doctrine of the 'inner light', to the Word beyond words, a movement away from the text of the protestant Bible. Milton's educated reader is created in the image of his author: before the publication of *De doctrina*, only such a reader could assimilate the religious and political unorthodoxy of *Paradise Lost*.

Areopagitica is like the manna Milton cites as a circumstance conducive to temperance: 'God committs the managing so great a trust, without particular Law or prescription, wholly to the demeanour of every grown man. And therefore when he himself tabl'd the Jews from heaven, that Omer which was every mans daily portion of Manna, is computed to have bin more then might have well suffic'd the heartiest feeder thrice as many meals.'[132] *Exodus* 16, the passage to which Milton alludes, describes how the excess manna rotted during night and melted during day (vv. 20-1). It was a most delicate substance, demanding temperance and subject to quite as much decay as Milton's text. The allusion demonstrates Milton's intent to make the reader as judicious in his consumption of the text as the Israelites were in the wilderness. Any

---

[131] *Geneva Bible* (1602), note on Revelation 11:7.
[132] Milton, *Works*, iv. 309-10.

textual excess would cause the decay of the argument. But the cause is ultimately fruitless, and closure can never be achieved: 'he who were pleasantly dispos'd could not well avoid to lik'n it to the exploit of that gallant man who thought to pound up the crows by shutting his Parkgate.'[133]

Trevor-Roper has noted that the reception of *Areopagitica*, and the ensuing events in the political arena, marked a turning-point in Milton's own millenarianism.[134] The tract represents the poet's passage from the heady apocalypticism of 1641-2 to his repudiation of such ideology after 1645. This explains Hill's perplexity: 'it is disconcerting to try to depict a man who has strong moral principles, for which he would die, without being able to state clearly what these principles are, and so being unable to submit them to precise rational analysis.'[135] This is exactly Milton's intention in *Areopagitica*, scrutinising the eschatologies of his contemporaries, and toying with the theoretical implications of each.

But Milton attempts this investigation at the risk of his own text's integrity. Like the 'imprimaturs' he criticises, *Areopagitica* begins a dialogue with itself and with its readers; as his monster stumbles from its source, 'the Author ... stands by in perplexity at the foot of his Epistle.'[136] *Areopagitica* projects a time when the people in the besieged city of English puritanism will be 'wholly tak'n up with the study of highest and most important matters to be reform'd, should be disputing, reasoning, reading, inventing, discoursing, ev'n to a rarity, and admiration, things not before discourst or writt'n of'.[137] *Paradise Lost* would take this mood one step beyond, to things 'unattempted yet in prose or rhyme'; there, Milton's thoughts would be upon his own millennial role, the 'high strains in new and lofty Measures' he had earlier anticipated.[138] Perhaps this is the main importance of Milton's tract; its exploration of the resources of language would be more powerful and enduring than the subversion of the millenarian ideas they (struggle to) contain. Milton delighted in his linguistic triumph over his enemies: he was 'in word mightier than they in Armes'.[139]

Areopagitica evidences the 'answerable style' which Milton developed to contain the transcendent and the super-natural.[140] *Areopagitica* evidences Milton's 'discourse without control', but disguises the fact

---

[133] Milton, *Works*, iv. 314.
[134] Trevor-Roper, *Catholics, Anglicans and Puritans*, p. 253.
[135] Hill, *Milton and the English Revolution*, p. 472.
[136] Milton, *Works*, iv. 304.
[137] Milton, *Works*, iv. 343.
[138] *PL* i. 16; Milton, *Works*, iii. 78.
[139] *PL* vi. 32.
[140] *PL* ix. 20.

that, in the terms of *Paradise Lost*, this is a Satanic literary strategy: Milton was using the forms and expressing the ideas suggested by the Devil, just as Satan would be charged with the Arianism Milton elsewhere supported.[141] But irrespective of concessions to get past the censor, Milton was compelled to involve himself in the linguistic forms he opposed. He may well have been 'standing by in perplexity'; for all his literary genius, he had left his successors a difficult heritage. Even in later years, he would call for 'that warning voice, which he who saw / Th' Apocalyps, heard cry in Heaven aloud'.[142] Milton pushed millenarian reality from his texts, from his Bible, and even from himself. It was left to the more radical of the brethren to expound the 'paradise within thee, happier farr' .[143]

---

[141] *PL* v. 803; v. 820ff.
[142] *PL* iv. 1-2.
[143] *PL* xii. 587.

CHAPTER 7

John Rogers and Irish Puritan Conversions

It was inevitable that the Westminster divines and their supporters should respond to the eschatological turbulence caused by Milton's evolving worldview. Robert Baillie, in his *Dissausive*, warned readers of Milton's doctrines of divorce. One year later, in 1646, the English Presbyterian Thomas Edwards published his *Gangræna*, a substantial three-volume catalogue of the heresies he found in those voices dissenting from the Westminster settlement. Though not himself a member of the Westminster Assembly, Edwards was a fierce proponent of their ecclesiological views, and was quick to castigate their opponents. Significantly, Edwards dated the rise of the 'whirlegigg spirits' around 1643, one year before the last printing of the Geneva Bible.[1] He listed monster births, sacrilegious soldiers, and even poor literary style as evidence of the decay caused by their sectarian thought. Socially as well as theologically, he believed, everything about the Independents was opposed to godly order: 'let but a man turne Sectary now adayes, and within one halfe year he is so metamorphosed in apparell, hair, &c. as a man hardly knows him.'[2] All these ideas had a common source on the 'Millenary conceit'; it was, Edwards claimed, 'the common subject of Sermons'.[3] In *Gangræna* the results were plain to see. Edwards despaired that England 'is become already in many places a Chaos, a Babel, another Amsterdam, yea, worse; we are beyond that, and in the highway to Munster.'[4]

Despite the dangers inherent to such apocalyptic excess, Milton's disillusionment with the Scottish Commissioners spread quickly throughout the English sectarian constituency. John Owen was following Milton's path from Presbyterianism to Independency when he noticed that the Covenanters' 'ambition to rule and to have all under their power, even in conscience, is quickly mistaken for zeal to the kingdom of Christ'.[5] Influential voices within the rising Independent

---

1 Edwards, *Gangræna*, i. A4v.
2 Edwards, *Gangræna*, i. 73.
3 Edwards, *Gangræna*, ii. 23.
4 Edwards, *Gangræna*, i. 120.
5 Owen, *Works*, viii. 329.

movement were seeing the Scots no more as an ally, but as an eschatological enemy which had to be defeated. In their eyes, those Presbyterians in Ireland were betraying their Antichristian roots in a pan-Royalist alliance with Roman Catholic rebels against the English Parliamentarians in the late 1640s. England's apocalyptic tensions exploded at the news. The Irish apocalypse gave a massive impetus to the hermeneutical and theological development of puritan eschatology as the sectarian groups who formed the backbone of Cromwell's revolutionary forces redirected England's latent millenarian zeal. *Areopagitica* had problematised textual authority; these new radicals would problematise the audience-personality their earlier texts assumed.

Although Ireland's place in the English apocalyptic imagination had been fostered by Ussher's endorsement of Brightman's thinking in *Gravissimae Quaestionis* (1613) and by the opportunities his church had provided for English puritan refugees, it was only secured by reports of horrific massacres of protestants from the rebellion of 1641. Contemporary estimates of two hundred thousand casualties, Baxter noted, 'astonished those that heard it'.[6] Patrick Adair, who began his Presbyterian ministry in Ulster four years after the rebellion, later cited claims that 'about 300,000 persons, men, women, and children, [were] destroyed one way or another.'[7] These problems, caused on England's least secure border, were pivotal in the breakdown between Charles and his Parliament. As the influence of Parliament grew, English puritans became acutely aware of the indignity which the Irish rebellion had caused and were keen to extirpate its Antichristian threat. Jeremiah Burroughs, in 1643, imagined 'what vengeance then doth hang over that Antichrist, for all the blood of the Saints that hath beene spilt by him! the scarlet whore hath dyed her selfe with this blood, yea and vengeance wil come for that blood that hath beene shed of our brethrens in Ireland upon any whosoever have beene instrumentals in it great or small.'[8] His prophecy did not long lack fulfilment in Ireland's apocalyptic landscape.

By the end of the 1640s Edwards was no longer alone in maintaining the conservative eschatologies of Brightman and 'Bishop Usher that learned and godly Divine'.[9] He was joined by many more Presbyterians who had moved away from apocalyptic immediacy, leaving the

---

[6] Baxter, *Autobiography*, p. 32.

[7] Patrick Adair, *A True Narrative of the Rise and Progress of the Presbyterian Church in Ireland* (Belfast: Aitchison, 1866), p. 74.

[8] Jeremiah Burroughs, *An Exposition upon the eight, ninth, and tenth chapters of ... Hosea* (1650), i. 36.

[9] Edwards, *Gangræna*, iii. 87.

Independents to adapt its rhetoric in circumstances conducive to theological and political extremism. The annotations of the Geneva Bible, whose last English edition was printed in 1644, could not contain puritanism's spiralling eschatological consciousness. By the end of the decade, when Cromwell was claiming that England was a nation 'at the edge of the promises', apocalyptic themes were again the common currency of political debate.[10] In December 1648 George Cockayn, referring to the King, had claimed that when God arises in judgement 'no Murderer shall then plead Prerogative to exempt him from Trial before this Judg.'[11] Similarly, while military and religious leaders were considering the question of toleration at the Whitehall debates of the winter of 1648-9, *Certain Queries Presented by many Christian People* advised them that 'the Antichristian empire, is about the extirpation, the time allotted (1,260 years) being about to finish.' The revolution's leaders were encouraged to prepare the way for the fifth monarchy, the rule of the saints, whose system of government was to be exercised through general assemblies 'of such officers of Christ, and representatives of the churches, as they shall choose and delegate; which they shall do till Christ come in person'.[12] The increasing juxtaposition of eschatological and socio-political concerns created an environment which could contemplate that most unparalleled of political actions – Parliament's trial and execution of its king. But, as a consequence, England's regicides were compelled to annihilate his every basis of support. The need to defend their emerging republicanism drove them to invade Ireland.

The English Radicals in Ireland

It is surprising that so little work has been published on the millenarian nature of the Commonwealth's Irish policies, given the nature of the conflict and the personalities it involved.[13] Cromwell's apocalyptic predilections, which had been fostered by Mede, Brightman, and the sermons of Stephen Marshall, were excited by the Irish war.[14] Amidst

---

[10] Oliver Cromwell, *The Writings and Speeches of Oliver Cromwell: With an Introduction, Notes and an Account of his Life*, ed. W.C. Abbott (1939; rpt. Oxford: Clarendon Press, 1988), iii. 64.

[11] *The English Revolution: Fast Sermons to Parliament, November 1648 to April 1649*, ed. R. Jeffs (London: Cornmarket Press, 1971), xxxii. 32.

[12] Woodhouse (ed.), *Puritanism and Liberty*, pp. 244-5.

[13] This context is explored in Crawford Gribben, *God's Irishmen: Theological debates in Cromwellian Ireland* (Oxford: Oxford University Press, 2007).

[14] Hill, *The Experience of Defeat*, p. 179; Mason I. Lowance, *The Language of Canaan: Metaphor and Symbol in New England from the Puritans to the Transcendentalists* (Cambridge: Harvard University Press, 1980), p. 123.

the confusion of changing loyalties, contemporaries reported, Cromwell 'looked upon the design of the Lord in this day ... He was now accomplishing what was prophesied in the 100th Psalm.'[15] John Owen, Cromwell's favourite preacher, understood events in a similar way to his leader. As Owen's biographer, Peter Toon, has recorded, Owen 'held that in opposing and then executing the King as well as in the invasion of Ireland and then Scotland the army had been doing the will of God ... Indeed, the battles fought and the victories won, were clearly prophesied in Revelation 17-19 as part of God's programme for the last days.'[16] In 1649, as the English army left their native shores, Owen reminded them that 'Ireland was the first of the nations that laid in wait for the blood of God's people ... therefore "their latter end shall be to perish for ever".'[17] They were the 'sworn vassals of the man of sin', the 'followers of the beast'.[18] The result of this thinking, Hill notes, was that 'the Irish people, through no fault of their own, found themselves on the wrong side in an international war between England and Antichrist.'[19]

With his most influential army chaplains promoting such a robustly apocalyptic programme, Cromwell's course of action quickly acquired an eschatological belligerence. There was even speculation from some quarters that Cromwell would attempt a European crusade to sack the Vatican. In December 1648 Hugh Peter called for the Army's uprooting of monarchy throughout Europe.[20] As one Independent minister put it, 'Jesuits, Cardinals, Pope, yea, Rome itself trembles to hear of England, and at the troubles that are arising in all Europe.'[21] Ireland was to be the first conquest in this international revolution.

Its conquest would certainly be a challenge. The English troops faced natural hazards as well as several different armies, each of them falling in and out of alliances. Reports which survive from the period complain of fevers, the conscription of aged and infirm soldiers, and the seizing of supply ships by pirates.[22] But internal weakness was matched by external threat. The soldiers of Cromwell's apocalypse were confronted in Ireland by an unlikely and uneasy alliance of Irish Catholics, English

---

[15] Oliver Cromwell, *Speeches of Oliver Cromwell*, ed. Ivan Roots (London: Dent, 1989), p. 204.

[16] Peter Toon, *God's Statesman: The Life and Work of John Owen: Pastor, Educator, Theologian* (Exeter: Paternoster Press, 1971), p. 49.

[17] Owen, *Works*, viii. 231.

[18] Owen, *Works*, viii. 235.

[19] Hill, *A Nation of Change and Novelty*, p. 150.

[20] *The English Revolution: Fast Sermons to Parliament*, xxxii. 5.

[21] Rogers, *Ohel*, p. 526.

[22] Robert Dunlop (ed.), *Ireland under the Commonwealth: being a selection of documents relating to the Government of Ireland from 1651 to 1659* (London: Manchester University Press, 1913), i. 133-4.

Royalists, and Scottish Covenanters from Ulster, all of them united in disgust at the regicide.[23] Previously, Cromwell had operated on a prioritisation of his enemies: he 'had rather be over-run with a Cavalierish interest than a Scotch interest; I had rather be over-run with a Scotch interest than an Irish interest ... For all the world knows their barbarism.'[24] In Ireland he was faced with all three enemies at once.

Each of these forces, nevertheless, were subsumed into the same eschatological personality - they were all the soldiers of Antichrist. Even the Ulster Covenanters were 'a part of Antichrist, whose Kingdom the Scripture so expressly speaks should be laid in blood'.[25] These Presbyterians were 'vicious spirits', full of 'corrupt humours', 'generally disaffected' and distrusted quite as much as the native Irish.[26] The pact which had united Presbyterians and Independents at the beginning of the Westminster Assembly had irretrievably broken down by 1649.

This Parliamentary hostility to the forces of covenanted reformation ensured that Irish puritans outside Ulster enjoyed the liberty for which Milton had argued in *Areopagitica*. Freedom for new light was deliberately incorporated into the Parliamentarian programme for the spiritual renewal of the Irish population. In a sermon on 28th February 1650, Owen spurred M.P.s to recruit young preachers to help facilitate a national puritan revival in Ireland; these preachers should be sent into 'blind and ignorant places', he thought, where the English settlers and soldiers were 'not capable of the care of their own souls'.[27] As a consequence, the Parliamentary Commissioners in Ireland actively pursued the ablest of the godly, almost instinctively turning to the New England exiles for help. In September 1651, the Commissioners gave them the assurances for which Milton had longed from the Westminster divines. They guaranteed that those settlers 'whose hearts the Lord shall stir up to look back again toward their native country ... shall enjoy free liberty of conscience in all religious or spiritual matters, as fully as they do now in New England, or as the Lord hereafter shall further make known to them to be his will'.[28] The English authorities were promising a legal indemnity for whatever revelation the returning exiles would yet receive. They were also invoking an eschatological justification for the Independent ecclesiology many of these exiles advanced: they should return, the Commissioners argued, to promote 'the more high exalting of the kingdom of Jesus Christ in the power and purity of gospel

---

[23] Bennett, *The Civil Wars in Britain and Ireland, 1638-1651*, p. 328.

[24] Cromwell, *Speeches of Oliver Cromwell*, p. 7.

[25] Cromwell, *The Writings and Speeches of Oliver Cromwell*, ii. 199.

[26] Rogers, *Ohel*, p. xxxv; Dunlop (ed.), *Ireland under the Commonwealth*, i. 23.

[27] Woodhouse (ed.), *Puritanism and Liberty*, p. 253.

[28] Dunlop (ed.), *Ireland under the Commonwealth*, i. 54-5.

ordinances and church fellowship'.[29] Parliament's deliberate cultivation of Independent fellowships was part of its larger apocalyptic programme in Ireland.

With all this official endorsement, the influence of the Independents would have been much greater in Ireland than at home, where the role of the English Presbyterians in the existing balance of power had to be respected. Barnard records that Parliament's Irish legislation left the pro-Independent Commissioners 'room for improvisation'; between 1649 and 1655, he claims, 'religious policy reflected their unorthodox tastes.'[30] Trinity College, for example, developed a keen millenarian edge. Although it had fostered an apocalyptic atmosphere since the days of Ussher, the historian J.D. Seymour has argued that in the early 1650s its ethos 'approximated to the Independents and their tenets'.[31] Owen, who was already a trustee of the college, was asked to undertake its reformation with the help of Thomas Goodwin.[32] They were ordered to suppress 'idolatry, popery, superstition and profaneness', to encourage preachers of the Gospel, and to 'consider all due ways and means for the advancement of learning and training up of youth in piety and literature'.[33]

The choice of Goodwin and Owen was significant. With the latter reaching the peak of his millenarian ideology, and the former having already demonstrated his apocalyptic virulence in a string of Parliamentary sermons, *A Glimpse of Sions Glory* (1641) and his commentary on *Revelation* (1639), the Commissioners were deliberately tapping the rich vein of millenarian fervour which the Independent movement housed. Indeed, it is ironic that a group so vigorously refuting the formal identification of church and state should find themselves in a position where their theology dominated and determined national political endeavour throughout Ireland. Their policies in the early 1650s were rooted in the expectation of an imminent eschatological moment.

But the course of Independent eschatology was to change in 1653. Independent leaders retreated from their earlier radicalism and consequently isolated the radicals from their influence. Owen was increasingly reversing his early commitment to eschatological literalism

---

[29] Dunlop (ed.), *Ireland under the Commonwealth*, i. 54.

[30] T.C. Barnard, *Cromwellian Ireland: English Government and Reform in Ireland 1649-1660* (London: Oxford University Press, 1975), p. 98.

[31] J.D. Seymour, *The Puritans in Ireland, 1647-1661* (Oxford: Clarendon Press, 1921), p. 28.

[32] Barnard, *Cromwellian Ireland*, p. 97; Dunlop (ed.), *Ireland under the Commonwealth*, i. 10-11.

[33] Dunlop (ed.), *Ireland under the Commonwealth*, i. 1-2.

and began to take measures against the more radical of the brethren. Goodwin, too, reneged on his earlier apocalyptic vision at the same time as the radicals were pirating some of his earlier sermons which, they believed, endorsed their programme. Goodwin had once argued, for example, that 'we shall one day be the top of nations ... we shall reign on earth';[34] the radicals published this in *A Sermon on the Fifth Monarchy* in 1654.

At the same time, the range of sects and radical groups in Ireland was swelling with the massive influx of 34,000 Parliamentary soldiers by 1653. Independent and Baptist ideologies were most prominent among these sectaries, and some of this new thinking was quick to take root.[35] One historian claims that Baptists in Ireland have never numbered more than they did during the Cromwellian period.[36] Their influence was certainly strong in the army: extant reports allege that many soldiers 'were re-baptized as the way to preferment'.[37] Nevertheless, the millenarianism of both groups was frequently expressed across denominational boundaries, as we have seen, as Baptist and Independent believers united to form 'Fifth Monarchist' groups.

These 'Fifth Monarchy Men' maintained exuberant eschatological hopes of the imposition of godly rule in an imminent millennial reign of Christ. Although they have gained notoriety as 'extremists' in popular historical thought, they were unique in their time only in their methodology. These millenarians saw *themselves* - rather than kings or bishops or parliaments - as the divine agents who should initiate godly rule in preparation for the imminent millennium. The saints, and the saints alone, were capable of government. At times their theory exploded into violence, as in Venner's rising in 1661; mostly it was contained within the confines of fairly conventional political lobbying. Capp argues that their interest in a system of social legislation founded upon the ten commandments was unique; but, as we have seen, interest in this type of legal reform can be traced back through the Covenanters, through Ussher, to Calvin and the magisterial Reformers.[38] The Fifth Monarchists emerged at the logical end of Calvinism's theocratic temper.

The other significant source of eschatological ideas in Ireland in the

---

[34] Quoted in Hill, *The Experience of Defeat*, p. 175.

[35] K.L. Carroll, 'Quakerism and the Cromwellian Army in Ireland', *Journal of the Friends Historical Society* 54:3 (1978), pp. 135-7.

[36] Kevin Herlihy, 'The Early Eighteenth Century Irish Baptists: Two Letters', *Irish Economic and Social History* 19 (1992), p. 72.

[37] William C. Braithwaite, *The Beginnings of Quakerism* (London: Macmillan, 1912), p. 213.

[38] Capp, *The Fifth Monarchy Men*, p. 163.

1650s was the embryonic Quaker movement. Initially, Quaker ideas do not appear to have enjoyed significant support among the English soldiers; it appears that they first entered Ireland through a merchant who imported elements of their thought from England in 1653. Itinerant Quaker missionaries arrived in Ireland to consolidate his witness one year later.[39] Quaker ideology popularised the concept of a 'realised eschatology', which claimed that the traditional elements of puritan apocalyptic discourse were metaphors for experiences which the believer could pass through in this life. Quakers developed Goodwin's idea that contemporary puritans had present access to the blessings of the millennial age, and, apparently on this basis, rejected sacraments as expressions of a 'mediation' which had no place in the millennium. Inner light had little need for ritualistic symbol.

There was a great deal of rivalry and competition between the various sectarian groups. In 1653, the Fifth Monarchist leaders Christopher Feake, John Simpson and George Cockayn together published *A Faithful Discovery of Treacherous Design of Mystical Antichrist*, alleging that their Quaker rivals were a manifestation of Antichrist.[40] Anabaptist groups among the Irish Parliamentary forces were also intent on upsetting the status quo. A group of Baptists in Waterford, for example, launched a ferocious attack upon the legitimacy of those Independent groups in Dublin which included in their membership both those who sprinkled children and those who immersed believers. Consistency, they argued, demanded that those saints who were Baptists should withdraw from those fellowships which included among their number those who sprinkled children. The congregation which met in Dublin's Christ Church Cathedral was critically divided over the issue; the healing of this division was the objective given to the young preacher John Rogers (1627-c.1665).

Rogers and Eschatology

Rogers had already gained the reputation of being a fiery orator when the English Parliament sent him to Dublin in 1651. His father had been a subscribing Laudian, and had expelled Rogers from his household, repelled by his puritan convictions. Narrowly escaping death by starvation, and having pursued studies at Cambridge, Rogers was ordained as a Presbyterian minister in Essex but was quickly frustrated by his congregation's conservatism. He moved to London, where his Independent and millenarian inclinations soon gained him a following among the radical brethren. Being ordered to Dublin, Rogers continued

---

[39] Carroll, 'Quakerism and the Cromwellian Army in Ireland', pp. 135-7
[40] Braithwaite, *The Beginnings of Quakerism*, p. 281.

to explore his millenarian interests, utilising their influence to attempt to re-unite the Christ Church congregation. By the end of that crucial year, he would be the only leading Independent divine to have advanced into the Fifth Monarchist party. He was turning to millenarian ideology at precisely the moment when the other Independent leaders were spurning it, fearing for the safety of their positions in a movement which was suddenly becoming far more radical than its leadership. *Ohel or Bethshemesh* (1653), a textbook of Independent ecclesiology and soteriology, was Rogers' record of his experiences in Dublin.

Although *Ohel* has been the subject of scholarly discussion in a variety of contexts, the most central and influential aspect of the book has been passed over in silence. Rogers wrote his book to demonstrate the eschatological basis of the entire Independent project, and to illustrate his thesis with references to the experiences of the Dublin saints. Millenarianism permeates Rogers' book: eschatology constantly informs his discussions of ecclesiastical and soteriological themes.

This foregrounding of eschatological themes was the basis of his criticism of the Presbyterians. He lamented that Presbyterian leaders kept their people from *Revelation*, 'pretending the difficulty and danger of meddling with hard places in Scripture, they telling them they are obscure and not to be ventured on, as the Revelation and the like, keep off many poor souls, who stand (in ignorance) at a distance from them'.[41] Realising that this eschatological silence was a direct challenge to his ecclesiology, Rogers construed this exegetical omission as evidence of his rivals' lack of salvation. If the Presbyterian laity would not read *Revelation*, and if their ministers would not preach it, it was hid; and 'if it be hid, it is hid to them that are lost'.[42] Once again, the increasing polarity among the erstwhile brethren of the puritan pact was being registered within an apocalyptic paradigm.

But Rogers also exploited eschatological themes to consolidate the claims of Independency. Referring to a variety of sources - including the works of Thomas Brightman - Rogers echoed *Gangræna*'s claim that the most significant year in modern English history was 1643. In *Gangræna* Thomas Edwards had berated that year as the beginning of the rise of the 'whirlegigg spirits'.[43] Rogers gave a more positive description of the same phenomena - for him it was the year when the 'the Congregational Churches got upon their feete'. Rogers shared George Gillespie's calculation that the end of the 1260 years of the beast's reign and the subsequent rise of the pure ecclesiology could be dated to 1643, but

---

[41] Rogers, *Ohel*, p. 502 [falsely 462].

[42] Rogers, *Ohel*, p. 465.

[43] Edwards, *Gangræna*, i. A4v.

differed quite radically as to the type of ecclesiastical government which would replace the Church of England. In 1643, Rogers claimed, 'Deliverance and Freedom came running in.'[44] Rogers understood that the Independent polity would enter a new realm of glory by 1652: 'Gospel-Discipline is to begin to be restored, & the Abomination to be eradicated root and branch ... Then is the blessednesse to begin, and gradually to go on until one thousand three hundred and thirty dayes, i.e. for five and forty yeers longer ... at the expiration of which ... the Kingdome of Christ shall bee glorious indeed.'[45] Believers were at most forty-five years from the beginning of the millennial rule: 'we live on the brinke of the times promised.'[46] It was this breathtaking expectation which was to unite the Christ Church congregation. That church, Rogers claimed, was built on this apocalyptic ecclesiology: 'there the Bride saith, O! come Lord Jesus! come quickly!'[47]

As the millennial reign approached, Rogers believed, Independent churches would enjoy increasing access to the privileges of the new age. Following *A Glimpse of Sions Glory*, apologists for the Independent order came to claim that their saints' experience of re-entry to Eden was almost a matter of course. Though 'the brambles of ambition and traditions grew thick and thronging out at both ends', the church was Christ's 'garden enclosed'.[48] Rogers imagined the church as a life in perpetual summer: 'The Meadows (me thinks) begin to look green, the chirping of birds, and the Turtle-dove is heard in our land, the young Figs that are (but) green, and tender grapes give a good smell, and much sweetnesse'.[49]

One of the most radical implications of the Independents' re-occupation of Eden was the role this afforded to the women of their congregations. Different understandings of the role of women in the church was 'one thing that helped to set at a distance the two societies in Dublin'.[50] Rogers accused the pastor of Dublin's other Independent church, Samuel Winter, of attempting to 'rob sisters of their just rights and privileges'. Both pastors were agreed that women should 'keepe silence in the Churches' (1 *Corinthians* 14:34), but, Rogers claimed, 'they are not forbid to speak, when it is obedience, and subjection to the church.'[51] Winter did not agree, and Rogers' defence argued that his

---

[44] Rogers, *Ohel*, pp. 19-20.
[45] Rogers, *Ohel*, p. 23.
[46] Rogers, *Ohel*, pp. 23-4.
[47] Rogers, *Ohel*, p. 392.
[48] Rogers, *Ohel*, pp. 30, 40.
[49] Rogers, *Ohel*, p. 28.
[50] Rogers, *Ohel*, p. 464.
[51] Rogers, *Ohel*, p. 249.

rival's traditionalism was an attack on the millenarian foundations of the Independent way both pastors shared. As far as Rogers was concerned, the fulfilment of 'these last-days promises' demanded the freedom of women in church.[52] To this end he quotes the prophecy recorded in *Joel* 2:29 and interpreted in *Acts* 2:18 as a reference to the Gospel age: 'and on my servants, and on mine handmaides I will powre out my spirit in those days, and they shall prophecie.' The 1602 Geneva Bible's note on the 'all flesh' of the preceding verse reminded readers, 'that is, men.' But Rogers claims that it referred to 'women as well as men, being restored by Christ to that equal liberty (in the things of God, and in the church of Christ) with men, which they lost by the Fall; and they are now again to become meet and mutual helps: for all are one in Christ, says the text'.[53] Progressive revelation was undermining the Genevan heritage.

Rogers' radical attitude to the role of women in the church was matched by his innovative presentation of the conversions of his church members. These 'conversion narratives' - forming the centrepiece of Rogers' account in *Ohel* - were also explicitly millenarian and were grounded in the common experiences of Independents in Ireland. The Dublin believers, for example, spoke of the ministries of other millenarian brethren 'awakening' them to their danger under sin. Ruth Emerson was awakened by John Archer, and Captain John Spilman had been a member of the Fifth Monarchist congregation in Yarmouth, pastored by William Bridges.[54] These narratives of conversion generally passed through several stages. Major Andrew Manwaring, for example, was 'prepared' by Sidrach Simpson and Walter Cradock, given 'conviction of sin' through John Owen, and 'received great comforts and assurance of Christ' eventually through Rogers.[55]

These narratives were not primarily formal autobiographical accounts. Their function was twofold. Traditionally, they outlined to the curious the evidences of salvation by which they could scrutinise God's work in their souls. The conservative Presbyterian Thomas Manton reduced the concept to its simplest - and most popular - metaphor: 'there is a golden chain, the chain of salvation, which is carried on from link to link, till the purposes of eternal grace do end in the possession of eternal glory ... there is an iron chain of reprobation, which begins in God's own voluntary preterition, and is carried on in the creature's

---

[52] Rogers, *Ohel*, p. 464.
[53] Rogers, *Ohel*, p. 472.
[54] Rogers, *Ohel*, pp. 411, 412[4]. A gathering of several pages is inserted between pp. 412 and 413. Citations to this gathering are noted as p. 412[...], with the number in square brackets indicating the number of the extra page.
[55] Rogers, *Ohel*, pp. 412[2-3].

voluntary apostasy, and endeth in their just damnation.'[56] This 'teleology of grace', as the historian Tom Webster has described it,[57] was a description of the constituent elements of what the theologians called the *ordo salutis* - effectual calling, regeneration, conversion, justification, sanctification - which arrived finally upon the plateau of assured election. This type of writing exercised profound influence. The young Richard Baxter, for example, worried that he could not trace 'the workings of the Spirit upon my heart in that method which Mr. Bolton, Mr. Hooker, Mr. Rogers and other divines describe'.[58] The John Rogers to whom Baxter alluded published *The Doctrine of Faith* in 1627. His later namesake used the conversionist genre to advance an additional type of thinking: by the 1650s, conversion narratives had become highly stylised applications for membership of Independent churches.

Conversion accounts had developed a distinct literary form among the Independent churches of New England, and would remain a salient feature of the lingering puritan temper as the movement descended into 'Nonconformity'.[59] Several collections of such accounts were published in the 1650s, mainly originating from the more radical of the saints, and demonstrating similar membership criteria among the Independent churches - Henry Walker, for example, published his *Experience of Sundry Believers* (1652). Rogers, quite typically of this group, maintained that 'every one to be ADMITTED' to church membership should relate 'some EXPERIMENTAL evidences of the work of GRACE upon his SOUL (for the Church to judge of) whereby he (or she) is convinced that he is regenerate, and received of God.'[60] *Ohel* uses these conversion accounts to defend Rogers' church government and justify his ministry. Following the example of St. Paul, Rogers looked to the experiences of his congregation for evidence of his divine vocation: 'yee are the seale of mine Apostleship in the Lord' (*1 Corinthians* 9:2). The conversions of his people - and their subsequent experiences of Edenic bliss - were to be the ultimate justification of his millenarian ministry.

Rogers and Eschatological Soteriology

Most of the scholarly attention *Ohel* has received has been due to the recent upsurge of interest in conversion narratives. Some of the studies

---

[56] Manton, *Works*, v. 202.

[57] Tom Webster, 'Writing to Redundancy: Approaches to Spiritual Journals in Early Modern Spirituality', *The Historical Journal* 39 (1996), pp. 33-56.

[58] Baxter, *Autobiography*, p. 10.

[59] Alan Simpson, *Puritanism in Old and New England* (Chicago: University of Chicago Press, 1955), p. 2.

[60] Rogers, *Ohel*, p. 354.

which have mentioned *Ohel* include Patricia Caldwell's *The Puritan Conversion Narrative* (1983), C.L. Cohen's *God's Caress* (1986), Elaine Hobby's *Virtue of Necessity* (1988) and Nigel Smith's *Perfection Proclaimed* (1989). Each of these studies has approached the text from a different angle. Caldwell has pointed to conversion accounts as the beginnings of American self-expression; Cohen has situated the text within a psychoanalytical framework. Hobby and Smith have figured the conversion accounts as primary documents of radical self-expression: Hobby, pursuing a feminist agenda, values their immediacy and their direct access to unmodified female self-fashioning; Smith, in passing, mentions their contribution to the hermeneutical debates of the English civil war. None of this scholarship has documented the extraordinary eschatological consciousness of Rogers' conversion accounts. Scholars have consistently failed to notice that Rogers' accounts are testimonies to the truth of his eschatology, and evidences of the millennial dawn breaking in upon the Dublin church. *Ohel's* narratives are crucial in the evolving literary representation of the puritan apocalypse, manipulating the established characteristics of the conversion narrative genre to create a distinctly apocalyptic puritan identity.

The most significant feature of civil war conversion narratives is their juxtaposition of soteriology and eschatology. Even the conservative Thomas Manton could link soteriology and eschatology in the 1650s: 'writing is a great help to promote the common salvation. ... The goose-quill hath smote antichrist under the fifth rib.'[61] The combination of these elements, which came to be known as 'realised eschatology', employed the traditional elements of puritan eschatology as metaphors for experiences which the individual might enjoy in the present life of faith. This was anticipating a trope which would be popular in eighteenth-century New England. James West Davidson, in his study of *The Logic of Millennial Thought: Eighteenth Century New England* (1977), noted the New Englanders' belief that the 'pattern behind the grand history of the Revelation, when examined more closely, was in fact the same pattern which shaped the birth of every believer ... the close relationship between the larger and smaller works of redemption was partly reflected in the sometimes ambiguous definition of the coming kingdom.' God, in other words, 'redeemed history the same way he redeemed individuals'.[62] This was the basic assumption underpinning the conversion narratives of both Quakers and Fifth Monarchists.

Conversion narratives from both groups tended to find closure with the individual's consciousness of union with Christ. As a consequence,

---

[61] Manton, *Works*, v. 98.
[62] James West Davidson, *The Logic of Millennial Thought: Eighteenth-Century New England* (New Haven: Yale University Press, 1977), pp. 129, 136.

these reports typically enlarged upon the negation of sinful characteristics - their 'old man' - and of the emerging glimpses of the new. The prospective believer's sinful personality was to be subjected to an othering process of godliness in what Owen called 'the renovation of our natures'.[63] This process of continuing repentance and increasing holiness was regularly described in Biblical terms. *Colossians* 3:9-10 was a frequently cited text: 'lie not to one another, seeing that yee have put off the olde man with his works, And have put on the new, which is renewed in knowledge after the image of him that created him.' The 1602 Geneva Bible's interpretative notes explained this verse as providing 'a definition of our new birth taken of the parts thereof, which are the putting off of the olde man, that is to say, of the wickednesse which is in us by nature, and the restoring, and repairing of the new man, that is to say, of pureness which is given us by grace'. Jeremiah Burroughs encouraged those who sought salvation to pray 'Lord, I am nothing, Lord, I deserve nothing, Lord, I can do nothing, I can receive nothing, and can make use of nothing, I am worse than nothing, and if I come to nothing and perish I will be no loss at all.'[64] The Presbyterian Thomas Watson spoke of such humility as 'a kind of self-annihilation'.[65] Self-denial, therefore, meant exactly that - in some instances denying the self's existence as much as its preferences.

In recounting their conversions, then, the Dublin puritans were engaged in a 'writing to redundancy', describing the negation of the self. The New England puritan tradition, which the Dublin congregation reflected, theorised that a state of 'void' should characterise the repenting sinner. This 'void' state has recently been described by R.T. Kendall as 'an emptiness' in which 'man has nothing he can point to, or even reflect upon, including his preparedness.'[66] Consequently, Rogers argued that 'a true and full perswasion of the way of Christ makes thee see an emtinesse, and a worthlessnesse in all other wayes, and an excellency and usefullnesse of this way (which is Christs) that all others fall short of'.[67] This soteriological innovation effected a challenge to the puritan representation of conversion, as prospective saints struggled to adequately depict this sense of emptiness. Nigel Smith has commented that 'at their most extreme the radical prophets looked beyond human

---

[63] Owen, *Works*, v. 9.

[64] Jeremiah Burroughs, *The Rare Jewel of Christian Contentment* (1648; rpt. Edinburgh: Banner of Truth, 1964), p. 89.

[65] Thomas Watson, *A Body of Divinity* (1692; rpt. London: Banner of Truth, 1958), p. 316.

[66] R.T. Kendall, *Calvin and English Calvinism to 1649* (New York: Oxford University Press, 1981), p. 172.

[67] Rogers, *Ohel*, p. 250.

language in an attempt to capture divine ... substance itself.'[68] As we shall see, attempts to represent the inner 'void' and its consequent abandonment of closure were the catalysts for the millenarian radicalisation of puritan self-fashioning.

The biblical discourse certainly provided Rogers with the tropes to invoke the spiritual inadequacy of the unconverted. He describes his conversion accounts as 'discourses and discoveries of the dead hearing the voice of the Son of God'.[69] Like Lazarus, his congregation waited in the darkness and impotence of spiritual death for the voice of God to call them to salvation. John Bywater, for example, 'was exceedingly cast down ... till the Lord himself brought me out of it, and gave me to be given up to Jesus Christ'.[70] Others, whose experience echoed that of John Bunyan in *Grace Abounding*, found themselves the passive subjects of the assaults of dreams and texts. Cohen argues that Rogers encouraged such 'heightened emotionality' as evidence of the operations of grace.[71]

Thus Raphael Swinfeild 'could find no comfort at all, by any means, until that place in *Isa. 50.10.* came into me, How he that sitteth in darkness, and seeth no light, should trust in the Name of the Lord, and stay himself upon his God: which did much fall upon me, and me upon God; whereby I had abundance of comfort, but yet never free from many temptations, and fears, and doubts, and such sometimes as made me I could not tell what to say; until once, that I had a sweet dream, which done my soul good to this day; and in my dream I was told, that God's love was free in Christ Jesus, and I need not fear, for his grace was granted in Christ, and he puts none by that comes.'[72] Since 1560 the Geneva Bible had taught puritans, from this passage, that 'it is a rare thing that anie shuld obey aright Gods true ministers, thogh they labour to bring them from hel to heaven.' It is significant that Rogers should choose to highlight in his selection one record which consolidates his own status as pastor-editor.

Another of the congregation, John Spilman, 'fell into great trouble ... and thought I was damned, and utterly lost for all this, still wanting faith, and looking upon my own actings and graces, till the Lord laid these sayings of Paul to Corinth home close to my heart, Covet the best things ... then I discovered the most excellent way, which is Christ and

---

[68] Nigel Smith, *Perfection Proclaimed: Language and Literature in English Radical Religion 1640-1660* (Oxford: Clarendon Press, 1989), p. 18.

[69] Rogers, *Ohel*, p. 392.

[70] Rogers, *Ohel*, p. 395.

[71] Charles Lloyd Cohen, *God's Caress: the psychology of Puritan religious experience* (Oxford: Oxford University Press, 1986), p. 213 n. 47.

[72] Rogers, *Ohel*, p. 397.

nothing but Christ, and then I grew confident, and full of courage and assurance, and loved Christ, in all, and all that was Christ's, and Christ more than all.'[73] Spilman's experience literally enacts his theology. If the subject of his sentence is himself and his object is Christ, the verb silenced by the incantatory parallelism of the final clauses demonstrates that in speaking of Christ he silences himself. His salvation demands a similar evacuation of his own 'works'.

The prominence of women's stories in Rogers' compilation of 'such as are the most remarkable' among his congregation demonstrates how untypical the radical groups were of their age.[74] Capp notes that most members of Fifth Monarchist congregations were women.[75] Significantly, *Ohel*'s female narratives offer the most millenarian interpretations of regeneration. In these accounts Rogers marries two discourses, merging ideas of prophecy fulfilled with the common puritan topos of conversion effecting a restoration of its subjects to the status humans enjoyed before the Fall. He implies that for believers, the curse incurred by Adam has been reversed, that the Christian is re-entering Paradise, and that this has, necessarily, social and spiritual implications. Unlike the most radical of puritan groups, Rogers limits the application of these ideas to the scope of the elect within the Independent order, and by their standards his claim that regeneration transports women to the status they enjoyed in Eden is still deeply conservative - Rogers' 'equal liberty' is only freedom to 'become meet and mutual helps'. Eve, after all, was only a 'help-meet'.

Nevertheless, the effects of the church re-entering Eden were profound:

> Paradise is the place wherein God did most familiarly appeare, and acquaint himselfe to Man, and manifest his love and glory. Three wayes we read of by which God spoke to men, by dreams, by visions, or else face to face; and in this manner, whereby his Love, and wherein his Glory did most appear, viz. face to face did the Lord manifest himself in Paradise, although his face was seen but as in a Glasse, 2 Cor. 3.18 under the similitude of an Angel, or some other bodily appearance ... Then the Saints in the Churches shall have the most familiar presence of God, discourses with him, discoveries of him walking in the Garden.[76]

There was no more need for Scripture - dreams were the inner light of the new revelation. But Rogers had to close in on this radical dynamic. By their very nature, conversion narratives were open to the most

---

[73] Rogers, *Ohel*, p. 5, insert.
[74] Rogers, *Ohel*, p. 355.
[75] Capp, *The Fifth Monarchy Men*, p. 82.
[76] Rogers, *Ohel*, p. 547.

radical of uses - the protestant privileging of the interior witness of the Spirit ensured that this was so. As a consequence, they became intensively policed. Hobby has noted how 'spiritual autobiographies were often published posthumously and they enter the public domain more carefully surrounded by a bevy of masculine praise, exhortation and interpretation than any other body of women's writing in the period.'[77] She cites Thomas Brooks' introduction to Susannah Bell's *Legacy of a Dying Mother* which was twice as long as Bell's narrative. Rogers is not immune from this type of prefacing - he always introduces his female candidates through their association with men, confirming that even in the millennium would women be a subjected sex.

Nevertheless, from time to time Rogers actively capitalises upon the millenarian edge of the conversion accounts, demonstrating the Independents' unique enjoyment of the enriched spirituality of 'those his latter Golden Days'.[78] Thus Tabitha Kelsall telescopes her personal apocalypse:

> I lay long under a sad condition, and so as I could not read, nor pray, nor hear, but found all unprofitable to me; many ways did God shake me sore and I lay under heavy trials and shakings long till the Lord came in by himself, and settled that in my mind, which is in He. 12.26. Yet once more I will shake not the earth only, but also heaven, that those things which cannot be shaken may remain. For the Lord by his voice did thus comfort me, that although heaven as well as earth, inward, and outward man, my spirit as well as my flesh, and all my works, and righteousnesses were shaken, yet it was to make way for what could never be shaken.[79]

Kelsall's experience is situated as a site for final judgement. In this she had radicalised the puritan doctrine of justification, in which assurance of salvation was based on the final verdict of Judgement Day revealed in advance. Justification - the essence of Calvinist conversion - here becomes the nexus in which the temporal and eternal collide, and the prophecy of the last day becomes instead a 'type' of the experience of Kelsall's soul. Agonising conviction of sin is figured as the shaking of heaven and earth, and the resulting eternal state signifies the enduring infusion of grace in the soul: the anonymous author of *Hebrews* was not writing so much about the last day as about her conversion.

In editing Kelsall's account, Rogers is radically re-writing the puritan understanding of Biblical hermeneutics; he is re-introducing the multi-level hermeneutic of scholasticism in a feature which William Scheick

---

[77] E. Hobby, *Virtue of Necessity: English Women's Writing 1649-88* (London: Virago, 1988), p. 67.
[78] Rogers, *Ohel*, p. 538.
[79] Rogers, *Ohel*, p. 412 [2].

has described as a 'logogic site', an 'intersection of historical connotation and allegorical denotation'.[80] Though Scheick was describing a feature of American puritan discourse, his analysis is pertinent to Rogers' narratives and highlights the continuing New England influence upon the literary representation of Rogers' Irish situation. Kelsall's account anticipates the 'realised eschatology' which was beginning to typify the Quaker apocalypse. It would seem that the Genevan heritage's preference for the 'interpretation' of apocalypse had ultimately proved unsuccessful in redirecting readers away from radical eschatologies. Interregnum groups were using 'interpretative strategies' to reinforce an alternative - though equally radical - apocalypse. A non-literal 'spiritualising' hermeneutic had become as dangerous as a strictly literal millenarianism.

Another of the 'sweet posie of some of the chiefest flowers that I have met with' was Elizabeth Avery, whose record of experience is one of the most extended in Rogers' collection.[81] Like most of the female entries, she is identified by her relationship to patriarchal figures. Rogers is keen to highlight her establishment connections: 'Mr. Parker was her father, that able divine that wrote *De Eccles. Polit.* so largely; but she married Master Avery a Commissionary in Ireland'. The 'able divine', she claims, 'was a godly man' who seems to have brought up his child in a solidly puritan atmosphere.[82] Avery recalls the rebuke of conscience for an early violation of the fourth commandment: 'on one Sabbath-day I was playing, but I was soon and soundly checked for it in my spirit; and went home, but I was a great while troubled, and lay under bondage all along.' About the age of 16 she resolved to improve her lifestyle - she became 'very strict' and displayed 'an entire love to the preaching of the Gospel', but was, she bemoans, 'yet under the Law, and Works'. Conversion was effected through her 'hearing something spoken of Free-grace', and the result was that Avery 'melted'. Her account subsequently details the manner in which 'Gods rod was laid heavy upon me' in the death of her three children. Avery was reminded of her own mortality - 'I was left in an horror, as if I were in Hell' - and finds comfort only when she receives a letter from a minister.[83] Her experiences fluctuate between the subjective and objective, the interior and exterior: heaven and hell are both inside her, in emotions, and at the same time hell is outside herself, a place to which she can be banished and 'ruined'.

---

[80] William J. Scheick, *Design in Puritan American Literature* (Lexington: University Press of Kentucky, 1992), p. 2.
[61] Rogers, *Ohel*, p. 391. See also chapter seven in Gribben, *God's Irishmen*.
[82] Rogers, *Ohel*, p. 403.
[83] Rogers, *Ohel*, p. 403.

Nevertheless the real world impinges upon her eschatological fusion. Another child dies, testing her renewed faith, but Avery meets her trial with assurance: 'I could bear it very well, and was not troubled, but rather did rejoyce within me to be thus tried.'[84] Like the Old Testament patriarch Job, however, her faith begins to disintegrate when friends abandon her and she herself is troubled: 'my friends slighted me, and one thing added to another, made me begin to despair again.' Her pain is relieved only when she, like Job, has the privilege of a private theophany: 'And the very next morning as I was at prayer, God wonderfully appeared; and then was it, that Christ was manifested to my spirit, and I was in a trance for a while, but after I awakened full of joy; and yet for all this, I was somewhat under bondage (me thoughts,) but the Word and Means of Grace did confirm me, and comfort me. In the times of the Wars in England, I was brought out of Egypt into the Wilderness.'[85]

Avery's experience offers an intriguing insight into the biblical discourse of idolatry-adultery. Her narrative describes how she displaced her confidence in God, preferring the certainty given by the ministers. She 'doted on them', 'followed and hunted after my lovers, having mens persons in admiration; and thus God suffered me for a little while to go on after them.'[86] Such extended Biblical allusion may cloak an admission of some impropriety on Avery's part. Colonel Lambert had offered to take Avery to Oxford, where her 'desire for communion with godly people there' excited her curiosity. Few details of the intriguing trip remain - Rogers has left ellipses in the original. But Brooks had glossed a similar case: 'It is natural for the soul to rest upon everything below Christ; to rest upon creatures, to rest upon graces, to rest upon duties, to rest upon divine manifestations, to rest upon celestial consolations, to rest upon gracious evidences, and to rest upon sweet assurances. Now the Lord, to cure His people of this weakness, and to bring them to live wholly and solely upon Jesus Christ, denies comfort, and denies assurance, etc., and for a time leaves His children to walk in darkness.'[87]

When the narrative picks up again, Avery is suffering the disappointment of finding nothing of God in the proceedings at Oxford, and retires to a garden to mourn. While in the garden she is met by three men who 'wondered to see me so', and who 'asked me many questions ----.' Again Rogers deletes the details of the incident. Avery simply relates that she was left in a 'passion', and found no comfort in

---

[84] Rogers, *Ohel*, p. 403.

[85] Rogers, *Ohel*, p. 404.

[86] Rogers, *Ohel*, p. 404.

[87] Thomas, *Golden Treasury*, p. 23.

the public ordinances of the church: 'I was so tormented that I could not bear it; for I could not joyn with them, nor hear, nor pray, nor had no rest, no comfort, no ease, nor could I eat or drink, but went (as I was wont) to bewail in a Garden, where I was moaning, when there came one unto me, and presently told me, That I was under the opening of the fifth seal, and very near the sixth, in the condition which I was in, and should be in. ----------.'[88]

Again Rogers' ellipses obscure a passage of potentially enormous interest. The anonymous person instructs Avery of her apocalyptic judgements; it is very likely that he suggests a protean form of the 'realised eschatology' which was, in the late 1640s and early 1650s, beginning to characterise the discourses of Quakers and other radical groups. The anonymous person's reference was to *Revelation* 6: 'And when hee had opened the fifth seale, I saw under the altar the soules of them that were killed for the word of God, and for the testimonie of the which they maintained. And they cryed out with a loud voice, saying, How long, Lord, which art holy and true! doest thou not judge and avenge our blood on them that dwell on the earth? And long white robes were given unto every one' (vv. 9-11).

Avery's moaning in the garden is, for her addressee, a figure of the souls under the altar crying out for vengeance on their persecutors. Thomas Goodwin, in his exposition of *Revelation*, had explained the significance of the white robes. They were given for glory, joy, and as a sign of the nobility of the martyrs: 'this giving them white robes is an allusion to the bringing the priests first into the temple when their thirty years were expired; they clothed them in white.'[89] Perhaps Avery's counsellor was alluding to this passage to hint that she would soon be received into congregational fellowship. This would usefully corroborate Rogers' claims for the conversion narratives as tickets of admission to the gathered church - he persistently argues that the church is a latter-day Temple. But Goodwin's exposition was silent on any 'realising' of the eschatology, any application of it to symbolise conversion. Avery, it seems, was drawing on a tradition more radical than that of her pastor.

Revelation's sixth seal presages a shaking reminiscent of that experienced by Tabitha Kelsall: 'And I beheld when he had opened the sixt seale, and loe, there was a great earthquake, and the Sunne was as blacke as sackecloth of haire, and the Moone was like blood. And the starres of heaven fell unto the earth, as a figge tree casteth her greene figges, when it is shaken of a mightie winde. And heaven departed away, as a scroule, when it is rolled, and every mountaine and yle were

---

[88] Rogers, *Ohel*, p. 405.
[89] Goodwin, *Works*, iii. 41.

mooved out of their places' (vv. 12-14). Goodwin was careful to note that 'there is never a phrase here used but is frequently and ordinarily used to express great mutations and overturnings in kingdoms, and great calamities brought upon men in those kingdoms by God, long before the day of judgement.'[90] Nevertheless he refused to personalise his application to the wayfaring believer. Rogers had followed Goodwin as the most radical exponent of an Independent eschatology, but here, in the pick of his crop of conversion narratives, the influence was felt of more innovative endings still.

Certainly the reference to the fifth and sixth seals could be read either way, either as promises of glory in the commentators or threatenings of judgement in the Biblical text. Avery's response was one of fear; she records a retreat into domesticity, and for the first time her narrative mentions her 'Husband', to whom she wrote that she wanted to return from Oxford. But God frustrates her attempts at escape - 'the Letter was burnt' - and she is certain that 'Gods wrath [was] in every thing against me'. Avery becomes resigned to her destruction, hoping only that all might be done to the glory of God, and found herself stranded in Oxford 'three quarters of a year'. After that time, though she had no assurance of salvation, 'it appeared my deliverance was near at hand.'[91] The actual moment of assurance is presaged by 'terrible shakings ... which lit altogether upon the flesh, for the spirit was free', and a voice which promised 'sorrow thou shalt see no more'. Actually the voice said more than that, if the recurring ellipses are to be believed, but again Rogers interferes in Avery's history and, as we shall later see, hints that his parishioners hear words which cannot be re-spoken. Avery then 'writ down what God had done for me, and writ about to my friends' and 'found Christ in me, ruling and reigning'. She seems passive in this operation, simply noting that 'God came in upon my spirit' - her assurance is not based on the observation of a holy life, for it had been 'strict' from her youth, but rather on the witness of an inner light.

The conclusion of Avery's narrative - a history of how she has been acted upon by men - describes how Christ 'hath caught the man-childe up to God, which I brought forth. i.e. The flesh, (by his incarnation) and I have found in me (and do yet) his judgement-seat set, to judge and sentence sin, and lust, and corruption, and his throne is there for himself to sit, and to rule by his own Laws.'[92] Like Kelsall, and following the method suggested by her anonymous advisor, she locates herself as the site of apocalypse, as the stage on which the final drama should be played. Her allusion is to *Revelation* 12, where a 'woman clothed with

---

[90] Goodwin, *Works*, iii. 43.

[91] Rogers, *Ohel*, p. 405.

[92] Rogers, *Ohel*, p. 406.

the sun, and the moone ... under her feete', wearing a 'crowne of twelve starres', bears a male child 'which should rule all nations with a rod of yron : and that her child was taken up unto God and to his throne' (vv. 1-5). Traditional exegesis had identified the woman variously as Israel, the Church or the Virgin Mary, and regularly argued that her son was the Messiah, the reign of a Christian emperor, or the settlement of a pure ecclesiology.

Avery stands this history of interpretation on its head, proclaiming herself as the apocalyptic woman and confusing with her silence the identity of her 'son'. As we have seen, the death of her children had taught Avery the transitory nature of this dull, sublunary world; perhaps the reference to her 'flesh' draws on Adam's description of a life brought forth from his, of 'bone of my bones, and flesh of my flesh' (*Genesis* 2:23), in which case she is referring to those children who had preceded her to death. Alternatively, as in common New Testament terminology, she may be using the 'flesh' to refer to the sinful nature, in which case she is representing her sanctification, her increasing experience of holiness as God gradually removes the power of her sin. The sentence is ambiguous, but the mystery of new birth is a highly symbolic puzzle for Rogers to leave his puritan reader. It certainly implies a claim for Avery's active role in the drama of her salvation; while *Revelation* is re-enacted in her psyche, her outward physical existence also contributes to the prophetic meaning of her words.

As a consequence, her experiences balance the external and internal as equal parts in divine revelation. She is within Christ, who leads her 'higher and higher in himself', but she is also outwith him, able to see him manifest in a church of which she is not yet a part.[93] Again the interior and exterior worlds conflate in a manner which, as Smith has shown in *Perfection Proclaimed* (1989), typifies the Old Testament discourse of the prophet, who often used gesture as well as words to communicate the divine. This assignation was common amongst radical religious groups of the period, but Avery is unusual in that her method of exegesis (where events are 'spiritualised' to refer to the immediate experience of the individual believer rather than a literal future for the elect as a collective) owes more to the Quakers than it does to the mainstream Independency Rogers represented. So too as she 'found Christ in me' and as she moved 'higher in himself', the ultimate barrier between the spiritual and physical has been removed; she has become a part of the Godhead, and the Godhead has become a part of her. The inner 'void' has become a site for God's transcendence. Avery goes beyond orthodox Calvinism's negation of the believer in effecting salvation; she posits a situation in which her entire identity itself

---

[93] Rogers, *Ohel*, p. 406.

disappears into that of the divine. She has deconstructed the dichotomy of the material and spiritual, and constructed the personality of apocalypse. This is the ultimate marriage of, and deconstruction of, self-negation and self-elevation: granted, she has lost her identity, but she could hardly have found anyone more powerful with whom to identify. As Smith has noted of the Interregnum period, 'visions of self were created which moved increasingly towards the merging of the individual with the Godhead, the ultimate claim for perfection ... undoubtedly the language of radical religion was founded upon irrationality in theory and in practice as the difference between the internal and the external, the literal and the figurative, disappeared. Self, Church and Godhead became one.'[94]

Thus Rogers' adaptation of the theology of the 'void' led to a movement away from the Goodwinian eschatology in which he had initially grounded his book towards a more radical Quaker hermeneutic. Man's void had become subsumed into deity - his soul had merged with God - and his hermeneutic had to be adjusted accordingly. It was a theme reflected in circumstances far away from Rogers' circle of radical sectarians in Dublin: *A Wonderful Pleasant and Profitable Letter Written by Mrs Sarah Wight* is a doctrinal exposition based on the premise that 'a Christian's true happiness lies in being emptied of all self, self refined, as well as gross self; and being filled with a full God.'[95] Traditional female subsuming of personality was fusing with the beginning of sectarian missionary movements to effect a self-perception on the outer edge of historic Christianity.

This extended theme of union with the Godhead is to some extent symptomatic of Rogers' control of the narratives. He does not disguise his role in mediating the accounts: 'I must contract much their experiences as they were taken, least they be too voluminous ... I shall gather out the flower only, and give you the sum of what they said.'[96] Rogers' role also explains why many of the claims for assurance are eschatologically informed and often result in the negation of the subject: as the pastor-catalyst of conversion, or as the mediator of these accounts, Rogers would (by his preaching) have exercised strong control over the theology they present and (by his editing) over the manner in which it is presented. His first sermon in Dublin, we are told, focused on 'Christ within' and the 'inward revealings' of his presence.[97] Each of the congregational 'experiences' is a variation upon this initial theme - but it is certain that the voice we hear is Rogers' all along.

---

[94] Smith, *Perfection Proclaimed*, p. 18.
[95] Quoted in Hobby, *Virtue of Necessity*, p. 67.
[96] Rogers, *Ohel*, p. 392.
[97] Rogers, *Ohel*, p. 407-8.

Rogers and the Poetics of Apocalypse

As puritans were called to read themselves as they had earlier been called to read Scripture, traditional Calvinistic introspection fused with millenarian tropes to create a dynamic hermeneutic. As a consequence, as well as creating a specifically apocalyptic identity, Rogers' narratives also worked towards a millenarian aesthetic. The conversion narratives in particular assure us that the essence of the millennial experience cannot be linguistically contained: Mary Barker, for example, had 'great experiences of God, though at present I am not able to express them'.[98] This is another echo of Goodwin, whose *Glimpse* had suggested the temporary nature of language and mediating thought. Richard Sibbes had been glad of mediation; he considered it 'the ground of all comfort' that 'we have all at the second hand.'[99] Rogers, and most of the radical millenarians, did not share his enthusiasm. Their illumination was 'first-hand', in the pages of the Bible and in the immediate revelation of the Spirit. The hermeneutic Rogers espouses conflates the interior and exterior: 'by comparing the providences and prophecies together, God's works, with God's words in these latter days, there by we shall attain to much light (I say, not infallible) to foretell what is to come.'[100] In the balance of inner and outer light, the liminality of personality and Scripture are deliberately blurred.

Thus Rogers' compilation of conversion narratives concludes with a frank address to the reader: 'you have heard but stutterings and stammerings to what are to come, and have seen but a jelly and imperfect embryo to that degree and measure which the saints shall shortly meet with; which will afford us matter of wordless worth, and too high for any language to delineate.'[101] Rogers returns to the old problem of Christian poetics, of how the finite might contain the infinite, and combines it with a deep ambivalence about closure. His argument was eschatological - but it was also typical of the Renaissance. Scheick has summarised a related problem: 'a straightforward divine meaning underlies all temporal words and events, a signification that will be disclosed, or unfolded, at the Second Coming; but in the meantime, humanity struggles with the subtle sinuous ambiguities of Satanic influence in the world and in the human word.'[102] Puritan theories of representation were founded on the possibility of mimesis and the iconic power of language. Reformation polemics had focused the problem of interpretation in the understanding of Scripture;

---

[98] Rogers, *Ohel*, p. 413.
[99] Sibbes, *Works*, iii. 27.
[100] Rogers, *Ohel*, pp. 27-8.
[101] Rogers, *Ohel*, p. 449.
[102] Scheick, *Design in Puritan American Literature*, p. 19.

contemporary hermeneutical debates within puritanism found a more immediate relevance in the challenge to understand God's providences both in the changing circumstances of the civil war and in the life of the individual believer.

Puritan divines cut the ground from under this debate when they suggested that literariness - the textuality of language, history and personality - would no longer exist in the imminent millennium. In *A Glimpse of Sions Glory*, Goodwin had asserted that sacramental symbols would no longer be needed in the overwhelming immediacy of God's presence in the millennium. More radically, the Seeker Lawrence Clarkson 'vilified the Scriptures, and would not have the people live upon white and black'.[103] When orthodox puritan divines developed this idea, they cut the ground from under Reformation polemics and contemporary eschatology. The problem of Biblical hermeneutics would be redundant when explicit statements in dreams subverted the believer's reliance upon Scripture - as was happening in Rogers' church. A human hermeneutic of providence was needless when inner voices explained it all. Sacraments, providence, and even language itself were ultimately only means of mediation, of interpreting and understanding a reality which existed beyond. When that reality interpreted itself, all men had to do was sit and wait for the witness of the inner voice. This was exactly the teaching of the Seekers. *Finitum non est capax infiniti* was now of little relevance - nothing now was finite. The capacity of the receiver to get now matched that of the sender to give.

At the same time, however, Rogers was pursuing a more radical solution to the problem of the puritan aesthetic. In his millennium, when all men shared one language, their books would simply cease to exist. If, as Smith has claimed, 'the search for the true church was also a quest for true signification',[104] the Independents' millennium had finally settled the question. There would be no need to find the 'true church' - no false one would exist - and with the annihilation of books and sacraments, there would be no need for any theory of signs. Rogers had already noted the temporary necessity of books in the continuing process of progressive revelation: 'the day is coming when Kiriath-Sepher shall be smitten, whose name signifies the City of Books, and our City and Country are full these times, which by the next age will all be out of date, and lie moulding like old almanacs in corners; for then the Lamb shall be our light, and the Lord our Temple.'[105] Language would lie exhausted in the immediate presence of God. There could be no more need for Clarkson's 'white and black'.

---

[103] Edwards, *Gangræna*, ii. 165.
[104] Smith, *Perfection Proclaimed*, p. 13.
[105] Rogers, *Ohel*, p. 217.

The proto-deconstructive method of Rogers' prose is confirmed by its affinity with Derridean thought. Derrida argued that 'the sign, which defers presence, is conceivable only on the *basis* of the presence that it defers and *moving toward* the deferred presence that it aims to reappropriate.'[106] Words, then, are a barrier to 'presence' and are only ever an echo of the reality to which they refer. Rogers' linguistic philosophy confirms this: the presence to which *Ohel* moves is the *parousia*, the 'presence' or 'coming' of Christ. When Christ returned, there would be no more need for any type of mediation of the divine, whether that be in sacraments or in Rogers' book. This is the puritan aesthetic in microcosm: in the struggle to efface the signifier and dissolve *différance*, iconoclasts struggled to abolish the deferral of the second coming. *Différance* opposes apocalypse, and it was the purpose of millenarian texts to witness to the dissolution of *différance* and to make imminent the advent of Christ. When the sign was replaced by the signified, there could be no more delay - the apocalypse was happening. John Rogers' literary theory charts the signs of the times: whether in sacraments or in words, there was no need for the sign when the signified was at hand, no need to contain or mediate the infinite. Now the infinite spoke for himself.

Having thus cast such a net of inescapable textuality, Rogers invites his reader into his book, attempting to confuse him or her with the same technique he uses elsewhere to construct the apocalyptic personality of the applicants for church membership. Human lives, having been paralleled with human productions, lose their inherent difference from the outer world. This subversion of the dichotomy of the interior and exterior world is developed in Avery's account, where, as we have seen, the self-divine dichotomy disappeared. Self-negation in the conversion narratives - representative of the expected 'void' - is paralleled by the self-negation of the author, and his attempt to seduce the reader into the same experience. His inclusion of Avery's account profoundly challenges his authorial situation. Avery has already fused her personality with God: how can Rogers invest himself with the authority to challenge that? Thus *Ohel* ultimately becomes its own most expressive 'example of experience', a series of conversion narratives whose form destabilises the role and personality of the reader as much as the writer. *Ohel* deconstructs the oppositions most basic to the creation of individuality and seeks to project its conclusion - and confusion - onto the reader.

This denial of stasis is representative of the essential nature of the Independent temper. Goodwin, with the other authors of the

---

[106] Jacques Derrida, *A Derrida Reader: Between the Blinds*, ed. Peggy Kamuf (New York: Harvester Wheatsheaf, 1991), p. 61.

Apologeticall Narration, whom Woodhouse considers 'the most moderate of Independents', resolved 'not to make our present judgement and practice a binding law unto ourselves for the future'. William Dell addressed Cromwell, Fairfax and the Council of War with similar intent: 'though through God's especial goodness the doctrine of the Gospel be again revived among us at this present time, yet ought we not to sit down content with the present state of things, but to search and see if our present doctrine do not yet err from the primitive purity and brightness of the Gospel.'[107] In politics and church order, quite as much as personal salvation, progressive revelation denied the possibility of stasis, and without stasis the possibility of assurance becomes a complex goal to pursue. Thus the doctrine of progressive revelation - underpinning much of *Ohel*'s argument - actually challenges its very existence. Like *Areopagitica*, *Ohel* would have fallen already behind the continuing revelation of the Spirit. Progressive revelation was inimical to the production of closed texts.

The year 1653, in which *Ohel* was published, marked the high-tide of the influence of the Independent brotherhood. Cromwell began the year as the darling of the Fifth Monarchists: his 'Barebones' Parliament, hand-picked from lists of saints submitted by puritan congregations, was commonly imagined as the catalyst of apocalypse, the instrument by which England might again be restored to its pristine primitive innocence. It could have been the beginning of the rule of the saints the Fifth Monarchists expected. But the increasing radicalisation of the saints resulted in Cromwell's turning against Parliament. Rogers assured the Commissioners that Biblical precedents made good legislation: 'the Acts of the Apostles had been your best statute-book in this business ... You use not God's Word.'[108] Others asked Thomas Fairfax how it could 'be lawful to patch up the old worldly government ... according to its own natural principles': something new would soon be taking its place.[109] Moderates were certain that the radical Independents aimed at nothing less than establishing theocracy according to the principles of the Fifth Monarchists.

The prospect of theocracy proved too much for certain of the godly. In a secret meeting early on the morning of the 12 of December, moderate M.P.s voted for the dissolution of the Barebones Parliament, and handed government back into the hands of Cromwell. The conservative backlash had begun. In Ireland Rogers' cause was overwhelmed when Thomas Patient, leader of the Waterford Baptists,

---

[107] Woodhouse (ed.), *Puritanism and Liberty*, pp. 45, 313.
[108] Rogers, *Ohel*, pp. 221-2.
[109] Woodhouse (ed.), *Puritanism and Liberty*, p. 246.

took over Rogers' old pulpit in Christ Church.[110] In England, Cromwell was invested as Lord Protector and set about demolishing the millenarian movement. Major-General Harrison, who in April had expelled the Presbyterians, found himself ejected from Parliament, and, with Rogers, was implicated in a plot in February 1654.[111] Rogers furiously slandered Cromwell as a 'Bastard of Ashdod' and an 'illegitimate Monster',[112] but it was all to no avail. Imprisoned without charge in July 1654, he was told by Cromwell that he 'suffered as a railer, as a seducer, and a busybody in other men's affairs, and a stirrer up of sedition ... not for the testimony of Jesus Christ'.[113] Rogers' words were at issue; Cromwell felt them 'as sharp as swords'.[114] 'You fix the name of Antichristian upon anything', the Protector complained, frustrated by the fluid heart of millenarian thought. But Rogers refused to retreat into closure, faithful to his millenarian aesthetic if not to his theology: 'that Fifth-Monarchy principle, as you call it, is of such a latitude as takes in all Saints, all such as are sanctified in Christ Jesus.'[115]

And so in an instant, in the twinkling of an eye, radical millenarianism was eclipsed as the establishment which had destroyed the old world refused to move into the new. Fifth Monarchism was driven underground, and, once again, the baton of the radical eschatology was passed on. As the eventual Restoration of Charles II signalled the eclipse of puritan influence, the squabbling brethren of the puritan pact were called again to unity. The Fifth Monarchists, who had branded Cromwell's coterie as Antichrists in the 1650s, later found themselves working alongside Owen and renegade Covenanters in the Rye House plot.[116] In the experience of defeat, puritans were compelled to recognise that the real enemy - Antichrist's fifth column - lay inside the self. The 'paradise within' imagined by Milton had become the site of innumerable eschatological conflicts.

---

[110] Phil Kilroy, 'Radical Religion in Ireland, 1641-1660', in Jane Ohlmeyer (ed.), *Ireland from Independence to Occupation, 1641-1660* (Cambridge: Cambridge University Press, 1995), pp. 210-1.

[111] P.G. Rogers, *The Fifth Monarchy Men* (London: Oxford University Press, 1966), pp. 37, 43.

[112] Rogers, *The Fifth Monarchy Men*, p. 140.

[113] Cromwell, *Speeches of Oliver Cromwell*, p. 228.

[114] Cromwell, *Speeches of Oliver Cromwell*, p. 229.

[115] Cromwell, *Speeches of Oliver Cromwell*, pp. 230-1.

[116] Capp, *The Fifth Monarchy Men*, pp. 220, 101.

CHAPTER 8

John Bunyan and the Realized Apocalypse

In the early 1650s, when members of Rogers' congregation were struggling for assurance of salvation, a similar spiritual crisis was being experienced by the young John Bunyan (1628-1688).[1] If we are to believe Hale White, his Edwardian biographer, Bunyan was eventually admitted to membership of the independent Bedford church in 1653, the year in which its pastor, John Gifford, was given a parish benefice and, as the vicar of St John's, entered the newly incorporated Cromwellian national church.[2] 1653 was also the high tide of the radical millenarian movement. As John Rogers was publishing his *Ohel*, the Bedford congregation were demonstrating their approbation of the theocratic ideology underpinning his thought. Gifford and other leading members of his congregation, for example, signed a letter encouraging Cromwell to ensure that men 'hating covetousness' would 'govern these nations in righteousness': they were participating in the millenarian aspirations which were to lead to the utopian hopes invested in the Nominated Assembly of 1653, the 'Sanhedrin' for which the Fifth Monarchists had called.[3] Recent historians have begun to explore the relationship between Bunyan's church and the apocalyptic radicals. The Bedford congregation certainly enjoyed strong links with like-minded fellowships in the capital: in 1658 one member was recommended to John Simpson's congregation in London, while another, who had only 'questionable reasons' for a transfer, was encouraged to seek the advice of Simpson, Henry Jessey and John Rogers.[4] (Rogers, by late 1653, had returned to London and had assumed his previous lectureship in the pulpit of St Thomas Apostles when Thomas Brooks, its previous

---

[1] On the dynamics of Bunyan's conversion, see R.L. Greaves, *Glimpses of Glory: John Bunyan and English Dissent* (Stanford: Stanford University Press, 2002).

[2] [Hale White], *John Bunyan* (London: Hodder and Stoughton, 1905), p. 28; Michael Mullett, *John Bunyan in Context* (Keele: Keele University Press, 1996), p. 44

[3] Mullett, *John Bunyan in Context*, p. 52. Note the allusion to Exodus 18:21.

[4] Greaves, *Saints and Rebels*, p. 127.

occupant, ceased his ministry there.[5]) There were strong similarities between the Bedford and Dublin churches. Both were independent, and both practised 'open communion', allowing into membership both those who had been sprinkled as covenant children and those who were immersed as believing adults - provided they could offer a narrative of God's dealings with their soul. The twin themes of Rogers' *Ohel* - soteriology and eschatology - would reach a mature complexity in the writing of the later Bunyan.

Grace Abounding (1666), Bunyan's spiritual autobiography, displays many of the distinctive features of the highly stylised conversion narrative genre. Like the other participants in the publication of conversion narratives, Bunyan foregrounded the tensions instilled by puritan exegesis, and sought to create order from the chaos of his spiritual experience. His pastoral theology was well within the mainstream Calvinist tradition and does not seem to have evolved throughout his life. Like many of his forebears, for example, he insisted on the dangers of false faith. In *A Holy Life the Beauty of Christianity* (1684), he describes 'non-saving faith [which] standeth in speculation and naked knowledge of Christ, and so abideth idle: but the other truly seeth and receives him, and so becometh fruitful.' The fruitfulness he demanded - the sanctification which was to evidence one's election - was of a high standard. He notes that 'there are a great many professors now in England that have nothing to distinguish them from the worst of men, but their praying, reading, hearing of sermons, baptism, church-fellowship, and breaking of bread.' For Bunyan, the marks so typical of a 'visible saint' were not in themselves sufficient: faith was to be evidenced by a holier walk than this. He explained that 'when Christ is truly received and embraced to the justifying of the sinner, in that man's heart he dwells by his word and Spirit, through the same faith also. Now Christ by his Spirit and word must needs *season* the soul he thus dwells in: so then the soul being seasoned, it seasoneth the body; and body and soul, the life and conversation.'[6]

Bunyan had already applied these standards to himself. Three decades earlier, events which were subsequently described in *Grace Abounding* had convinced the narrator that although he was 'an ignorant sot ... yet, at a venture, I will conclude that I am not altogether faithless, though I know not what faith is.'[7] While his experience 'commanded a great calm in my soul, it persuaded me there might be hope'.

---

[5] Brooks, *Works*, i. xxxi; Edward Rogers, *Some Account of the Life and Opinions of a Fifth-Monarchy-Man. Chiefly Extracted from the Writings of John Rogers, Preacher* (London: Longmans, Green, Reader and Dyer, 1867), p. x.

[6] Bunyan, *Works*, ii. 507-8.

[7] GA §48.

Nevertheless Bunyan was too wise to pin his hopes solely upon an emotion: 'I lay not the stress of my salvation thereupon, but upon the Lord Jesus, in the promise.' But he could not enjoy the assured faith Rogers had described: his peace only lasted 'three or four days, and then I began to mistrust and to despair again'.[8] By the time of writing *Of the Resurrection of the Dead* (1665) Bunyan had grown more cautious: 'If thou miss but one letter in thy evidence, thou art gone; for though thou mayest deceive thy own heart with brass, instead of gold, and with tin instead of silver, yet God will not be so put off.'[9] One of the strongest themes of his account is the insufficiency of the external evidence of 'works' or 'godly walking'. Prioritising the witness of the inner light, Bunyan's introspection was constantly frustrated in its search for the evidences of election.

This was the same pastoral theology which Rogers had propounded. We have already seen that the atmosphere among these early Independents and Baptists, combining traditional Calvinistic self-scrutiny with a sense that the millenarian kingdom of Christ was about to be established, accounts for much of the literary instability of their conversion narratives. Bunyan's experience is particularly fraught and was to prove seminal for all his subsequent writing. As Vincent Newey has observed, Bunyan's preparation of *Grace Abounding* was 'a great seminal experience: there is hardly an ingredient in his two other works, *The Pilgrim's Progress* and *The Holy War*, which did not originate in the earlier text.'[10]

It is consequently true, as one recent critic has noted, that soteriology remains 'the focal point of Bunyan's theology' throughout his life.[11] Nevertheless, in its focus in *Grace Abounding*, Bunyan's spiritual experience does not easily conform to the progress through the morphology of conversion which Calvinistic puritans propounded. This is no simple movement from wrath to grace, from sin to salvation. Bunyan's spiritual interests extend over a long period of time. When 'but a child of but nine or ten', the young Bunyan was awakened to his dire predicament, 'greatly afflicted and troubled with the thoughts of the day of judgement, and that both night and day'.[12] He recounts

---

[8] *GA* §174.

[9] Bunyan, *Works*, ii. 120.

[10] Vincent Newey, '"With the eyes of my understanding: Bunyan, experience, and acts of interpretation', in N.H. Keeble (ed.), *John Bunyan Conventicle and Parnassus: Tercentenary Essays* (Oxford: Clarendon Press, 1988), p. 208.

[11] Gordon Campbell, 'Fishing in Other Men's Waters: Bunyan and the Theologians', in N.H. Keeble (ed.), *John Bunyan Conventicle and Parnassus: Tercentenary Essays* (Oxford: Clarendon Press, 1988), p. 146.

[12] *GA* §6-7.

shutting out the voice of conscience, and turning from all religious interest until his marriage. His wife was so poor that her dowry consisted only of two classics of puritan spirituality, *The Plain Man's Pathway to Heaven* and *The Practice of Piety*. In reading these texts, Bunyan's heart was again touched by concern about his 'sad and sinful state', yet 'because I knew no better, I fell in very eagerly with the religion of the times; to wit, to go to church twice a day'.[13] Michael Mullet has claimed that the services which Bunyan attended, whose description evokes the Church of England's despised Laudian elaborations, were most likely conducted in the later 1640s, after the Book of Common Prayer had been replaced by the Calvinistic simplicity of the Westminster divines' *Directory of Worship*.[14] But this strict ecclesiology was not enough to 'awaken' Bunyan. The mature author could look back and lament that 'all this while, I was not sensible of the danger and evil of sin.'[15] External reformation - giving up swearing - amounted to his gaining an impressive reputation: 'our neighbours did take me to be a very godly man, a new and religious man, and did marvel much to see such a great and famous alteration in my life and manners.' Bunyan himself regarded the change as a 'conversion', but admitted 'I was nothing but a poor painted hypocrite, yet I loved to be talked of as one that was truly godly.'[16] The rest of *Grace Abounding* continues this oscillation of hope and despair, a cyclical pattern repeated time after time, so that those engaged in 'reading his work upon me'[17] cannot even be sure when it is saving: the moment of Bunyan's regeneration is a closely guarded secret. Bunyan's account of conversion is far removed from that described in the 1644 Baptist confession of faith, where a sudden awareness of free grace transports an individual from one level of living to another. What Bunyan presents is a series of steps so minute they might almost be an inclined plane. Vincent Newey has noticed that this 'pattern of mis-taking and the deferral of predicted ends is repeated over and over again in *Grace Abounding*'.[18] Dayton Haskin has commented upon the text's 'belatedness'.[19] In her study of the double-conversion motif in *Grace Abounding*, Anne Hawkins has described 'little sense of structure' in

---

[13] *GA* §16.

[14] Mullett, *John Bunyan in Context*, p. 26.

[15] *GA* §19.

[16] *GA* §31-2.

[17] *GA* Preface.

[18] Newey, '"With the eyes of my understanding: Bunyan, experience, and acts of interpretation', p. 194.

[19] Dayton Haskin, '"Thou must feed upon my Word": Bunyan and the Bible', in N.H. Keeble (ed.), *John Bunyan Conventicle and Parnassus: Tercentenary Essays* (Oxford: Clarendon Press, 1988), p. 158.

Bunyan's conversion - 'a kind of conversion which is by definition diffuse, repetitive, and cumulative'.[20] Remarkably, as a narrative of spiritual journey, *Grace Abounding* consistently refuses to offer closure.

As Hawkins implies, this continual frustration of closure finds its source in traditional puritan evangelical theology. Bunyan's continued uncertainty as to whether or not he was saved simply enacted William Perkins' teaching that 'every new act of sin requires a new act of faith and repentance.'[21] Perkins viewed conversion as more of a cyclical process than a linear teleology: the converted could always be reconverted. The irony is, of course, that Perkins himself had popularised the metaphor of the 'golden chain of salvation', which even found its way into that most definitive of reformed creeds, the Canons of the Synod of Dort.[22] Perkins' treatise of *The Golden Chain* (1591) included a diagram which emphasised the explicit linearity of spiritual experience - a logical movement either towards glory or perdition.[23] Bunyan's *Mapp of Salvation* (1663) mirrors its main themes, reiterating the puritan construction of the self as a text: if the conversion narratives had encouraged saints to look into their hearts and write, Bunyan's *Mapp* urged them to 'look / Into thy heart, as in a book / And see if thou canst read the same.'[24] Bunyan's *Mapp* is a flow chart demonstrating the temporal development of the eternal decrees of election and reprobation - enabling the discerning reader to compare his experience with that described on the *Mapp* as one text with another. Yet the *Mapp* is explicitly teleological; Bunyan gives no hint of its opposition to his own cyclical experience in *Grace Abounding*. He could defend his course by claiming to find both ideas in Perkins.

There is a sense, of course, in which this frustration of closure was just part of the general puritan difficulty of expressing the transcendent. Believers were mystified by the divine operation of salvation: Rogers, we noted, ends his narratives protesting that 'you have heard but stutterings and stammerings to what are to come, and have seen but a jelly and imperfect embryo to that degree and measure which the Saints shall shortly meet with; which will afford us matter of wordlesse worth, and too high for any language to delineate.'[25] We have already noted

---

[20] Anne Hawkins, 'The Double-Conversion in Bunyan's *Grace Abounding*', *Philological Quarterly* 61 (1982), p. 259.

[21] William Perkins, *The Art of Prophesying* (1606; rpt. Edinburgh: Banner of Truth, 1996), p. 62.

[22] Hall (ed.), *Harmony of the Protestant Confessions*, p. 547.

[23] Gordon Campbell, 'The Source of Bunyan's *Mapp of Salvation*', *Journal of the Warburg and Courtauld Institutes* 44 (1981), pp. 240-1.

[24] Bunyan, *Works*, iii. unpaginated frontispiece.

[25] Rogers, *Ohel*, p. 449.

that other millenarians - more radical than Bunyan - expressed hope that the day would soon come when books would be altogether redundant in the immediate presence of God when there would be no need for any finite medium to convey an infinite message. The radicals expected that every book would self-consume as the distinctions between sign and signifier collapsed and human language reverted to its pre-Babel unity.[26] Locating itself within this common millenarian discourse, *Grace Abounding* foregrounds its inability to capture the reality of the events it describes. After one particularly sweet spiritual experience, when his heart was 'filled full of comfort and hope', Bunyan 'said in my soul, with much gladness, I would write this down before I go any farther, for surely I will not forget this forty years hence; but alas! within less than forty days, I began to question all again; which made me begin to question all still.'[27]

Bunyan and Eschatology

That Bunyan should at least allude to the millenarian trope of 'the end of books' highlights the connection between *Grace Abounding* and the apocalyptic environment of the radical sects. The year in which *Grace Abounding* was published, 1666, was the year in which, according to Henry Archer and the Fifth Monarchist Henry Danvers, the millennium would begin. The year also marked the end of the first period of Bunyan's direct involvement with millenarian thought - a phase which had begun with his arrest in 1660 and which reached its high point in his anticipation of the collapse of papacy in *The Holy City* (1665). As we have seen, in the 1650s Bunyan's Bedford congregation had forged strong links with many of the most apocalyptically-minded saints in London, and, by association, many critics have pointed to the radicalism of Bunyan's earlier eschatology. By 1661, however, the leading Independents had opened a considerable critical distance from the extremists. 1661 was the year in which Thomas Venner led an ultimately unsuccessful Fifth Monarchist rising in London, centred, significantly, on Rogers' old preaching centre at St Thomas Apostle's. Thomas Goodwin repudiated the attempted coup; he was joined by Brooks and Bunyan.[28] The newly restored government, nevertheless, was

---

[26] James Knowlson, *Universal Language Schemes in England and France, 1600-1800* (Toronto: University of Toronto Press, 1975), p. 8.
[27] GA §92.
[28] Brooks, *Works*, i. xxxii; R.L. Greaves, 'Conscience, Liberty, and the Spirit: Bunyan and Nonconformity', in N.H. Keeble (ed.), *John Bunyan Conventicle and Parnassus: Tercentenary Essays* (Oxford: Clarendon Press, 1988), p. 28; Rogers, *Some Account of the Life and Opinions of a Fifth-Monarchy-Man*, p. 327.

immediately suspicious of all dissent, and Bunyan, with many other nonconformists, was imprisoned the same year.[29]

Bunyan's subsequent millenarian interests have been widely discussed in the larger programme to situate him within the radical context. William York Tindall's *John Bunyan, Mechanick Preacher* (1934) initiated this movement and his concerns have been adopted by contemporary scholars such as Christopher Hill. Tindall was keen to foreground his own distance from the frankly partisan nineteenth-century portrait of his subject. Before writing the first draft of his book, he claims, he had read only one secondary source. Nevertheless, Tindall recognised the importance of apocalyptic thought in Bunyan's writing, devoting two chapters of his total nine to an exploration of that subject. Unfortunately he seems to have popularised a reading of Bunyan which evinces little sympathy to the nuances of seventeenth-century eschatological debate.

A recognition of what Hill has described as the 'trail-blazing'[30] character of *John Bunyan, Mechanick Preacher* need not imply that each one of Tindall's arguments have been uncritically accepted. Both Bob Owens and Richard Greaves, for example, take issue with Tindall's claim that Bunyan's repeated protestations of loyalty to King and Government were mere facades concealing a hidden militarism. Although Tindall 'regards these expressions of political loyalty as being purely pragmatic', Owens claims that 'it remains difficult to accept that Bunyan's repeated expressions of loyalty to the King were cynically dishonest, as Tindall suggests.'[31] Furthermore, Greaves suggests, although 'Bunyan was radical in many respects, such as his open-membership policy, his pronounced dislike of most rich and powerful people, and his determination to hold conventicles, we have no evidence that he ever asserted the right of Christians to take up arms against an antichristian government.'[32] It would appear that Tindall could not anticipate the possibility that Bunyan's commitment to monarchy - as an eschatological instrument of vengeance - was itself a radical apocalyptic agenda in the early 1680s. His descriptions of what Charles II should be - the international defender of the protestant cause - clearly contrasts what he was. Nor need we assume that Bunyan was ignorant of court trends. His links with John Owen - who was involved

---

[29] Toon, *God's Statesman*, p. 123.

[30] Hill, *A Tinker and a Poor Man*, p. 64.

[31] W.R. Owens, 'Antichrist must be Pulled Down: Bunyan and the Millennium', in A. Lawrence et al (eds), *John Bunyan and his England, 1628-88* (London: The Hambledon Press, 1990), pp. 90-1.

[32] R.L. Greaves, *John Bunyan and English Nonconformity* (London: The Hambledon Press, 1992), p. 201.

a radical anti-government conspiracy network[33] - could have kept him in touch with developments in the palace.

Given Bunyan's reputation as a socio-political radical, it is perhaps surprising that his vision of the godly prince was drawn from his life-long adherence to the ideology outlined in the Geneva Bible and Foxe's 'Book of Martyrs'. Only in his final years would he abandon the politico-eschatology of the Marian exiles. Consequently, aspects of his thinking were grounded in their conservative thought. Even the imagery of his most radical text, *The Holy War* (1682), had conservative roots. Bunyan's description of Christian man as a besieged city clearly drew on the context which had emerged from Calvin's discussion of a believer's mind as a 'citadel'.[34] John Donne, as an Anglican cleric, had built on Calvin's metaphor, begging God to 'batter my heart', advising him that 'I, like a usurped town, to another due, / Labour to admit you'.[35] Presbyterian Manton continued the idea in the 1650s: 'when a commander hath taken a strong castle, and placed a garrison in it, he suffereth none to enter but those of his own side, keeping the gate shut to his enemies. So we must open the heart to none but God, and those that are of God's party and side, keeping the gate shut to others.'[36] Perhaps this is why Greaves has had to defend Bunyan from a charge of implicit conservatism: as he cautiously asserted, 'nothing in Bunyan's millenarianism is incompatible with a radical stance'.[37] Nevertheless, while Bunyan's relation to radical puritanism remains ambiguous, as Roger Sharrock has suggested, the 'test case' remains his millenarianism.[38] Defining the origins and implications of Bunyan's eschatology will position him within the complex matrix of ideas in nonconformist England.

Unfortunately, the recent critical debate seems to have obscured the most helpful historical evidence in its excessive dependence upon often confused second-hand observations. Concern expressed at such imprecision is not merely a case of splitting theological hairs - it is indisputable that this misunderstanding has spilled over into Bunyan criticism and has detrimentally influenced modern evaluations of the writer's influences and interests. At times it still appears that Bunyan

---

[33] Capp, *The Fifth Monarchy Men*, pp. 101, 220.

[34] Calvin, *Institutes*, ii. i. 9; ii. ii. 3.

[35] Donne, 'Batter my heart', ll. 5-6; in *The Oxford Authors: John Donne*, ed. John Carey (Oxford: Oxford University Press, 1990), p. 177; Donne is cited in Rogers, *Ohel*, p. 390.

[36] Manton, *Works*, v. 85.

[37] R.L. Greaves, *Secrets of the Kingdom: British Radicals from the Popish Plot to the Revolution of 1688-1689* (Stanford: Stanford University Press, 1992), p. 50.

[38] Greaves, *Secrets of the Kingdom*, p. 49.

himself was more aware of competing eschatologies than are many of his twentieth-century critics. There was, Bunyan claims, much 'lingering and disputing about the glorious state of the Church in the latter days: Some being for its excellency to consist chiefly in outward glory; and others swerving on the other side, concluding she shall not have none of this; some conceiving that this City will not be built until the Lord comes from Heaven in Person; others again concluding that when he comes, there shall be no longer any tarrying here, but that all shall forthwith, even all the Godly, be taken up to Heaven; with diverse other opinions in these matters'.[39]

What is certain is that Bunyan was the only one of our selection of puritan writers to have invoked the (now stereotypical) idea of a six-thousand-year universal history. In the posthumous *Exposition of the First Ten Chapters of Genesis* (1692), he notes that the 'sabbath' of the creation week typified

> the seventh thousand of years, which are to follow immediately after the world hath stood six thousand first: for as God was six days in the works of creation, and rested the seventh; so in six thousand years he will perfect his works and providences that concern this world. Also he will finish the toil and travel of his saints, with the burthen of the beasts, and the curse of the ground; and bring all into rest for a thousand years. A day with the Lord, is as a thousand years: wherefore this blessed and desirable time is also called 'a day,' 'a great day,' 'that great and notable day of the Lord,' Ac. ii. 20. which shall end in the eternal judgement of the world.[40]

Of Antichrist, and his Ruine, published in the same year, highlighted the role of godly monarchs in the destruction of the 'man of sin', but taught that, at this point, 'there will be such ruins brought both upon the spirit of Christianity, and the true Christian church state, before this Antichrist is destroyed, that there will for a time scarce be found a Christian spirit, or a true visible living church of Christ in the world: Nothing but the dead bodies of these will be to be seen of the nations.'[41] Nevertheless, his work on *Genesis* finished on an optimistic note. He noted that the length of Adam's life was a type of Christ, who would reign in the church for a similar period of time: 'the world therefore beginning thus, doth shew us how it will end; namely, by the reign of the second Adam, as it began with the reign of the first.' Bunyan was acutely conscious of the 'glory that the church shall have in the latter day, even in the seventh thousand years of the world, that sabbath when Christ shall set up his kingdom on earth.' It would be the time

[39] Bunyan, *Works*, iii. 408-9.
[40] Bunyan, *Works*, ii. 424.
[41] Bunyan, *Works*, ii. 66.

referred to in *Revelation* 20, when 'the wicked in the world shall forbear to persecute', when the dragon would be bound, and when 'Christ shall reign in and among his saints till all his enemies be destroyed.'[42] This seventh millennia of world history was to be the time when 'the kingdoms of the earth shall ALL at last become the kingdoms of our Lord, and of his Christ.'[43] Quite where the resurrection and second coming fit in to this chronology is not clear. Bunyan, after his death, hovers ambiguously between pre- and postmillennialism. He never informs the reader whether Christ's reign is spiritual - *through* his saints - or physically *with* them. Perhaps, like that other Bedford millenarian Thomas Brightman, he maintained both positions simultaneously. Nevertheless, Hill is certain that Bunyan, like Napier and Mede, believed that 'the last days' - whether of this world or merely of this age - were to be expected in the seventeenth century.[44]

Thus a sustained mis-reading of the eschatologies of Bunyan's contemporaries has hindered a true understanding of his own eschatological beliefs. Roger Pooley notes that 'twenty years earlier, the millennialist flavour of some of *The Holy War* could have signalled a Fifth Monarchist message, a call to uprising. In fact the principal political allusion is to the remodelling of the Bedford corporation - though the principal events happened shortly after the book was published.'[45] But there is far more to *The Holy War* (1682) than political analogy - its scope and power extend far beyond the concerns of local politics. Bunyan's allegory became a fable enacting the tableau of cosmic history, the history of the church, dramatising the fears of seventeenth-century protestantism, and highlighting problems of representation which remain at the heart of critical theory. Much of its radical power came from Bunyan's powerful fusion of soteriological and prophetic modes. Evidencing his emerging metaphorical consciousness, *The Holy War* exemplified the difficulties of puritan writing at the edge of the promises.

Realised Eschatology and *The Holy War*

The fruit of Calvinistic puritanism's increasingly self-reflexive literary practice was a semiological explosion which, ironically, seemed to parallel the hermeneutics of their rivals. Distinguished by their competing interpretative strategies, the nonconformist groups contested

---

[42] Bunyan, *Works*, ii. 456.
[43] Bunyan, *Works*, ii. 423.
[44] Hill, *A Tinker and a Poor Man*, p. 94.
[45] Roger Pooley, *English Prose of the Seventeenth Century, 1590-1700* (London: Longman, 1992), p. 43.

the methods involved in coding and decoding meaning. As Hugh Ormsby-Lennon has affirmed, 'Quakers rendered themselves immediately identifiable by their speechways (passionately espoused and defended) rather than by their doctrines, which did not approach any fixity of definition until well after Charles II was restored in 1660.'[46] Richard Bauman agrees: 'ways of speaking were ... an identifying feature of the Quaker movement.'[47] In *The Holy War*, Bunyan engaged with their rhetorical slippage and invoked representative methods which typified their discourse. The consequent self-consumption of *The Holy War* was as much the product of a Quaker-like realised eschatology as it was the fruit of puritanism's original Calvinistic ideology of aesthetics.

Of course it is highly ironic that Bunyan - the hammer of the Quakers - should develop a hermeneutic which affirmed one crucial aspect of their 'speechways'. His antipathy towards their semiotic challenge was made clear in his first published texts. *Gospel Truths Opened* (1656), and its subsequent *Vindication* (1657), attacked 'certain men newly started up in our days, called quakers' whose understanding of the resurrection went no further than the raising of believers 'from the state of nature to a state of grace.' Again, he claimed, when they claim to 'own the second coming of Christ to judge the world' they mean 'only to own him in his coming in spirit, within.'[48] Bunyan warned of the danger of such non-literal reading while an increasingly metaphorical strain among his puritan brethren provided the context for a substantial hermeneutical revision within the confines of orthodoxy.

As the 1650s progressed, mainstream puritans were increasingly taking metaphors of Christian life from the records of Scriptural history. Several decades earlier, Richard Sibbes had compared conversion - the beginning of the Christian life - to the initial act of creation. Just as God 'created all out of nothing, order out of confusion', Sibbes claimed, 'God ... raiseth an excellent frame in the heart of a man, he scatters his natural blindness, he sets in order his natural confusion, that a man becomes a new creature.'[49] With similar exegetical technique, Scriptural descriptions of the world's end were also being referred to experiences

---

[46] Hugh Ormsby-Lennon, 'From Shibboleth to Apocalypse: Quaker Speechways during the Puritan Revolution', in Peter Burke and Roy Porter (eds), *Language, Self and Society: A Social History of Language* (Cambridge: Polity Press, 1991), p. 74.

[47] Richard Bauman, *Let Your Words Be Few: Symbolism of Speaking and Silence among Seventeenth-Century Quakers* (Cambridge: Cambridge University Press, 1983), p. 7.

[48] Bunyan, *Works*, ii. 176-7.

[49] Sibbes, *Works*, iii. 10.

within the Christian life. Some years after Sibbes, Thomas Brooks described his wife's experience of a 'realised' millennium:

> The gracious presence of God was signally manifested in the chaining up of Satan; for the greatest part of her sickness, her body being very low, her spirits low, and her strength low, and by reason of her great and many weaknesses, she was cast unavoidably under great indispositions, both as to civil and sacred things; the greater was the mercy in God's chaining up of Satan; and if now and then Satan began to be busy, the Lord quickly rebuked him, and laid a law of restraint upon him.[50]

Just as Sibbes revisited the act of creation in his meditation on conversion, Brooks' wife experienced the latter-day binding of Satan as a transcendence of illness before death.

As this increasingly metaphorical consciousness increased in influence among the puritans, Bunyan's own eschatological and soteriological concerns continued to develop. In *The Holy War* Bunyan attempted to combine both interests, and fused a mode of discourse which appears to have been the ultimate attempt to impose linearity upon his cyclical conversion experience. The theology of Perkins, as we noted, allowed space for constant cyclicism. To counter this influence, Bunyan seems to have attempted to invoke the complexities of his conversion while involving the teleological assumptions of Biblical eschatology. Creation's movement from genesis to apocalypse would paradigm the sinner's movement through the *ordo salutis* from condemnation to glory. This combination of soteriological and eschatological themes would certainly demonstrate Bunyan's affinity with the eighteenth-century New England puritans in their understanding of 'the close relationship between the larger and smaller works of redemption'. God, as they understood it, 'redeemed history the same way he redeemed individuals'.[51]

Bunyan's change of attitude towards 'realising' eschatology appears to have developed through his network of personal contacts. Both Brooks and Bunyan, we have seen, had links with the same London radicals, and it may have been that their influence encouraged Bunyan in his movement towards metaphor.[52] Certainly his early hostility to the Quakers - whose distinctive 'speechways' were constructed on the basis of realised eschatology - seems to have been overcome as nonconformists of all varieties suffered together under unsympathetic

---

[50] Brooks, *Works*, i. lxxx.
[51] Davidson, *The Logic of Millennial Thought*, pp. 129, 136.
[52] Brooks preceded John Rogers in the pastorate of St Thomas Apostles in the early 1650s.

Restoration governments.[53] By the 1670s Bunyan had languished in prison alongside many of the ablest Quaker defenders,[54] and those works published after the experiences of this imprisonment seem to owe a debt to their literary strategy. Some aspects of their discourse had always been a feature of Bunyan's writing. His work had never particularised details, for example - Michael Mullett has described *Grace Abounding* as a 'tantalizing fragment' lacking both dates and location, and the landscape of *The Pilgrim's Progress* as a 'neutral nowhere'.[55] Similarly, Jackson Cope has argued that Quaker writing also transcended detail: 'personal histories are made so vague that they seem almost to lose reality.'[56] But by the time of writing *The Holy War*, Bunyan's debt to Quakerism had gone far beyond this mere omission of detail.

In the latter allegory, Bunyan presents his most radical hermeneutic to date - not a method of 'literalising' Biblical apocalyptic, but an exegesis which finds in *Revelation* only a tableau of his own spiritual history, an annotated psychodrama. Perhaps, as Michael Watts has suggested, Bunyan found consolation in 'the meaning which the Quaker emphasis on realizing the kingdom of God within had for men and women whose hopes of establishing the kingdom of God on earth had been thwarted.'[57] Bunyan's allegory compares his individual regeneration with the great 'regeneration' of all things (*Matthew* 19:28) - and tries to convince the reader that there is little difference. In this attempt to conflate the sign and thing signified, *The Holy War* enacts Cope's observation that Quaker writing tends 'to break down the boundary between literalness and metaphor, between conceptions and things'.[58] Pointing the reader back past Babel to the time when the original universal language posited a unique identification between description and object, Bunyan's last allegory provides us with the logical culmination of the metaphysical trend within puritan literature, the tail end of the movement towards the total conflation of sign and thing signified. It juxtaposes radically diverse registers and argues, apparently, for the identification of personal and universal histories. But the result of this identification was a failure to represent the closure of unfinished experience. Despite its invocation of teleological patterns, *The Holy War* continues to frustrate what Webster has described as 'the

---

[53] Mullett, *John Bunyan in Context*, p. 100.
[54] Mullett, *John Bunyan in Context*, p. 100.
[55] Mullett, *John Bunyan in Context*, pp. 27, 192.
[56] Jackson I. Cope, 'Seventeenth-Century Quaker Style', *PMLA* 76 (1956), p. 745.
[57] Michael R. Watts, *The Dissenters: From the Reformation to the French Revolution* (Oxford: Clarendon Press, 1978), p. 207.
[58] Cope, 'Seventeenth-Century Quaker Style', p. 726.

effort of the diarist ... to make experience conform to a teleology of grace.'[59] Indeed, Hawkins has noted that *The Holy War* 'manifests the pattern of a double conversion even more clearly than does *The Pilgrim's Progress'*.[60] Despite its apocalyptic register, *The Holy War* cannot supply an ending. Bunyan's text undermines the certainties it posits on every level of its allegory.

Thus the self-consumption of *The Holy War* and its demonstration of the insufficiency of reading epitomises Bunyan's faithfulness to Calvinism's aesthetic practice and iconoclastic temper. Following the tradition of the puritan eschatologists, Bunyan situated his text as a discussion of the Calvinistic aesthetic maxim: *finitum non est capax infiniti*. Nevertheless, as we will later see, the narrator's manoeuvrings to compel the reader to destroy *The Holy War* as a remnant of the Diabolonian invasion of Mansoul typify Bunyan's sense that his book is still an icon - albeit an icon grounded in transformative power. Bunyan's interest in *The Holy War* involves issues which diverge widely from a study of the application of soteriology. Rooted in complexities, *The Holy War* is so much more than a Quaker *Grace Abounding*.

The ambivalence of this method is usefully noted in Bunyan's treatment of the millennium in *The Holy War*.[61] Perhaps the most confusing of the text's episodes, this invocation of the binding of Satan in *Revelation* 20 suggests to the reader that the allegory is almost over - certainly in its Biblical setting, the millennium introduces the last act in the drama of redemption. Bunyan's narrator, nevertheless, seems to confuse both the timing and the nature of this future golden age. In so far as time is concerned, *The Holy War*'s millennium does not occur at the end of its narrative, as an orthodox puritan reader might have expected, but signals the experience of the believer within time. Side-stepping the linear historiography the millenarians advanced, Bunyan applied the golden age ideology to Mansoul in the period *between* its redemption and its eschatological closure - as Brooks had earlier described his wife's transcendence of illness in similar terms. Thus, far from demonstrating a linear historiography culminating in a millennium and an apocalypse, as we might expect from a text purporting to be an allegory of universal history, *The Holy War* mirrors the more cyclical experience of *Grace Abounding*'s protagonist.

Similarly, Bunyan seems to undermine the nature of the golden age described in *Revelation*. The inspired Apostle envisaged the millennium

[59] Webster, 'Writing to Redundancy', p. 43.
[60] Anne Hawkins, 'The Double-Conversion in Bunyan's *Grace Abounding'*, *Philological Quarterly* 61 (1982), p. 271.
[61] Page numbers cite John Bunyan, *The Holy War*, eds. Roger Sharrock and James F. Forrest (Oxford: Clarendon Press, 1980), p. 92.

as a period in which the Devil was to be 'cast ... into the bottomless pit ... that he should deceive the nations no more, till the thousand years should be fulfilled' (*Revelation* 20:3). But in *The Holy War*, when they 'took Diabolus and bound him fast in chains, the better to reserve him to the Judgement that he had appointed for him', their binding was noticeably less successful.[62] Diabolus was immediately able to gather support from other of his estranged followers, summoning them again to the town for a new assault, which is very nearly successful, and which involves the entire second half of the text. The rest of Bunyan's details do closely follow the biblical precedent:

> And when the thousand years are expired, Satan shall be loosed out of his prison, And shall go out to deceive the nations which are in the four quarters of the earth, Gog and Magog, to gather them together to battle: the number of whom is as the sand of the sea. And they went up on the breadth of the earth, and compassed the camp of the saints about, and the beloved city: and fire came down from God out of heaven and devoured them. And the devil that deceived them was cast into the lake of fire and brimstone (*Revelation* 20:7-10).

Diabolus' extended action around 'the beloved city' continually hints that the end is near, but continually refuses to provide it. Bunyan's narrator was abandoning the sense of teleological bliss towards which puritan conversion and history was imagined to move. In the outworkings of providence in universal history and individual experience, the puritan reader is left baffled, confused by each turn of events, and utterly unable to predict the future. It was a situation curiously analogous to Calvinistic conversion and the realities of political machinations under successive Restoration governments. Bunyan's puritans were not actors in a 'teleology of grace',[63] but in a never-ending cycle. The puritan life could be seen as teleology only when viewed from outside itself. Necessarily, *The Holy War* undermines the end-closed certainties it posits, and constructs a reading strategy at odds with its supposed intentions. Having adopted a Quaker-like hermeneutic, Bunyan involves narrative form in his apocalyptic apparatus. Ironically, his Quaker-like realisation of eschatology functions as a catalyst in the construction of a Calvinistic poetics.

Bunyan and the Poetics of Apocalypse

The introductory poem 'To the Reader' opens *The Holy War* with a striking assertion of the importance of Bunyan's text:

---

[62] Bunyan, *The Holy War*, p. 92.
[63] Webster, 'Writing to Redundancy', p. 43.

'Tis strange to me, that they that love to tell
Things done of old, yea, and that do excell
Their Equals in Historiology,
Speak not of Mansoul's wars, but let them lye
Dead, like old Fables, or such worthless things,
That to the Reader no advantage brings:
When men, let them make what they will their own,
Till they know this, are to themselves unknown.[64]

There is some confusion as to the identity of the object to which the narrator points in line ten. Many readers would assume that the reference - 'this' - is to the story of 'Mansoul's wars' which the poem goes on to summarise, but other readings are also possible.[65] Noting that lines nine and ten are set off from the rest of the poem (of 172 lines) as the only ones not printed in italics, we might wonder whether the lines are signalling themselves: perhaps Bunyan is drawing attention to the vital role this preface plays in the reader's understanding of his book, as it draws attention to the use of the margin and the importance of the interpretative power of Scripture in his construction of the complexities of the Christian life. Alternatively, Bunyan may be pointing to the fact that his preface articulates his plot, and that the reader, having read the poem, will find few surprises in perusing the main text of *The Holy War*. These lines do, after all, introduce a discussion of Bunyan's creative methods, and the narrator, it seems, does highlight the repetitive nature of his work, the extent to which it tells and then re-tells the same story, quite unsympathetic to chronological concerns. Pursuing this type of thinking, we might argue that the narrator is insisting that the reader should admit to an awareness that the linear unfolding of plot is not the allegory's primary concern. The reader's construction of self-knowledge should be based on foregrounding Bunyan's claim that Mansoul's wars are not the book's focus. Inviting the reader to share his rhetorical flourishes, the preface is arguing that *The Holy War*, like *The Pilgrim's Progress*, elevates discourse over events and that the reader's self-knowledge is based on the awareness of this priority. Like the ballad tradition, with which Bunyan was so familiar, the interest of the succeeding pages must lie not so much in the story as in the manner in which it is told.

Thus while the narrative ostensibly relates the 'Town of Mansoul and her state, / How she was lost, took captive, made a slave', its 'events' are interspersed with set-piece dialogues, letters, speeches and

---

[64] Bunyan, *The Holy War*, p. 1, ll. 1-10.
[65] Bunyan, *The Holy War*, p. 1, l. 6.

petitions.[66] Bunyan's allegory continually explores the vexed question of communication. His interest was typical of his age: Lois Potter's *Secret Rites and Secret Writings* (1989) has voiced the common observation that seventeenth-century 'writers themselves frequently represent the civil war as a conflict about language.'[67] Thus the most potent weapons in Diabolus' siege of Mansoul were 'big and ruffling words' and a 'ruffling language'.[68] One battle, in fact, seems almost entirely verbal:

> Diabolus commanded that his Drummer should beat a Charge against the Town, and the Captains also that were in the Town sounded a Charge against them, but they had no Drum, they were Trumpets of Silver with which they sounded against them. Then they which were of the Camp of Diabolus came down to the Town to take it, and the Captains in the Castle, with the slingers at Mouthgate played upon them amain. And now there was nothing heard in the Camp of Diabolus but horrible rage and blasphemy; but in the Town good words, Prayer and singing of Psalms: the enemy replied with horrible objections, and the terribleness of their Drum.[69]

Such 'horrible rage and blasphemy' characterises the 'language of Diabolus', a hazy, ambivalent and ambiguous discourse, typifying the uncertainty and moral confusion of life in a fallen world. Bunyan is playing on a Scriptural analogy: 'Yee are of your father the devill, and the lusts of your father yee will doe: hee hath beene a murtherer from the beginning, and abode not in the trueth, because there is no trueth in him. When hee speaketh a lie, then speaketh he of his owne: for hee is a liar, and the father thereof' (*John* 8:44). Diabolus, Emanuel says, is a 'fountain of deceit'.[70]

Certainly Diabolus' first approach to Mansoul was grounded in 'pretended fairness, covering of our intentions with all manner of lies, flatteries, delusive words'.[71] He came to Mansoul claiming to be 'bound by the King to do you my homage' but began immediately to question the credibility of the God he claimed to serve: 'all that he hath said to you, is neither true, nor yet for your advantage.'[72] He indicates that there are inconsistencies in God's speech - 'he saith first, you may eat of all; and yet after, forbids the eating of one' - and consequently he is

---

[66] Bunyan, *The Holy War*, 'To the Reader', ll. 32-3.

[67] Lois Potter, *Secret Rites and Secret Writings* (Cambridge: Cambridge University Press, 1989), p. xii.

[68] Bunyan, *The Holy War*, pp. 41, 63.

[69] Bunyan, *The Holy War*, pp. 197-98.

[70] Bunyan, *The Holy War*, p. 75.

[71] Bunyan, *The Holy War*, p. 13.

[72] Bunyan, *The Holy War*, pp. 14-15.

hostile to the literary representation of Shaddai's thoughts.[73] After his successful invasion of Mansoul, his servants set about the destruction of Shaddai's words: 'Mr. Mind had some old, rent, and torn parchments of the Law of good Shaddai in his house, but when Willbewill saw them, he cast them behind his back.'[74] Diabolus is given ample space to display his rhetorical flourishes, but the reader is always warned of their intent. As Emanuel says: 'know thou, O Diabolus, that nothing must be regarded that thou canst propound, for nothing is done by thee but to deceive.'[75]

This positing of uncertainty within the discourses of *The Holy War* involves the reader in the complexities of Mansoul's world. Outwith the allegory, in the margin of the text, Satan's presence is felt in disrupting the normal processes of linear linguistic cognition: 'Satan reads all backwards' and his 'Satanical Rhetorick' 'sometimes makes Saints eat their words'.[76] The reader's awareness of his danger only slowly emerges. By the time he has reached these warnings, the reader has already been involved in his own recapitulation of plot, as he has moved from the summary of the plot in 'To the Reader' to return again to the beginning of the plot in the first pages of the allegory. Like Satan, the narrator has reversed narrative linearity: he, rather than Satan, is making his reader read backwards. Similarly, his identification with the Diabolonians is certainly marked. The Diabolonians in general - and Atheism and Self-conceit in particular - are described by Bunyan as 'brisk', just as Bunyan characterised himself as a 'brisk talker' in *Grace Abounding*.[77] Thus Bunyan's narrator is deeply involved in the destabilisation of *The Holy War*.

This elision between voices also presents the reader with difficulty. The following extract moves between the point of view most suited to Diabolus and that most suited to the narrator:

> When Diabolus heard this, and perceived that he was discovered in all his deceits, he was confounded and utterly put to a nonplus; but having in himself the fountain of iniquity, rage, and malice against both Shaddai and his Son, and the beloved Town of Mansoul, what doth he but strengthen himself what he could to give fresh Battel to the noble Prince Emanuel? So then, now we must have another fight before the Town of Mansoul is taken. Come up then to the Mountains you that love to see military actions, and behold by both sides how the fatal blow is given;

---

[73] Bunyan, *The Holy War*, p. 15.

[74] Bunyan, *The Holy War*, p. 23.

[75] Bunyan, *The Holy War*, p. 84.

[76] Bunyan, *The Holy War*, pp. 20, 193, 201.

[77] Bunyan, *The Holy War*, pp. 120, 150, 201; *GA* §37.

while one seeks to hold, and the other seeks to make himself the master of the famous Town of Mansoul.[78]

Although it seems clear that there is a movement from the voice of Diabolus to that of the narrator, the reader is left with uncertainty as to the categorisation of the middle sentence, beginning 'So then ...' Indeed, the logical structure of the three sentences - in which each 'then' makes the previous sentence a premise for the next - clearly confuses the independence of each speaker, and demonstrates the extent to which the development of the narrative and the positioning of the reader within the narrative ('Come up then') are rooted in Diabolus' rhetoric. This silencing of clear distinctions between the voice of Satan, of the narrator, and the experience of the reader disguise profound hermeneutical difficulties. The reader's experience, Bunyan implies, is ultimately determined by the speech of Diabolus.

Some of the implications of this rhetorical-ideological disturbance are highlighted in the prefatory poem 'To the Reader'. There the fictive narrator grounds his own construction of identity in his involvement in the experiences his allegory describes:

> When Mansoul trampled upon things Divine,
> And wallowed in filth as doth a swine:
> When she betook her self unto her arms,
> Fought her Emanuel, despis'd his charms,
> Then I was there, and did rejoice to see
> Diabolus and Mansoul so agree.[79]

Thus, at the re-enactment of the Fall archetype with *The Holy War*, 'when the Townsfolk saw that the Tree was good for food, and that it was pleasant to the eye, and a Tree to be desired to make one wise' (an echo of *Genesis* 3:6), the narrator admits to his readers that he shares in their new ignorance. He admits that he is uncertain as to how Lord Innocency died, 'whether by a shot from the Camp of the Giant, or from some stinking qualm that suddenly took him, or whether by the stinking breath of that Treacherous Villain old Ill-pause, for so I am most apt to think'.[80] Ill-pause's previous promise of wisdom for those who ate the forbidden fruit proved disappointingly hollow - fallen ignorance reaches out to implicate the narrator of *The Holy War*.

Similarly, the narrator foregrounds his own investment in ambiguity when describing the Doubters, 'such as have their name from their nature, as well as from the Lord and Kingdom where they are born;

---

[78] Bunyan, *The Holy War*, pp. 85-6.
[79] Bunyan, *The Holy War*, p. 2, ll. 12-17.
[80] Bunyan, *The Holy War*, p. 16.

their nature is to put a question upon every one of the Truths of Emanuel'.[81] As personifications of anti-Calvinist theological objections, they represent the trial of faith faced by Restoration nonconformists. The narrator capitulates to their confusion: 'But there were three of those that came from the land of Doubting ... (Three did I say, I think there were four.)'.[82] Elsewhere *The Holy War* fudges over details - 'several slings and two or three Battering-Rams' - and elides the reader's attention over unnecessary self-correction, discussing 'this matter, I mean this purpose of the King and his Son'.[83] But the reader can never be certain that the truth of *The Holy War* is actually couched in error - that would be too certain a conclusion. Instead, rhetorical amnesia everywhere colours the plot. The narrator's note that he 'must not forget to tell' highlights his uncertainty whether 'I remember my tale aright'.[84]

The picture that emerges from this text is of a narrator who is heavily involved in sympathetically representing the Diabolonian position. The very possibility that readers can question the accuracy of his account highlights the extent to which he is engaged with the enemies of Mansoul: 'these Diabolonian Doubters turned the men of Mansoul out of their Beds, and now I will add, they wounded them, they mauled them, yea, and almost brained many of them. Many, did I say, yea most, if not all of them.'[85] Is the narrator speaking truth? Were all the Mansoulian men 'almost brained'? If so, he is a Doubter, for only they survived unharmed. If not, he is still a Doubter, for he would be speaking untruth, and Doubters deal in lies. 'Question the truth of all', Diabolus exhorts the Mansoulians;[86] but as Bunyan's narrator forces his reader into the same position, he mirrors the Devil and positions his readers with Mansoul's impotent and captive citizens. It is a positioning entirely consistent with puritan evangelical concerns - the reader is positioned with those most in need of redemption and is denied a narrator who can help him or her make ultimate sense of their world. The key to interpreting Bunyan's allegory then moves beyond his text. Its evangelical interests demand its denial of closure.

Nevertheless, the reader is constantly forced to interrogate the text. He is, like Mansoul, in 'perplexity': 'one would go by now, and as he went, if he heard his neighbour tell his tale, to be sure he would tell the quite contrary, and both would stand in it that he told the truth'.[87] The

---

[81] Bunyan, *The Holy War*, p. 227.
[82] Bunyan, *The Holy War*, p. 234.
[83] Bunyan, *The Holy War*, pp. 29, 51.
[84] Bunyan, *The Holy War*, pp. 21, 116.
[85] Bunyan, *The Holy War*, p. 205.
[86] Bunyan, *The Holy War*, p. 35.
[87] Bunyan, *The Holy War*, p. 97.

extract typifies the destabilised hermeneutic: the reader is left uncertain as to whether both neighbours agreed on the first story, or whether they disagreed, each maintaining their original story. The extract ultimately tells us nothing.

But Emanuel too becomes involved in *The Holy War*'s interpretative morass. Although we read his claim that 'all my words are true', the fact that this is represented by our Diabolonian reporter demands that we must question the veracity of the account.[88] Even *The Holy War*'s mediation of objective Scripture - the words of God outside the allegory - is vague. The flux of Biblical allusion proves a potential difficulty. Diabolus recognises the power of divine discourse and seeks to situate himself within it, even using it to argue against Emanuel for lordship of the town: 'this Town of Mansoul, as thou very well knowest, is mine, and that by a two-fold Right. 1. It is mine by right of Conquest, I won it in the open field. And shall the prey be taken from the mighty, or the lawful Captive, be delivered?'[89] While Bunyan fails to note the source of this reference in his margin, Diabolus' quotation is taken from *Isaiah* 49:24: 'shall the prey be taken from the mighty, or the lawful captive delivered?' As in the temptation of Christ, the Devil is happy to quote Scripture when it suits his purpose. Elsewhere, echoing the Messianic words of *Psalm* 2:3, Diabolus warns Mansoul that having 'broken [Shaddai's] bonds, and cast his cords away', they need expect only judgement - unless they make Diabolus their defender.[90] Later, he

> summons the whole Town into the Market place, and there with deceitful Tongue thus he addresses himself unto them.
>
> Gentlemen, and my very good Friends, You are all as you know my legal Subiects, and men of the famous Town of Mansoul; you know how from the first day that I have been with you until now, I have behaved myself among you.[91]

Ironically, it was St. Paul who wrote in *1 Thessalonians* 2:10, 'Ye are my witnesses, and God also, how holily and justly and unblameably we behaved ourselves among you.' Here, Bunyan is demonstrating the subtlety of the devil, who could appear even as 'an angel of light' (*2 Corinthians* 11:14).[92]

Even the representatives of good are involved in this reversal of Scripture. The forces of Emanuel, when seeking to release Mansoul from Diabolonian bondage, echo the words of the ungodly Assyrians laying

---

[88] Bunyan, *The Holy War*, p. 77.
[89] Bunyan, *The Holy War*, p. 72.
[90] Bunyan, *The Holy War*, p. 17.
[91] Bunyan, *The Holy War*, p. 32.
[92] Bunyan, *The Holy War*, p. 84.

siege to Jerusalem: 'but the Trumpeter soon replyed, saying, 'Our message is, not to the Gyant Diabolus, but to the miserable Town of Mansoul: nor shall we at all regard what answer by him is made; nor yet by any for him.'[93] The Biblical archetype displays a similar preference to address the population over their leader: 'then said Rabshakeh, Hathe my master sent me to thy master, & to thee to speake these wordes, and not to the men that sit on the wall?' (*Isaiah* 36:12). The allusion is quite startling: the forces of good allude to the wicked, and the wicked allude to the good. Such reversal dramatises the uncertainty of the puritans in the aftermath of the civil war, a dilemma whose hermeneutical basis was heightened when Mansoul's troubles are traced, in *The Holy War*, to poor interpretation of language: 'ah poor Mansoul! now thou feelest the fruits of sin, and what venom was in the flattering words of Mr. Carnal Security!'[94] The trouble had started when Diabolonians approached who 'could speak the language of Mansoul well'. 'Take heed Mansoul', Bunyan's margin had warned.[95]

Thus *The Holy War*'s constant flux of Biblical allusion creates its own uncertainties and problematises the Scriptural authority which *The Holy War* was attempting to exploit. This mirrors the experience of the English public during the civil wars, as the explosion of publishing thrust upon them a confusing cacophony of pamphlets and broadsheets. Many of these texts claimed Biblical justification for often mutually incompatible ideas; critics ever since have related their appearance to the decline of Biblical authority. Richard Baxter wondered whether this might be the product of some malevolent influence: 'I confess', he wrote in 1653, 'I am ... apprehensive of the luxurious fertility of licentiousness of the press of late, as being a design of the enemy to bury and overwhelm ... those judicious, pious, excellent writings, that before were so commonly read by the people.'[96] More recently, Hill has claimed - contentiously - that the Bible 'lost its universal power once it had been demonstrated that you could prove anything from it'.[97] This culture of questions, and the subsequent tussle for ownership of the cultural media, undermined protestant Biblicism by the end of the seventeenth century.

In the same way, the narrator of *The Holy War* plays with his readers, alluding to Scriptural passages and disappointing the hopes which their

---

[93] Bunyan, *The Holy War*, p. 42.
[94] Bunyan, *The Holy War*, p. 204.
[95] Bunyan, *The Holy War*, p. 168.
[96] Quoted in J.I. Packer, *Among God's Giants: The Puritan Vision of the Christian Life* (Eastbourne: Kingsway, 1991), p. 78.
[97] Christopher Hill, *The English Bible and Seventeenth-Century Revolution* (Harmondsworth: Allen Lane 1993), p. 428.

contexts might have raised. In a series of references which readers might understand as closing the plot, the narrator repeatedly invokes and undermines the hope of imminent apocalypse: 'no sooner had the Captain made this Speech to his Souldiers, but one Mr. Speedy came post to the Captain from the Prince, to tell him that Emanuel was at hand.'[98] This expression, lifted from *Philippians* 4:5, suggests at last the final descent, the winding up of the age, and would be confirmed by the description of the tired soldiers rising up 'like men raised from the dead'.[99] It is, nevertheless, followed by another allusion which would tend to undermine this connotation. Emanuel's entry to Mansoul is explicitly modelled on the Triumphal Entry of Christ to Jerusalem: 'every door also was filled with persons who had adorned every one of their forepart against their house with something of variety, and singular excellency to entertain him withal as he passed in the streets; they also themselves as Emanuel passed by, did welcome him with shouts and acclamations of joy, saying, Blessed be the Prince that cometh in the name of his Father Shaddai.'[100] The situation affords some keen dramatic irony, requiring the reader to suspect the townsmen of the same capriciousness as that of the Jerusalem crowds, welcoming Christ on 'Palm Sunday', and shouting for his crucifixion less than one week later. This hardly raises any expectation of an imminent 'happy ending'.

This difficulty of determining final meaning is a topic to which Bunyan's treatises regularly return. The '&c.' of page nine, for example, is repeated frequently throughout Bunyan's commentaries and treatises, explicitly delegating the creation of meaning away from the author - a useful technique in a climate of censorship. Within *The Holy War* closure is problematised in plot as much as in allusion: the ending of the allegory clouds the future of the town. Ultimately, of course, Emanuel withdraws from Mansoul, denying eschatological resolution and encouraging her citizens to 'hold fast till I come'.[101] With responsibility thrust upon the citizens, Emanuel's final return is indefinitely delayed, and the attempt at eschatological or hermeneutical finality is abandoned. Neither are Bunyan's readers encouraged to expect an untroubled future for the period of waiting: given that the second siege of the town occurred after Incredulity's first escape, it is surely more than ominous that in the final episode, the Diabolonian 'Princes, and the Captains with old Incredulity their General, did all of them make their

---

[98] Bunyan, *The Holy War*, p. 221.
[99] Bunyan, *The Holy War*, p. 221.
[100] Bunyan, *The Holy War*, p. 224.
[101] Bunyan, *The Holy War*, p. 250.

escape'.[102] This breakout is followed by a string of others. Carnal-sense, we are to believe, 'will not yet quit the Town, but lurks in the Diabolonian dens a days, and haunts like a Ghost honest mens houses a nights'.[103]

Thus *The Holy War* ends as it began, *in medias res*. Engaging with mimesis, the fictive narrator is denied access to knowledge of which his character-peers would be ignorant. As a consequence, his allegory is rooted in the experience of the elect in time. As he cannot script the future, his allegory is only a history of the past. The reader is left as vulnerable as the book's protagonists, with no promise that providence will not again prove so capricious - this obscured 'sense of an ending' underpins Bunyan's invocation of millenarian tropes in *The Holy War*. But the text, most of all, is left vulnerable to attack.

The narrator reports that every other trace of the Doubters is removed after the Diabolonian commanders 'make their escape': 'they that buried them, buried also with them their arms, which were cruel instruments of death, (their weapons were arrows, darts, mauls, fire-brands, and the like) they buried also their armour, their colours, banners, with the standard of Diabolus, and what else soever they could find that did but smell of a Diabolonian Doubter.'[104] But the victory is less complete than the narrator pretends. Readers are not told why it is that the manuscript of *The Holy War* managed to avoid the purge of the Doubter relics. The narrator's persistent instability and rhetorical deviousness has not concealed his Doubter intentions. *The Holy War*, in this sense, is the last of the Doubter manuscripts, the last victim of puritanism's iconoclastic ire. Only when this is recognised can the final irony of Bunyan's ambivalence be seen: celebrating the extermination of the Doubter presence, *The Holy War* requires the reader to disapprove of its own existence. The narrator is seeking the annihilation of his own text: this is the real 'writing to redundancy'. Rarely does reading become so destabilised.

Thus the result of Bunyan's poetics was to force the reader into adapting the familiar millennial trope of the 'end of books'. A Quaker-like realised eschatology was adopted and invoked to demonstrate the oscillation of narrative and allusion and to point the reader past the allegory towards its signified, highlighting the continual frustration of closure. In the poetics of *The Holy War* Bunyan dramatises the Calvinistic aesthetic - *finitum non est capax infiniti*. It is in the poetics of the text, rather than in the somewhat flat characterisation or the rigidly detailed allegory, that the value of *The Holy War* is found, for the power

---

[102] Bunyan, *The Holy War*, pp. 133, 227.
[103] Bunyan, *The Holy War*, p. 243.
[104] Bunyan, *The Holy War*, p. 227.

of *The Holy War* lies in the fact that the effects of its subject matter could not and cannot be restricted to the page. In its form, as much as its content, the text is implicitly - and problematically - theological.

Thus *The Holy War* emerges as a text exemplifying many of the characteristics of puritan writing in its troubled maturity. The result is not simply an allegory revealing coded Fifth Monarchist messages for Bunyan's persecuted brethren, or a Quaker version of *Grace Abounding*, but a text which betrays a more radical stance still. *The Holy War* requires readers to approve of its own dissolution and demonstrates that, for all his antipathy towards their heresies, Bunyan was able to invoke the 'speechways' of the Quakers to demonstrate the veracity of his orthodox Calvinistic heritage.

Bunyan's 'fit reader' was to recognise his depiction of a Quaker-esque conversion narrative, complete with invocations of the millennium as an experience in time, and was to have been able to identify the distance between Bunyan and narrator, between the related but distinct concerns of *Grace Abounding* and *The Holy War*. Bunyan's reader should have constructed his reading on *The Holy War*'s problematising of epistemology, and its ironic investigation of the concerns of Quaker thought. Thus involving his reader, Bunyan was refusing to allow the objectivity of critical distance.

Six years after the publication of *The Holy War*, radicals welcomed the Glorious Revolution in glowing apocalyptic terms. In the same year, Baptist leaders gathered in synod to adopt a new confession of faith. It was closely worded, abandoning their previous creed to echo instead the form and content of the more conservative Westminster Confession. They amended the first chapter, 'Of the Holy Scriptures', to argue that the Bible is 'the only sufficient, certain, and infallible rule of all saving knowledge'. They moderated the robust eschatological thrust of the 1644 confession. Positing the certainty of its infallible text, they may have been responding to the subjectification of knowledge texts like *The Holy War* seemed to advance.[105] It would have been a paradox entirely appropriate in the ambivalent world of *The Holy War*.

---

[105] Michael A.G. Haykin, *Kiffin, Knollys and Keach* (Leeds: Carey, 1996), p. 68.

CHAPTER 9

Conclusion

Throughout the three kingdoms, the aesthetic and apocalyptic revolution which puritanism engendered had struck at the root of the existing social order. The established pattern of ecclesiastical and social control foundered upon the application of puritanism's iconoclastic theory. Its political implications were unparalleled. Never before had a king been tried and executed by his subjects. The Calvinist international shuddered; the Scottish Covenanting movement split into opposing pro- and anti-monarchical factions. The radical millenarianism which was used as a foil for the rise of the Genevan hegemony proved to be the catalyst for its fall.[1] If, as Hill claims, English Calvinism was crumbling in the 1590s,[2] then after the 1640s both strict church discipline and Calvinist theology finally 'lost their grip': 'Calvinism broke down when the Revolution established freedom of discussion.'[3] The situation was not to be salvaged. Post-Restoration nonconformist bodies were voluntary organisations, very different from the national church envisaged by the Westminster Assembly divines: 'after the overthrow of the hierarchy, the preachers had little to say to those of the lower orders who felt the need for social reform; the latter were driven to organise themselves in sectarian organisations with a very different theology from the predestinarianism of the orthodox Calvinists.'[4]

The revolution's literary implications were also enormous. The closure unpinning Calvinist theology - of elect and reprobate, of material and spiritual, of this world and the next - had been interrogated and problematised the puritan literary engagement. The Geneva Bible's notes had envisaged Antichrist's efforts to 'wound and pierce through with cursings, both [the] names and writings' of holy men; Junius would have been surprised to hear that 'holy men' had themselves undermined their textual project.[5] As Thomas Manton noted in 1655, 'the press is an excellent means to scatter knowledge, were it

---

[1] Hill, *Society and Puritanism in Pre-Revolutionary England*, p. 243.
[2] Hill, *Society and Puritanism in Pre-Revolutionary England*, p. 167.
[3] Hill, *Society and Puritanism in Pre-Revolutionary England*, pp. 241-2.
[4] Hill, *Society and Puritanism in Pre-Revolutionary England*, p. 428.
[5] *Geneva Bible* (1602), note on Revelation 11:7.

not so often abused. All complain there is enough written, and think
that now there should be a stop. Indeed, it were well if in this scribbling
age there were some restraint. Useless pamphlets are grown almost as
great a mischief as the erroneous and profane'.[6] Hill has noted that

> The collapse of censorship saw a fantastic outpouring of books, pamphlets
> and newspapers. Before 1640, newspapers were illegal; by 1645 there were
> 722. Twenty-two books were published in 1640; over 2,000 in 1642. As
> both sides in the Civil War appealed for support from the ordinary people,
> the issues at stake had to be discussed. But it went much farther than that
> ... No old shibboleths were left unchallenged in this unprecedented
> freedom.[7]

Perhaps Owen had been right in hoping 'we might have less writing,
and more praying'.[8]

Yet, despite sometimes grave doctrinal differences, puritans of the
civil wars shared a common affiliation in the pursuit of a Biblical
worldview. If by nothing else, they can be identified by their common
emphasis on the need to establish a holistic biblical hermeneutic. As this
concern permeated their work, the discussion of closure and
eschatological certainty came to characterise a substantial body of
seventeenth-century literature. The movement collapsed when it was
recognised that the Genevan hermeneutic was, after all, only one theory
amongst many possibilities. Cutting across genre, and lingering long
after the movement suffered eclipse, the crumbling edifice of puritanism
was united, if in nothing else, by an exploration of writing's inherent
infinite.

This hegemony was nevertheless challenged. The Restoration
reasserted England's allegiance to the Episcopal hierarchy and another
Irishman counteracted Ussher's earlier influence. In 1660, Bishop
Williams of Ossory published his treatise on 'Ο ΑΝΤΙΧΡΙΣΤΟΣ, 'The
Antichrist'. His title page illustrated his belief that 'the Assembly of
Presbyterians consulting at Westminster, together with the
Independents, Anabaptists, and Lay-Preachers' were the 'false Prophet,
and the mystical soul of that Great Antichrist'. Texts of this sort,
radically revising the radical's eschatology, became a sign of the times.
Rutherford lamented the passing of the late Presbyterian settlement: 'for
ten thousand worlds,' he declared in 1661, 'I dare not venture to pass
from the protestation against the corruptions of the time, nor go along
with the shameless apostasy of the many silent and dumb watchmen of
Scotland ... Know that the overthrow of the sworn Reformation, the

---

[6] Sibbes, *Works*, iii. 3.
[7] Quoted in Owens, 'Antichrist must be Pulled Down', p. 6.
[8] Owen, *Works*, viii. 33.

introducing of Popery and the mystery of iniquity, is now set on foot in the three kingdoms ... but I believe he cometh quickly who will remove our darkness, and shine gloriously in the Isle of Britain, as a crowned King, either in a formally sworn covenant, or in his own glorious way.'[9] But dissension was creeping through the former allies. Rutherford's former companion Robert Baillie took a different view of the past two decades: he noted, on 31st January 1661, 'it was the justice of God that brought ... to disgrace the two Goodwins, blind Milton, Owen, Sterrie, Lockier and other of the maleficent crew.'[10]

By the 1680s the puritans were labouring under renewed censorship from the Restoration government. The Covenanter murder of Archbishop Sharp in 1679, the Rye House plot of 1683, and Monmouth's rebellion in 1685 all served to discredit their constituency. Even the eschatologically-optimistic Owen was expecting the return of Popery: 'if a time of going into Smithfield should again come, - if God shall call us to that fiery trial or any other, whatever it may be, - remember that to suffer against Antichrist is as great and glorious as to suffer against Paganism.' But always the hope remained. The Whore of Babylon would certainly fall. 'It may be tomorrow; it may be not these hundred years ... When she is boasting herself, destruction shall come.'[11] The accession of the Prince of Orange was rooted in apocalyptic thought. So too Increase Mather, debating eschatology with Richard Baxter in 1690, could still refer his friend to Thomas Goodwin's sermons 'concerning the world to come'.[12]

Signs of the Times

There were of course profound literary and philosophical problems for each of these puritans, living the 'at the edge of the promises'.[13] Having surveyed the topography of puritan apocalypse from the 1550s to the 1680s, we can trace an overarching movement from the careful Genevan hermeneutic towards the radical Quaker conflation of sign and thing signified. But there is also continuity - the iconoclastic storm of the early Reformation paralleled the regicide in its attempt to root the new and replacement sign in the immediate presence of the transcendent signifier. The Stuarts had promoted their dynasty on the premise that they were rulers by divine right - God's representatives on earth. The

---

[9] Rutherford, *Letters*, p. 703.
[10] Baillie, *Letters and Journals*, iii. 443.
[11] Owen, *Works*, ix. 507-8.
[12] Richard Baxter, *Calendar of the Correspondence of Richard Baxter*, eds N.H. Keeble and Geoffrey F. Nuttall (Oxford: Clarendon Press, 1991), ii. 309.
[13] Cromwell, *The Writings and Speeches of Oliver Cromwell*, iii. 64.

regicides, fuelled by millenarian fervour, took advantage of this to argue that this was all the more reason for replacing the royal dynasty with the one they represented. The regicide was nothing less than a clearing of the way for the second coming of Christ, England's rightful king.

It is exactly this trend which is evidenced in the selection of texts this book has examined. The Genevans were careful to delineate the boundaries of figurative speech and literalness, but found the next century increasingly ready to challenge the closure of their argument. Ussher - the arch-conservative - paradoxically fostered hermeneutical disturbance by gathering into the Irish church those radicals most keen to take advantage of their liberty to renegotiate the complex Genevan ideology. His suggestion of a futuristic millennium prepared the way for the hermeneutical spiral of the 1640s, when Brightman, Archer, Mede and Goodwin appeared in English giving multiple expositions of the same Scripture. The 'vortex of history' these books engendered swept puritan writers into an increasingly self-reflexive literary strategy, which combined with the rapid theological developments of the middle decades of the seventeenth century to produce a body of literature of unparalleled intensity. This was the basis for the conversion narratives presented by Rogers and Bunyan, which invested individual experience with elements of the most transcendent discourse available to the puritans, with descriptions of an event they had yet to witness. These were signs that had a meaning no-one could anticipate or absolutely define.

Perhaps an awareness of this literary strategy provides moderns with another tool in the continuing quest to define the puritan: perhaps puritans were proponents of a worldview continually in pursuit of the transcendent, the ultimate signifier in literature, politics, and the psychology of the self. Based on the Calvinist dictum that *finitum non est capax infiniti*, their search was for the one reality which would underpin every other reality. It was nothing less than the pursuit of God.

But it was a pursuit driven by collapsing assumptions. The Geneva Bible generated a momentum which drew puritans into a centripetal whirlpool of interiorisation. *Revelation* began as a description of universal history and culminated as little more than a paradigm for personal conversion: the meta- became a micro-narrative. Renaissance literary awareness combined with the beginnings of a scientific historiography to make expositions of 'universal history' increasingly fraught with difficulty. Successive interpreters shed 'exterior' eschatological controls - like the function of the 'godly prince' - until interior factors predominated. Foxe had adapted an historical narrative which dated back to Augustine to position the millennium securely in the past. This interpretation continued until the beginning of the seventeenth century, when Ussher, with others, revitalised the ancient millennial hope. The Christian 'golden age' was being projected into the future: Ussher's *Gravissimae Quaestionis* implied both a past and a present millennium. All the millenarian debates of the 1640s were founded upon this premise, and it was only with the emergence of the Quaker movement in the early 1650s, promoting a 'realised' eschatology, that *Revelation* was understood to refer to events in the individual's present. Rogers was another transitional figure: his *Ohel* alludes to both a future and a present apocalypse. From a metanarrative of universal history, *Revelation* was reduced to a model of appropriate spiritual experience.

Significantly, however, it was this appropriation of Quaker eschatology by the puritan mainstream which promoted those ideas of modern 'personality' with which the puritans have been credited. Several studies on the evolution of autobiography have noted the crucial role of conversion narratives in the literary construction of a definable self. In the thought of Rogers and Bunyan, the individual's personal experience - though always at the mercy of the editor - remained the only sphere untouched by the critical world. The reason it remained untouched was because it invoked concepts which could not be challenged. It operated beyond closure. Thus the seventeenth century's secularisation of history generated the apocalyptic investment in personality: as Foxe's past was reworked by Clarendon, *Grace Abounding* became *The Holy War*. The apocalyptic puritan personality was to be a haven for self-consciousness, critical in the evolving Romantic temper.

All this demonstrates the crucial need to understand the evolution of puritan thought - a flux of meaning generated by a discourse intimately concerned with 'literalness' and figurative language. After the Genevans trained British Christians in linguistic and critical awareness, the saints became increasingly self-reflexive and self-aware. Milton's *Areopagitica* might be its most brilliant production, but Bunyan's *Holy War* represents the logical culmination of the hermeneutical awareness the Geneva Bible first advanced.

Nevertheless, as the puritan movement was drawn inexorably towards the eighteenth century, its millenarian interests slipped, in popular estimation, from threat to entertainment. Four years later, when John Mason assembled his followers to await the millennium, his neighbours found him only an object of ridicule.[14] Within half a century, the ideology which had underpinned a revolution was dismissed as folly.

---

[14] Keith Thomas, *Religion and the Decline of Magic* (1971; rpt. Harmondsworth: Penguin, 1991), p. 171.

Millennialism in the Puritan Confessions*

From the Marxism of Christopher Hill to the Anglicanism of J. I. Packer, puritan studies have been the victim of confessional bias. Since the rediscovery of the puritan literary corpus in the mid-twentieth century, historical and theological scholars have regularly culled source documents for confirmation of their own theological predispositions.[1] In this struggle between objectivity and appropriation, perceptions of puritan eschatology have become a critical focus of discussion – especially in the rush to own the *gravitas* conferred by the most influential of the puritan creedal statements, the Westminster Confession of Faith (1646). In his study of puritan eschatology, Bryan W. Ball noted that the reference to the *parousia* of Jesus Christ in this 'ultimate official pronouncement of Puritan dogma' indicates 'the measure of its respectability' in seventeenth-century orthodoxy.[2] But others have sought to go beyond this, and, in a series of competing claims, historical theologians from backgrounds as diverse as Calvinism and Seventh-day Adventism have attempted to articulate the meaning of WCF 33:1-3. R. G. Clouse, arguing that the confession is 'clearly' amillennial, found 'no suggestion of a period of latter-day glory or of a millennium connected with the conversion of the Jews'.[3] LeRoy Froom has viewed the confession as 'the strongest premillennialist symbol of Protestantism'.[4] James de Jong has argued that 'Westminster's formulation must be seen as a deliberate choice of mild, unsystemized, postmillennial expectations.'[5] As this debate illustrates, in spite of all that has been written about puritan eschatology - and the literature is, by now, extensive - it is still a subject fogged by obscurity.

---

* This appendix originally appeared as 'The eschatology of the puritan confessions', *Scottish Bulletin of Evangelical Theology* 20:1 (2002), pp. 51-78, and is reprinted here, with minor amendments, with the permission of the editor.

[1] Coffey, *Politics, Religion and the British Revolutions*, pp. 5-15.

[2] Bryan W. Ball, *A Great Expectation: Eschatological Thought in English Protestantism to 1660* (Leiden: Brill, 1975), p. 44.

[3] Clouse, 'The Rebirth of Millenarianism', p. 60.

[4] Froom, *The Prophetic Faith of our Fathers*, ii. 553.

[5] de Jong, *As the Waters Cover the Sea*, p. 38 n. 11.

In part this confusion is due to the often a-historical nature of theological discussions of 'the Puritan movement' and the confessions it produced. Popular-level evangelicalism often presents the movement as homogenous, assuming an essential identity, for example, in 'the puritan view' of family, work, church, or state. Packer thus eulogizes 'God's giants':

> The Puritans ... were great souls serving a great God. In them clear-headed passion and warm-hearted compassion combined. Visionary and practical, idealistic and realistic too, goal-orientated and methodical, they were great believers, great hopers, great doers, and great sufferers.[6]

But of which puritans is he speaking? One is tempted to imagine that Packer, like so many other writers on puritan themes, has cast his subjects in his own image.

As the debate about the meaning of the term 'puritan' suggests, therefore, there is little scholarly consensus in understanding what the movement actually was. It is difficult to be more specific than to suggest that the movement represented a broad spectrum of protestant ecclesiastical discontent and a call for further reformation over a wide range of issues in the early modern period.[7] It would be surprising indeed if such a broad movement produced any substantial degree of ideological concurrence.

At a more scholarly level, conservative theologians perpetuate a milder form of the same kind of a-historical analysis when they cite the Westminster Confession as a document charged with transcendent meaning, the first port of call in the storm of theological debate. Their approach often shows little sense of the context out of which the Confession emerged or the fact that it was deliberately designed as a generally acceptable compromise between parties convinced of various – and often mutually incompatible – systems. The documents of the Westminster Assembly could never have been dispassionate attempts to delineate objective truth when the disproportionate influence of the Scottish Commissioners' theology was more than partly due to the English Parliament's need to win the support of their Presbyterian army.[8] Perhaps to signal their temporizing ambitions, the divines themselves disclaimed any notion of creedal finality (WCF 31:4) and were reluctant to provide their conclusions with Scriptural proofs when the English Parliament insisted that they should.[9] Many modern

---

[6] Packer, *Among God's Giants*, p. 24.
[7] See the discussion of the definition of 'puritan' in chapter one of this volume.
[8] R. S. Paul, *The Assembly of the Lord: Politics and Religion in the Westminster Assembly and the 'Grand Debate'* (Edinburgh: T&T Clark, 1985), *passim.*
[9] Paul, *The Assembly of the Lord*, p. 518.

readings of the Confession, however, overlook these historical complexities. This lack of historical sensitivity and anachronistic application of contemporary intellectual paradigms cannot fail to be misleading.[10] The disagreement between Clouse, Froom and de Jong is symptomatic of a wider and contemporary problem.

As a consequence, although their insights are often powerful and compelling, the interpretive frameworks in which Clouse, Froom and de Jong operate cripple the validity of their conclusions. Each of these scholars misrepresent the confession's eschatology because they each underestimate the extent to which puritan readings of Revelation could defy and transcend the contemporary concepts of pre-, post- or amillennialism. These three positions, largely constructed by more recent eschatological enquiry, cannot be used as uncomplicated heuristic tools to explicate puritan texts.[11] Their inutility is registered by the fact that their most basic presupposition – that Revelation 20:1-7 refers to only one period of a thousand years – was not shared by every puritan who wrote on the passage. Thomas Brightman, one of the most influential of the puritan expositors of Revelation, argued instead that the thousand years of Satan's captivity (Rev. 20:2-3) and the thousand years of the reign of the saints (Rev. 20:4-6) referred to two historically distinct but contiguous periods of time stretching from the years 300 to 1300, and 1300 to 2300, respectively.[12] A-, pre- and postmillennial paradigms, however useful they may be for current debate, should be used with care when explaining puritan apocalyptic thought. Puritan eschatology is much less precise, much more ambiguous, than contemporary terminology allows.

This revision of methodology and terminology, however, calls also for a revision of privileged texts. The variety of puritan readings of eschatology requires a new canon of source documents to balance the individualistic focus promoted by previous scholarship in this area. Ideas of puritan eschatology have too often been extrapolated from the writings of theologians deemed representative by modern historians, while the type of puritan deemed representative has largely been

---

[10] Aspects of this problem have also been manifest in the recent debate about the proper interpretation of the 'six days' of creation among conservative Presbyterians in the USA. For responses to this context, see Robert Letham, '"In the space of six days": The Days of Creation from Origen to the Westminster Assembly', *Westminster Theological Journal* 61 (1999), pp. 149-74, and William S. Barker, 'The Westminster Assembly on the Days of Creation: A Reply to David W. Hall', *Westminster Theological Journal* 62 (2000), pp. 113-20.

[11] The term 'eschatology' itself is a nineteenth-century invention. Alan E. Lewis, 'Eschatology', in Donald M. McKim (ed.), *Encyclopaedia of the Reformed Faith* (Edinburgh: St Andrews Press, 1992), pp. 122-24.

[12] See pp. 40-41 below.

determined by the (often unconscious) presuppositions which historians bring to the text (and consequently leave undefined).[13] Paradoxically, and perhaps in an earnest attempt to avoid the difficulties of the Clouse–Froom–de Jong debate, studies of puritanism often ignore the documents which were self-consciously created as defining the acceptable boundaries of the movement's constituent subgroups – the jointly-prepared, deliberately debated statements of denominational faith. It is at this point that the system of compromise upon which the confessions were founded becomes their most useful asset. When properly historicized, the puritan confessions are seen to express the negotiated centres of important theological cultures within puritanism.

Thus historians are well-placed to study the puritan confessions. There is plenty of material; the very existence of the movement depended upon their careful articulation of the distinctive doctrines which made up their ecclesiastical manifesto. The publication of their conclusions, often supplied with detailed biblical proofs, acted as an invitation to contrast and compare each text with those other documents published with the same purpose, and called upon the reader to realign their denominational loyalties in accordance with the results of this inquiry.

Of course, there are distinct advantages, as well as limitations, in this 'survey of confessions' approach. Perhaps the most major difficulty is, paradoxically, that it underplays the importance of eschatology. The puritan end-of-the-worldview encompassed themes as diverse as epistemology, church government, foreign policy, and individual piety. In the confessions, eschatology is reduced to a two-dimensional subject of academic enquiry. Nevertheless, the study of the confessions does illustrate the extent to which an interest in eschatology was not the monopoly of the poor and dispossessed. Instead, it was part of the essential cultural and ecclesiastical capital of the age, invested in the very fabric of the reform the movement was demanding. The publication of puritan creeds, doctrinal articles and confessions of faith offers an unparalleled opportunity to position the constituent groupings of the movement as collective entities in terms which their members would themselves recognize as authentic. It is surprising, therefore, that despite all the secondary literature in the area, the eschatology of the puritan confessions has never been examined. This appendix offers a contribution to that end.

---

[13] Note the reception given to Murray, *The Puritan Hope*. Murray's study is often cited by conservative evangelical postmillennialists to support the notion that 'the puritans' were postmillennialists.

Reformation Contexts

The continuing debate about 'Calvin and the Calvinists' is pushing the acceptable boundaries of puritan studies deep into the sixteenth century.[14] A number of recent studies have located the origins of seventeenth century debates in a reformation context. But this movement of relocating crucial centres of discussion has not been balanced across the theological loci. While perceived discontinuities in soteriology continue to generate scholarly discussion across the chronological contexts, secondary treatments of early reformation eschatology are less numerous than those concentrating on its seventeenth-century variant.

Curiously, contemporary lack of interest in the subject is almost inversely proportional to the appeal it exercised in the sixteenth century. Those studies of Luther and Calvin which have been undertaken have illustrated the extent to which 'the Reformation was spawned in and nurtured by an atmosphere of intense hopes and fears about impending universal upheaval, disaster, transformation, judgment, and the end of the world.'[15] Varieties of eschatology – at both popular and scholarly levels – were therefore both a cause and a consequence of the factors driving reformation. The lingering medieval worldview attached transcendental importance to the appearance of Halley's comet in 1531;[16] descriptions of the new world were often couched in the language of eschatological hope, such as the anti-Islamic millenarianism of Christopher Columbus;[17] and reformation rhetoric developed metaphors already employed to describe the cosmic battle of good against evil.

---

[14] For representative positions in the 'Calvin and the Calvinists' debate see R. T. Kendall, *Calvin and English Calvinism*, and Paul Helm, *Calvin and the Calvinists* (Edinburgh: Banner of Truth, 1982). More recent assessments can be found in Richard A. Muller, *The Unaccommodated Calvin: Studies in the Formation of a Theological Tradition* (Oxford: Oxford University Press, 2000), pp. 6, 64; and Carl R. Trueman and R. S. Clark, 'Introduction', in Trueman and Clark (eds), *Protestant Scholasticism: Essays in Reassessment* (Carlisle: Paternoster, 1999), pp. xiii-xix.

[15] Robin B. Barnes, 'Apocalypticism', in Hans J. Hillerbrand (ed.), *The Oxford Encyclopaedia of the Reformation* (Oxford: Oxford University Press, 1996), iii. 63; Quistorp, *Calvin's Doctrine of the Last Things*; Torrance, 'The Eschatology of the Reformation', pp. 36-62. For a recent study of reformation eschatology, as well as an up-to-date bibliography, see Irena Backus, *Reformation Readings of the Apocalypse: Geneva, Zurich, and Wittenberg* (Oxford: Oxford University Press, 2000).

[16] Barnes, 'Apocalypticism', iii. 65.

[17] Felipe Fernández-Armesto, *Columbus* (Oxford: Oxford University Press, 1991), p. 26.

Despite this medieval impulse, the eschatology of the reformation movement also developed in startling discontinuity with the past. This is the most obvious factor about the reformation's creedal statements on eschatology. Given the confusion of the Clouse-Froom-de Jong debate, it is rather ironic that one of the most important areas in the reformation's intellectual advance was its simplification of eschatology. Under the influence of Augustine, medieval Catholicism had abandoned the chiliasm of the Church Fathers and, in course of time, implicitly challenged the definition of eschatology as a discussion of the 'four last things' by developing an elaborate complex of spiritual destinations alongside the more traditional termini of death, judgment, heaven and hell.[18] With historic Christendom, it argued that those who died in the guilt of mortal sin were damned. With more novelty, it contended that those whose guilt was merely venial were instead ushered into purgatory, where their souls were cleansed in preparation for the beatific vision. There were various minor modifications to this scheme. In the Old Testament dispensation, for example, the souls of believers who died without guilt could not enter directly into glory. Before the death of Christ, both those who died without guilt and those who had passed through the purification of purgatory waited in *limbus patrum* for Christ's 'harrowing of hell' and his 'leading captivity captive'. Although *limbus patrum* was now empty, the Church continued to posit a third – and eternal – destination alongside heaven and hell. This *limbus infantum* held the souls of un-baptized children and others who died in the state of original sin but without grievous personal guilt. There they remained eternally, in perfect natural happiness, but without ever enjoying the beatific vision.[19] With the reformation, however, protestants began to abandon these accretions to the Biblical faith.

In this as in many other areas of reformation debate, protestant leaders developed their thinking in response to both the monolithic hostility of Roman Catholicism and the frenetic instability of the Anabaptists. As the reform movement progressed across Europe, a series of protestant confessions reiterated the ban on millenarianism that was mistakenly believed to have been first imposed by the Council

---

[18] Michael J. Scanlon, 'Eschatology', in Allan D. Fitzgerald (gen. ed.), *Augustine through the Ages: An Encyclopaedia* (Grand Rapids: Eerdmans, 1999), pp. 316-18; Brian E. Daley, 'Chiliasm', in Everett Ferguson (ed.), *Encyclopaedia of Early Christianity*, 2nd ed. (New York: Garland, 1997), i. 238-41; B.E. Daley, *The Hope of the Early Church: Eschatology in the Patristic Age* (Cambridge: Cambridge University Press, 1991).

[19] P.J. Toner, 'Limbo', in *The Catholic Encyclopaedia* (1910; rpt. New York: The Encyclopaedia Press, 1913), ix. 256-59; 'Limbo', in Richard P. McBrien, *The HarperCollins Encyclopaedia of Catholicism* (New York: HarperCollins, 1995), p. 771.

of Ephesus in 431 A.D. – and consequently indicated the continuing appeal such ideas possessed.[20] The takeover of Münster by millenarian Anabaptists in 1534 and 1535 graphically illustrated the social and political dangers of unfettered apocalypticism.[21] Protestant leaders reacted so vigorously to the danger of radical millenarianism that, for a time, it seemed to many Catholic scholars, a rejection of the canonicity of Revelation seemed to hallmark the reformation movement.[22] Zwingli denied that John's visions were in any way canonical; Luther's initial hostility to their contents was only slowly overcome.[23] But as reformers developed their readings of Scripture and providence, the rhetorical possibilities which apocalyptic tropes afforded seemed to eclipse the initial hesitancy about how best to read – or even whether to read – Revelation. William Perkins was perhaps unique among British expositors in defending the canonicity of Revelation in a preface to his *Godly and Learned Exposition of the three first Chapters in the Revelation* (1595), an eschatologically-driven jeremiad over the Laodicean state of English Christianity.[24] His defense illustrated the compelling utility of Biblical apocalyptic in the campaign to promote the puritan cause. Why should reformers ignore Biblical apocalyptic when it so clearly described England's 'signs of the times' and the fall of an influential religious empire based in a city with seven hills?

This revival of interest in Biblical eschatology was also accompanied by a growing enthusiasm for the apocalyptic teaching of various non-canonical sources. Not all puritans shared these esoteric interests; and the fears of those who did not suggest the interests of those who did. Readers of Thomas Hayne's *Christs Kingdom on Earth* (1645) were warned off the 'senseless' teaching of 'Rabbi Elias', who argued that the world would last only for six thousand years.[25] Others, like Thomas Hall in *A Confutation of the Millenarian Opinion* (1657), exposed the excessive credulity of some towards the eschatologies of Jewish Targums and Talmuds, Sibylline Oracles, the Koran, and astronomy.[26] Perkins' *A Fruitfull Dialogue Concerning the Ende of the World* (1587) imagined a

---

[20] The classic study of medieval millenarian movements is still Cohn, *The Pursuit of the Millennium*.

[21] Cohn, *The Pursuit of the Millennium*, pp. 278-306. See also Klaus Deppermann, *Melchior Hoffman: Social Unrest and Apocalyptic Visions in the Age of the Reformation* (Edinburgh: T&T Clark, 1987).

[22] Backus, 'The Church Fathers and the Canonicity of the Apocalypse in the Sixteenth Century', p. 662.

[23] Firth, *The Apocalyptic Tradition in Reformation Britain*, p. 9.

[24] Perkins, *Works*, iii. 207-208.

[25] Hayne, *Christs Kingdom on Earth*, pp. 61-2. For Elias, see Leeman, 'Was Bishop Ussher's Chronology influenced by a Midrash?', pp. 127-30.

[26] Dallison, 'Contemporary Criticism of Millenarianism', p. 111.

discussion in which the credulous Worldling sources 'olde prophecies of this yeare found in olde stone walls' and other 'Anabaptisticall revelations' in support of his apocalyptic fears.[27] The very fact that Perkins felt the need to refute these kinds of arguments demonstrates something of the impact he felt they were having among his contemporaries.

Such sources enjoyed an international respectability. While lists of English publications from the 1650s demonstrate the popularity of texts attributed to Nostradamus, the Scottish expositor John Napier – now better known for the system of logarithms his millenarian exegesis developed – included the Sybilline oracles in the appendix of *A Plaine Discovery of the Whole Revelation* (1593). His writings exercised some influence in the French Reformed Church, which would itself debate millenarianism throughout the seventeenth century.[28] Similarly, as a German delegate to the Synod of Dort, Johann Heinrich Alsted's Reformed credentials were never in doubt; but he managed to combine his millenarian enthusiasms with a fascination for the occult, while repeated citations of his work illustrate the pervasive influence he exercised on the development of puritan eschatology within the three kingdoms.[29]

Against the complexities of these trends, the puritan confessions of faith evidence the movement's eschatology at its most guarded, operating most closely within the controls of Scripture. However popular religion developed at ground level or in the scholar's attic, it was vital for the movement's leaders to express their doctrines in terms buttressed by careful (if not convincing) biblical exegesis. In a study of their reception of biblical apocalyptic texts, the puritan confessions offer an unparalleled insight into a complex exegetical tradition.

But, as we have noted, the study of puritan eschatology co-exists ambiguously with the findings of the 'Calvin and the Calvinists' debate on the broader plane of intellectual history. Richard Muller has comprehensively answered R. T. Kendall's allegation that a basic discontinuity should be posited between the soteriology of Calvin and the Calvinists, largely by deconstructing the implied dichotomy.[30] Nevertheless, the charge of discontinuity can be brought against the eschatology of Calvin and the 'Calvinists'. Eschatology was one of the few theological loci where such divergence was tolerated in early

---

[27] Perkins, *Works*, iii. 467.

[28] Kevin C. Robbins, *City on the Ocean Sea: La Rochelle, 1530-1650: Urban Society, Religion and Politics on the French Atlantic Frontier* (Leiden: Brill, 1997), pp. 131, 181.

[29] Hotson, *Johann Heinrich Alsted, passim.*

[30] Muller, *The Unaccommodated Calvin*, pp. 11-17.

modern Reformed dogmatics. Nevertheless, as official statements, the puritan confessions illustrate the extent to which protestants in the three kingdoms proved reluctant to move beyond Calvin's caution. Louis Berkhof has claimed that amillennialism 'is the only view that is either expressed or implied in the great historical Confessions of the Church, and has always been the prevalent view in Reformed circles.'[31] Qualifying his a-historical terminology, we can nevertheless test his assertion. To the extent that puritanism's official formulae diverge from a nervous reluctance even to consider the meaning of Revelation 20:1-7 or the existence of a distinctive future period of blessing, we can posit a discrepancy between the reformation and its seventeenth-century descendants, between Calvin and the Calvinists.

The Scots Confession (1560)[32]

The first of the British puritans were acutely aware of their debt to Calvin. Fleeing from the persecution of Mary in the 1550s, Geneva offered the tired refugees a haven of both physical reprieve and theological stimulation. With British refugees in other safe cities across the Continent, the Genevan exiles developed a distinctive worldview which they advanced through the publication of a wide variety of texts – from historical studies to biblical commentaries and drama. Their potential for radicalism was nevertheless tempered by the conservatism of the protestant authorities who had given them shelter. The exiles' development of resistance theory and revolutionary apocalyptic was governed by conclusions like those reached by the Augsburg Confession (1530), drafted by Calvin's friend Melancthon and published with the approval of Luther. It had explicitly condemned those 'Anabaptists' who 'scatter Jewish opinions, that, before the resurrection of the dead, the godly shall occupy the kingdoms of the world, the wicked being everywhere suppressed'.[33] The exigencies of their situation meant that even with all their interest in apocalyptic, the exiles never turned to millenarianism.[34]

In part this is surprising. Before his participation in the exile, John Knox had already demonstrated an interest in radical eschatology. His first sermon had dwelt on the apocalyptic historiography of Daniel 7:24-

---

[31] Louis Berkhof, *Systematic Theology* (1939; rpt. Edinburgh: Banner of Truth, 1958), p. 708.

[32] A Latin text of the Scots Confession can be found in Philip Schaff (ed.), *The Creeds of the Evangelical Protestant Churches* (London: Hodder and Stoughton, 1877), pp. 437-79.

[33] Schaff (ed.), *Creeds of the Evangelical Protestant Churches*, p. 18.

[34] Backus, *Reformation Readings of the Apocalypse, passim.*

25, charging history with providential meaning.[35] His concerns paralleled the exiles' starkly apocalyptic literary project, intended, apparently, to combat native apathy by disseminating pro-puritan propaganda in belligerently apocalyptic tropes.[36] In *The Image of Both Churches* (1547), John Bale had found in Revelation a history of the true church of God in constant warfare with the 'devil's chapel'. Ten years later, in 1557, the apocalyptic momentum had visibly increased: John Olde authored a *Short Description of Antichrist*, Bartholomew Traheron published his lectures on Revelation 4, and Robert Pownall's *Admonition to the Towne of Callys* warned the English outpost of impending divine judgment. The preface to the first edition of the Geneva Bible (1560) described the exiles as a remnant that 'love the comming of Christ Jesus our Lord'.[37]

Nevertheless, when Knox, together with other leaders of the Scottish Reformation, came to agree upon a statement of their common doctrine, the apocalyptic themes which elsewhere dominated his thinking were clearly underplayed. The Scots Confession, adopted by the Scottish Parliament on 17 August 1560 as 'hailsome and sound doctrine groundit vpoune the infallibill trewth of Godis word', seems, at first glance, to continue Calvin's apparent neglect of apocalyptic.[38] Knox, after all, wrote not as a 'speculative theologian which desires to give you courage, but even your Brother in affliction'.[39] The confession reflects this pastoral concern.

Thus the articles of the confession follow the redemptive-historical chronology outlined in Scripture, and expound the work of Christ as the teleology of creation and redemption before moving on to the work of the Spirit, the Christian life, and the sacraments. Eschatological interests are limited to the ninth article, 'Of the Ascension', which deals with Christ's session, present glory, and coming judgment:

> To the Execution [of judgement] we certainlie beleve, that the same our Lord JESUS sall visiblie returne, as that hee was sene to ascend. And then we firmely beleve, that the time of refreshing and restitutioun of all things

---

[35] Geddes MacGregor, *The Thundering Scot: A Portrait of John Knox* (Philadelphia: Westminster Press, 1957), p. 43.

[36] Dawson, 'The Apocalyptic Thinking of the Marian Exiles', pp. 75-91. See also idem, 'Trumpeting Resistance: Christopher Goodman and John Knox', in Roger A. Mason (ed.), *John Knox and the British Reformations*, St Andrews Studies in Reformation History (Aldershot: Ashgate, 1998), pp. 131-153.

[37] The Geneva Bible (1560), sig. iiiv.

[38] Quoted in G.D. Henderson (ed.), *Scots Confession, 1560* (Edinburgh: Church of Scotland Committee on Publications, 1937), p. 8.

[39] John Knox, *Works*, ed. David Laing (Edinburgh: Wodrow Society, 1846-64), iii. 10.

sall cum, in samekle that thir, that fra the beginning have suffered violence, injurie, and wrang, for richteousness sake, sal inherit that blessed immortalitie promised fra the beginning.

There follows an application of the doctrine:

The remembrance of quhilk day, and of the Judgement to be executed in the same, is not onelie to us ane brydle, whereby our carnal lustes are refrained, bot alswa sik inestimable comfort, that neither may the threatning of worldly Princes, nether zit [yet] the feare of temporal death and present danger, move us to renounce and forsake that blessed societie, quhilk we the members have with our Head and onelie Mediator CHRIST JESUS.[40]

Despite Knox's fearsome reputation, the eschatology of the Scots Confession was a recipe for the martyrs' endurance, not a programme for a revolution of the saints.

We should thus be careful of descriptions of Knox's eschatology. From his first sermon, he himself seems to have preferred the apocalyptic mode, which influences even his *History of the Reformation* (1586).[41] But there is no evidence of millenarianism. Quite the opposite appears to be the case. As part of the pan-Calvinist international, the Scottish Reformed Church was also to adopt the second Helvetic Confession in 1566 alongside the Reformed churches of Hungary, Poland and Geneva. The importance of this document is that it was deeply hostile to the type of millenarian extremism displayed at Münster, roundly condemning the 'Jewish dreams, that before the Day of Judgment there shall be a golden world in the earth; and that the godly shall possess the kingdoms of the world, their wicked enemies being trodden under foot'.[42] The eschatology of the Scots Confession – by contrast rather muted, even in the heresies it condemns – illustrates the extent to which sixteenth-century denunciations of millenarianism were necessary only on the Continent. Knox did not need to follow Calvin that far.

---

[40] Schaff (ed.), *Creeds of the Evangelical Protestant Churches*, p. 449-50; Henderson (ed.), *Scots Confession, 1560*, pp. 57-59.

[41] Carol Edington, 'John Knox and the Castilians: A Crucible of Reforming Opinion?', in Roger A. Mason (ed.), *John Knox and the British Reformations*, St Andrews Studies in Reformation History (Aldershot: Ashgate, 1998), p. 46.

[42] Hall (ed.), *Harmony of the Protestant Confessions*, p. 88. 'Damnamus præterea Judaica somnia, quod ante judicii diem aureum in terries sit futurum seculum, et pii regna mundi occupaturi, oppressis suis hostibus impiis', Schaff (ed.), *Creeds of the Evangelical Protestant Churches*, p. 257.

The Irish Articles (1615)[43]

As their situation developed, and Antichrist's influence was recognized within the ritualism still being tolerated in the established churches, English and Irish puritans could not but be dissatisfied with the limitations of their state-church's creed. Their stripped-down Thirty-nine Articles (1562) seemed to pale in comparison with models like the Scots Confession. But there was little momentum for change. The hotter sort of Elizabethan protestants produced the Lambeth Articles (1595) as a manifesto of their hopes, but in 1604 James refused to include them as part of the foundational documents of the Church of England.[44]

Although the Lambeth Articles were unsuccessful in influencing the official structures of the Church of England, they did gain creedal status in Ireland, where the Irish church's convocation included them in its Irish Articles (1615). These comprehensive statements – one hundred and four in comparison to the English articles' thirty-nine – were the position paper of a church which was struggling to balance acceptability to refugee nonconformists with loyalty to the English establishment. Their commitment to Calvinistic soteriology, witnessing the beginnings of covenant theology, together with their refusal to outline any system of *jure divino* church government, created a broad church structure attractive to the puritan ministers expelled from the churches of England and Scotland. As the articles demonstrate, the protestant community of early modern Ireland was not slow to pragmatically adapt the contours of existing reformed thought. Existing as a tiny minority in a land dominated by traditional loyalties to Rome, though nevertheless organising themselves as a state church and enjoying governmental support, the Irish Reformed were compelled to negotiate with their inheritance as they attempted to bring protestant thought to bear on their very different situation.[45] They were influenced by both Geneva and Canterbury. Composed under the shadow of the Thirty-nine Articles, the Irish Articles' silences are almost as illuminating as its explicit statements. Exercising profound influence throughout the course of the seventeenth century, the Irish Articles' contouring of protestant orthodoxy would provide a basic pattern for subsequent puritan confessions to follow.

The composition of the articles was dominated by the leading theologian of the Irish church – the future archbishop James Ussher

---

[43] A text of the Irish Articles can be found in Schaff (ed.), *Creeds of the Evangelical Protestant Churches*, pp. 526-44.

[44] A text of the Lambeth Articles can be found in Schaff (ed.), *Creeds of the Evangelical Protestant Churches*, pp. 523-25.

[45] Ford, *The Protestant Reformation in Ireland, 1590-1641, passim.*

(1581-1656).[46] Like Knox, Ussher was fascinated by history, chronology and eschatology. In his D.D. oration at Trinity College Dublin in 1613, he chose as his subjects the 'seventy weeks' of Daniel 9, a passage whose eschato-chronological importance was unsurpassed in the sixteenth and seventeenth centuries, as well as the disputed Revelation 20.[47] In the same year, in his first published text, *Gravissimae Quaestionis de Christianarum Ecclesiarum Successione et Statu* (1613), Ussher had cautiously suggested the possibility of a second millennium, 'de nova ligatione Satanæ per Evangelii restaurationem sub medium secundi millenarii ... fieri coepta.'[48] With changing circumstances at court making the articulation of radical ideas imprudent, Ussher never published that part of his history which its contents pages promised most controversial.

Instead, in composing the articles, Ussher remained on safe ground, with standard Reformed teaching on individual eschatology. Judgment is taken in under the work of Christ, where 'he will return to judge all men at the last day' (IA 30):

> 101. After this life is ended, the soul's of God's children be presently received into heaven, there to enjoy unspeakable comforts; the souls of the wicked are cast into hell, there to endure endless torments.
>
> 103. At the end of this world, the Lord Jesus shall come in the clouds with the glory of his Father: at which time, by the almighty power of God, the living shall be changed, and the dead shall be raised; and all shall appear both in body and soul before his judgment-seat, to receive according to that which they have done in their bodies, whether good or evil.
>
> 104. When the last judgment is finished, Christ shall deliver up the kingdom to his Father, and God shall be all in all.

In general eschatology the articles offered the standard condemnation of Roman Catholicism:

> 102. The doctrine of the Church of Rome concerning limbus patrum, limbus puerorum, purgatory, prayer for the dead, pardons, adorations of images and relics, and also invocations of saints, is vainly invented with all warrant of holy scripture, yea, and is contrary to the same.

---

[46] On Ussher, see Knox, *James Ussher: Archbishop of Armagh*; Trevor-Roper, *Catholics, Anglicans and Puritans*, pp. 120-164; and Ford, *James Ussher: Theology, history and identity in early-modern Britain and Ireland*. On Ussher and the Irish Articles, see Capern, 'The Caroline Church: James Ussher and the Irish Dimension', pp. 57-85.

[47] Ussher, *Works*, i. 33, 321; cf. xv. 108.

[48] Ussher, *Works*, ii. xi.

The inclusion of this article illustrated the dangers facing the tiny remnant of Ireland's protestants, and understates the extent to which Ussher's life of study was grounded upon his enduring antipathy to Roman Catholicism: 'Rome (whose faith was once renowned throughout all the world) [had] become "Babylon the mother of whoredoms and abominations of the earth".' Indeed, his reading of Revelation convinced him that her further reformation was impossible: 'Rome is not to cease from being Babylon, till her last destruction shall come upon her; and that unto her last gasp she is to continue in her spiritual fornications, alluring all nations unto her superstition and idolatry.'[49] It was perhaps this radicalism which underlay the most important creedal innovation in the Irish Articles – their insistence that the Pope was the 'man of sin, foretold in the holy scriptures, whom the Lord shall consume with the Spirit of his mouth, and abolish with the brightness of his coming' (IA 80). For the first time, the protestant conviction that the Pope was Antichrist had gained creedal status.

This identification, however, did not gain universal approval. It would be debated at the Synod of Dort (1618-19), where Ussher's friend and correspondent Samuel Ward was one of the British delegation, which argued in favour of the Pope being described as 'an antichrist' rather than as 'the antichrist'.[50] Ussher himself would later lament his foregrounding of the Antichrist trope. By the mid-seventeenth century, he had cause to complain that nothing was 'so familiar now a days, as to father upon Antichrist, whatsoever in church matters we do not find to suite with our own humours'.[51] But Ussher perhaps never realized the extent to which the revolutionary atmosphere of the 1640s had been created by the Calvinistic and apocalyptic theology harnessed by his own Irish Articles.

The First London Confession (1644)[52]

Ussher's reluctance to publicly commit himself to an innovative eschatology was necessarily prudent given the changing climate of the Stuart court. James VI, who had published a commentary on Revelation 20 in 1588, turned from his ebullient Presbyterianism after his removal

---

[49] Ussher, *Works*, xii. 542-3.
[50] M.W. Dewar, 'The British Delegation at the Synod of Dort: Assembling and Assembled; Returning and Returned', *Irish Biblical Studies* 13 (1991), p. 75.
[51] Ussher, *Works*, vii. 45.
[52] The text for this confession is taken from *The First London Confession of Faith* (Rochester, NY: Backus Book Publishers, 1981).

to the English throne in 1603.[53] With the support of his prelates, he pursued policies advancing the uniformity of the churches throughout the three kingdoms – a policy which seemed to justify his burning of two millenarian Anabaptists in 1612.[54]

Throughout the period of Laud's supremacy, from his appointment as Bishop of London in 1628 to his imprisonment in 1641, Baptist groups remained largely underground. After the recalling of the Long Parliament in 1640, however, radical groups could once more raise their heads. The Long Parliament unleashed its programme of deliberate apocalyptic provocation, publishing translations of Joseph Mede and Thomas Brightman, as well as new editions of John Foxe, John Cotton, and other writers banned under the Laudian regime. With the older models of the reformation's Augustinian apocalyptic being thus increasingly challenged, the staple elements of the older Marian exile ideology broke down completely in the free market of ideas created by the collapse of state censorship in the 1640s. As the three kingdoms entered the vortex of revolution, the Augustinian theology and Constantinian church-state settlement hanging over from the reformation were finally swept away.

Baptist rhetoric was all the while developing in a robustly eschatological tenor. John Smyth's *The Character of the Beast* (1609) had condemned the baptism of infants in a series of allusions to Revelation. By the 1640s, however, it was evident that for some Baptists the influence of Antichrist had pervaded far beyond Rome, far beyond the prelates, even into the puritan brotherhood. Christopher Blackwood's *The Storming of Antichrist in his two last and strongest Garrisons, of Compulsion of Conscience and Infants Baptism* (1644) argued that even the Presbyterian and Independent divines meeting at Westminster were under his nefarious influence. The 1644 confession refused to claim that the Pope was Antichrist.

It was with some caution, therefore, that English Baptists emerged from the puritan underground. Their very survival depended upon their ability to distinguish themselves from the destabilizing forces which had wreaked such havoc at Münster. Among their puritan brethren, distrust and suspicion could be overcome only by a careful articulation of the Calvinistic faith they shared. Rumours of their Arminianism were due to an inability to differentiate them from the General Baptists; rumours of their immorality, in the repeated stories of

---

[53] For a recent study of James' intellectual interests, see W.B. Patterson, *King James VI and I and the Reunion of Christendom* (Cambridge: Cambridge University Press, 1997).
[54] Hill, *A Nation of Change and Novelty*, p. 256

naked baptisms, were simply untrue.[55] Thus the leadership of the English Baptists – based mostly in London – met to articulate the respectability and orthodoxy of their common faith in 1644.

Their confession, which was republished with minor editions in 1646, was prepared mostly by John Spilsbury, William Kiffin and Samuel Richardson.[56] Against the lingering shadow of Münster, the *Confession of Faith of Seven Congregations or Churches of Christ in London, which are commonly (but unjustly) called Anabaptists* (1644) affirmed the right of private property (1644 31) and advocated obedience to civil authorities whose divine institution it recognized (1644 48).[57] Doctrinally, it affirmed the common Calvinism of puritan dissent and rejected the Pelagianism which seemed to characterize the General Baptists.

The most important aspect of the confession, however, was its presentation as an eschatological document. Its title's description of seven subscribing churches was an historical accident which provided for future rhetorical investment. In Revelation 2-3, the ascended Christ addressed seven churches in Asia Minor. Puritan and Reformed writers had repeatedly taken the state of each of the seven churches as a paradigm for periods of church history as a whole, or for the universal church. Nor were the Baptist churches ignorant of this; as one historian has noted, 'if at first the coincidence was accidental, it was soon remarked upon, and the churches accepted the hint, so that they began to speak of themselves as the Seven ... The peculiar retention of the number Seven, hints at a prediction [sic] for allegory and mysticism, if not for the warlike Fifth-Monarchy doctrines outright.'[58] This should be contested. Some Fifth Monarchists urged violent revolution as a necessary means to establish the political expression of the millennial kingdom for which the group longed.[59] But the Baptist confession is markedly different. The confession did not allow a civil role for the moral law; the only subversion it allowed was passive resistance (1644 48); and it made no identification of its enemy. The Antichrist is never mentioned, presumably because they thought his seat of influence much nearer than the Vatican.

---

[55] White, 'The Origins and Convictions of the First Calvinistic Baptists', pp. 39-47.

[56] Haykin, *Kiffin, Knollys and Keach*, p. 33.

[57] Samuel E. Waldron, *A Modern Exposition of the 1689 Baptist Confession of Faith* (Darlington: Evangelical Press, 1989), p. 427.

[58] W.T. Whitely, 'The Seven Churches of London', *The Review and Expositor* 7:3 (1910), pp. 384, 405.

[59] The best study of the Fifth Monarchy movement is Capp, *The Fifth Monarchy Men*.

Nevertheless, the confession retained strong links to the Reformed tradition. Its structure advanced on Calvin's three-fold division of the work of Christ into the offices of prophet, priest and king. Like the Scots Confession, the Baptists linked Christ's kingly office to his future rule (1644 19-20): 'This his kingly power shall be more fully manifested when He shall come in glory to reign among his saints, and when He shall put down all rule and authority under His feet' (1644 20). The Scriptural proofs which the confession cited in this article included 1 Corinthians 15:24, 28, Hebrews 9:28, 2 Thessalonians 1:9-10, 1 Thessalonians 4:15-17, John 17:21, 26 – but, significantly, no reference was made to Revelation 20. With similar caution, the resurrection was dealt with in a general way, again without reference to the first or second resurrections which Revelation 20 put at either end of the millennium (1644 52). Its statements ended with the prayer, 'Come, Lord Jesus, come quickly.'[60] Its mood was definitely apocalyptic – but any reference to the political millenarianism of the Fifth Monarchists is clearly overstated.

The Westminster Confession (1646)

At the same time as Spilsbury, Kiffin and Richardson were working on their confession, a much larger assembly of divines was also meeting in London to produce a statement of faith and associated documents designed to ensure the uniformity of the church throughout the three kingdoms in accordance with 'the word of God and the best reformed churches'. First called in 1643, and publishing its confession only in 1647, the Westminster Assembly continued mainstream puritanism's interest in eschatological study and undertook its work in a self-consciously millenarian atmosphere. Its divines were acutely aware of the Baptist confession, and specifically wanted to redress its theological system.[61] Nevertheless, despite their movement far beyond the relative conservatism of the 1644 Baptist confession, the Westminster divines' careful, deliberate exposition of biblical apocalyptic must be seen as contrasting with the more radical mood among many of its delegates and within the puritan brotherhood more generally. One of its most prominent delegates, Thomas Goodwin, had already published *An Exposition of the Revelation* (1639) as an articulate defense of Independent ecclesiology, suggesting several dates for important apocalyptic

---

[60] *The First London Confession of Faith*, p. 21.
[61] S. W. Carruthers, *The Everyday Work of the Westminster Assembly* (Philadelphia: Presbyterian Historical Society, 1943), p. 103.

events.[62] On the other side of the ecclesiological divide, George Gillespie, the youngest and most vocal of the Scottish Commissioners, announced in a sermon to Parliament in March 1644 that biblical chronology proved that the building of Ezekiel's millennial temple had begun the year before, in 1643.[63] As in many other areas of their deliberation, however, the divines recognized some merit in advancing a system of biblical theology capable of sustaining several rather different readings – a necessary compromise if the confession was, after all, to sustain a broad national church.

Drawn up with 'an eye on the Irish Articles', the Westminster Confession was a statement of puritan theology in its maturity.[64] Couched and nuanced as the consequence of extended debate, its negotiations took longer than those of other documents which the Assembly produced. Several items produced in the interim displayed an evolution of thought even within the narrow chronological confines of the Assembly's meetings. *The Directory for the Publick Worship of God*, which was published in 1644, exhibited the optimistic influence of the Scottish Commissioners and the English Independents, who had worked together on its completion.[65] It instructed parish ministers to pray for

> the conversion of the Jews, the fullness of the Gentiles, the fall of Antichrist, and the hastening of the second coming of our Lord; for the deliverance of the distressed churches abroad from the tyranny of the antichristian faction, and from the cruel oppressions and blasphemies of the Turk; for the blessings of God upon the reformed churches, especially upon the churches and kingdoms of Scotland, England, and Ireland, now more strictly and religiously united in the Solemn National League and Covenant.[66]

The Confession itself was more guarded. Like the Scots Confession, Irish Articles and the 1644 Baptist confession, it did not refer to the conversion of the Jews, or the hoped-for deliverance from Islamic and

---

[62] This text is reprinted as Thomas Goodwin, 'An Exposition of the Revelation', in Goodwin, *Works*, iii. 1-226.

[63] George Gillespie, 'A Sermon Preached ... March 27, 1644', in Gillespie, *Works*, i. 23.

[64] Jan Rohls, *Reformed Confessions: Theology from Zurich to Barmen*, trans. John Hoffmeyer, Columbia Series in Reformed Theology (Louisville, Kentucky: Westminster John Knox Press, 1998), p. 26. See also A.A. Hodge, *Evangelical Theology: A Course of Popular Lectures* (1890; rpt. Edinburgh: Banner of Truth, 1976), p. 165.

[65] Murray, *Puritan Hope*, p. 44.

[66] 'The Directory for the Publick Worship of God', in *The Westminster Confession of Faith* (1967), p. 377.

Roman Catholic hostility. But neither did it restrict eschatological themes to the discussion of Christ's kingly office, as previous English and Scottish puritan confessions had. Instead, as in the Irish Articles, eschatology was given a separate discussion; form was matching content, locating the discussion at the end of the confession, in chapters 32-33. There the divines advanced a conservative Augustinian reading of eschatology, locating 'the last day' as the single day for judgment (WCF 32:2, 33:1) and guarding against any attempt to fix dates:

> As Christ would have us to be certainly persuaded that there shall be a day of judgment, both to deter all men from sin; and for the greater consolation of the godly in their adversity: so He will have that day unknown to men, that they may shake off all carnal security, and be always watchful, because they know not at what hour the Lord will come; and may be ever prepared to say, Come Lord Jesus, come quickly. Amen. (WCF 33:3)

With this prayer, echoing the finale of the Baptist confession three years before, the Confession concluded.

In the later documents these pietistic and soteriological emphases were expanded upon. The Longer Catechism (1648) expounded individual eschatology – death, the intermediate state and the resurrection – under its section on communion with Christ (LC 84-90). The Assembly's most vibrant statement of general eschatology was expounded in the section outlining of the Lord's Prayer:

> In the second petition, (which is, *Thy kingdom come*,) acknowledging ourselves and all mankind to be by nature under the dominion of sin and Satan, we pray, that the kingdom of sin and Satan may be destroyed, the gospel propagated throughout the world, the Jews called, the fullness of the Gentiles brought in; the church furnished with all gospel-officers and ordinances, purged from corruption, countenanced and maintained by the civil magistrate: that the ordinances of Christ may be purely dispensed, and made effectual to the converting of those that are yet in their sins, and the confirming, comforting, and building up of those that are already converted: that Christ would rule in our hearts here, and hasten the time of his second coming, and our reigning with him for ever: and that he would be pleased so to exercise the kingdom of his power in all the world, as may best conduce to these ends. (LC 191)

In its most extensive treatment of the topic to this point, eschatology is linked to the Assembly's wider project, involving world evangelism and a last-days revival, proper ecclesiology, the theonomic rule of the 'godly prince', and the eternal reign of the saints. It was an ebullient statement of the Assembly's comprehensive programme for reform and a marked advance upon earlier confessional statements.

The Savoy Declaration (1658)[67]

For many of its delegates, however, the documents produced by the Westminster Assembly were insufficiently exact. The publication of *An Apologeticall Narration* (1644) by the 'Dissenting Brethren' – leaders of the Independent faction at Westminster – indicated that all was not well in the citadel of English puritanism. The Independents believed that the Westminster confession could be more closely refined.

After two decades of Dutch exile and Anglican expulsion, and with a heady rise to dizzying influence during the Commonwealth period, the Independent divines were rapidly radicalized. The success of their polemic was also vigorously advancing. By the 1650s they had become the leading English denomination; in East Anglia, some thirty new congregations had been established between 1650 and 1658.[68] But when they met in convocation in 1658, they were sensing the gradual eclipse of their power. John Owen, their leading divine, had been Vice-Chancellor of the University of Oxford for five years when the Chancellor, Richard Cromwell, replaced him with the Presbyterian John Conant in 1657. Despite his sympathy for their distinctives, Oliver Cromwell himself was hoping to achieve the union of Presbyterians and Independents.[69] As in Ireland, so in England, the Independents were losing ground.[70]

Their tradition had, however, tended to be more radical than the Presbyterians. The first of the expression 'the Congregational way', for example, was made in the epistle to the reader prefacing *A Glimpse of Sions Glory* (1641), a radically millenarian sermon published anonymously but attributed, in its own day and since, to Thomas Goodwin.[71] Goodwin had preached the sermon while in Dutch exile alongside William Bridge, Jeremiah Burroughes, Philip Nye and Sidrach Simpson, all of whom were later Westminster delegates and signatories of *An Apologeticall Narration*.[72] At the Westminster Assembly they opposed both Episcopalianism and Separatism, arguing instead for the inclusion of independent churches within a comprehensive state church. All were vibrantly millenarian. Anthony Dallison's study of Goodwin's sermons before 1658 has emphasized that 'the subject of the latter-day

---

[67] A text of the Savoy Confession can be found in Schaff (ed.), *Creeds of the Evangelical Protestant Churches*, pp. 707-29.

[68] A.G. Matthews, 'Introduction', in A.G. Matthews (ed.), *The Savoy Declaration of Faith and Order 1658* (London: Independent Press, 1959), p. 24.

[69] Matthews, 'Introduction', p. 16.

[70] Matthews, 'Introduction', p. 10.

[71] G.F. Nuttall, *Visible Saints* (Oxford: Oxford University Press, 1957), p. 8 n. 4. The sermon is reprinted in Goodwin, *Works*, xii. 61-79.

[72] Watts, *The Dissenters*, pp. 99-100.

glory was not a mere speculative theory but a doctrine which supplied the churches of the Congregational way with a powerful motive for reformation and a glorious hope for the future.'[73]

While in exile in Holland, Goodwin had preached the sermons which were published as *An Exposition of the Revelation* (1639).[74] One of these sermons was pirated and published as *A Sermon on the Fifth Monarchy, proving by invincible arguments that the saints shall have a Kingdom here on earth which is yet to come* (1654). One year later, several of Goodwin's sermons on Ephesians were pirated and published as *The World to Come; or, the Kingdom of Christ Asserted in two expository lectures on Eph. i. 21, 22* (1655). Both of these editions seem to have been published to further the cause of the radical and often amorphous Fifth Monarchist group. John Owen, too, was an apocalyptic enthusiast.[75] His sermons to Parliament were bald statements warning of 'the shaking and translating of heaven and earth'. His increasing political radicalism co-existed uneasily with Goodwin's belief that Cromwell should take the throne.

Despite these tensions, when the leaders of the Independent churches met to forge a theological alliance at the end of the Commonwealth, they found their job much easier thanks to the efforts some of them had already made as part of the Westminster Assembly. Sessions of the Savoy Conference lasted from 29 September to 12 October 1658.[76] The end product of the discussion was a revision of the Westminster Confession, carried out by Thomas Goodwin, Philip Nye, William Bridge, William Greenhill, Joseph Caryl (all of whom had attended the Westminster Assembly) and John Owen.[77] The committee's conclusions were read every morning to the one hundred and twenty delegates to synod, debated, and then adopted.[78] It was designed as a common front against the perception of weakness and division: Owen led the delegation which presented the Savoy Declaration to Richard Cromwell in October 1658.[79]

The Savoy Confession largely reiterates the Westminster's pronouncements on the intermediate state and the last judgment (Savoy 31-32, WCF 32-33). Its most innovative eschatological statements are included in chapter twenty-six, 'Of the Church'. Here, evidencing their

---

[73] Dallison, 'The Latter-day Glory in the Thought of Thomas Goodwin', p. 54.

[74] Dallison, 'The Latter-day Glory in the Thought of Thomas Goodwin', pp. 53-68. See also comments on Goodwin in Hill, *The Experience of Defeat*, pp. 172-7.

[75] For Owen's eschatology, see Watts, *The Dissenters*, pp. 134-42. See also Hill, *The Experience of Defeat*, pp. 164-172. The most recent biography of Owen is Toon, *God's Statesman*.

[76] Matthews, 'Introduction', p. 22.

[77] Matthews, 'Introduction', p. 34.

[78] Matthews, 'Introduction', pp. 34, 22.

[79] Matthews, 'Introduction', p. 11.

distinctive patterns of ecclesiology, the Savoy divines expansively modified the Westminster Confession's formulae. They affirmed only the first paragraph of WCF 25, replacing subsequent paragraphs with a definition of the church which excluded baptized children from church membership and denied that the authority for the administration of ordinances or church government were given to the universal church, instead locating the foci of church authority in the local congregation (Savoy 26:2, contra WCF 25:2-3). Savoy 26 was also the closest the puritan confessions came to outright millennialism:

> IV. There is no other Head of the Church but the Lord Jesus Christ; nor can the Pope of Rome in any sense be Head thereof; but is that Antichrist, that man of sin, and son of perdition, that exalteth himself in the Church against Christ, and all that is called God, whom the Lord shall destroy with the brightness of his coming.
>
> V. As the Lord in his care and love towards his Church, hath in his infinite wise providence exercised it with great variety in all ages, for the good of them that love him, and his own Glory; so according to his promise, we expect that in the later days, Antichrist being destroyed, the Jews called, and the adversaries of the Kingdom of his dear Son broken, the Churches of Christ being inlarged [sic], and edified through a free and plentiful communication of light and grace, shall enjoy in this world a more quiet, peacable and glorious condition then [sic] they have enjoyed.

Although the confession refuses to treat of Revelation 20:1-7 – it avoids offering any Scriptural proofs whatsoever – it clearly posits a period of earthly blessing after the return of Christ. This is not to say, however, that it is premillennial: it does not assert a millennial reign of Christ upon earth, and could allude to Goodwin's belief that the millennium would be inaugurated by Christ without his presence on earth throughout its duration.[80] In an addition to WCF 25:6, the Savoy states that Antichrist will be destroyed at the second coming (Savoy 26:4), thereby linking ecclesiology to their eschatological hopes. Those Independents who were eschatologically-minded did not hesitate to claim that the millennium would bring true church government.[81] The 'later days' (Savoy 26:5) will see the conversion of the Jews, the expansion of biblical churches, and the benefits of progressive revelation leading to increasing knowledge, grace and glory. Historians would be glad to know which Scriptural texts the Savoy divines were thinking of when they referred to 'his promise' as the basis for these hopes (Savoy 26:5). This silence notwithstanding, the Savoy Confession was the most closely millenarian of the puritan confessions.

---

[80] Dallison, 'The Latter-day Glory in the Thought of Thomas Goodwin', p. 62.
[81] Dallison, 'The Latter-day Glory in the Thought of Thomas Goodwin', p. 59.

The Second Baptist Confession (1677/1689)[82]

Part of the difficulty facing the Independents was the increasing influence of the Baptists at both popular level and in the state administration. Through the period of Parliament's ascendancy, the Baptist cause was rapidly expanding. By the late 1650s they had grown from seven churches in London to around one hundred and thirty throughout England, Wales and Ireland.[83] By 1660, there were around two hundred and twenty Baptist churches in existence, one hundred and thirty of whom were Calvinistic. But not many of these churches had entered Cromwell's national church. In 1662, only nineteen Baptist ministers were ejected from the state church.[84] They had proved themselves more independent than the Independents.

Despite their separatism, the Restoration's clampdown on dissent encouraged Baptist leaders to demonstrate the essential unity of the nonconformists. By the 1670s, the 1644 confession was clearly out-of-step with the developing form and content of dissenting Calvinism. Covenant theology had developed through its refinements in the Westminster and Savoy confessions. Similarly, the 1644 confessions' advocacy of 'closed' communion – the idea that the benefits of church membership were open only to candidates who had been immersed as believers – was clearly out-of-step with the increasingly ecumenical spirit of co-operation among dissenters.[85] A new confession of faith would articulate Baptist-Independent ecclesiology more carefully, while taking account of the theological developments of the previous thirty years. Thus Baptist leaders turned to the Savoy confession as a basic model for Baptist faith. This revision of the Savoy was carried out in 1677, largely by William Collins, although signatories included the prominent leaders Hanserd Knollys, William Kiffin and Benjamin Keach. This 'most influential and important of all Baptist Confessions'[86] was reaffirmed by English Baptist leaders in 1689 and adopted by American Baptists in 1742 as the Philadelphia Confession of Faith.

With all the sources at their disposal – the 1644, Westminster and Savoy confessions – it is interesting to note that on no occasion do the 1677 revisers privilege the statements of Westminster above those of the Savoy.[87] The revised confession was composed of one hundred and

---

[82] A text of the 1677/1689 Baptist Confession can be found in William L. Lumpkin, *Baptist Confessions of Faith* (Chicago: Judson Press, [1959]).
[83] Haykin, *Kiffin, Knollys and Keach*, p. 40.
[84] Watts, *The Dissenters*, p. 160.
[85] Matthews, 'Introduction', p. 19.
[86] W.J. McGlothlin, *Baptist Confessions of Faith* (Philadelphia: American Baptist Publication Society, 1911), p. 219.
[87] Waldron, *1689 Baptist Confession of Faith*, p. 428.

sixty paragraphs. Of this total, one hundred and forty six are derived from the Savoy confession, eight from the 1644 confession, and only six appear to be original.[88] Retaining Calvinism, the revisers refined Westminster's covenant theology;[89] rejected the Presbyterian government which was common to the Scottish church and the General Baptists (1677/1689 26:7); supported lay-preaching, with due qualifications (1677/1689 26:11); and, in contrast to the 1644 and Westminster confessions, no longer demanded that every church member had to be baptized (1677/1689 26:6), or even that baptism was necessary before the individual could participate in communion (1677/1689 30).[90] The 1677/1689 confession demonstrates the distance which Baptists had traveled on the road from their Anabaptist reputation – no-one now could doubt their status as a fully-fledged puritan denomination.

Like the other confessions, it was composed amid millennial excitement and disappointment. The radically millenarian Fifth Monarchists had always drawn the support of Baptists and were still suspected of fomenting rebellion one decade after the failure of Venner's London rising in 1661.[91] Leading Baptists, like John Bunyan, joined leading Independents, like Thomas Brooks and Thomas Goodwin, in distancing themselves from his Fifth Monarchism.[92] Nevertheless, these radical hopes were maintained after the Restoration. In 1688, Baptist leader Hanserd Knollys (who had signed the 1644 confession) was expecting the imminent commencement of the millennium.[93] Benjamin Keach, another Baptist leader, viewed the Glorious Revolution in vibrantly eschatological terms.[94] One year later, William and Mary's introduction of religious freedom was the context in which the confession was adopted by 'messengers' from one hundred and seven churches in the first general assembly of the Particular Baptists of England, in 1689.[95] Nevertheless, the 1677/1689 confession evidences a retreat from the heady apocalypticism of the Savoy divines.

---

[88] Waldron, *1689 Baptist Confession of Faith*, p. 429.

[89] Waldron, *1689 Baptist Confession of Faith*, p. 429.

[90] Whitely, 'The Seven Churches of London', p. 390.

[91] B.R. White, 'John Pendarves, the Calvinistic Baptists and the Fifth Monarchy', *Baptist Quarterly* 25 (1974), pp. 251-69.

[92] Brooks, *Works*, i. xxxii; Greaves, 'Conscience, Liberty and the Spirit: Bunyan and Nonconformity', p. 28; Rogers, *Some Account of the Life and Opinions of a Fifth Monarchy Man*, p. 327.

[93] Howson, 'Eschatology in Sixteenth and Seventeenth Century England', p. 331.

[94] Kenneth G.C. Newport, 'Benjamin Keach, William of Orange and the Book of Revelation: A Study in English Prophetical Exegesis', *Baptist Quarterly* 36 (1995-96), pp. 43-51.

[95] Lumpkin, *Baptist Confessions of Faith*, pp. 235-8.

They simply omitted Savoy 26:5 from their discussion of the church. Again ignoring Revelation 20, their erstwhile millennial hope was being replaced by an increasing concentration upon ecclesiology. It does not take any explicit position on the millennium, but its position can be inferred from its identification of one day of judgment, not two separated by one thousand years. A thousand year reign was implicitly denied.

The second Baptist confession's emphatic statement of a single judgment (1677/1689 32:1) echoes the Westminster/Savoy repudiation of date-setting: 'he will have the date of that day kept unknown to men, that they may shake off all carnal security, and always be watchful, because they know not at what hour the Lord will come' (1677/1689 32:3). But its caution did not preclude its ending on the 1644/Westminster/Savoy's final note of joyful hope: 'Come, Lord Jesus, come quickly!' (1677/1689 32:3).

Conclusion

For a movement of ecclesiastical radicalism, the eschatology of the puritan confessions of faith is remarkably conservative. Revealing the gradual rise and fall of the movement's eschatological priorities, Richard Sibbes' remark that 'we are fallen into the latter end of the world' seemed again and again to signal the sense of imminence upon which the hopes of the movement were grounded and also the caution which guarded against the inclusion of such hopes within the movement's confessional documents.[96] Puritans seemed able to distinguish between that understanding of prophecy which was of 'private origin' and the more cautious expression of hope which was appropriate to collective statements of faith. Despite the number of detailed expositions of the subject, puritan eschatology never attained the finality afforded to the movement's statements of soteriology or even ecclesiology. Puritan confessions repeatedly refuse to endorse the radical eschatologies defended in the individual writings of some of the very theologians who composed them.

But the confessions were conservative also in their method. Despite the popularity and respectability of interest in non-canonical sources, the writers of the puritan confessions sought to remove the influence of pagan apocalyptic and replace it with data more firmly derived from Scripture. The puritan confessions can be judged successful by the extent to which subsequent generations of believers and unbelievers alike have looked to the Bible alone as sufficient in defining the Christian's blessed hope.

---

[96] Sibbes, *Works*, iv. 43.

This repudiation of non-canonical sources is also illustrated in the extent to which puritan theology did not regard Calvin – or, indeed, any other expositor – as an infallible touchstone. Believing themselves to be at the end of history, when 'knowledge shall increase', puritan theologians advanced on the basis of progressive revelation to proffer readings of Revelation often unlike any maintained before. Sharing Calvin's rejection of the medieval past, puritan expositors showed themselves more open to rehabilitating the patristic millenarian tradition – but, remarkably, never in their confessions. To that extent, historians can posit a dichotomy between Calvin and the Calvinists, if not in the eschatology the confessions contain, then certainly in the mood the confessions represent.

So the confusion between Clouse, Froom and de Jong can be seen to misrepresent the very nature of the debate. With none of the puritan confessions ever citing Revelation 20, it is difficult to see how any of them could be properly described as either pre-, post- or amillennial. They were, nevertheless, all conservative in comparison to what some of their compositors would commit themselves to elsewhere.

In a web of intertextuality, the puritan confessions emerged as highly-referential developments of a common set of themes. As this survey has illustrated, in their tensions and dissensions the puritan confessions are snapshots of - if not monuments to - the developing puritan theological tradition in its movement of eschatology toward its modern position at the focus of Reformed dogmatics. They may not be amillennial, as Berkhof suggested, but they were certainly nervous about committing themselves to any exposition of Revelation 20 that could at all be definite. The millennialism of the puritan confessions seems as obscure as ever.

Bibliography

Primary Sources

Alleine, Joseph, *An Alarm to the Unconverted* (1671; rpt. Edinburgh: Banner of Truth, 1959).

Alsted, John, *The Beloved City* (London, 1643) STC A2924.

[Anon.], *Reverend Mr. Brightman's Judgement ... on the Revelations* (London, 1642) STC 4683.

Archer, John, *The Personall Reign of Chist upon Earth* (London, 1643) STC A3614.

Aspinwall, William, *The Work of the Age* (London, 1655) STC A4010.

Augustine, *Concerning the City of God Against the Pagans* (1467; rpt. trans. Henry Bettenson, Harmondsworth: Penguin, 1972).

Bale, John, *Select Works of John Bale*, ed. Henry Christmas (Cambridge: University Press, 1849).

Baillie, Robert, *The Letters and Journals of Robert Baillie*, ed. David Laing (Edinburgh: Robert Ogle, 1841-2).

— *A Dissausive from the Errors of the Times* (London, 1645) STC B456.

Bastwick, John, *The Beast is Wounded* (London, 1638) STC 22032.

Baxter, Richard, *Reliquiae Baxterianae, or Mr. Richard Baxter's narrative of the most memorable passages of his life and times* (London, 1696) STC B1370.

— *Gildas Salvianus: The Reformed Pastor* (1656; rpt. London: Epworth Press, 1939).

— *The Autobiography of Richard Baxter*, ed. N.H. Keeble (London: Dent, 1974).

— *Calendar of the Correspondence of Richard Baxter*, eds N.H. Keeble and Geoffrey F. Nuttall (Oxford: Clarendon Press, 1991).

Bolton, Robert, *The Four Last Things: Death, Judgement, Hell and Heaven* (1830; rpt. Pittsburgh: Soli Deo Gloria, 1994).

Bolton, Samuel, *The True Bounds of Christian Freedom* (1645; rpt. Edinburgh: Banner of Truth, 1964).

Bradshawe, William, *English Puritanisme* (1605; rpt. Farnborough: Gregg International Publishers, 1972).

Bridge, William, *A Lifting up for the Downcast* (1649; rpt. Edinburgh: Banner of Truth, 1961).

— *The Works of the Rev. William Bridge* (London: Thomas Tegg, 1845).

Brightman, Thomas, *A Most Comfortable Exposition of ... Daniel* (Amsterdam, 1635; rpt. 1644) STC 3753.

— *A Revelation of the Revelation* (Amsterdam, 1615) STC 3755.

Brooks, Thomas, *The Works of Thomas Brooks*, ed. A.B. Grosart (1861-67; rpt. Edinburgh: Banner of Truth, 1980).

Bunyan, John, *The Works of John Bunyan*, ed. George Offor (Glasgow: Blackie and Son, 1860).

— *Grace Abounding to the Chief of Sinners*, ed. Roger Sharrock (Oxford: Clarendon Press, 1962).

— *The Pilgrim's Progress*, ed. James Blanton Wharey; 2nd ed. Roger Sharrock (Oxford: Clarendon Press, 1960).

— *The Life and Death of Mr Badman*, eds James F. Forrest and Roger Sharrock (Oxford: Clarendon Press, 1988).

— *The Holy War*, eds Roger Sharrock and James F. Forrest (Oxford: Clarendon Press, 1980).

— *The Miscellaneous Works of John Bunyan*, vol. i, eds T.L. Underwood and Roger Sharrock (Oxford: Clarendon Press, 1980).

— *The Miscellaneous Works of John Bunyan*, vol. ii, ed. Richard L. Greaves (Oxford: Clarendon Press, 1976).

— *The Miscellaneous Works of John Bunyan*, vol. iii, ed. J. Sears McGee (Oxford: Clarendon Press, 1987).

— *The Miscellaneous Works of John Bunyan*, vol. vi, ed. Graham Midgley (Oxford: Clarendon Press, 1980).

— *The Miscellaneous Works of John Bunyan*, vol. viii, ed. Richard L. Greaves (Oxford: Clarendon Press, 1979).

— *The Miscellaneous Works of John Bunyan*, vol. ix, ed. Richard L. Greaves (Oxford: Clarendon Press, 1981).

— *The Miscellaneous Works of John Bunyan*, vol. x, ed. Owen C. Watkins (Oxford: Clarendon Press, 1988).

— *The Miscellaneous Works of John Bunyan*, vol. xi, ed. Richard L. Greaves (Oxford: Clarendon Press, 1985).

— *The Miscellaneous Works of John Bunyan*, vol. xii, ed. W.R. Owens (Oxford: Clarendon Press, 1994).

— *The Miscellaneous Works of John Bunyan*, vol. xiii, ed. W.R. Owens (Oxford: Clarendon Press, 1994).

Burgess, Cornelius, *The First Sermon, Preached to the Honorable House of Commons ... Novemb. 17. 1640* (1641) STC B5671.

— *Another Sermon Preached to the Honorable House of Commons* (1641) STC B5668.

Burroughs, Jeremiah, *Sions Joy ... For the PEACE concluded between ENGLAND and SCOTLAND* (1641) STC B6119.

— *The Rare Jewel of Christian Contentment* (1648; rpt. Edinburgh: Banner of Truth, 1964).

— *An Exposition upon the Eight, Ninth, and Tenth Chapters of ... Hosea ...* (1650) STC B6070B.

Calvin, John, *Institutes of the Christian Religion*, eds J.T. McNeill and F.L. Battles (1559; rpt. London: SCM, 1960).

— *Calvin's Commentaries: The Epistles of Paul the Apostle to the Romans and to the Thessalonians*, trans. Ross Mackenzie (Edinburgh: St. Andrew Press, 1972).

Cotton, John, *The Churches Resurrection* (London, 1642) STC C6419.

Cromwell, Oliver, *The Writings and Speeches of Oliver Cromwell: With an Introduction, Notes and an Account of his Life*, ed. W.C. Abbott (1939; rpt. Oxford: Clarendon Press, 1988).

— *Oliver Cromwell's Letters and Speeches*, ed. Thomas Carlyle (London: Chapman and Hall, 1893).

— *Speeches of Oliver Cromwell*, ed. Ivan Roots (London: Dent, 1989).

Dickson, David, *Sermons Preached at a Communion in Irvine* (c. 1635) rpt. *Anthology* v (1992), pp. 294-328.

— *A Brief Exposition of ... Matthew* (1647; rpt. Edinburgh: Banner of Truth, 1981).
— *A Commentary on the Psalms* (1653-5; rpt. Edinburgh: Banner of Truth, 1959).
Donne, John, *The Oxford Authors: John Donne*, ed. John Carey (Oxford: Oxford University Press, 1990).
Edwards, Thomas, *Gangræna* (1646; rpt. *The Rota* and the University of Exeter, 1977).
The English Revolution: Fast Sermons to Parliament, November 1648 to April 1649, ed. R. Jeffs, vol. xxxii (London: Cornmarket Press, 1971).
Finch, Sir Henry, *The Calling of the Jews* (1623) STC 10874.
Foxe, John, *Acts and Monuments* (1563; 9th ed. London, 1684).
— *The Acts and Monuments of John Foxe*, ed. George Townsend (1563; rpt. New York: A.M.S. Press, 1965).
— *Christus Triumphans* (1556; rpt. in Smith [trans.] [1973]), pp. 199-371.
Frese, James, *A Packet of News* (London, 1651) STC F2197DA.
Gauden, John, *The Love of Truth and Peace* (1640) STC G362.
Gillespie, George, *The Works of George Gillespie: The Presbyterian's Armoury*, ed. W.M. Hetherington (Edinburgh: Robert Ogle, and Oliver & Boyd, 1846).
— 'A Sermon Preached ... March 27, 1644' in *Works* i: 1-26.
— *A Treatise of Miscellany Questions* (1649; rpt. in *Works* [1846]).
Goodwin, Thomas, *The Works of Thomas Goodwin* (Edinburgh: James Nichol, 1861-66).
— *A Glimpse of Sions Glory* (London, 1641) STC G1245A.
Goodwin, Thomas, et al, *An Apologeticall Narration* (1644) STC G1225.
Hayne, Thomas, *Christs Kingdom on Earth* (London, 1645) STC H1217.
Hobbes, Thomas, *Behemoth* (1679; rpt. New York: Burt Franklin, 1975).
James I, *Works* (1616) STC 14344.
Knox, John, *Works*, ed. David Laing (Edinburgh: Wodrow Society, 1846-64).
— *The First Blast of the Trumpet Against the Monstrous Regiment of Women* (1558; rpt. Dallas: Presbyterian Heritage Publications, 1993).
Manton, Thomas, *The Complete Works of Thomas Manton* (London: James Nisbet, 1870-75).
Marshall, Stephen, *A Sermon Preached before the Honourable House of Commons ... November 17. 1640* (1641) STC M776A.
— *A Peace-Offering to God ... for the PEACE concluded between ENGLAND and SCOTLAND* (1641) STC M766.
Mede, Joseph, *The Key of the Revelation* (London, 1643) STC M1600.
Works (London, 1664) STC M1586.
Milton, John, *The Works of John Milton*, gen. ed. Frank A. Patterson (New York: Columbia University Press, 1931-40).
Minutes of the Sessions of the Westminster Assembly of Divines, eds A.F. Mitchell and J. Struthers (Edinburgh: Blackwood and Sons, 1874).
Napier, John, *A Plaine Discovery of the Whole Revelation* (London, 1593; 2nd ed. 1611) STC 18356.
Owen, John, *The Works of John Owen*, ed. W.H. Goold (London: Johnstone and Hunter, 1850-53).
Perkins, William, *The Art of Prophesying* (1606; rpt. Edinburgh: Banner of Truth, 1996).
— *The Workes of ... Mr. William Perkins* (London, 1612) STC 19650.

Petrie, Alexander, *Chiliasto-mastix* (Rotterdam, 1644) STC P1878.

Preston, John, *The Breastplate of Faith and Love* (London, 1630) STC 20208.

Rogers, John, *Ohel or Bethshemesh* (1653) STC R1813.

Rutherford, Samuel, *Quaint Sermons of Samuel Rutherford*, ed. Andrew Bonar (London: Hodder and Stoughton, 1885).

— *Letters of Samuel Rutherford*, ed. Andrew Bonar (1891; rpt. Edinburgh: Banner of Truth, 1984).

Savoy Declaration of Faith and Order, ed. A.G. Matthews (1658; rpt. London: Independent Press, 1959).

Sibbes, Richard, *The Complete Works of Richard Sibbes*, ed. A.B. Grosart (Edinburgh: James Nichol, 1862-64).

Sidney, Philip, *An Apology for Poetry* (1595; rpt. London: Sangam Books, 1975).

Subordinate Standards and Other Authoritative Documents of the Free Church of Scotland (Edinburgh: Blackwood, 1973).

Ussher, James, *The Whole Works of James Ussher*, eds C.R. Elrington and J.R. Todd (Dublin, 1847-64).

— *Confessions and Proofes of Protestant Divines of Reformed Churches, That Episcopacy is in respect of the Office according to the word of God, and in respect of the Use of the Best* (Oxford, 1644) STC M2835.

Venning, Ralph, *The Plague of Plagues* (1669; rpt. London: Banner of Truth, 1965).

Watson, Thomas, *A Body of Divinity* (1692; rpt. London: Banner of Truth, 1958).

— *The Doctrine of Repentance* (1668; rpt. Edinburgh: Banner of Truth, 1987).

Williams, Griffith, *The Great Antichrist Revealed* (1660) STC W2662.

Secondary Sources

Abrams, M.H., *A Glossary of Literary Terms* (1957; 9th ed. London: Holt, Rinehard and Winston, 1988).

Achinstein, Sharon, *Milton and the Revolutionary Reader* (Princeton: Princeton University Press, 1994).

Adair, Patrick, *A True Narrative of the Rise and Progress of the Presbyterian Church in Ireland* (Belfast: Aitchison, 1866).

Aers, David et al, *Literature, Language and Society in England 1580-1680* (Dublin: Gill and Macmillan, 1981).

Alexander, J.H., 'Christ in *The Pilgrim's Progress'*, *Bunyan Studies* 1:2 (1989), pp. 22-29.

Alumni Dublinenses, eds G.D. Burtchaell and T.U. Sadlier (Dublin: Alex. Thom and Co., 1935).

[Anon.], 'How the Year 2000 Bug will Hurt the Economy', *Business Week* 2 March 1998, pp. 46-51.

[Anon.], 'Bank boss fears global crash in 2000', *Sunday Times: Money* 29 March 1998, p. 1.

Anthology of Presbyterian and Reformed Literature v, ed. Christopher Coldwell (Dallas: Naphtali Press, 1992).

Antognazza, Maria Rosa and Howard Hotson, *Alsted and Liebniz on God, the Magistrate and the Millennium* (Wiesbaden: Harrassowitz Verlag, 1999).

Armitage, David, et al (eds), *Milton and Republicanism* (Cambridge: Cambridge

University Press, 1995).

Armstrong, Brian G., *Calvinism and the Amyraut Heresy: Protestant Scholasticism and Humanism in Seventeenth-Century France* (Madison: University of Wisconsin Press, 1969).

Armstrong, Nancy, and Leonard Tennenhouse, *The Imaginary Puritan: Literature, Intellectual Labor, and the Origins of Personal Life* (Berkeley: University of California Press, 1992).

Backus, Irena, *Les Sept Visions et la Fin des Temps: Les Commentaires Genevois de l'Apocalypse entre 1539 et 1584* (Geneva: Revue de théologie et de philosophie, 1997).

— 'The Church Fathers and the Canonicity of the Apocalypse in the Sixteenth Century: Erasmus, Frans Titelmans, and Theodore Beza', *Sixteenth Century Journal* 29 (1998), pp. 651-665.

— *Reformation Readings of the Apocalypse: Geneva, Zurich and Wittenberg* (Oxford: Oxford University Press, 2000).

Bailie, W.D., *Presbyterian Worship in Ulster prior to the Introduction of the Westminster Directory in 1647* (Belfast: Presbyterian Historical Society of Ireland, 1987).

Baird, Charles W., *John Bunyan: A Study in Narrative Technique* (London: National University Publications, 1977).

Baker, Derek (ed.), *Reform and Reformation: England and the Continent c.1500-c.1750* (Oxford: Blackwell, 1979).

Balentine, Samuel E. and John Barton (eds), *Language, Theology, and the Bible: Essays in Honour of James Barr* (Oxford: Clarendon Press, 1994).

Ball, B. W., *A Great Expectation: Eschatological Thought in English Protestantism to 1660* (Leiden: Brill, 1975).

— *The English Connection: The Puritan Roots of Seventh-Day Adventist Belief* (Cambridge: James Clarke, 1981).

— *The Seventh-day Men: Sabbatarians and Sabbatarianism in England and Wales, 1600-1800* (Oxford: Clarendon Press, 1994).

Ban, Joseph, 'Was John Bunyan a Baptist? A Case-Study in Historiography', *Baptist Quarterly* 30 (1984), pp. 367-76.

Barbour, Hugh and Arthur Roberts (eds), *Early Quaker Writings* (Grand Rapids: Eerdmans, 1973).

Barnard, T.C., *Cromwellian Ireland: English Government and Reform in Ireland 1649-1660* (London: Oxford University Press, 1975).

— 'The Uses of 23 October 1641 and Irish Protestant Celebrations', *English Historical Review* (1991), pp. 898-9.

— 'The Protestant Interest, 1641-1660', in Ohlmeyer (ed.) (1995), pp. 218-240.

Barnes, Robin B., *Prophecy and Gnosis: Apocalypticism in the Wake of the Lutheran Reformation* (Stanford, CA: Stanford University Press, 1988).

Barker, Francis et al (eds), *Uses of History: Marxism, Postmodernism and the Renaissance* (Manchester: Manchester University Press, 1991).

Barker, William S., 'The Westminster Assembly on the Days of Creation: A Reply to David W. Hall', *Westminster Theological Journal* 62 (2000), pp. 113-20.

Barr, James, 'Why the World was Created in 4004 B.C.: Archbishop Ussher and Biblical Chronology', *Bulletin of the John Rylands University Library of Manchester* 67 (1985), pp. 575-608.

Baskerville, Stephen, *Not Peace but a Sword: The Political Theology of the English Revolution* (London: Routledge, 1993).

Bath, Michael, *Speaking Pictures: English Emblem Books and Renaissance Culture* (London: Longman, 1994).

Batson, E. Beatrice, *John Bunyan: Allegory and Imagination* (London: Croom Helm, 1984).

Bauckham, Richard, *Tudor Apocalypse: Sixteenth-century Apocalypticism, Millenarianism and the English Reformation: From John Bale to John Foxe and Thomas Brightman* (Appleford: Sutton Courtenay Press, 1978).

Bauman, Richard, *Let your Words be Few: Symbolism of Speaking and Silence among Seventeenth-Century Quakers* (Cambridge: Cambridge University Press, 1983).

Baumgartner, Frederic, *Longing for the End: A History of Millennialism in Western Civilization* (New York: St. Martin's Press, 1999).

Beeke, Joel R., *Assurance of Faith: Calvin, English Puritanism, and the Second Dutch Reformation* (New York: Peter Lang, 1991).

Bell, M. Charles, *Calvin and Scottish Theology: The Doctrine of Assurance* (Edinburgh: Handsel Press, 1985).

Bell, Mark R., *Apocalypse how? Baptist Movements during the English Revolution* Macon, GA: Mercer University Press, 2000).

Bennett, Martyn, *The Civil Wars in Britain and Ireland, 1638-1651* (Oxford: Blackwell, 1997).

Bercovitch, Sacvan, *The Puritan Origins of the American Self* (New Haven: Yale University Press, 1975).

— (ed.), *The American Puritan Imagination: Essays in revaluation* (London: Cambridge University Press, 1974).

Berkhof, Louis, *Systematic Theology* (1939; rpt. Edinburgh: Banner of Truth, 1958).

Berkouwer, G. C., *Studies in Dogmatics: The Person of Christ*, trans. John Vriend (Grand Rapids, MI: Eermans, 1954).

Bernard, G.W., 'The Church of England c.1529-c.1642', *History* 35 (1990), pp. 183-206.

Berry, Lloyd E., *The Geneva Bible: A Facsimile of the 1560 Edition* (Madison: University of Madison Press, 1969).

Berthoff, A.E., *The Resolved Soul: A Study of Marvell's Major Poems* (Princeton: Princeton University Press, 1970).

Biographical Dictionary of British Radicals in the Seventeenth Century, eds Richard L. Greaves and Robert Zaller (Brighton: Harvester Press, 1982-84).

Blum, Abbe, 'The Author's Authority: *Areopagitica* and the Labour of Licensing', in Nyquist and Ferguson (eds) (1987), pp. 74-96.

Boesky, Amy, *Founding Fictions: Utopias in Early Modern England* (Athens: University of Georgia Press, 1996).

Boran, Elizabethanne, 'An Early Friendship Network of James Ussher, Archbishop of Armagh, 1626-1656', in Robinson-Hammerstein (ed.) (1998), pp. 116-134.

— 'The Libraries of Luke Challoner and James Ussher: 1595-1608', in Robinson-Hammerstein (ed.) (1998), pp. 75-115.

Bostick, Curtis V., *The Antichrist and the Lollards: Apocalypticism in late Medieval and Reformation England* (Leiden: Brill, 1998).

Boulger, James D., *The Calvinist Temper in English Poetry* (The Hague: Montoun, 1980).

Boyer, Paul, *When Time Shall Be No More: Prophecy Belief in Modern American Culture* (Cambridge: Belknap Press, 1992).

Bozeman, Theodore Dwight, *To live Ancient Lives: The Primitivist Dimension in Puritanism* (Chapel Hill, NC: University of North Carolina Press, 1988).

Bradshaw, Brendan, et al (eds), *Representing Ireland: Literature and the Origins of Conflict, 1534-1660* (Cambridge: Cambridge University Press, 1993).

Bradshaw, Brendan and Peter Roberts (eds), *British Consciousness and Identity: The Making of Britain, 1533-1707* (Cambridge: Cambridge University Press, 1998).

Brady, David, 'The Number of the Beast in Seventeenth- and Eighteenth-Century England', *Evangelical Quarterly* 45 (1973), pp. 219-240.

— *The Contribution of British Writers between 1560 and 1830 to the Interpretation of Revelation 13.16-18* (Tübingen: J.C.B. Mohr, 1983).

Braithwaite, William C., *The Beginnings of Quakerism* (London: Macmillan, 1912).

Brannigan, John, *New Historicism and Cultural Materialism* (London: Macmillan, 1998).

Bremer, F., 'To Live Exemplary Lives: Puritans and Puritan Communities as Lofty Heights', *The Seventeenth Century* 7 (1992), pp. 27-39.

Brooke, Peter, *Ulster Presbyterianism: The Historical Perspective 1610-1970* (Dublin: Gill and Macmillan, 1987).

Bull, Malcolm (ed.), *Apocalypse Theory and the Ends of the World* (Oxford: Blackwell, 1995).

Burdon, Christopher, *The Apocalypse in England: Revelation Unravelling, 1700-1834* (London: Macmillan, 1997).

Burke, Peter, and Roy Porter (eds), *Language, Self and Society: A Social History of Language* (Cambridge: Polity Press, 1991).

Burrage, C., 'The Fifth Monarchy Insurrections', *English Historical Review* 25 (1910), pp. 722-47.

Burrell, S.A., 'The Apocalyptic Vision of the Early Covenanters', *Scottish Historical Review* 43 (1964), pp. 1-24.

Bush, D., *English Literature in the Earlier Seventeenth Century* (Oxford: Oxford University Press, 1962).

Cain, T.G.S. and Ken Robinson (eds), *Into Another Mould: Change and Continuity in English Culture 1625-1700* (London: Routledge, 1992).

Caldwell, Patricia, *The Puritan Conversion Narrative: The Beginnings of American Expression* (Cambridge: Cambridge University Press, 1983).

Cameron, James K., 'The Commentary on the Book of Revelation by James Durham (1622-58)', in Wilks (ed.) (1994), pp. 123-129.

Cameron, Nigel et al (eds), *Dictionary of Scottish Church History and Theology* (Edinburgh: T&T Clark, 1993).

Campbell, Gordon, 'The Source of Bunyan's *Mapp of Salvation*', *Journal of the Warburg and Courtauld Institutes* 44 (1981), pp. 240-41.

— 'Fishing in Other Men's Waters: Bunyan and the Theologians', in Keeble (ed.) (1988), pp. 137-51.

Capern, Amanda L., 'The Caroline Church: James Ussher and the Irish Dimension', *Historical Journal* 39 (1996), pp. 57-85.

Capp, B.S., 'Extreme Millenarianism', in Toon (ed.) (1970), pp. 66-90.
— 'Godly Rule and English Millenarianism', *Past and Present* 52 (1971), pp. 106-17.
— *The Fifth Monarchy Men: A Study in Seventeenth-Century Millenarianism* (London: Faber and Faber, 1972).
Carlton, Charles, *Archbishop William Laud* (London: Routledge and Kegan Paul, 1987).
— *Going to the Wars: The Experience of the British Civil Wars 1638-1651* (London: Routledge, 1992).
Carroll, K.L., 'Quakerism and the Cromwellian Army in Ireland', *Journal of the Friends Historical Society* 54:3 (1978), pp. 135-54.
Carruthers, S. W., *The Everyday Work of the Westminster Assembly* (Philadelphia: Presbyterian Historical Society, 1943).
Christianson, Paul, *Reformers and Babylon: English Apocalyptic Visions from the Reformation to the Eve of the Civil War* (Toronto: University of Toronto Press, 1978).
Christopher, Georgia B., *Milton and the Science of the Saints* (Princeton: Princeton University Press, 1982).
Clarke, Aidan, 'Ireland and the General Crisis', *Past and Present* 48 (1970), pp. 79-100.
Clifford, Alan C., *Atonement and Justification: English Evangelical Theology 1640-1790: An Evaluation* (Oxford: Clarendon Press, 1990).
— *Calvinus: Authentic Calvinism: A clarification* (Norwich: Charenton Reformed Publishing, 1996).
Clouse, R.G., 'Johann Heinrich Alsted and English Millenarianism', *Harvard Theological Review* 62 (1969), pp. 189-207.
— 'The Rebirth of Millenarianism', in Toon (ed.) (1970), pp. 42-65.
— 'The Apocalyptic Interpretation of Thomas Brightman and Joseph Mede', *Fides et Historia* 13:1 (1980), pp. 181-93.
— 'The New Christian Right, America, and the Kingdom of God', *Christian Scholar's Review* 12:1 (1983), pp. 3-16.
Coats, Catharine Randall, *(Em)bodying the Word: Textual Resurrections in the Martyrological Narratives of Foxe, Crespin, de Bèze and d'Aubigné* (New York: Peter Lang, 1992).
Coffey, John, *Politics, Religion and the British Revolutions: The mind of Samuel Rutherford* (Cambridge: Cambridge University Press, 1997).
Cogley, Richard, 'The Fall of the Ottoman Empire and the Restoration of Israel in the "Judeo-centric" strand of Puritan Millenarianism', *Church History* 72 (2003), pp. 303-32.
Cohen, Charles Lloyd, *God's Caress: The Psychology of Puritan Religious Experience* (Oxford: Oxford University Press, 1986).
Cohn, Norman, *The Pursuit of the Millennium* (1957; rpt. London: Mercury Books, 1962).
— *Cosmos, Chaos and the World to Come: The Ancient Roots of Apocalyptic Faith* (London: Yale University Press, 1993).
Colker, Martin L., *Descriptive Catalogue of the Medieval and Renaissance Latin Manuscripts* (Aldershot: Scolar Press, 1991).
Collinson, Patrick, *The Elizabethan Puritan Movement* (London: Jonathan Cape,

1967).

— *From Iconoclasm to Iconophobia: The Cultural Impact of the Second English Reformation* (Reading: University of Reading, 1986).

— *The Puritan Character: Polemics and Polarities in Early Seventeenth-Century English Culture* (Los Angeles: William Andrews Clark Memorial Library, 1989).

— 'Biblical Rhetoric: The English Nation and National Sentiment in the Prophetic Mode', in McEachern and Shuger (eds) (1997), pp. 15-45.

Coolidge, John S., *The Pauline Renaissance in England: Puritanism and the Bible* (Oxford: Clarendon Press, 1970).

Cooper, B.G., 'The Academic Re-discovery of Apocalyptic Ideas in the 17th Century', *Baptist Quarterly* 18 (1959-60), pp. 351-57.

Cope, Jackson I., 'Seventeenth-Century Quaker Style', *PMLA* 76 (1956), pp. 725-54.

Corish, P.J., *Radicals, Rebels and Establishments* (Belfast: Historical Studies, 1985).

Corns, T.N., *Regaining Paradise Lost* (London and New York: Longman, 1994).

— (ed.), *The Cambridge Companion to English Poetry: From Donne to Marvell* (Cambridge: Cambridge University Press, 1993).

Cowan, Ian B., *The Scottish Covenanters 1660-1688* (London: Victor Gallancz, 1976).

Crump, G.M., *The Mystical Design of Paradise Lost* (London: Associated University Presses, 1975).

Cummins, Juliet (ed.), *Milton and the Ends of Time* (Cambridge: Cambridge University Press, 2003).

Cunningham, Harold G., 'Liberty of Conscience: A Problem for Theonomy', *Reformed Theological Journal* 13 (1997), pp. 44-57.

Daley, Brian E., *The Hope of the Early Church: Eschatology in the Patristic Age* (Cambridge: Cambridge University Press, 1991).

— 'Chiliasm', in Everett Ferguson (ed.), *Encyclopedia of Early Christianity*, 2nd ed. (New York: Garland, 1997), i. 238-41.

Dallison, A.R., 'Contemporary Criticism of Millenarianism', in Toon (ed.) (1970), pp. 104-114.

— 'The Authorship of 'A Glimpse of Syons Glory'', in Toon (ed.) (1970), pp. 131-136.

— 'The Latter-day Glory in the Thought of Thomas Goodwin', *Evangelical Quarterly* 58:1 (1986), pp. 53-68.

Damrosch, Leopold, *God's Plot and Man's Stories: Studies in the Fictional Imagination from Milton to Fielding* (Chicago: University of Chicago Press, 1985).

Daniell, David, *The Bible in English: Its History and Influence* (New Haven: Yale University Press, 2003).

Danielson, Dennis (ed.), *The Cambridge Companion to Milton* (Cambridge: Cambridge University Press, 1989).

Danner, Dan G., 'The Later English Calvinists and the Geneva Bible', in Graham (ed.) (1994), pp. 489-504.

Davidson, James West, *The Logic of Millennial Thought: Eighteenth-Century New England* (New Haven: Yale University Press, 1977).

Davies, Julian, *The Caroline Captivity of the Church: Charles I and the Remoulding of*

Anglicanism, 1625-41 (Oxford: Clarendon Press, 1992).

Dawson, Jane E. A., 'The Apocalyptic Thinking of the Marian Exiles', in Wilks (ed.) (1994), pp. 75-91.

— 'Trumpeting Resistance: Christopher Goodman and John Knox', in Roger A. Mason (ed.), *John Knox and the British Reformations*, St Andrews Studies in Reformation History (Aldershot: Ashgate, 1998), pp. 131-53.

Deppermann, Klaus, *Melchior Hoffman: Social Unrest and Apocalyptic Visions in the Age of the Reformation* (Edinburgh: T&T Clark, 1987).

Derrida, Jacques, 'Of an Apocalyptic Tone Recently Adopted in Philosophy', *Semeia* 23 (1982), pp. 63-97.

— *A Derrida Reader: Between the Blinds*, ed. Peggy Kamuf (New York: Harvester Wheatsheaf, 1991).

Dobbins, A.C., *Milton and the Book of Revelation* (Alabama: University of Alabama Press, 1975).

Docherty, Thomas, *Postmodernism: A Reader* (Hemel Hempstead: Harvester Wheatsheaf, 1993).

Dow, F.D., *Cromwellian Scotland 1651-1660* (Edinburgh: John Donald, 1979).

Dowling, Paul M., *Polite Wisdom: Heathen Rhetoric in Milton's Areopagitica* (Lanham: Rowman and Littlefield, 1995).

Duke, Alastair et al (eds), *Calvinism in Europe, 1540-1610: A Collection of Documents* (Manchester: Manchester University Press, 1992).

Dunlop, Robert (ed.), *Ireland under the Commonwealth: Being a Selection of Documents relating to the Government of Ireland from 1651 to 1659* (London: Manchester University Press, 1913).

Dwyer, John et al (eds), *New Perspectives on the Politics and Culture of Early Modern Scotland* (Edinburgh: John Donald, n.d. [1982?]).

Eagleton, Terry, 'The god that failed', in Nyquist and Ferguson (eds) (1987), pp. 342-49.

Ebner, Dean, *Autobiography in Seventeenth-Century England: Theology and the Self* (The Hague: Mouton, 1971).

Edington, Carol, 'John Knox and the Castilians: A Crucible of Reforming Opinion?', in Roger A. Mason (ed.), *John Knox and the British Reformations*, St Andrews Studies in Reformation History (Aldershot: Ashgate, 1998).

Edwards, Michael, *Towards a Christian Poetics* (London: Macmillan, 1984).

Eire, Carlos, *War against the Idols: The Reformation of Worship from Erasmus to Calvin* (Cambridge: Cambridge University Press, 1986).

Eley, Geoff and William Hunt (eds), *Reviving the English Revolution: Reflections and Elaborations on the Work of Christopher Hill* (London: Verso, 1988).

Emmerson, Richard K. and Richard McGinn (eds), *The Apocalypse in the Middle Ages* (Ithaca: Cornell University Press, 1992).

Felperin, Howard, "Cultural Poetics' versus 'Cultural Materialism': The two New Historicisms in Renaissance Studies', in Barker et al (eds) (1991), pp. 76-100.

Ferguson, Sinclair B., *John Owen on the Christian Life* (Edinburgh: Banner of Truth, 1987).

Fernández-Armesto, Felipe, *Columbus* (Oxford: Oxford University Press, 1991).

Ferrell, Lori Anne and Peter McCullough (eds), *The English Sermon Revised: Religion, Literature and History 1600-1750* (Manchester: Manchester University

Press, 2000).

Festinger, Leon et al, *When Prophecy Fails* (Minneapolis: University of Minneapolis Press, 1956).

Fincham, Kenneth (ed.), *The Early Stuart Church, 1603-1642* (London: Macmillan, 1993).

Fincham, Kenneth, and Peter Lake, 'The Ecclesiastical Policy of James I', *Journal of British Studies* 34:2 (1985), pp. 169-207.

Finlayson, Michael G., *Historians, Puritanism, and the English Revolution: The Religious Factor in English Politics before and after the Interregnum* (Toronto: University of Toronto Press, 1983).

The First London Confession of Faith (Rochester, NY: Backus Book Publishers, 1981).

Firth, Katherine, *The Apocalyptic Tradition in Reformation Britain, 1530-1645* (Oxford: Oxford University Press, 1979).

Fish, Stanley E., *Surprised by Sin: The Reader in Paradise Lost* (London: Macmillan, 1967).

— *Self-Consuming Artifacts: The Experience of Literature in the Seventeenth Century* (Berkeley: University of California Press, 1972).

— 'Driving from the Letter: Truth and Indeterminacy in Milton's *Areopagitica*', in Nyquist and Ferguson (eds) (1987), pp. 234-254.

Fitter, Chris, *Poetry, Space, Landscape: Toward a New Theory* (Cambridge: Cambridge University Press, 1995).

Fitzpatrick, Brendan, *Seventeenth-Century Ireland: The War of Religions* (Dublin: Gill and Macmillan, 1988).

Fixler, Michael, *Milton and the Kingdoms of God* (London: Faber and Faber, 1964).

— 'The Apocalypse Within Paradise Lost', in Kranidas (ed.) (1969), pp. 131-178.

Fleming, David Hay, *The Story of the Scottish Covenant in Outline*, in *Anthology* v (1992), pp. 44-61.

Fleming, Robert, *The Millennium* (1701; rpt. Dublin: Philip Dixon Hardy, 1849).

Folz, Robert, *The Concept of Empire* (London: Edward Arnold, 1969).

Force, J. E. and R. H. Popkin (eds), *Millenarianism and Modernism in Early Modern Europe, vol. 3: The Millenarian Turn: Millenarian Contexts of Science, Politics and everyday Anglo-American life in the Seventeenth and Eighteenth Centuries* (Dordrecht: Kluwer, 2001).

Ford, Alan, 'Correspondence between Archbishops Ussher and Laud', *Archivium Hibernicum* 46 (1991-2), pp. 5-21.

— 'Dependent or Independent? The Church of Ireland and its Colonial Context, 1536-1649', *Seventeenth Century* 9 (1995), pp. 163-87.

— 'The Church of Ireland, 1558-1641: A Puritan Church?', in Ford et al (eds) (1995), pp. 52-68.

— *The Protestant Reformation in Ireland, 1590-1641* (Dublin: Four Courts Press, 1997).

— 'James Ussher and the Creation of an Irish Protestant Identity', in Bradshaw and Roberts (eds) (1998), pp. 185-212.

— *James Ussher: Theology, History and Identity in early modern Britain and Ireland* (Oxford: Oxford University Press, 2007).

Ford, Alan et al (eds), *As by Law Established: The Church of Ireland since the Reformation* (Dublin: Lilliput Press, 1995).

Foster, Walter Ronald, *Bishop and Presbytery: The Church of Scotland 1661-1688* (London: S.P.C.K., 1958).

— *The Church before the Covenants* (Edinburgh: Scottish Academic Press, 1975).

Fotheringham, J.G., *The Diplomatic Correspondence of Jean De Montereul and the Brothers De Bellievre French Ambassadors in England and Scotland 1645-48* (Edinburgh: Scottish Historical Society, 1898).

Foulner, Martin A., *Theonomy and the Westminster Confession: An Annotated Sourcebook* (Edinburgh: Marpet Press, 1997).

— 'Goat Hunting with Samuel Rutherford: A Response to Dr. Harold G. Cunningham's *Liberty of Conscience*', *Christianity & Society* 8:4 (1998), pp. 14-20.

Fox, Peter (ed.), *Treasures of the Library: Trinity College Dublin* (Dublin: Royal Irish Academy, 1986).

Freeman, Thomas S., 'A Library in Three Volumes: Foxe's 'Book of Martyrs' in the Writings of John Bunyan', *Bunyan Studies* 5 (1994), pp. 47-57.

Froom, L.E., *The Prophetic Faith of Our Fathers: The Historical Development of Prophetic Interpetation*, 4 vols (Washington: Review and Herald, 1948).

Fuller, Robert C., *Naming the Antichrist: The History of an American Obsession* (New York: Oxford University Press, 1995).

Geist, Charles R., *The Political Thought of John Milton* (London: Macmillan, 1984).

Gentles, I., *The New Model Army in England, Ireland and Scotland 1645-1653* (Oxford: Blackwell, 1992).

Giblin, Cathaldus, O.F.M., 'Aegidius Chaissy, O.F.M., and James Ussher, Protestant Archbishop of Armagh', *Irish Ecclesiastical Record* 85 (1956), pp. 393-405.

Gilbert, S.M. and S. Gubar, *Shakespeare's Sisters: Feminist Essays on Women Poets* (Bloomington: Indiana University Press, 1979).

Gillespie, Raymond, *Devoted People: Belief and Religion in Early Modern Ireland* (Manchester: Manchester University Press, 1997).

Gilpin, W. Clark, *The Millenarian Piety of Roger Williams* (Chicago: University of Chicago Press, 1979).

Goldish, M. and R. H. Popkin (eds), *Millenarianism and Messianism in early modern European Culture, vol. 1: Jewish Messianism in the early modern World* (Dordrecht: Springer, 2001).

Goodbody, Olive C., 'Anthony Sharp, Wool Merchant, 1643-1707 and the Quaker Community in Dublin', *Journal of the Friends Historical Society* 48:1 (1956), pp. 38-50.

Gould, Philip, *Covenant and Republic: Historical Romance and the Politics of Puritanism* (Cambridge: Cambridge University Press, 1996).

Gordon, Bruce (ed.), *Protestant Identity and History in Sixteenth-century Europe* (Brookfield: Scolar Press, 1996).

Grace, William J., *Ideas in Milton* (Notre Dame: University of Notre Dame Press, 1968).

Graham, Elspeth, et al (eds), *Her Own Life: Autobiographical Writings by Seventeenth-Century Englishwomen* (London: Routledge, 1989).

Graham, W. Fred (ed.), *Later Calvinism: International Perspectives* (Kirksville: Sixteenth Century Journal Publishers, 1994).

de Grazia, Margarita et al (eds), *Subject and Object in Renaissance Culture*

(Cambridge: Cambridge University Press, 1996).

Greaves, R.L., 'John Bunyan and Covenant Thought in the Seventeenth Century', *Church History* 36 (1967), pp. 151-69.

— *John Bunyan* (Appleford: Sutton Courtney Press, 1969).

— 'John Bunyan's "Holy War" and London Nonconformity', *Baptist Quarterly* 26 (1975), pp. 158-68.

— *Saints and Rebels: Seven Nonconformists in Stuart England* (Macon: Mercer University Press, 1985).

— *Deliver us from Evil: The Radical Underground in Britain, 1660-1663* (Oxford: Oxford University Press, 1986).

— 'Conscience, Liberty, and the Spirit: Bunyan and Nonconformity', in Keeble (ed.) (1988), pp. 21-43.

— *Enemies under his Feet: Radicals and Nonconformists in Britain, 1664-1677* (Stanford: Stanford University Press, 1990).

— *Secrets of the Kingdom: British Radicals from the Popish Plot to the Revolution of 1688-1689* (Stanford: Stanford University Press, 1992).

— *John Bunyan and English Nonconformity* (London: The Hambledon Press, 1992).

— 'The Rye House Plotting, Nonconformist Clergy, and Calvin's Resistance Theory', in Graham (ed.) (1994), pp. 505-524.

— *God's Other Children: Protestant Nonconformists and the Emergence of Denominational Churches in Ireland, 1660-1700* (Stanford: Stanford University Press, 1997).

— *Glimpses of Glory: John Bunyan and English Dissent* (Stanford: Stanford University Press, 2002).

Greenblatt, Stephen, *Renaissance Self-Fashioning: From More to Shakespeare* (Chicago: University of Chicago Press, 1980).

— 'Remnants of the Sacred in Early Modern England', in de Grazia et al (eds) (1996), pp. 337-45.

— (ed.), *Representing the English Renaissance* (Berkeley: University of California Press, 1988).

Greene, Thomas M., *The Vulnerable Text: Essays on Renaissance Literature* (New York: Columbia University Press, 1986).

Gregerson, Linda, *The Reformation of the Subject: Spenser, Milton and the English Protestant Epic* (Cambridge: Cambridge University Press, 1995).

Grell, Ole Peter, *Calvinist Exiles in Tudor and Stuart Britain* (Aldershot: Scolar Press, 1996).

Gribben, Crawford, *God's Irishmen: Theological Debates in Cromwellian Ireland* (Oxford: Oxford University Press, 2007).

— 'Puritanism in Ireland and Wales', in John Coffey and Paul Lim (eds), *Cambridge companion to Puritanism* (Cambridge: CUP, 2008).

— 'Rhetoric, fiction and theology: James Ussher and the death of Jesus Christ', *The Seventeenth Century* 20:1 (2005), pp. 53-76.

Griffith, Gwilym O., *John Bunyan* (London: Hodder and Stoughton, 1927).

Hadfield, Andrew, 'Briton and Scythian: Tudor Representations of Irish Origins', *Irish Historical Studies* 28:12 (1993), pp. 390-408.

Haigh, Christopher, *English Reformations: Religion, Politics and Society under the Tudors* (Oxford: Clarendon Press, 1993).

Hall, Peter (ed.), *Harmony of the Protestant Confessions* (1842; rpt. Edmonton: Still

Waters Revival Books, 1992).

Haller, William, *Tracts on Liberty in the Puritan Revolution 1638-1647* (New York: Columbia University Press, 1933).

— *The Rise of Puritanism: Or, the Way to the New Jerusalem as set forth in Pulpit and Press from Thomas Cartwright to John Lilburne and John Milton, 1570-1643* (1938; rpt. New York: Columbia University Press, 1957).

— *Foxe's Book of Martyrs and the Elect Nation* (London: Jonathan Cape, 1963).

Halley, Janet E., 'Heresy, Orthodoxy, and the Politics of Religious Discourse: The Case of the English Family of Love', in Greenblatt (ed.) (1988), pp. 303-327.

Hancock, Maxine, 'Bunyan as Reader: The Record of *Grace Abounding*', *Bunyan Studies* 5 (1994), pp. 68-84.

Hardin, Richard F, *Civil Idolatry: Desacralizing and Monarchy in Spenser, Shakespeare, and Milton* (London: Associated University Presses, 1992).

Harding, William Henry, *John Bunyan: Pilgrim and Dreamer* (London: Oliphants, [n.d.]).

Haskin, Dayton, 'Bunyan, Luther, and the Struggle with Belatedness in *Grace Abounding*', *University of Toronto Quarterly* 50 (1981), pp. 300-13.

— 'The Burden of Interpretation in *The Pilgrim's Progress*', *Studies in Philology* 79 (1982), pp. 256-78.

— '"Thou must Feed upon my Word": Bunyan and the Bible', in Keeble (ed.) (1988), pp. 153-170.

Hawkins, Anne, 'The Double-Conversion in Bunyan's *Grace Abounding*', *Philological Quarterly* 61 (1982), pp. 259-76.

— *Archetypes of Conversion: The Autobiographies of Augustine, Bunyan, and Merton* (Lewisburg: Bucknell University Press, 1985).

Haykin, Michael A.G., *Kiffin, Knollys and Keach: Rediscovering our English Baptist Heritage* (Leeds: Carey, 1996).

Healy, Thomas, *New Latitudes: Theory and English Renaissance Literature* (London: Edward Arnold, 1992).

Healy, Thomas, and Jonathan Sawday (eds), *Literature and the English Civil War* (Cambridge: Cambridge University Press, 1990).

Helgerson, Richard, *Forms of Nationhood: The Elizabethan Writing of England* (Chicago: University of Chicago Press, 1992).

Helm, Paul, *Calvin and the Calvinists* (Edinburgh: Banner of Truth, 1982).

Henderson, G.D. (ed.), *Scots Confession, 1560* (Edinburgh: Church of Scotland Committee on Publications, 1937).

Hendricks, Margo and Patricia Parker (eds), *Women, "Race", and Writing in the Early Modern Period* (London: Routledge, 1994).

Herlihy, Kevin, 'The Early Eighteenth Century Irish Baptists: Two Letters', *Irish Economic and Social History* 19 (1992), pp. 71-76.

— (ed.), *The Irish Dissenting Tradition, 1650-1750* (Dublin: Four Courts Press, 1995).

Hetherington, William Maxwell, *History of the Westminster Assembly of Divines* (1856; rpt. Edmonton: Still Waters Revival Books, 1993).

Hibbard, G.R., 'The Country House Poem of the Seventeenth Century', *Journal of the Warburg and Courtnauld Institute* 19 (1956), pp. 159-74.

Hill, Christopher, *Puritanism and Revolution* (London: Martin Secker and

Warburg, 1958).
— *Society and Puritanism in Pre-Revolutionary England* (1964; rpt. Harmondsworth: Penguin, 1991).
— *God's Englishman: Oliver Cromwell and the English Revolution* (1970; rpt. Harmondsworth: Penguin, 1990).
— *Antichrist in Seventeenth-Century England* (London: Oxford University Press, 1971).
— *The World Turned Upside Down: Radical Ideas during the English Revolution* (1972; rpt. Harmondsworth: Penguin, 1991).
— *Milton and the English Revolution* (London: Faber and Faber, 1977).
— *Some Intellectual Consequences of the English Revolution* (London: Weidenfield and Nicolson, 1980).
— *The Experience of Defeat: Milton and some Contemporaries* (London: Faber and Faber, 1984).
— *A Tinker and a Poor Man: John Bunyan and his Church 1628-1688* (New York: Albert A. Knopf, 1989).
— *A Nation of Change and Novelty: Radical Politics, Religion and Literature in Seventeenth-Century England* (London and New York: Routledge, 1990).
— *The English Bible and Seventeenth-Century Revolution* (Harmondsworth: Allen Lane 1993).
Hill, John Spencer, *John Milton: Poet, Priest and Prophet: A Study of Divine Vocation in Milton's Poetry and Prose* (London: Macmillan, 1979).
Hillerbrand, Hans J. (ed.), *The Oxford Encyclopedia of the Reformation* (Oxford: Oxford University Press, 1996).
Hinds, Hilary, *God's Englishwomen: Seventeenth-century Radical Sectarian Writing and Feminist Criticism* (Manchester: Manchester University Press, 1996).
Historical Catalogue of Printed Editions of the English Bible 1525-1961 (1903; 2nd. ed. rev. A.S. Herbert) (London: British and Foreign Bible Society, 1968).
Hobby, E., *Virtue of Necessity: English Women's Writing 1649-88* (London: Virago, 1988).
Hodge, A.A., *Evangelical Theology: A Course of Popular Lectures* (1890; rpt. Edinburgh: Banner of Truth, 1976).
Hodge, R.I.V., *Foreshortened Time: Andrew Marvell and Seventeenth Century Revolutions* (Cambridge: Brewer, 1978).
Holstun, James, *A Rational Millennium: Puritan Utopias of Seventeenth-century England and America* (New York: Oxford University Press, 1987).
Horn, Siegfried H., 'From Bishop Ussher to Edwin R. Thiele', *Andrews University Seminary Studies* 18 (1980), pp. 37-49.
Hotson, Howard, 'The Historiographical Origins of Calvinist Millenarianism', in Gordon (ed.) (1996), pp. ii. 159-181.
— *Johann Heinrich Alsted, 1588-1638* (Oxford: Oxford University Press, 2000).
— *Paradise postponed: Johann Heinrich Alsted and the Birth of Calvinist Millenarianism* (Dordrecht: Kluwer, 2000).
Howe, Susan, *The Birth-mark: Unsettling the Wilderness in American Literary History* (Hanover: Wesleyan University Press, 1993).
Huehns, Gertrude, *Antinomianism in English History: With Special Reference to the Period 1640-1660* (London: Cresset Press, 1951).
Hughes, Merrit Y., *Ten Perspectives on Milton* (New Haven: Yale University

Press, 1965).

Hunter, W.B. (gen. ed.), *A Milton Encyclopedia* (London: Associated University Presses, 1978-80).

Hurtgen, John E., *Anti-language in the Apocalypse of John* (Lewiston: Mellen Biblical Press, 1993).

Hutcheon, Linda, *A Poetics of Postmodernism: History, Theory, Fiction* (London: Routledge, 1988).

Hutton, Sarah, 'The Appropriation of Joseph Mede: Millenarianism in the 1640s', in Force and Popkin (eds) (2001), pp. 1-14.

Jameson, Fredric, 'Postmodernism, or The Cultural Logic of Late Capitalism' (1991; rpt. in Docherty [ed.] [1993]), pp. 62-92.

Jasper, David, *The Study of Literature and Religion* (London: Macmillan, 1989; 2nd ed. 1992).

Jensen, Michael, '"Simply" Reading the Geneva Bible: The Geneva Bible and its Readers', *Literature and Theology* 9 (1995), pp. 30-45.

Johnson, Ellwood, *The Pursuit of Power: Studies in the Vocabulary of Puritanism* (New York: Peter Lang, 1995).

Jong, James de, *As the Waters Cover the Sea: Millennial Expectations in the Rise of Anglo-American Missions 1640-1810* (Kampen: Kok, 1970).

Jonge, C. de, 'Franciscus Junius (1545-1602) and the English Separatists at Amsterdam', in Baker (ed.) (1979), pp. 165-73.

Johnson, Warren, 'Apocalypticism in Restoration England' (unpublished PhD thesis, University of Cambridge, 2000).

— 'The patience of the saints, the apocalypse and moderate nonconformity in Restoration England', *Canadian Journal of History* 38:3 (2003), pp. 505-16.

— 'The Anglican apocalypse in Restoration England', *Journal of Ecclesiastical History* 55:33 (2004), pp. 467-501.

Jue, Jeffrey K., *Heaven upon Earth: Joseph Mede (1586-1638) and the Legacy of Millenarianism* (Dordrecht: Springer, 2006).

Katz, David S. and Richard H. Popkin (eds), *Messianic Revolution: Radical Religious Politics to the End of the Second Millennium* (New York: Hill and Wang, 1991).

Kearney, Hugh F., *Strafford in Ireland 1633-41: A Study in Absolutism* (Manchester: Manchester University Press, 1959).

Keeble, N.H., *The Literary Culture of Nonconformity in Later Seventeenth-Century England* (Leicester: Leicester University Press, 1987).

— (ed.) *John Bunyan, Conventicle and Parnassus: Tercentenary Essays* (Oxford: Clarendon Press, 1988).

Kendall, R.T., *Calvin and English Calvinism to 1649* (New York: Oxford University Press, 1981).

Kendrick, Christopher, *Milton: A Study in Ideology and Form* (London: Methuen, 1986).

Kent, Stephen A., 'The 'Papist' Charges against the Interregnum Quakers', *Journal of Religious History* 12 (1983), pp. 180-90.

Kenyon, John, *The History Men: The Historical Profession in England since the Renaissance* (London: Weidenfeld and Nicolson, 1983; 2nd ed. 1993).

Kermode, Frank, *The Sense of an Ending: Studies in the Theory of Fiction* (New York: Oxford University Press, 1967).

Kerrigan, John, *Revenge Tragedy: Aeschylus to Armageddon* (Oxford: Clarendon Press, 1996).

Kevan, Ernest F., *The Grace of Law: A Study in Puritan Theology* (London: Carey, 1964).

Kilroy, P., 'Sermon and Pamphlet Literature in the Irish Reformed Church, 1613-34', *Archivium Hibernicum* 33 (1975), pp. 110-21.

— *Protestant Dissent and Controversy in Ireland 1660-1714* (Cork: Cork University Press, 1994).

— 'Radical Religion in Ireland, 1641-1660', in Ohlmeyer (ed.) (1995), pp. 201-17.

Kinney, Arthur F., and Dan S. Collins, *Renaissance Historicism: Selections from English Literary Renaissance* (Amherst: University of Massachusetts Press, 1987).

Klaassen, W., *Living at the End of the Ages: Apocalyptic Expectation in the Radical Reformation* (New York: University Press of America, 1992).

Knappen, M.W., *Tudor Puritanism: A Chapter in the History of Idealism* (1939; rpt. Chicago: University of Chicago Press, 1965).

Knott, John R., *The Sword of the Spirit: Puritan Responses to the Bible* (Chicago: University of Chicago Press, 1986).

Knowlson, James, *Universal Language Schemes in England and France, 1600-1800* (Toronto: University of Toronto Press, 1975).

Knox, R. Buick, *James Ussher: Archbishop of Armagh* (Cardiff: University of Wales Press, 1967).

— (ed.) *Reformation Conformity and Dissent: Essays in Honour of Geoffrey Nuttall* (London: Epworth Press, 1977).

Korshin, Paul J., *Typologies in England* (Princeton: Princeton University Press, 1982).

Kranidas, T. (ed.), *New Essays on Paradise Lost* (Berkeley: University of California Press, 1969).

Lamont, William M., *Godly Rule: Politics and Religion, 1603-60* (London: Macmillan, 1969).

— 'Puritanism as History and Historiography: Some Further Thoughts', *Past and Present* 44 (1969), pp. 133-146.

— 'Richard Baxter, the Apocalypse and the Mad Major', *Past and Present* 55 (1972), pp. 68-90.

— *Richard Baxter and the Millennium: Protestant Imperialism and the English Revolution* (London: Croom Helm, 1979).

— *Puritanism and historical controversy* (London: U.C.L. Press, 1996).

Lander, Jesse, '"Foxe's" *Book of Martyrs*: Printing and Popularising the *Acts and Monuments*', in McEachern and Shuger (eds) (1997), pp. 69-92

Laurence, A., et al (eds), *John Bunyan and his England, 1628-88* (London: The Hambledon Press, 1990).

Lawton, David, *Faith, Text and History: The Bible in English* (London: Harvester Wheatsheaf, 1990).

Le Comte, Edward, *Milton's Unchanging Mind: Three Essays* (Port Washington: Kennikat Press, 1973).

Leeman, Saul, 'Was Bishop Ussher's Chronology Influenced by a Midrash?', *Semeia* 8 (1977), pp. 127-130.

Lenz, Joseph M., *The Promised End: Romance Closure in the* Gawain-*poet, Malory,*

Spenser, and Shakespeare (New York: Peter Lang, 1986).

Letham, Robert, '"In the Space of Six Days": The Days of Creation from Origen to the Westminster Assembly', *Westminster Theological Journal* 61 (1999), pp. 149-74.

Levin, Carole, 'Women in *The Book of Martyrs* as Models of Behaviour in Tudor England', *International Journal of Women's Studies* 4:2 (1980), pp. 196-207.

Lewalski, Barbara Kiefer, 'Innocence and Experience in Milton's Eden', in Kranidas (ed.) (1969), pp. 86-117.

Lewis, Alan E., 'Eschatology', in Donald M. McKim (ed.), *Encyclopedia of the Reformed Faith* (Edinburgh: St Andrews Press, 1992), pp. 122-24.

Lienhard, Marc (ed.), *The Origins and Characteristics of Anabaptism: Proceedings of the Colloquium organised by the Faculty of Protestant Theology of Strasbourg* (The Hague: Martinus Nijhoff, 1977).

Lindenbaum, Peter, *Changing Landscapes: Anti-Pastoral Sentiment in the English Renaissance* (Athens: University of Georgia Press, 1986).

Liu, Tai, *Discord in Zion: The Puritan Divines and the Puritan Revolution* (The Hague: Martinus Nijhoff, 1973).

Lloyd-Jones, D.M., *The Puritans: Their Origins and Successors: Addressed Delivered at the Puritan and Westminster Conferences, 1959-1978* (Edinburgh: Banner of Truth, 1987).

Loades, David, 'John Foxe and the Traitors: The Politics of the Marian Persecution', in Wood (ed.) (1993), pp. 231-258.

Loewenstein, David, *Milton and the Drama of History: Historical Vision, Iconoclasm, and the Literary Imagination* (Cambridge: Cambridge University Press, 1990).

— *Milton: Paradise Lost* (Cambridge: Cambridge University Press, 1993).

Loewenstein, David, and James Grantham Turner (eds), *Politics, Poetics and Hermeneutics in Milton's Prose* (Cambridge: Cambridge University Press, 1990).

Lotz, David W., "*Sola Scriptura*: Luther on Biblical Authority", *Interpretation* 35 (1981), pp. 258-73.

Lotz-Heumann, Ute, 'The Protestant Interpretation of History in Ireland: the Case of James Ussher's *Discourse*', in Gordon (ed.) (1996), ii. 107-20.

Lowance, Mason I., *The Language of Canaan: Metaphor and Symbol in New England from the Puritans to the Transcendentalists* (Cambridge: Harvard University Press, 1980).

Lumpkin, William L., *Baptist Confessions of Faith* (Chicago: Judson Press, [1959]).

Lunham, Thomas A., 'Early Quakers in Cork', *Journal of the Cork Historical and Archaeological Society* 10 (1904), pp. 103-10.

Lupton, Lewis, *A History of the Geneva Bible* (London: Fauconberg Press, 1966-81).

Luxon, Thomas H., *Literal Figures: Puritan Allegory and the Reformation Crisis in Representation* (Chicago: University of Chicago Press, 1995).

Lyall, Francis, 'Of Metaphors and Analogies: Legal Language and Covenant Theology', *Scottish Journal of Theology* 32 (1979), pp. 1-17.

Lyotard, Jean-François, 'Answering the Question: What is Postmodernism?' (1983; rpt. in Docherty [ed.] [1993]), pp. 38-46.

Macgregor, J. F. and Barry Reay (eds), *Radical Religion in the English Revolution* (Oxford: Oxford University Press, 1984).

Macinnes, Allan I., *Charles I and the Making of the Covenanting Movement, 1625-41* (Edinburgh: John Donald, 1991).

Maclean, Gerald M., *Time's Witness: Historical Representation in English Poetry, 1603-1660* (Madison: University of Wisconsin, 1990).

— (ed.), *Culture and Society in the Stuart Restoration: Literature, Drama, History* (Cambridge: Cambridge University Press, 1995).

Maclear, J.F., 'New England and the Fifth Monarchy: The Quest for the Millennium in Early American Puritanism', in Vaughan and Bremer (eds) (1977), pp. 66-91.

Macleod, John, *Scottish Theology in Relation to Church History since the Reformation* (Edinburgh: Knox Press and Banner of Truth, 1974).

Macpherson, John, *The Doctrine of the Church in Scottish Theology* in *Anthology* v (1992), pp. 126-97.

MacQueen, John, *Numerology: Theory and Outline History of a Literary Mode* (Edinburgh: Edinburgh University Press, 1985).

Makey, Walter, *The Church of Scotland 1637-1651: Revolution and Social Change in Scotland* (Edinburgh: John Donald, 1979).

Manuel, Frank E. and Fritzie P., *Utopian Thought in the Western World* (Oxford: Blackwell, 1979).

Matchinske, Megan, 'Holy Hatred: Formations of the Gendered Subject in English Apocalyptic Writing, 1625-1651', *English Literary History* 60:2 (1993), pp. 349-77.

Marlowe, John, *The Puritan Tradition in English Life* (London: The Cresset Press, 1956).

Martin, Randall, *Women Writers in Renaissance England* (London: Longman, 1997).

McBrien, Richard P., *The HarperCollins Encyclopedia of Catholicism* (New York: HarperCollins, 1995).

McCoy, F.N., *Robert Baillie and the Second Scots Reformation* (Berkeley: University of California Press, 1974).

McEachern, Claire, and Debora Shuger (eds), *Religion and Culture in Renaissance England* (Cambridge: Cambridge University Press, 1997).

McGinn, Bernard et al (eds), *Encyclopedia of Apocalypticism*, 3 vols (New York: Continuum, 1998).

McGlothlin, W.J., *Baptist Confessions of Faith* (Philadelphia: American Baptist Publication Society, 1911).

McGrath, Gavin J., *'But We Preach Christ Crucified': The Cross of Christ in the Pastoral Theology of John Owen 1616-1683* (London: St. Antholin's Lectureship Charity Lecture, 1994).

MacGregor, Geddes, *The Thundering Scot: A Portrait of John Knox* (Philadelphia: Westminster Press, 1957).

McKay, W.D.J., 'George Gillespie and the Westminster Assembly: The Defence of Presbyterianism', *Scottish Bulletin of Evangelical Theology* 13 (1995), pp. 51-71.

— *An Ecclesiastical Republic: Church Government in the Writings of George Gillespie* (Edinburgh: Rutherford House, 1997).

McMillan, William, *The Worship of the Scottish Reformed Church, 1550-1638* (London: Lassodie Press, n.d. [1930?]).

McNeill, John T., *The History and Character of Calvinism* (Oxford: Oxford University Press, 1967).

Meigs, Samantha A., *The Reformation in Ireland: Tradition and Confessionalism 1400-1690* (Houndmills: Macmillan, 1997).

Miller, Perry, *Errand into the Wilderness* (Cambridge: Harvard University Press, 1956).

Milner, A., *John Milton and the English Revolution: A Study in the Sociology of Literature* (London: Macmillan, 1981).

Milton, Anthony, 'The Church of England, Rome, and the True Church: The Demise of a Jacobean Consensus', in Fincham (ed.) (1993), pp. 187-205.

— *Catholic and Reformed: The Roman and Protestant Churches in English Protestant Thought 1600-1640* (Cambridge, Cambridge University Press, 1995).

Morgan, Edmund S., *Visible Saints: The History of a Puritan Idea* (London: Cornell University Press, 1963).

Morgan, Irvonwy, *Puritan Spirituality* (London: Epworth Press, 1973).

Morrill, John, *Oliver Cromwell and the English Revolution* (London: Longman, 1990).

— *The Nature of the English Revolution: Essays by John Morrill* (London: Longman, 1993).

— (ed.), *The Oxford Illustrated History of Tudor and Stuart Britain* (Oxford: Oxford University Press, 1996).

Morrissey, Mary, 'Elect Nations and Prophetic Preaching: Types and Examples in the Paul's Cross Jeremiad', in Ferrell and McCullough (eds) (2000), pp. 43-58.

Mueller, Janel M., 'Pain, Persecution and the Construction of Selfhood in Foxe's *Acts and Monuments*', in McEachern and Shuger (eds) (1997), pp. 161-87.

Muir, Edwin, *John Knox: Portrait of a Calvinist* (London: Jonathan Cape, 1929).

Mullan, David G., '"Uniformity in Religion": The Solemn League and Covenant (1643) and the Presbyterian Vision', in Graham (ed.) (1994), pp. 249-266.

Muller, Richard A., 'Perkins' *A Golden Chaine*: Predestinarian System or Schematized *Ordo Salutis*?', *Sixteenth Century Journal* 9 (1978), pp. 69-81.

— *Christ and the Decree: Christology and Predestination in Reformed Theology from Calvin to Perkins* (Durham: Labyrinth, 1986).

— *The Unaccommodated Calvin: Studies in the Formation of a Theological Tradition* (Oxford: Oxford University Press, 2000).

Mullett, Michael, *John Bunyan in Context* (Keele: Keele University Press, 1996).

— (ed.), *New Light on George Fox (1624 to 1691)* (York: The Ebor Press, n.d. [1993?]).

Murray, Iain H., *The Puritan Hope: Revival and the Interpretation of Prophecy* (Edinburgh: Banner of Truth, 1971).

— 'The Scots at the Westminster Assembly', *Banner of Truth* 371-2 (1994), pp. 6-40.

Newey, Vincent, '"With the Eyes of my Understanding: Bunyan, Experience, and Acts of Interpretation', in Keeble (ed.) (1988), pp. 189-216.

Newport, Kenneth G.C., 'Benjamin Keach, William of Orange and the Book of Revelation: A Study in English Prophetical Exegesis', *Baptist Quarterly* 36 (1995-96), pp. 43-51.

— *Apocalypse and Millennium: Studies in Biblical Eisegesis* (Cambridge: Cambridge

University Press, 2000).

North, Gary, 'Towards the Recovery of Hope', *Banner of Truth* 88 (1971), pp. 12-16.

— *Millennialism and Social Theory* (Tyler: Institute for Christian Economics, 1990).

Nuttall, Geoffrey F., *The Holy Spirit in Puritan Faith and Experience* (1946; rpt. Chicago: University of Chicago Press, 1992).

— *Visible Saints* (Oxford: Oxford University Press, 1957).

— 'The Heart of *The Pilgrim's Progress*', *American Baptist Quarterly* 7 (1988), pp. 472-83.

Nyquist, Mary and Margaret W. Ferguson (eds), *Re-membering Milton: Essays on the Text and Traditions* (London: Methuen, 1987).

Oberman, Heiko, 'The 'Extra' Dimension in the Theology of Calvin', *Journal of Ecclesiastical History* 21 (1970), pp. 43-64.

Ohlmeyer, Jane (ed.), *Ireland from Independence to Occupation, 1641-1660* (Cambridge: Cambridge University Press, 1995).

Olsen, Palle J., 'Was John Foxe a Millenarian?', *Journal of Ecclesiastical History* 45:4 (1994), pp. 600-24.

Olsen, V. Norskov, *John Foxe and the Elizabethan Church* (Berkeley: University of California Press, 1973).

Ormsby-Lennon, Hugh, 'From Shibboleth to Apocalypse: Quaker Speechways during the Puritan Revolution', in Burke and Porter (eds) (1991), pp. 72-112.

van Os, M., and G.J. Schutte, *Bunyan in England and Abroad* (Amsterdam: VU University Press, 1990).

Owens, W.R., 'Antichrist must be Pulled Down: Bunyan and the Millennium', in Laurence et al (eds) (1990), pp. 77-94.

Packer, J.I., *Among God's Giants: The Puritan Vision of the Christian Life* (Eastbourne: Kingsway, 1991).

Packer, John W., *The Transformation of Anglicanism, 1643-1660, with special reference to Henry Hammond* (Manchester: Manchester University Press, 1969).

Parker, Patricia and David Quint (eds), *Literary Theory/Renaissance Texts* (Baltimore: John Hopkins University Press, 1986).

Parry, Graham, *The Golden Age Restor'd: The Culture of the Stuart Court, 1603-42* (Manchester: Manchester University Press, 1981).

— *The Seventeenth Century: The Intellectual and Cultural Context of English Literature 1603-1700* (London: Longman, 1989).

— *The Trophies of Time: English Antiquarians of the Seventeenth Century* (Oxford: Oxford University Press, 1995).

Patrides, C.A., *Milton and the Christian Tradition* (Oxford: Clarendon Press, 1966).

— *Premises and Motifs in Renaissance Thought and Literature* (Princeton: Princeton University Press, 1982).

— (ed.) *Approaches to Marvell: The York Tercentenary Lectures* (London: Routledge and Kegan Paul, 1978).

Patrides, C.A. and Joseph Wittreich (eds), *The Apocalypse in English Renaissance Thought and Literature: Patterns, Antecedents and Repercussions* (Ithaca: Cornell University Press, 1984).

Patterson, W.B., *King James VI and I and the Reunion of Christendom* (Cambridge: Cambridge University Press, 1997).

Pauck, Wilhelm, 'Martin Bucer's Conception of a Christian State', *Princeton*

Theological Review 26 (1928), pp. 80-88.

Paul, R.S., *The Assembly of the Lord: Politics and Religion in the Westminster Assembly and the 'Grand Debate'* (Edinburgh: T&T Clark, 1985).

Paulin, Tom, *Minotaur: Poetry and the Nation State* (London: Faber and Faber, 1992).

Perceval-Maxwell, M., 'Strafford, the Ulster-Scots and the covenanters', *Irish Historical Studies* 18:72 (1973), pp. 524-51.

Petegorsky, David W., *Left-Wing Democracy in the English Civil War: Gerard Winstanley and the Digger Movement* (1940; rpt. Stroud: Alan Sutton, 1995).

Peterson, Rodney L., *Preaching in the Last Days: The Theme of 'Two Witnesses' in the Sixteenth and Seventeenth Centuries* (Oxford: Oxford University Press, 1993).

Pettegree, Andrew et al (eds), *Calvinism in Europe, 1540-1620: A Collection of Documents* (Cambridge: Cambridge University Press, 1994).

Pettegree, Andrew, *Marian Protestantism: Six Studies* (Aldershot: Scolar Press, 1996).

Pittock, Murray G.H., *The Invention of Scotland: The Stuart Myth and the Scottish Identity, 1638 to the Present* (London: Routledge, 1991).

Ponsford, Michael, '"Poetical Fury": The Religious Enthusiasts of the Late Seventeenth Century', *Christian Scholar's Review* 16:1 (1986), pp. 24-39.

Pooley, Roger, 'Spiritual Experience and Spiritual Autobiography', *Baptist Quarterly* 32 (1988), pp. 393-402.

— *English Prose of the Seventeenth Century, 1590-1700* (London: Longman, 1992).

Popkin, Richard H. (ed.), *Millenarianism and Messianism in English Literature and Thought, 1650-1800* (Leiden: E.J. Brill, 1988).

Potter, Lois, *Secret Rites and Secret Writings* (Cambridge: Cambridge University Press, 1989).

Prestwich, Menna (ed.), *International Calvinism, 1541-1715* (Oxford: Clarendon Press, 1985).

Quint, David et al (eds), *Creative Imagination: New Essays on Renaissance Literature in Honor of Thomas M. Greene* (Binghamton: Centre for Medieval and Early Renaissance Studies, 1992).

Quistorp, H., *Calvin's Doctrine of the Last Things* (London: Lutterworth Press, 1955).

Rajan, Balachandra, *The Form of the Unfinished: English Poetics from Spenser to Pound* (Princeton: Princeton University Press, 1985).

Rattansi, P.M., 'Paracelsus and the Puritan Revolution', *Ambix* xi (1963), pp. 24-32.

Reeves, Marjorie, *The Influence of Prophecy in the Later Middle Ages: A Study in Joachimism* (Oxford: Clarendon Press, 1969).

— 'History and Eschatology: Medieval and early Protestant Thought in some English and Scottish Writings', *Medievalia et Humanistica* 4 (1973), pp. 99-123.

Reeves, Marjorie and Warwick Gould, *Joachim of Fiore and the Myth of the Eternal Evangel in the Nineteenth Century* (Oxford: Clarendon Press, 1987).

Reid, James, *Memoirs of the Westminster Divines* (Paisley: Young, 1811).

Richardson, R.C., *The Debate on the English Revolution Revisited* (London: Routledge, 1988).

Richmond, Hugh M., *The Christian Revolutionary: John Milton* (Berkeley:

University of California Press, 1974).

Robbins, Kevin C., *City on the Ocean Sea: La Rochelle, 1530-1650: Urban Society, Religion and Politics on the French Atlantic Frontier* (Leiden: Brill, 1997).

Robinson-Hammerstein, Helga (ed.), *European Universities in the Age of Reformation and Counter-Reformation* (Dublin: Four Courts, 1998).

Rogers, Edward, *Some Account of the Life and Opinions of a Fifth-Monarchy-Man. Chiefly Extracted from the Writings of John Rogers, Preacher* (London: Longmans, Green, Reader and Dyer, 1867).

Rogers, P.G., *The Fifth Monarchy Men* (London: Oxford University Press, 1966).

Rohls, Jan, *Reformed Confessions: Theology from Zurich to Barmen*, trans. John Hoffmeyer, Columbia Series in Reformed Theology (Louisville, Kentucky: Westminster John Knox Press, 1998).

Ronberg, Gert, *A Way With Words: The Language of English Renaissance Literature* (London: Edward Arnold, 1992).

Rooy, Sidney H., *The Theology of Mission in the Puritan Tradition: A Study of Representative Puritans: Richard Sibbes, Richard Baxter, John Eliot, Cotton Mather, and Jonathan Edwards* (Delft: Meinema, 1965).

Rose, Mary Beth (ed.), *Women in the Middle Ages and the Renaissance: Literary and Historical Perspectives* (Syracuse: Syracuse University Press, 1986).

Rowse, A.L., *Milton the Puritan: Portrait of a Mind* (London: Macmillan, 1977).

Rumrich, John P., 'Mead and Milton', *Milton Quarterly* 20 (1986), pp. 136-41.

Russell, William R., 'Martin Luther's understanding of the Pope and Antichrist', *Archiv für Reformationsgeschichte* 85 (1994), pp. 32-44.

Ryken, Leland, *The Apocalyptic Vision in Paradise Lost* (London: Cornell University Press, 1970).

Sanderson, John, *'But the People's Creatures': The Philosophical Basis of the English Civil War* (Manchester: Manchester University Press, 1989).

Sawyer, Jack, 'Introduction to Bucer's *De Regno Christi*', *Journal of Christian Reconstruction* 5 (1978-9), pp. 8-16.

Scanlon, Michael J., 'Eschatology', in Allan D. Fitzgerald (gen. ed.), *Augustine through the Ages: An Encyclopedia* (Grand Rapids: Eerdmans, 1999), pp. 316-18.

Schaff, Philip (ed.), *The Creeds of the Evangelical Protestant Churches* (London: Hodder and Stoughton, 1877).

Scheick, William J., *Design in Puritan American Literature* (Lexington: University Press of Kentucky, 1992).

Schlissel, Steve (ed.), *Hal Lindsey and the Restoration of the Jews* (Edmonton: Still Waters Revival Books, 1990).

Scott, Otto J., *James I* (New York: Mason/Charter, 1976).

Scult, Mel, *Millennial Expectations and Jewish liberties: A Study of Efforts to Convert the Jews in Britain, up to the mid-nineteenth Century* (Leiden: Brill, 1978).

Seaver, Paul S., *The Puritan Lectureships: The Politics of Religious Dissent, 1560-1662* (Stanford: Stanford University Press, 1970).

Snell, Alan P.F., review of Clifford (1990), *Calvin Theological Journal* 27:1 (1992), pp. 117.

Seymour, J.D., *The Puritans in Ireland, 1647-1661* (Oxford: Clarendon Press, 1921).

Shaw, Duncan, *Reformation and Revolution: Essays Presented to The Very Reverend Principle Emeritus Hugh Watt, D.D., D.Litt. on the Sixtieth Anniversary of his Ordination* (Edinburgh: St. Andrews Press, 1967).

Short-Title Catalogue of Books Printed in England, Scotland and Ireland and of English Books Printed Abroad 1475-1640, eds A.W. Pollard and G.R. Redgrave; rvsd. W.A. Jackson et al (London: The Bibliographical Society, 1976-1991).

Short-Title Catalogue of Books Printed in England, Scotland, Ireland, Wales and British America and of English Books Printed in other Countries 1641-1700, ed. Donald Wing; rvsd. John J. Morrison et al (New York: Modern Language Association of America, 1994-1998).

Showalter, Elaine, 'Apocalypse Now and Then, Please', *The Times* April 16 1998, p. 38.

Shuger, Debora Kuller, *Habits of Thought in the English Renaissance: Religion, Politics and the Dominant Culture* (Berkeley: University of California Press, 1990).

— *The Renaissance Bible: Scholarship, Sacrifice and Subjectivity* (Berkeley: University of California Press, 1994).

Sinfield, Alan, *Literature in Protestant England, 1560-1660* (London: Croom Helm, 1983).

— *Faultlines: Cultural Materialism and the Politics of Dissident Reading* (Oxford: Clarendon Press, 1992).

Sim, Stuart, 'Isolating the Reprobate: Paradox as a Strategy for Social Critique in *The Life and Death of Mr. Badman*', *Bunyan Studies* 1:2 (1989), pp. 30-40.

— *Negotiations with Paradox: Narrative Practice and Narrative Form in Bunyan and Defoe* (New York: Harvester Wheatsheaf, 1990).

Simpson, Alan, *Puritanism in Old and New England* (Chicago: University of Chicago Press, 1955).

Smith, David E., *John Bunyan in America* (Bloomington: Indiana University Press, 1966).

Smith, Barabra Herrnstein, *Poetic Closure: A Study of How Poems End* (London: University of Chicago Press, 1968).

Smith, John Hazel (trans.), *Two Latin Comedies by John Foxe the Martyrologist: Titus et Gesippus, Christus Triumphans* (London: Cornell University Press, 1973).

Smith, Nigel, *Perfection Proclaimed: Language and Literature in English Radical Religion 1640-1660* (Oxford: Clarendon Press, 1989).

— '*Areopagitica*: Voicing Contexts, 1643-5', in Loewenstein (ed.) (1990), pp. 103-122.

— 'The Uses of Hebrew in the English Revolution', in Burke and Porter (eds) (1991), pp. 51-71.

— *Literature and Revolution in England 1640-1660* (London: Yale University Press, 1994).

Smout, T.C., *A History of the Scottish People 1560-1830* (London: Fontana, 1969).

Sprunger, Keith L., 'English and Dutch Sabbatarianism and the Development of Puritan Social Theology (1600-1660)', *Church History* 51 (1982), pp. 24-38.

Solt, Leo, 'The Fifth Monarchy Men: Politics and the Millennium', *Church History* 30 (1961), pp. 314-24.

— *Church and State in Early Modern England, 1509-1640* (Oxford: Oxford University Press, 1990).

Steadman, John M., *The Hill and the Labyrinth: Discourse and Certitude in Milton and his Near-Contemporaries* (Berkeley: University of California Press, 1984).

Stephen, W.P. (ed.), *The Bible, the Reformation and the Church: Essays in Honour of James Atkinson* (Sheffield: Sheffield Academic Press, 1995).

Stevenson, David, *Revolution and Counter-Revolution in Scotland, 1644-1651* (London: Royal Historical Society, 1977).

— *The Covenanters and the Western Association 1648-1650* (n.p.: Ayrshire Archaeological and Natural History Society, 1982)

— 'Cromwell, Scotland and Ireland', in Morrill (ed.) (1990), pp. 149-80.

— 'The Century of the Three Kingdoms', in Wormald (ed.) (1991), pp. 107-19.

— *King or Covenant? Voices from Civil War* (East Linton: Tuckwell Press, 1996).

— *Revolution and Religion in 17th-century Scotland* (Aldershot: Scolar Press, 1997).

Stocker, M.C., *Apocalyptic Marvell: The Second Coming in Seventeenth Century Poetry* (Brighton: Harvester, 1986).

Stranahan, Brainerd P., 'Bunyan's Special Talent: Biblical Texts as "Events" in *Grace Abounding* and *The Pilgrim's Progress*', *English Literary Renaissance* (1981), pp. 329-43.

— 'Bunyan and the Epistle to the Hebrews: His Source for the Idea of Pilgrimage in *The Pilgrim's Progress*', *Studies in Philology* 79 (1982), pp. 279-96.

Strier, Richard, *Resistant Structures: Particularity, Radicalism, and Renaissance Texts* (Berkeley: University of California Press, 1995).

Sturgis, Amy H., 'Prophesies and Politics: Millenarians, Rabbis and the Jewish Indian Theory', *The Seventeenth Century* 14:1 (1999), pp. 15-23.

Sutherland, N.M., 'The Marian Exiles and the Establishment of the Elizabethan Régime', *Archiv für Reformation Geschichte* 78 (1987), pp. 253-86.

Svigel, Michael J., 'The Phantom Heresy: Did the Council of Ephesus (431) condemn Chiliasm?', *Trinity Journal* 24 n.s. (2003), pp. 105-12.

Swann, Joel, 'Reading Revelation in the English Geneva Bibles' (unpublished BSc dissertation, University of Manchester, 2006).

Sykes, Norman, 'James Ussher as Churchman', *Theology* 60 (1957), pp. 54-60.

Tawney, R.H., *Religion and the Rise of Capitalism* (London: John Murray, 1926).

Thomas, I.D.E., *The Golden Treasury of Puritan Quotations* (Edinburgh: Banner of Truth, 1975).

Thomas, Keith, *Religion and the Decline of Magic: Studies in Popular Beliefs in Sixteenth and Seventeenth-century England* (1971; rpt. Harmondsworth: Penguin, 1991).

Thrupp, Sylvia L., *Millennial Dreams in Action: Studies in Revolutionary Religious Movements* (New York: Schocken Books, 1970).

Tillyard, E.M.W., *The Elizabethan World Picture* (1943; rpt. Harmondsworth: Penguin, 1972).

Tindall, William York, *John Bunyan, Mechanick Preacher* (1934; rpt. New York: Russell and Russell, 1964).

Todd, Margo, *Christian Humanism and the Puritan Social Order* (Cambridge: Cambridge University Press, 1987).

Toner, P.J., 'Limbo', in *The Catholic Encyclopedia* (1910; rpt. New York: The Encyclopedia Press, 1913), ix. 256-59.

Toon, Peter, 'Introduction', in Toon (ed.) (1970), pp. 8-22.

— 'The Latter-Day Glory', in Toon (ed.) (1970), pp. 23-41.

— *God's Statesman: The Life and Work of John Owen: Pastor, Educator, Theologian* (Exeter: Paternoster Press, 1971).

— *Puritans and Calvinism* (Swengel: Reiner, 1973).

— (ed.), *Puritans, the Millennium, and the Future of Israel* (Cambridge: James Clarke, 1970).

— (ed.) *The Correspondence of John Owen (1616-1683), pp. with an account of his life and work* (Cambridge: James Clarke, 1970).

Torrance, T.F., 'The Eschatology of the Reformation', *Eschatology: Scottish Journal of Theology Occasional Papers* 2 (1953), pp. 36-62.

Trevor-Roper, Hugh, 'The Fast Sermons of the Long Parliament', in Trevor-Roper (ed.) (1965), pp. 85-138.

— *Catholics, Anglicans and Puritans* (1987; rpt. London: Fontana, 1989).

— (ed.) *Essays in British History Presented to Sir Keith Fielding* (London: Macmillan, 1965).

Trinterud, Leonard J. (ed.), *Elizabethan Puritanism* (New York: Oxford University Press, 1971).

Trueman, Carl R. and R. S. Clark (eds), *Protestant Scholasticism: Essays in Reassessment* (Carlisle: Paternoster, 1999).

Tuttle, Elizabeth, 'Bibilical Reference in the Political Pamphlets of the Levellers and Milton, 1638-1654', in Armitage et al (eds) (1995), pp. 63-81.

Tyacke, Nicholas, *Anti-Calvinists: The Rise of English Arminianism, c.1590-1640* (Oxford: Clarendon Press, 1987).

Underdown, David, *Fire from Heaven: Life in an English Town in the Seventeenth Century* (London: Fontana, 1993).

Underwood, T.L., 'Early Quaker Eschatology', in Toon (ed.) (1970), pp. 91-103.

Vann, Richard T., 'Quakerism and the Social Structure in the Interregnum', *Past and Present* 43 (1960), pp. 71-91.

Vattimo, Gianni, 'The Structure of Artistic Revolutions' (1988; rpt. in Docherty [ed.] [1993]), pp. 110-119.

Vaughan, Alden T. and Francis J. Bremer (eds), *Puritan New England: Essays on Religion, Society and Culture* (New York: St. Martin's Press, 1977).

Veeser, H. Aram, *The New Historicism* (London: Routledge, 1989).

Waldron, Samuel E., *A Modern Exposition of the 1689 Baptist Confession of Faith* (Darlington: Evangelical Press, 1989).

Wallace, Dewey D., *Puritans and Predestination: Grace in English Protestant Theology, 1525-1695* (Chapel Hill: University of North Carolina Press, 1982).

Walsham, Alexandra, *Providence in early modern England* (Oxford: Oxford University Press, 1999).

Walzer, Michael, 'Puritanism as a Revolutionary Ideology', *History and Theory* 3 (1963-4), pp. 59-90.

— *The Revolution of the Saints: A Study in the Origins of Radical Politics* (London: Weidenfeld and Nicolson, 1965).

Waswo, Richard, *Language and Meaning in the Renaissance* (Princeton: Princeton University Press, 1987).

Watkins, Owen C., *The Puritan Experience: Studies in Spiritual Autobiography* (London: Routledge and Kegan Paul, 1972).

Watt, Diane, *Secretaries of God: Women Prophets in Late Medieval and Early Modern England* (Cambridge: Brewer, 1997).

Watt, Tessa, *Cheap Print and Popular Piety 1550-1640* (Cambridge: Cambridge University Press, 1991).

Watts, Michael R., *The Dissenters: From the Reformation to the French Revolution* (Oxford: Clarendon Press, 1978).

Webber, Joan, *The Eloquent "I": Style and Self in Seventeenth-Century Prose* (Madison: University of Wisconsin Press, 1968).

Weber, Max, *The Protestant Ethic and the Sprit of Capitalism* (1930; rpt. London: George Allen and Unwin, 1976).

Webster, Tom, 'Writing to Redundancy: Approaches to Spiritual Journals in Early Modern Spirituality', *The Historical Journal* 39 (1996), pp. 33-56.

Wells, Robin H., *Elizabethan Mythologies: Studies in Poetry, Drama and Music* (Cambridge: Cambridge University Press, 1994).

White, B.R., 'The Organisation of the Particular Baptists, 1644-1660', *Journal of Ecclesiastical History* 17 (1966), pp. 209-26.

— *The English Separatist Tradition* (London: Oxford University Press, 1971).

— 'John Pendarves, the Calvinistic Baptists and the Fifth Monarchy', *Baptist Quarterly* 25 (1974), pp. 251-71.

— 'The Origins and Convictions of the First Calvinistic Baptists', *Baptist History and Heritage* 25:4 (1990), pp. 39-47.

[White, Hale], *John Bunyan* (London: Hodder and Stoughton, 1905).

Whitely, W.T., 'The Seven Churches of London', *Review and Expositor* 7:3 (1910), pp. 384-413.

Wilding, M. (ed.), *Marvell: Modern Judgements* (London: Macmillan, 1969).

— *Dragon's Teeth: Literature in the English Revolution* (Oxford: Clarendon Press, 1987).

Wilks, Michael (ed.), *Prophecy and Eschatology: Studies in Church History, Subsidia 10* (Oxford: Blackwell, 1994).

Williams, Ann (ed.), *Prophecy and Millenarianism: Essays in Honour of Marjorie Reeves* (Harlow: Longman, 1980).

Williams, Neville, *John Foxe the Martyrologist: His Life and Times* (London: Dr. William's Trust, 1975).

Williamson, Arthur H., *Scottish National Consciousness in the Age of James VI: The Apocalypse, the Union and the Shaping of Scotland's Public Culture* (Edinburgh: John Donald, 1979).

Wilson, John F., 'A Glimpse of Syon's Glory', *Church History* 31 (1962), pp. 66-73.

— 'Comment on "Two Roads to the Puritan Millennium"', *Church History* 32 (1963), pp. 339-43.

— *Pulpit in Parliament: Puritanism during the English Civil Wars 1640-1648* (Princeton: Princeton University Press, 1969).

de Witt, J.R., *Jus Divinum: the Westminster Assembly and the Divine Right of Church Government* (Kampen: Kok, 1969).

Wittreich, Joseph Anthony, *Visionary Poetics: Milton's Tradition and His Legacy* (San Marino: Huntingdon Library, 1979).

Wood, Diana (ed.), *Martyrs and Martyrologies: Papers read at the 1992 Summer Meeting and the 1993 Winter Meeting of the Ecclesiastical History Society* (Oxford: Blackwell, 1993).

Woodhouse, A.S.P. (ed.), *Puritanism and Liberty: Being the Army Debates (1647-9) from the Clarke Manuscripts with Supplementary Documents* (1938; rpt. London: Dent, 1992).

Wormald, Jenny (ed.), *Scotland Revisited* (London: Collins and Brown, 1991).

Yule, George, *The Independents in the English Civil War* (Cambridge: Cambridge University Press, 1958).

Zacharias, Bryan G., *The Embattled Christian: The Puritan View of Spiritual Warfare* (Edinburgh: Banner of Truth, 1995).

Zagorin, Perez, *Milton: Aristocrat and Rebel: The poet and his politics* (New York: D.S. Brewer, 1992).

Zakai, Avihu, 'Reformation, History and Eschatology in English Protestantism', *History and Theory* 26:3 (1987), pp. 300-318.

— *Exile and Kingdom: History and Apocalypse in the Puritan Migration to America* (Cambridge: Cambridge University Press, 1992).

Zinck, Arlette M., "Doctrine by Ensample': Sanctification through Literature in Milton and Bunyan', *Bunyan Studies* 6 (1995-6), pp. 44-55.

Index

Studies in Christian History and Thought
(All titles uniform with this volume)
Dates in bold are of projected publication

David Bebbington
Holiness in Nineteenth-Century England
David Bebbington stresses the relationship of movements of spirituality to changes in their cultural setting, especially the legacies of the Enlightenment and Romanticism. He shows that these broad shifts in ideological mood had a profound effect on the ways in which piety was conceptualized and practised. Holiness was intimately bound up with the spirit of the age.
2000 / 0-85364-981-2 / viii + 98pp

J. William Black
Reformation Pastors
Richard Baxter and the Ideal of the Reformed Pastor
This work examines Richard Baxter's *Gildas Salvianus, The Reformed Pastor* (1656) and explores each aspect of his pastoral strategy in light of his own concern for 'reformation' and in the broader context of Edwardian, Elizabethan and early Stuart pastoral ideals and practice.
2003 / 1-84227-190-3 / xxii + 308pp

James Bruce
Prophecy, Miracles, Angels, *and* Heavenly Light?
The Eschatology, Pneumatology and Missiology of Adomnán's Life of Columba
This book surveys approaches to the marvellous in hagiography, providing the first critique of Plummer's hypothesis of Irish saga origin. It then analyses the uniquely systematized phenomena in the *Life of Columba* from Adomnán's seventh-century theological perspective, identifying the coming of the eschatological Kingdom as the key to understanding.
2004 / 1-84227-227-6 / xviii + 286pp

Colin J. Bulley
The Priesthood of Some Believers
Developments from the General to the Special Priesthood in the Christian Literature of the First Three Centuries
The first in-depth treatment of early Christian texts on the priesthood of all believers shows that the developing priesthood of the ordained related closely to the division between laity and clergy and had deleterious effects on the practice of the general priesthood.
2000 / 1-84227-034-6 / xii + 336pp

Anthony R. Cross (ed.)
Ecumenism and History
Studies in Honour of John H.Y. Briggs
This collection of essays examines the inter-relationships between the two fields in which Professor Briggs has contributed so much: history—particularly Baptist and Nonconformist—and the ecumenical movement. With contributions from colleagues and former research students from Britain, Europe and North America, *Ecumenism and History* provides wide-ranging studies in important aspects of Christian history, theology and ecumenical studies.
2002 / 1-84227-135-0 / xx + 362pp

Maggi Dawn
Confessions of an Inquiring Spirit
Form as Constitutive of Meaning in S.T. Coleridge's Theological Writing
This study of Coleridge's *Confessions* focuses on its confessional, epistolary and fragmentary form, suggesting that attention to these features significantly affects its interpretation. Bringing a close study of these three literary forms, the author suggests ways in which they nuance the text with particular understandings of the Trinity, and of a kenotic christology. Some parallels are drawn between Romantic and postmodern dilemmas concerning the authority of the biblical text.
2006 / 1-84227-255-1 / approx. 224 pp

Ruth Gouldbourne
The Flesh and the Feminine
Gender and Theology in the Writings of Caspar Schwenckfeld
Caspar Schwenckfeld and his movement exemplify one of the radical communities of the sixteenth century. Challenging theological and liturgical norms, they also found themselves challenging social and particularly gender assumptions. In this book, the issues of the relationship between radical theology and the understanding of gender are considered.
2005 / 1-84227-048-6 / approx. 304pp

Crawford Gribben
Puritan Millennialism
Literature and Theology, 1550–1682
Puritan Millennialism surveys the growth, impact and eventual decline of puritan millennialism throughout England, Scotland and Ireland, arguing that it was much more diverse than has frequently been suggested. This Paternoster edition is revised and extended from the original 2000 text.
2007 / 1-84227-372-8 / approx. 320pp

Galen K. Johnson
Prisoner of Conscience
John Bunyan on Self, Community and Christian Faith
This is an interdisciplinary study of John Bunyan's understanding of conscience across his autobiographical, theological and fictional writings, investigating whether conscience always deserves fidelity, and how Bunyan's view of conscience affects his relationship both to modern Western individualism and historic Christianity.

2003 / 1-84227-223-3 / xvi + 236pp

R.T. Kendall
Calvin and English Calvinism to 1649
The author's thesis is that those who formed the Westminster Confession of Faith, which is regarded as Calvinism, in fact departed from John Calvin on two points: (1) the extent of the atonement and (2) the ground of assurance of salvation.

1997 / 0-85364-827-1 / xii + 264pp

Timothy Larsen
Friends of Religious Equality
Nonconformist Politics in Mid-Victorian England
During the middle decades of the nineteenth century the English Nonconformist community developed a coherent political philosophy of its own, of which a central tenet was the principle of religious equality (in contrast to the stereotype of Evangelical Dissenters). The Dissenting community fought for the civil rights of Roman Catholics, non-Christians and even atheists on an issue of principle which had its flowering in the enthusiastic and undivided support which Nonconformity gave to the campaign for Jewish emancipation. This reissued study examines the political efforts and ideas of English Nonconformists during the period, covering the whole range of national issues raised, from state education to the Crimean War. It offers a case study of a theologically conservative group defending religious pluralism in the civic sphere, showing that the concept of religious equality was a grand vision at the centre of the political philosophy of the Dissenters.

2007 / 1-84227-402-3 / x + 300pp

Byung-Ho Moon
Christ the Mediator of the Law
Calvin's Christological Understanding of the Law as the Rule of Living and Life-Giving

This book explores the coherence between Christology and soteriology in Calvin's theology of the law, examining its intellectual origins and his position on the concept and extent of Christ's mediation of the law. A comparative study between Calvin and contemporary Reformers—Luther, Bucer, Melancthon and Bullinger—and his opponent Michael Servetus is made for the purpose of pointing out the unique feature of Calvin's Christological understanding of the law.

2005 / 1-84227-318-3 / approx. 370pp

John Eifion Morgan-Wynne
Holy Spirit and Religious Experience in Christian Writings, c.AD 90–200

This study examines how far Christians in the third to fifth generations (c.AD 90–200) attributed their sense of encounter with the divine presence, their sense of illumination in the truth or guidance in decision-making, and their sense of ethical empowerment to the activity of the Holy Spirit in their lives.

2005 / 1-84227-319-1 / approx. 350pp

James I. Packer
The Redemption and Restoration of Man in the Thought of Richard Baxter

James I. Packer provides a full and sympathetic exposition of Richard Baxter's doctrine of humanity, created and fallen; its redemption by Christ Jesus; and its restoration in the image of God through the obedience of faith by the power of the Holy Spirit.

2002 / 1-84227-147-4 / 432pp

Andrew Partington,
Church and State
The Contribution of the Church of England Bishops to the House of Lords
during the Thatcher Years
In *Church and State*, Andrew Partington argues that the contribution of the
Church of England bishops to the House of Lords during the Thatcher years was
overwhelmingly critical of the government; failed to have a significant influence
in the public realm; was inefficient, being undertaken by a minority of those
eligible to sit on the Bench of Bishops; and was insufficiently moral and
spiritual in its content to be distinctive. On the basis of this, and the likely
reduction of the number of places available for Church of England bishops in a
fully reformed Second Chamber, the author argues for an evolution in the
Church of England's approach to the service of its bishops in the House of
Lords. He proposes the Church of England works to overcome the genuine
obstacles which hinder busy diocesan bishops from contributing to the debates
of the House of Lords and to its life more informally.
2005 / 1-84227-334-5 / approx. 324pp

Michael Pasquarello III
God's Ploughman
Hugh Latimer: A 'Preaching Life' (1490–1555)
This construction of a 'preaching life' situates Hugh Latimer within the larger
religious, political and intellectual world of late medieval England. Neither
biography, intellectual history, nor analysis of discrete sermon texts, this book is
a work of homiletic history which draws from the details of Latimer's milieu to
construct an interpretive framework for the preaching performances that formed
the core of his identity as a religious reformer. Its goal is to illumine the
practical wisdom embodied in the content, form and style of Latimer's
preaching, and to recapture a sense of its overarching purpose, movement, and
transforming force during the reform of sixteenth-century England.
2006 / 1-84227-336-1 / approx. 250pp

Alan P.F. Sell
Enlightenment, Ecumenism, Evangel
Theological Themes and Thinkers 1550–2000
This book consists of papers in which such interlocking topics as the
Enlightenment, the problem of authority, the development of doctrine,
spirituality, ecumenism, theological method and the heart of the gospel are
discussed. Issues of significance to the church at large are explored with special
reference to writers from the Reformed and Dissenting traditions.
2005 / 1-84227-330-2 / xviii + 422pp

Alan P.F. Sell
Hinterland Theology
Some Reformed and Dissenting Adjustments
Many books have been written on theology's 'giants' and significant trends, but what of those lesser-known writers who adjusted to them? In this book some hinterland theologians of the British Reformed and Dissenting traditions, who followed in the wake of toleration, the Evangelical Revival, the rise of modern biblical criticism and Karl Barth, are allowed to have their say. They include Thomas Ridgley, Ralph Wardlaw, T.V. Tymms and N.H.G. Robinson.

2006 / 1-84227-331-0 / approx. 350pp

Alan P.F. Sell and Anthony R. Cross (eds)
Protestant Nonconformity in the Twentieth Century
In this collection of essays scholars representative of a number of Nonconformist traditions reflect thematically on Nonconformists' life and witness during the twentieth century. Among the subjects reviewed are biblical studies, theology, worship, evangelism and spirituality, and ecumenism. Over and above its immediate interest, this collection provides a marker to future scholars and others wishing to know how some of their forebears assessed Nonconformity's contribution to a variety of fields during the century leading up to Christianity's third millennium.

2003 / 1-84227-221-7 / x + 398pp

Mark Smith
Religion in Industrial Society
Oldham and Saddleworth 1740–1865
This book analyses the way British churches sought to meet the challenge of industrialization and urbanization during the period 1740–1865. Working from a case-study of Oldham and Saddleworth, Mark Smith challenges the received view that the Anglican Church in the eighteenth century was characterized by complacency and inertia, and reveals Anglicanism's vigorous and creative response to the new conditions. He reassesses the significance of the centrally directed church reforms of the mid-nineteenth century, and emphasizes the importance of local energy and enthusiasm. Charting the growth of denominational pluralism in Oldham and Saddleworth, Dr Smith compares the strengths and weaknesses of the various Anglican and Nonconformist approaches to promoting church growth. He also demonstrates the extent to which all the churches participated in a common culture shaped by the influence of evangelicalism, and shows that active co-operation between the churches rather than denominational conflict dominated. This revised and updated edition of Dr Smith's challenging and original study makes an important contribution both to the social history of religion and to urban studies.

2006 / 1-84227-335-3 / approx. 300pp

Martin Sutherland
Peace, Toleration and Decay
The Ecclesiology of Later Stuart Dissent
This fresh analysis brings to light the complexity and fragility of the later Stuart Nonconformist consensus. Recent findings on wider seventeenth-century thought are incorporated into a new picture of the dynamics of Dissent and the roots of evangelicalism.

2003 / 1-84227-152-0 / xxii + 216pp

G. Michael Thomas
The Extent of the Atonement
A Dilemma for Reformed Theology from Calvin to the Consensus
A study of the way Reformed theology addressed the question, 'Did Christ die for all, or for the elect only?', commencing with John Calvin, and including debates with Lutheranism, the Synod of Dort and the teaching of Moïse Amyraut.

1997 / 0-85364-828-X / x + 278pp

David M. Thompson
Baptism, Church and Society in Britain from the Evangelical Revival to
Baptism, Eucharist and Ministry
The theology and practice of baptism have not received the attention they deserve. How important is faith? What does baptismal regeneration mean? Is baptism a bond of unity between Christians? This book discusses the theology of baptism and popular belief and practice in England and Wales from the Evangelical Revival to the publication of the World Council of Churches' consensus statement on *Baptism, Eucharist and Ministry* (1982).

2005 / 1-84227-393-0 / approx. 224pp

Mark D. Thompson
A Sure Ground on Which to Stand
The Relation of Authority and Interpretive Method of Luther's Approach to Scripture
The best interpreter of Luther is Luther himself. Unfortunately many modern studies have superimposed contemporary agendas upon this sixteenth-century Reformer's writings. This fresh study examines Luther's own words to find an explanation for his robust confidence in the Scriptures, a confidence that generated the famous 'stand' at Worms in 1521.

2004 / 1-84227-145-8 / xvi + 322pp

Carl R. Trueman and R.S. Clark (eds)
Protestant Scholasticism
Essays in Reassessment

Traditionally Protestant theology, between Luther's early reforming career and the dawn of the Enlightenment, has been seen in terms of decline and fall into the wastelands of rationalism and scholastic speculation. In this volume a number of scholars question such an interpretation. The editors argue that the development of post-Reformation Protestantism can only be understood when a proper historical model of doctrinal change is adopted. This historical concern underlies the subsequent studies of theologians such as Calvin, Beza, Olevian, Baxter, and the two Turrentini. The result is a significantly different reading of the development of Protestant Orthodoxy, one which both challenges the older scholarly interpretations and clichés about the relationship of Protestantism to, among other things, scholasticism and rationalism, and which demonstrates the fruitfulness of the new, historical approach.

1999 / 0-85364-853-0 / xx + 344pp

Shawn D. Wright
Our Sovereign Refuge
The Pastoral Theology of Theodore Beza

Our Sovereign Refuge is a study of the pastoral theology of the Protestant reformer who inherited the mantle of leadership in the Reformed church from John Calvin. Countering a common view of Beza as supremely a 'scholastic' theologian who deviated from Calvin's biblical focus, Wright uncovers a new portrait. He was not a cold and rigid academic theologian obsessed with probing the eternal decrees of God. Rather, by placing him in his pastoral context and by noting his concerns in his pastoral and biblical treatises, Wright shows that Beza was fundamentally a committed Christian who was troubled by the vicissitudes of life in the second half of the sixteenth century. He believed that the biblical truth of the supreme sovereignty of God alone could support Christians on their earthly pilgrimage to heaven. This pastoral and personal portrait forms the heart of Wright's argument.

2004 / 1-84227-252-7 / xviii + 308pp

Paternoster
9 Holdom Avenue,
Bletchley,
Milton Keynes MK1 1QR,
United Kingdom
Web: www.authenticmedia.co.uk/paternoster